Developing Web Applications with ASP.NET and C#

Hank Meyne
Scott Davis

Wiley Computer Publishing

John Wiley & Sons, Inc.

Publisher: Robert Ipsen
Editor: Theresa Hudson
Developmental Editor: Kathryn A. Malm
Managing Editor: Angela Smith
Text Design & Composition: John Wiley Composition Services

Library of Congress Cataloging-in-Publication Data:

ISBN: 0-471-12090-1

Printed in the United States of America.

10 9 8 7 6 5 4 3 2 1

Scott Davis would like to dedicate this book to his wife, Sharon, and two sons, Cole and Carter, for the many hours he spent away from them to complete this project.

Hank Meyne dedicates this book to his wife, Stacy, who endured his many late nights and weekends at work completing this project.

Contents

About the Authors

Hank Meyne received his bachelor's degree from the University of North Florida College of Computing Science. Since then he has worked as a developer on projects ranging from low-level graphics applications to enterprise Windows systems, and particularly imaging and document management programs. He is an expert in C/C++, C#, and Web programming, and, of course, he has served time at the helm of Visual Basic projects as well. Hank's own software company is in its fourth year and staying busy developing .NET applications for clients in fast-growing Jacksonville, Florida.

Besides writing software, Hank is avidly interested in Formula 1 racing and sports cars in general, as well as hunting, fishing, hiking, and, most of all, travel.

Hank can be reached via email at hmeyne@mediaone.net.

Scott Davis obtained his bachelor's degree in Electrical Engineering from Michigan State University in 1993. He has spent the majority of his career developing and supporting applications for the manufacturing industry, particularly the automotive industry. Scott's interest and experience with computers dates back to the Commodore 64 era when getting online meant firing up your auto dialer to get into a local Bulletin Board System. Scott is an expert developer with C#, C++, ASP.NET, and relational databases. He obtained his Microsoft Certified Solutions Developer status in 1999. Scott is an independent contractor specializing in .NET solutions for corporations of all sizes, and he is currently based outside of Jacksonville, Florida.

When he is not sitting in front of his computer developing software, Scott is in front of his computer playing online PC games or tending to his fantasy football team. He is also an avid outdoorsman and sports fanatic who enjoys hunting, fishing, football, basketball, and NASCAR races.

Scott can be contacted via e-mail at davistech@mediaone.net.

Acknowledgments

We would like to thank the following people who made this project possible for us: Studio B, Wiley Computer Publishing and our editor Kathryn Malm, and Joe Healy, who helped us get through the early days of undocumented, pre-alpha .NET builds.

Introduction

From the beginning of the Internet's existence, the available technologies for Web-based application developers have been a mixed bag of various tools and languages. For this reason Web programming has been a tedious and error-prone task. Most Web applications have been developed with hard-to-read code that is not object oriented or event driven. Web programmers have longed for a way to harness the mature, object-oriented and event-driven techniques that have been available to traditional client/server programmers. Now, for the first time, Microsoft has created an entire suite of tools that achieve exactly this—the .NET Framework.

Microsoft's .NET Framework is poised to revolutionize the computing industry. ASP.NET and C# (C Sharp) are new ground-breaking technologies that are key components of the .NET Framework. Currently, Web programmers must choose between using less-than-elegant scripting languages and dealing with the complexities of server-side COM components. To provide any kind of friendly user interface on the Web, programmers must often resort to using bug-prone and nonportable client-side scripting languages.

ASP.NET picks up where ASP leaves off and provides a vast improvement over the former technology. ASP.NET provides the Web programmer with the tried and true event-driven programming model to which most Windows developers are accustomed. Furthermore, ASP.NET opens up the power of the entire Windows operating system to the Web developer, something that is not easily achieved using current technologies.

C# is Microsoft's new object-oriented programming language, available for the first time as part of the .NET Framework. C# is one of the two primary languages that can be used to create ASP.NET Web applications. C# successfully captures the power and robustness of C++ while eliminating its shortcomings and pitfalls.

We will take the reader through the process of developing an entire suite of enterprise applications using the .NET Framework. Specifically, we will go in depth on all key aspects of enterprise application development using the full power of ASP.NET and C#.

Each chapter will explain its topics by example, and at the end of the book, you will have an application that touches on many of the things that can be done in a Web application, and all in the .NET way. We believe that we can help the reader understand the theories behind the features of ASP.NET and, at the same time, give real-world examples that would likely be a part of a large-scale system. As each chapter progresses, we will add functionality to the overall system using the features that are relevant to the chapter. In addition, we will include multiple ways of doing things, where applicable, because your applications will have different requirements. We won't hold back on the .NET Framework either; although the book is specifically for teaching how to write ASP.NET Web apps, we will try to include as much of the base class functionality of .NET as we can while keeping with the overall sample. We will also try to do things in C# that show off the power and features of the language. We won't try to keep the examples too simple for fear of the reader's not knowing enough about the particular language. This is a book about C#, too, and it will include many nontrivial examples of the language throughout.

Many usable, real-world examples are provided to demonstrate the power of the technology and to help the reader get off to a running start with ASP.NET.

A Car Parts Locator Service

After having spent years developing Web application using CGI, ASP, and other technologies, our first project using .NET started in mid-2000, and it was one of the only .NET projects going on in the world at the time, outside of Microsoft, of course. The project was to build an e-commerce site that sold auto parts to customers all over the country. The back-end systems were done in .NET, too, including the call center, customer service, inventory, employee workflow, accounting, and purchasing apps. This was a large and fast-moving project; at times it was made very difficult by the fact that it was started on the earliest bits of the .NET products and tools. The project was a success, though, and .NET proved, even in its early stages, to be a boon for our development team. The apps could never have been done as quickly using any other technology, we believe. In addition to being a good project to work on, it was a great project to use as an example. It used many facets of .NET and leveraged many features that are available only in .NET. As soon as we decided to write this book, we knew that our examples would be based on this project. Throughout the book we will build on a system for selling auto parts over the Web. The applications we will create will be an e-commerce business-to-consumer (b-to-c) shopping-cart style Web site to sell parts and a set of Web services that expose the parts-buying functionality to other companies. We feel that with these sample applications, we can touch on some of the most powerful and interesting features that .NET has to offer.

How This Book Is Organized

The chapters of this book are organized to promote reading them in sequential order. Each chapter will build on the previous chapter's material. That doesn't mean that you can't skip around to sections that interest you the most and refer back to previous chapters when needed.

Chapter 1, Making Sense of .NET.   This chapter defines what the .NET Framework, ASP.NET, and C# are all about. We'll also make some comparisons between ASP.NET and its predecessor, ASP. Then we'll finish by explaining what we intend to accomplish in the rest of the book.

Chapter 2, Anatomy of an ASP.NET Page.   This chapter describes the various ways that an ASP.NET page can be developed. We'll see the pros and cons of the various methods. We'll take a deep look at the lifetime of an ASP.NET page from the time it is requested until the time it is delivered to the client.

Chapter 3, Server Controls.   Server Controls are the fundamental building blocks of an ASP.NET page. We'll cover the Server Controls that are supplied with ASP.NET in detail and see just how powerful they are.

Chapter 4, Database Access.   This chapter introduces you to using ADO.NET to access data sources and discusses how to bind server-side controls to data collections. We'll also cover the basics of error handling under the .NET Framework.

Chapter 5, Creating More Advanced ASP.NET Pages.   We'll move into some more advanced concepts that will be the final pieces to the ASP.NET puzzle that we will need to construct our own real-world Web application. We'll learn how to use cookies to remember users, how to store objects in Session, Application and View state, and see how to reuse our ASP.NET code on multiple pages with user controls.

Chapter 6, Applying What We've Learned So Far.   This chapter brings everything together into a working, real-world application. We'll see the usefulness of designing and creating a robust, reuseable object model using C# and how it will dramatically increase our ability to make changes and additions to a Web site. We will then use this object model to create an online store for a car parts business that we will build on throughout the remainder of the book.

Chapter 7, Web Services.   This chapter covers the very basics of SOAP and XML, which are used heavily by XML Web services. We'll then define what a Web service is, how we go about creating one, and letting other people know that we have a service, and then we'll see how easy it is to use a Web service from a client application. We'll finish up by creating some Web services for our online car parts store.

Chapter 8, Security and Membership.   This chapter will cover the different types of user authentication available. We'll look at the built-in authentication methods that are provided by Internet Information Server (IIS) and then see how ASP.NET works with IIS to provide further security options and enhancements.

Chapter 9, Adding E-Commerce Essentials.   We'll take a high-level look at the XML support that is built into the .NET Framework. We'll then use XML to communicate with UPS in real time for calculating shipping prices for merchandise and validating addresses. We'll also see how simple it is to send email to our customers. We'll round out the chapter by adding address validation, shipping calculation, and invoice emailing to our online car parts store.

Chapter 10, Debugging and Optimization.   Debugging is a fact of life for a programmer, so we'll cover how to use Tracing to help debug our ASP.NET pages. There are also several things that we can do to make our pages more efficient. We'll cover the ASP.NET cache and performance profiling and discuss how to use them effectively. We'll also see how to increase page performance by limiting what is stored in View state and cutting down on transmission time to the client.

Who Should Read This Book

This book is for programmers looking for an in-depth look at ASP.NET. The concepts and examples provided range from beginner to advanced level.

We will be using C# exclusively in this book. You won't find examples printed in both Visual Basic .NET and C#. If you don't know C# yet and you are an experienced C++ or Java programmer, you will have no problems picking up on the C# language. If you are coming from a VB background, the C# examples are clear enough for you to easily understand and translate to Visual Basic .NET code if you so desire.

You should also have a basic knowledge of HTML. Because the .NET Framework has been built with heavy emphasis on XML, a working knowledge of XML will come in handy; however, it is not required. You won't find any sections of the book that will leave you stranded on advanced XML topics.

Tools You Will Need

All examples in this book were written using Visual Studio .NET, on both Windows 2000 Professional and Windows 2000 Server. Before running any of the examples, make sure Internet Information Services is installed and running.

The majority of the book is written with the assumption that the user has a copy of Visual Studio .NET available. Some of the examples refer to tasks performed in the Visual Studio .NET IDE. Of course, you could write all of the book's examples without Visual Studio .NET, but it would be more difficult. The .NET Framework SDK contains the class libraries, runtimes, compilers, and linkers needed to create, compile, and run .NET applications, but using Visual Studio .NET wraps this all up into a RAD environment, and this is the way that most programmers will develop them. It is important to note that ASP.NET applications can be run on any machine that has the .NET Component Update (which is part of the Framework SDK install) or ASP.NET Premium (which is a standalone install to allow a machine to serve ASP.NET applications) installed, regardless of whether Visual Studio .NET is installed. If only the .NET Component Update or ASP.NET Premium is installed, you will be able to run the example applications, but you will have to view the code using a text editor such as Notepad. Even if you have Visual Studio .NET installed, you may still install ASP.NET Premium to take advantage of its extra features. In fact, many of the examples in this book were built on a machine with both Visual Studio .NET and ASP.NET Premium installed.

What's on the Web Site

The examples in the book are all available on the companion Web site, located at www.wiley.com/compbooks/meyne. All examples will be presented as complete Visual Studio .NET projects. In the cases throughout the book where the examples are simple and show only a code snippet, the companion Web site will include the entire example. In addition to the code are the database scripts needed to re-create the sample databases used. To create these databases in SQL Server, simply use the Query Analyzer tool, open the script files, and run them.

What Should You Get from This Book?

We hope you will learn what ASP.NET is and how it compares to its predecessor—classic ASP. You should understand the fundamental ways that ASP.NET works and its major features. You should be able to write both single ASP.NET pages and full ASP.NET applications, which utilize all of the standard controls and server features in ASP.NET. You will also understand how to make use of object-oriented programming in ASP.NET, as well as database access using ADO.NET. You should also be able to write and consume ASP.NET Web services. The knowledge learned in this book should be a springboard to allow you to create large, complex Web applications that take advantage of ASP.NET's most important features.

Up Next

Now it's time to move into what exactly ASP.NET is. The first chapter, "Making Sense of .NET," will provide the definition and explanation of both .NET and ASP.NET, and from there we move straight into coding examples in Chapter 2, "Anatomy of an ASP.NET Page."

CHAPTER 1

Making Sense of .NET

Before we can jump into writing Web applications, let's talk about what .NET is and what it means to a Web programmer. This chapter will give you a brief overview of what the move to .NET is and how .NET has changed ASP.NET, and it will introduce a powerful new programming language—C#.

The Microsoft .NET Vision

Microsoft .NET is not easily defined. It is not an API, programming environment, or even a specific program. Microsoft defines .NET as its vision for the next generation of distributed computing systems. But more than just a vision, .NET provides the foundation on which we will run these systems, as well as the programming environment with which they can be built. From a tangible standpoint, especially as far as the programmer is concerned, .NET consists mostly of a framework that is installed on Windows, which supports the runtime needs of .NET applications. In this framework are the classes, compilers, and linkers that allow us to create our executable applications. In addition, .NET includes Visual Studio .NET, which allows us to rapidly develop these applications.

At one end of the spectrum, .NET provides robust programming libraries and tools we can use to leverage new standards for interoperability and programmability across platforms in a distributed environment. .NET will allow the applications we write to receive functionality in the form of objects, properties, and methods over the Internet or any intranet as well. .NET allows us to leverage Web servers for much more than just static, or even dynamically created, data that resides on the other side of the server. This new idea is called Web services and allows us to access data and services over the Internet via full-featured applications as opposed to just using the limited functionality provided by browsers. The support for calling objects and data across the network is provided not by proprietary binary protocols (DCOM, CORBA) but by loosely coupled, system-independent open standards. Much of the power available within the .NET programming environment is heavily based on the industry standard and very robust Extensible Markup Language (XML). In fact, .NET takes on the complex tasks of performing communications between disparate applications by taking full advantage of the Simple Object Access Protocol (SOAP), which itself is heavily tied to XML.

But .NET is not only about using new technologies to build distributed systems. Included in the .NET Framework, which is a basic building block of .NET itself, is support for writing all kinds of applications, from Windows rich-client programs, to browser-based Web applications. ASP.NET is the new version of the ever-popular Active Server Pages (ASP) model that has been the corner stone of Web programming within the Microsoft world. But ASP.NET is not just an enhancement on last year's product; it is a major evolution that provides very powerful mechanisms for writing Web server-based applications with performance and speed that have been near impossible until now. In addition to all of the support for building powerful applications across the Web, .NET introduces a new programming language: C# (pronounced C Sharp). This book focuses on building Web applications using all of the powerful features of .NET, and it does so entirely using C#.

Web Services

While .NET provides us with a robust and powerful framework for building all kinds of applications, one of the most significant shifts is to what is called Web services. When we say that .NET gives us a way to use object-oriented functionality across the Web, as opposed to just Web pages, we are talking about Web services. In simple terms, a Web service is a specialized Web application, which runs on a Web server. Instead of serving pages with a human-usable user interface, Web services serve methods and objects, complete with properties. The protocol used for using these objects across the network is SOAP and is heavily tied to XML.

SOAP uses XML as the default format of the objects, properties, and data when communicating via Web services. Instead of fulfilling requests for pages by a browser, or other simple rendering client, Web services are designed to fulfill requests made by other applications that will use the served objects in their runtime processing.

For a simple example, think of a shipping company. In the past, this company would most likely provide its prices and services over the Web via a standard Web application, meant to be viewed by a human using a browser, complete with a formatted user interface to display the data. With .NET, this company can still provide a browser-readable Web application as before, but it also has an additional means to allow access to its data. By creating a Web service, the company can now provide its shipping prices and services as objects and properties to other applications. The Web service would not format the data or add a user interface to it at all. It would provide business objects, loaded with data, so the calling program could display or use the information as needed. This provides a whole new level of power and flexibility both for the company providing the Web services and for the calling application. Even simple functionality fits nicely into the Web services model. For example, instead of keeping a local database of ever-changing area codes or zip codes and city names, a company could call a Web service that offers this up-to-date data as objects over the Web and consume them in their applications.

When we install .NET on a Windows server, enhancements are added to Internet Information Server, which allow us to create and serve Web services easily. Likewise, we can consume Web services easily from our applications written for .NET by utilizing the fully featured SOAP client classes in the .NET Framework. Microsoft's .NET strategy will be key to moving away from the current client/server-based world of information to a truly distributed network architecture, all the way down to the application level.

We all use distributed networks everyday by accessing our company's customer accounts while at work or checking our bank statements over the Internet at home. We use a client application such as a browser, which is installed locally, to read and write data on a Web server. For example, when you transfer money between your bank accounts over the Internet, your browser reads the stream of HTML data from the server and displays the data about your current account balances on the screen. Then, you would make changes in the fields and press a button to invoke the changes back on the server. At this point in the game, all the work is done on the server—the browser only sends a stream of data back to the server, where the real work will happen to actually change your balance.

The difference between today's technology and .NET is on what level the distribution occurs. With .NET, there is a shift from having large silos of data on servers to having real functionality on the remote systems. With .NET, we will no longer be limited to requesting a stream of formatted data from the Web server; instead, we can actually call functions on the server in an object-oriented way. Think of the banking example just described. With .NET, the bank could make not only this data, but also the functionality and logic related to it, available as a Web service. Then, it could provide a user interface in the form of a Web application as before. If the system is exposed as services, the bank could also create a rich client application for its users that would provide more advanced features than can easily be built in Web browser output. Or, maybe the bank would create an application that plugs into a personal manager program, so that you can check your bank balance from there. These are just some of the things that Web services can provide; we will discuss how to create and consume Web services later in the book.

While Web services are the underlying backbone to .NET's idea of a massive distributed system, the Web as most of us know it today will remain unchanged for a long time. We will still be accessing applications by using our Web browsers to request pages of information. For these reasons, Web sites must become more feature rich while at the same time support a diverse set of client devices, each with its own abilities and limitations. This is where ASP.NET steps in, and this is what this book will focus on, and particularly how it is used when a Web browser is the client. In the very near future, many people will be accessing the Web from their cell phones, cars, and pocket computers, but those topics are outside the scope of this book. With ASP.NET, Web programming has taken a large evolutionary step in the right direction. And with the release of .NET, ASP has been upgraded to a serious programming tool that just happens to support all of the other great features of .NET and the distributed systems of tomorrow.

ASP in .NET

ASP.NET is the successor to Microsoft's popular Web technology, Active Server Pages (ASP). Its purpose is to deliver dynamic and active content in Web pages. Microsoft has made some major advances with Active Server Pages. Let's take a brief look at some of the major differences between ASP and ASP.NET. You'll need to have some understanding of these new features before we move on to building the application in the rest of the book.

Compiled Code

One of the major changes with ASP.NET is how the code is interpreted. Previous versions of ASP pages were written using scripting languages. The Microsoft Scripting Host engine interpreted these scripts entirely at runtime through the COM dispatch interface. The drawback to this was the known overhead and limitations inherent in interpreted code.

ASP.NET pages are compiled to native code and are not interpreted at runtime. The default way to write ASP.NET pages with Visual Studio .NET is to use code-behind classes. Code-behind classes are real, full-blown, object-oriented code classes that provide the functionality of each page and make up your ASP.NET application. When we write ASP.NET applications this way, we compile them, link them, and then deploy them to the server. When the application is compiled, it is output as an intermediate language form called the *Microsoft Intermediate Language* (MSIL). This intermediate language is then read by the .NET runtime and compiled to native Windows 32-bit code. The result? A huge increase in performance—so much so that on complex Web applications, there is a noticeable increase in reaction time over that of ASP.

In addition to the performance increase, compiling your code at design time is the tried and true method of software development. Instead of failing at runtime, as with ASP, you will be forced to correct your code before it ever reaches the runtime environment.

Because ASP.NET applications are compiled, the developer has to ship only a minimal set of files needed to run the application on the server. The source code written to build the application is never required in the production environment. This makes deployment easy, and it allows vendors that sell ASP.NET applications to keep their source code private. This is in contrast to ASP, where all of the source code for the application must be shipped and deployed onto the Web server.

The Common Language Runtime

ASP has been written in one of two languages supported by the Microsoft Scripting Host: Visual Basic or JavaScript. Although popular, both of these languages are fairly limited in their functionality.

.NET is based on the common language runtime. This is the heart of programming in .Net, and it is the set of features and rules to which all .NET languages will adhere and within which run. Currently, Visual Basic .NET, Managed Visual C++, and C# all support the common language runtime. Although these languages each have their own syntax, style, and virtues, they all have the same base set of object-oriented characteristics, support the same base class library, and run within the same environment. In fact, the lines between the capabilities of different languages have blurred substantially in .NET. For example, in the past, it was easy to see when it was better to use C++ versus VB. Now, because Managed C++ running in the common language runtime and Visual Basic .NET support the same class library and object-oriented features, both tools could most often be used to accomplish many of the same programming tasks. The language choice will now be much more a programmer preference than a decision made based on language features and capabilities. Any language can be made to compile and run in the common language runtime. Many companies are developing common language runtime compilers for their languages, including Perl, COBOL, Eiffel, Java, and others.

ASP.NET gains the full benefit of common language runtime. ASP.NET programmers can use Visual Basic .NET, C#, or any other language that supports common language runtime. The key is the code-behind classes. Remember, these are the compiled object-oriented classes that make up an ASP.NET application. Each page in an ASP.NET application is explicitly linked to a common-language-runtime-based class (the code-behind class), it doesn't matter which language was used to create that class. In addition, the standard type system defined by the common language runtime allows all of your ASP.NET applications to use a uniform set of types, so programmers won't have to be concerned with remembering which type in one language matches which type in another. The robust garbage collection engine ensures that memory is managed and objects are allocated consistently across all .NET applications, in all languages, including ASP.NET. This also removes the burden of deallocation from the programmer, although no garbage collection system is a complete substitute for proper program design.

Truly Object Oriented

Another major change from ASP is a move to true object-oriented programs. All .NET applications, including ASP.NET, are fully object oriented. Here are just a few examples of the object-oriented features inherent in the code running in the common language runtime. All code lives inside some class. Everything is an object, even simple data types. There is full support for static and instance properties, static and instance methods, events, virtual functions, abstract classes, polymorphism, data hiding, and inheritance. Using these features allows us to create far more robust applications than were possible with ASP. Although covering the full explanation of the object-oriented paradigm is outside the scope of this book, you will see its use throughout the examples.

By moving to an object-oriented design in our Web applications, we also get away from the tight binding between the user interface and the business logic that was inevitable in ASP. ASP applications consisted of the ASP files that contained both the user interface code in the form of HTML and special tags to mark the beginning and end of dynamically executed code. To write object-oriented code, programmers either had to use the very limited and sometimes nonintuitive objects that can be created within the ASP scripting languages or write runtime-callable COM objects that would be called by the scripting code. This allowed for black-box objects to be used in ASP applications, but the only truly object-oriented code is confined to living inside the

COM object itself. A nice (and fundamental) feature of COM is that objects can be written using various languages and tools, but not ASP scripting languages. Because of this, creating object-oriented Web applications with ASP required programming in at least two different tools and languages. Doing this also subjected the programmer to the complexities of calling COM objects by their dispatch interface, as well as the inherent dangers of calling code at runtime with no early binding type safety. Also, in these cases, an ASP programmer who did not possess the skills to create COM objects would have to rely on another programmer to provide this portion of the application.

In ASP.NET, and in all .NET applications, COM is no longer the foundation for discovering, loading, and using binary black-box objects at runtime. .NET has retooled the way this works and has its own native way to handle this using meta data that is compiled into each and every object built on the common language runtime. Legacy COM objects are still accessible from any .NET application including ASP.NET; however, to really leverage the power that .NET provides, programmers can write objects of virtually unlimited complexity directly in the ASP.NET code.

In addition, to use objects without code, meaning to use a binary object that exists in a DLL, you only need to reference it; .NET takes care of discovering and exposing its capabilities for your use. One difference between this and COM is that the registry is consulted to identify the interfaces exposed by a COM object, as well as its location on the machine so it may be loaded. .NET objects are not referenced via the registry, but they are referred to directly by the physical location of the DLL. This allows several major advantages over COM. First, different versions of .NET objects can reside in different directories on the same machine without breaking the different versions of the calling code. Also, .NET objects have meta data compiled into them so that the calling code can learn about their interfaces without having to ask them through complex OLE calls at runtime. This meta data also eliminates the need for header files, type libraries, or wizards to create unfriendly wrapper code to which you must bind. And because .NET natively supports this type of object binding, no special service has to be invoked first as in nonmanaged C++, where an application must first initialize the COM environment before even attempting to use an object.

Access the Entire Windows System

ASP applications were limited to access to functionality built into the scripting languages and interfaces exposed by COM objects provided by vendors or themselves. For example, if an ASP application were to access the email subsystem, it would do so by calling on interfaces exposed by COM objects that wrapped MAPI, or Microsoft's Collaboration Data Objects (CDO), or some other email client object by some other vendor. Not so in ASP.NET, whose base class library provides native access to an object that handles email services.

An ASP.NET application has access to a huge class library called the .NET Framework Base Class Library (BCL). Like many large and robust class libraries such as those in Microsoft Foundation Classes (MFC) or Java, much of the underlying functionality of the host OS is wrapped and available for use. For the first time in the ASP world, applications have native access (as opposed to COM object access) to almost the entire Windows OS and everything that it provides. Even a full-featured fat client Windows application written in .NET has no more power than an ASP.NET application in terms of using system services and resources. (Of course, the UI in a Windows app is more robust than that in a browser, although .NET makes huge leaps to narrow even that gap.)

There are sometimes cases when a programmer wants to access the Win32 or other API directly, in cases where there is no access to a class object that wraps the desired functionality. This could be for many reasons; an ASP.NET program may need to call functions that are contained in a legacy non-COM Win32 DLL. Or, there may be some rarely used functions in the Win32 set of APIs that are not included in the .NET Base Class Library (BCL). In these instances, the Win32 Interop classes allow an ASP.NET, or any .NET app for that matter, to call the function directly from the DLL in a simple, elegant, code-light way. Those who are familiar with the VB style of calling DLL functions via the Declare statement will see that .NET Win32 Interop works in a similar fashion.

Proper Error Handling

ASP applications traditionally have had very poor support for error handling because of the limited features supported by the scripting languages. In VBScript, for example, the support for On Error leaves a lot to be desired and is not at all extensible. In ASP.NET, the application is running within the .NET runtime, which supports a very robust exception-handling mechanism using a try-catch-finally-and-throw syntax. In fact, the exception handling in .NET has been honed over many years of Microsoft's providing programming languages that support exceptions. And due to the full object support in .NET, programmers can implement powerful, custom error-handling routines.

Server-Side Controls

To provide the user interfaces, ASP programmers have had to include standard HTML controls in their ASP files and access them via their IDs within the DOM or create the HTML to render the control directly using script code. The latter method is similar to writing CGI code, which can be tedious. To use a control in an object-oriented way, you would have to call a COM object that exposes an interface. In this case, however, the object is wrapping up the details of writing HTML control code onto the stream headed back to the browser.

.NET adds a host of feature-rich controls called *Server Controls*. These controls are implemented and accessible as objects in the .NET Framework. To lay these controls out in your UI, special tags are added to the HTML user interface files. These controls are also flagged in code such that they will be run on the server. When the page is processed, the ASP.NET engine creates the correct HTML code to render the controls and sends it back to the browser for you. Throughout the code for your page, you can access these controls very much as you would a Windows control in an MFC or VB6 app, by referring to them by their variable names and calling methods and accessing properties on them.

In addition to the benefit of having real object-oriented access to your Web UI, ASP.NET will automatically detect the browser devices' capabilities and then render the control appropriately. This frees programmers from the trouble of managing code for detecting different versions of HTML and DHTML, for example. There are controls for almost any type of UI item you could need for your Web apps, and some complex controls as well. For example, several controls render data in grid fashion, without the programmer's having to create complicated and hard-to-maintain tables, divs, and spans.

State in a Nonstate Environment

In ASP, each time a page is loaded, the code is executed in a top-down fashion, and the response, including the dynamically generated HTML code, is sent to the browser. There is no state held between a browser and the server because HTTP is a connectionless protocol. The problem with this is that when the user reloads the page for any reason, including action taken on some UI item like a form submit button that causes a trip to the server, the page has to be completely reloaded. The programmer is responsible for making sure the UI elements are in the same state each subsequent time the server resends the page. For example, think of some ASP code that creates and fills a list box with some text items, selects the first item, then sends it and a button to the browser. The button is clicked, which submits a form, which causes a trip back to the server. The same page is loaded again, and the same code executes. Now the list box is created again, filled, and the first item is selected. What if the user had selected another item in the list before hitting the submit button? The code should reflect this by selecting the correct list item before sending it to the browser on the second trip around; this task is the programmer's responsibility in ASP.

In ASP.NET, this is handled automatically and quite nicely. The ASP.NET page framework makes the stateless HTTP protocol appear to have state. What this means for the programmer is that you no longer have to write code to keep the UI current with what the user has done to it between multiple server round trips on the same page. In ASP, programmers often jump to a new page when a user performs an action that will cause a round trip to the server. In ASP.NET, because the state of the UI is taken care of automatically, programmers will find themselves adding more functionality to a single page, even if it requires multiple trips to the server. In addition to the UI state as the user sees it, state is maintained in the UI objects that are in the code-behind the page as well. In ASP, form variables or a query string must be consulted to see what value was in a UI control when it was submitted. In ASP.NET, the values are in the most natural place, the control object variable itself. This adds a whole new level of UI programmability to Web apps. It also makes the code more like that of an MFC or VB Windows app, where the controls themselves are accessed as objects.

Event-Driven Programming

ASP provided nothing in the way of event-driven programming. In order to handle events, programmers had to rely on handling form submissions or handle the event on the client using VBScript, JavaScript, or Jscript. In ASP.NET, when a user causes an event by pressing a button or selecting an item in a list on the browser, for example, an event is fired in the code on the server. This occurs via some .NET-generated JavaScript and a form submittal, but that happens behind the scenes. Finally, Web programmers can handle real events all in one place: the server. All events in .NET are handled by what are called delegates, which are analogous to function pointers. Really, these delegates are just like the event handlers in VB apps, and for most standard events, they can even be added via point and click in the Visual Studio .NET IDE. But unlike last-generation VB event handlers, .NET event handlers can be added both at design time and runtime, so you can do much more robust things with the code than ever before, including creating your own custom events. This is fully supported in ASP.NET apps as well.

In most traditional apps, during an event handler, UI controls are updated to show changes in the state of the app. Because ASP.NET events are run on the server, the server-side controls reflecting your UI can be accessed, as mentioned in an earlier section. This again brings the robust programming styles we have enjoyed in traditional Windows app to the Web.

Processing the Pages

ASP pages are processed on the fly by an ISAPI DLL that is loaded by the Web server and passed the contents of ASP pages when they are requested. One problem with this design is that if the ISAPI DLL enters some sort of exception state, the whole Web server could hang because it is running in the same process. This can be made to run in an external surrogate process by modifying certain options in IIS for the app in question, but doing so can require more system resources and negatively affect performance overall.

ASP.NET uses a different approach. A separate Windows service executable runs and is passed the ASP.NET pages for processing. This service cannot bring down the Web server if it fails to respond or enters a state of exception because it is running in an entirely different process. If the ASP.NET service ever stops responding you will still be able to access non-ASP.NET content on the server. Basically, your HTML and legacy ASP pages will still function properly; however, you would not get any response when trying to access an ASP.NET page until the malfunctioning service was restarted. Because of this more robust way to process the pages, performance and reliability are substantially increased. Your Web apps will respond better, and they will stay running. In addition, the runtime services for ASP.NET are configurable such that they can be made to restart periodically, a feature that leads to a somewhat self-healing Web application.

Introducing C#

C# (pronounced C Sharp) is the newest addition to the Microsoft suite of Windows programming languages. C# is the first new language to support the .NET Framework and common language runtime. It was built from the ground up to mesh very well with the loyal Windows programmers as well as programmers of other environments. C# uses the familiar and robust C/C++-like syntax and in many ways is very similar to Sun's Java programming language. C# is a general-purpose language well suited to most types of application development. It has the simplicity to allow a programmer to create powerful, high-level apps in a short period of time, but it is also perfectly suited to low-level and system programming. In fact, most of ASP.NET itself was developed in C#.

Other than in its syntax, C# is different in many ways from C++, and it fixes some of the complexities in C++. For example, C++ programmers have the burden of keeping track of header files and initializing their variables. Header files and the circular reference headaches that they brought with them do not exist in C#. Variables are automatically initialized for you, numeric data types are initialized to 0, and string types are set to an empty string. As another example, dynamically determining object types in C++ can require advanced techniques and, in some cases, compiler switches (speaking of RTTI options). C# takes care of these complexities for you, allowing you to concentrate more on the logic rather than the plumbing of your application.

Unlike C++, which allows variables and code outside of any class, C# is completely object oriented. For example, although C++ allows for true multiple inheritance, meaning that a class in C++ can inherit implementation from more than one base class, this can get very complex very quickly and can cause problems that are difficult to solve. In fact, most of the programming community has learned that multiple implementation inheritance is rarely needed; Microsoft's flagship MFC doesn't even use it at all. In contrast, C# supports single implementation inheritance and multiple interface inheritance. C++ allows you to create an interface class, too, but by means of writing an abstract class with all pure virtual functions. C#, on the other hand, supports this with the much simpler and more readable interface keyword. With C++, some operators have several meanings, and often an operator itself is not at all descriptive of what it does. Sometimes it can be hard to see what is happening in code based solely on the syntax. In C#, however, there are distinct keywords and operators for the different features, and reading the code is usually much easier. Take, for example, C#'s ref keyword, which means that a function is taking a parameter by its reference. This is much more sensible than the pointer dereference or reference operators in C++, which are the vague * and & characters, respectively.

In addition to simplifying the language and supporting a well-defined set of objective features, C# has some nice examples of *syntactical sugar* throughout. For example, typically when iterating through a collection in C++, a programmer must deliberately code for getting the first item, then continuously getting the next item until the end is reached. C# introduces something entirely new to C++ programmers, the foreach construct, which has been in Visual Basic for years. This is a way to iterate through a collection with a very simple and readable syntax. Another example is indexers. Indexers are used in collections classes so that the caller can index an item in the collection without having to call a method or property explicitly. This doesn't enhance program performance, but it makes the code simpler and more readable. Plus, because a lot of these syntax enhancements lessen the amount of code that needs to be written, there is less chance for errors.

Clearly these are just some examples of how C# handles some things differently than C++, but we want you to have some idea of the design goals of the language. There are already good books on C#, so try one out. For now, know that C# is likely to become extremely popular with the huge base of C/C++ programmers, as well as with VB and Java programmers looking to move to something new. It supports the power and robustness of C++, with its familiar syntax, but helps alleviate some of the nastier parts of the former language so you can get on with the important matter of producing great apps.

Where Do We Go from Here?

Now that you've had a tour of .NET and seen how it has changed ASP, it's time to get our hands dirty and do some coding. In the next chapter, we will get right into the basics of writing ASP.NET pages, and then we will move quickly into the heavy technical content that will constitute the remainder of the book.

CHAPTER 2

Anatomy of an ASP.NET Page

Now that we know what ASP.NET is, let's take a look at the traditional Hello World application. This chapter will give you the very basics that we will build on in the remainder of the book. ASP.NET pages can be developed with a simple text editor or by using Visual Studio .NET. We'll cover these methods in depth.

The first few examples that we cover demonstrate how you can go about writing ASP.NET pages with a simple text editor. We then finish up the chapter by creating our first page with Visual Studio .NET. Although Visual Studio .NET is not required to develop ASP.NET pages, it does make things a lot easier. In addition, we'll take a look at what ASP.NET and the .NET Framework are doing for us behind the scenes. Some of the information we cover is fairly advanced, but it is necessary to fully understand all that ASP.NET does for you. It also might come in handy when something goes astray on your Web server at 2:00 in the morning. If you're like us, you'll want to know exactly how everything is working and where things are located. If you're not, then you can just pretend that the things you don't know or care about are simply a bit of Microsoft magic.

A Simple Page

In its absolutely simplest form, an ASP.NET page is nothing but pure HTML. Any file with the extension .aspx will be parsed by aspnet_wp.exe. If there isn't any script in the .aspx file and there are no references to a code-behind file, then the page simply passes through and is sent directly to the client in its raw form.

To test this theory, we'll create an ASP.NET page called HelloWorld.aspx and save it in the root directory of our default Web site. We'll then request the page from a browser and view the source of the page to verify that it has not been changed.

Start by firing up your trusty copy of Windows Notepad. Enter the following HTML:

```
<html>
  <head>
  </head>
  <body>
    Hello World
  </body>
</html>
```

Save the document as HelloWorld.aspx in the root directory of your default Web site (usually c:\inetpub\wwwroot). Now open your browser and navigate to http://localhost/HelloWorld.aspx. You should see a pretty boring page that says Hello World across the top. Now view the source for the page within your browser. If you are using Internet Explorer this can be done by selecting View, Source from the drop-down menu. If everything went correctly, you should see the exact same code that you typed into your HelloWorld.aspx file, completely unchanged.

Adding a Web Control

Now let's make a slight change to our HelloWorld.aspx file. We'll use an ASP.NET Web Control to display the "Hello World" text. We'll see how ASP.NET processes the page on the server and renders the appropriate HTML in place of the Web Server Control. Web Server controls provide us with a wide range of UI functionality from displaying a simple line of text to a very sophisticated data grid. In addition, Web Server Controls can be accessed programmatically in server-side code, which enables us to make our pages fully dynamic. We'll be covering Web Server Controls in detail in Chapter 3, "Server Controls."

```
<html>
  <head>
  </head>
  <body>
    <form runat=server>
      <asp: Label text="Hellow World" runat=server />
    </form>
  /body>
</html>
```

Save this file as HelloWorld2.aspx in the same directory as before. Now navigate to http://localhost/HelloWorld2.aspx with your Web browser. The page should look similar to your original page. The difference is "Hello World" is wrapped up inside of a <span> tag. There is also a hidden input element called VIEWSTATE, which we will cover in the next section. View the source of this page and you should see the following:

```
<html>
  <head>
  </head>
  <body>
    <form name="_ct10" method="post" action="HelloWorld2.aspx" id="_ct10">
      <input type="hidden" name="_VIEWSTATE" value=dDw5MjMzODA0MjI7Oz4="/>
```

```
  <span>Hello World</span>
 </form>
 /body>
</html>
```

Now let's examine what happened here at a high level. <asp:Label> is an ASP.NET Web Control. This is one of many Web Controls designed by Microsoft and included with the .NET Framework. When the HelloWorld2.aspx page is processed, the Web server creates a Label control. The Label control has a property called *text*, which contains the text that will be displayed by the control when the page is rendered. It also contains a property called *runat*, whose only valid value is *server*. This tells ASP.NET to process the control on the Web server. With Web and HTML controls, you must always set the runat property to server. As you can see from viewing the source of the rendered page, the <asp:Label> control renders its text inside of an HTML <span> block.

It is also important to note that Web Controls must be placed inside of a <form> tag that also has its runat attribute set to server.

We should also point out that anything on the page that does not require server-side processing is compiled into an instance of the LiteralControl object on the server. The purpose of this object is to act as a holder for text when the page is being processed on the server. Any HTML element that does not contain a runat="server" attribute/value pair in its opening tag, as well as any text on the page, will be compiled into a LiteralControl object.

Introducing In-Line Script

"Let's modify the page again. We'll add a button to our page using another Web Control <asp:Button>. When this button is clicked we'll change the text of our <asp:Label> control from "Hello World" to ".NET Rules!". We're going to do this with a little bit of C# code inside of a method that will be called when the button is clicked. For now, we are going to write this method within the .aspx file along with the HTML and ASP.NET content. This is called *in-line script*. In the next section, we'll see how to use code-behind to separate our code from the rest of the page.

Modify the HelloWorld2.aspx file as follows and save it as HelloWorld3.aspx.

```
<html>
  <head>
  </head>
  <body>
    <form method="post" runat="server">
      <asp:Label id=lblHelloWorld text="Hello World" runat=Server />
      <br>
      <asp:Button onclick=ClickedIt text="Submit" runat=Server />
    </form>
  </body>

<script Language=C# runat=server>
void ClickedIt(object sender, System.EventArgs e)
{
  lblHelloWorld.Text = ".NET Rules!";
```

```
        }
        </script>

        </html>
```

Once again, navigate to this page and view it with your Web browser. When the page is first rendered, the text at the top should be "Hello World". Click the Submit button, and the text should change to ".NET Rules!", as shown in Figure 2.1. Let's examine what we had to do to get this to work.

We included an HTML <form> block, which is the standard way to collect data from the user and send it back to the Web server. All of the controls for this page are contained within this <form> block. We set the *method* property of the form to *post* and set the runat property to server. Note that the action property of the <form> tag is omitted. In standard HTML, the action property sets the URL of the page that will process the form data on postback. Without it, the page doesn't know where to post to and the button won't work. Because the runat property of the <form> tag was set to server, ASP.NET will process it as an HTML Control. HTML Controls are very similar to Web Controls in that they can be programmatically accessed on the server; however, they retain the familiar look and feel of an HTML element. An HtmlForm control will be created on the server when this page is requested. The HtmlForm control has an *action* property, whose default value is the current page. We'll see this when we examine the rendered source of the page. The full set of Web Controls is covered in Chapter 3.

The second thing we did is to assign an ID to the <asp:Label> control. This will allow us to programmatically access the control by name in the C# code. We also added an <asp:Button> control to the page and set the *onclick* attribute to ClickedIt. The onclick attribute allows us to specify a method that will be called when the *click* event of the button is fired. ClickedIt is a method that belongs to our page. For this example, we have written it inside of a <script> block within the .aspx file. Finally, set the runat property to server.

The <script> tag has a *Language* property, which is used to designate the programming language that will be used inside the script block. For the initial release of ASP.NET, the valid languages are C#, Visual Basic .NET, and Jscript. In addition, you can't mix and match languages within the same page, so you can't have one script block written in C# and another written in Visual Basic .NET. Here we set the Language property to C# as that is the language that we will be using consistently throughout this book. Inside the <script> block we have one simple line of C# code.

```
        lblHelloWorld.Text = ".NET Rules!";
```

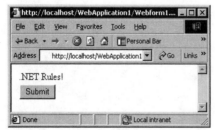

Figure 2.1   Our Hello World Application.

This line sets the text property of the Label control to the string ".NET Rules!". Note that we are still setting the text property of the Label control with this line of code:

```
<asp:Label id=lblHelloWorld text="Hello World" runat=Server />
```

This is why we see "Hello World" when we first request the page. After clicking the Submit button, the ClickedIt method is called and changes the text property of the Label control to ".NET Rules!".

Before we examine the rendered source of this page, let's try one more thing. Navigate to the page again with your browser and click the submit button once. Now refresh the page with your browser. (If you are using Internet Explorer, pressing F5 will do this. You may get a pop-up dialog with a Retry and a Cancel button. If you do, just click Retry.) Notice that the text at the top of the page is still ".NET Rules!". ASP.NET has maintained the state of the page for us and repopulated the Label control with the text that it contained before the postback. This is something that had to be handled entirely manually with ASP. Let's examine the rendered source and see how this all works. Here is the source of the rendered page on our machine.

```
<html>
  <head>
  </head>
  <body>
    <form name="ctrl1" method="post" action="HelloWorld3.aspx"
id="ctrl1">
<input type="hidden" name="__VIEWSTATE"
value="dDwtMTc5Njg3MTUyMjt0PDtsPDE8MT47PjtsPHQ8O2w8MTwxPjs+O2w8dDxwPHA8b
DxUZXh0Oz47bDwuTkVUIFJ1bGVzITs+Pjs+Ozs+Oz4+Oz62BKTiR3UtZabhkEbCIE3jS
lq7hA==" />

    <span id="lblHelloWorld">.NET Rules!</span>
    <br>
    <input type="submit" name="ctrl6" value="Submit" />
  </form>
  </body>
</html>
```

Notice that every HTML element on the page has been assigned either a name or an ID, or both. In the case of the Label control, a <span> tag was rendered with the same ID that we assigned to the Label control, lblHelloWorld. ASP.NET has auto-generated IDs for the rest of the elements because we did not assign any ourselves.

We can also see that the <form> element's action property has been given the value HelloWorld3.aspx, which is the name of the current page. Remember that we didn't set this ourselves; the HtmlForm control did this for us on the server.

The <asp:Button> control was rendered as an HTML <input> element. Its *type* property is set to submit, which causes the form to postback to the Web server when the button is clicked. Its *value* property is also set to "Submit," which is the caption that appears on the button and is the value that we assigned to the *text* property of the <asp:Button> control.

The last thing to look at is probably the most important thing. A hidden <input> element has been added to the form with the name __VIEWSTATE. This is how ASP.NET maintains the state of a page from postback to postback. The first time we request the page, ASP.NET encoded the values of all of the controls and stored them in the *value* property of this hidden <input> element. On every subsequent submit of the page, this is used to reinitialize the Web Controls and HTML Controls that are created on the server when the page is being processed. ASP.NET will allow us to store other things here as well, such as server side variable values that we want to maintain. We'll cover how to go about doing that in later chapters.

Code-Behind

In-line script is useful for putting together very small pages and maintaining the entire source in one single file. It has some shortcomings, though. Only one person can edit a single .aspx file at a time. That means that a page designer and a programmer can't be working on the same page at the same time. This could be a problem if the page designer and the programmer are two different people and are working collaboratively on a project. If the designer and the programmer are the same person, then it isn't a problem at all.

Another problem with in-line script is that compile errors are not detected until the page is requested for the first time with a Web browser. You can't precompile your in-line C# code to make sure that it is syntactically and semantically correct. The very first time that an ASP.NET page is requested, all of the code is compiled. It is not until this time that errors in your in-line code will be detected.

Also, in-line script does not provide you with the ability to protect your source code. If you are developing an application that will be distributed, you may very well be giving away intellectual property if you use in-line script.

ASP.NET provides us with the ability to separate the user interface from the code to a large degree. And, in fact, if you keep all of your code in the code-behind classes, you can achieve complete logic and user interface separation. This allows a page designer to work on the UI, while a programmer develops the functionality of the page. In addition, it allows us to precompile our code and protect our intellectual property. This feature was referred to in Chapter 1, "Making Sense of .NET," as *code-behind classes*. To use it, we must add a tag to the top of the .aspx file that tells ASP.NET where to find the code that supports the page. We then have a separate C# (.cs) file that contains all of the code for the page. This C# file must be precompiled into a class library (.dll file) and placed in the bin directory of the Web application. Precompiling this code means that we can work out any blatant C# coding mistakes ahead of time. Code-behind also helps promote code reuse and makes our pages much easier to understand and debug because the code is in a completely separate file.

Let's go ahead and work up a code-behind example building on the Hello World page. We'll rewrite the HelloWorld3 example, but this time we'll use code-behind instead of in-line script. First, let's modify the code from the HelloWorld3.aspx file. We'll remove the <script> block and add a Page Directive to the top of the file. Page directives allow us to specify various settings that should be used by the compilers when the page is processed. Modify the file as follows, and save it as HelloWorldCB.aspx.

```
<%@ Page Inherits="Wiley.ASPNET.HelloWorldCB" %>

<html>
  <head>
  </head>
  <body>
    <form method="post" runat="server">
      <asp:Label id=lblHelloWorld text="Hello World" runat=Server />
      <br>
      <asp:Button onclick=ClickedIt text="Submit" runat=Server />
    </form>
  </body>
</html>
```

All ASP.NET page directives must start with an opening tag <%@ and end with a closing tag %>. They can be located anywhere within the .aspx file, though the standard practice is to place them at the top of the file. Note that this is similar to ASP, where code is delimited by <% and %>. In ASP.NET, this too is the case although we will often have all of our code in the code-behind classes, rather than inside <% %> markers in the aspx file. We are using the @Page directive here, which is used by the ASP.NET page parser and compiler to set various page-specific options. The Inherits attribute has been set to Wiley.ASPNET.HelloWorldCB. This tells ASP.NET that the class or object that contains the code for this page is HelloWorldCB, which is located in the Wiley.ASPNET namespace. ASP.NET will look for a dll in the bin directory that implements this class when it processes the page.

Now we need to create a C# file to implement the HelloWorldCB class. Create a new file with the following code, and save it in the same directory with the Hello-WorldCB.aspx file. Name this file HelloWorldCB.cs.

```
namespace Wiley.ASPNET
{
  using System;
  using System.Web;
  using System.Web.UI;
  using System.Web.UI.WebControls;

  public class HelloWorldCB: System.Web.UI.Page
  {
    protected Label lblHelloWorld;

    protected void ClickedIt(object sender, System.EventArgs e)
    {
      lblHelloWorld.Text = ".NET Rules!";
    }
  }
}
```

The first line of code defines a *namespace* called Wiley.ASPNET. Namespaces provide us with a way to organize related code into logical groups. In addition, a namespace allows us to create globally unique types because all types declared within a namespace are specific to that namespace. For instance, in the preceding code a class called HelloWorldCB is declared. The fully qualified name for this class is Wiley.ASPNET. HelloWorldCB. This class would be completely distinguishable from another class with the name HelloWorldCB that is declared in a different namespace.

The next thing we see is several using directives (not to be confused with the using statement). The using directive can save us a lot of typing, and that is the only thing it does for us. It allows us to use names in a namespace without having to fully qualify them. For instance, in this example we declare a Label with this line of code.

```
protected Label lblHelloWorld;
```

The Label class is defined in the System.Web.UI.WebControls namespace. If we had not included this namespace with a using directive, we would need to fully qualify the Label class like this:

```
protected System.Web.UI.WebControls.Label lblHelloWorld;
```

Next, the HelloWorldCB class is defined. In this class, a Label control is defined and a ClickedIt method is implemented as in previous examples. This class is the one from which our .aspx page is inheriting, as we defined in the Page directive in .aspx file.

Now we need to compile this into a .NET library type assembly. An assembly is the primary building block of a .NET application. Not only does it contain compiled code, but it also contains meta data that makes it completely self-describing, such as how to resolve references to other code. We'll compile our code from the command line using the C# compiler. Open up a command prompt, navigate to the directory containing your HelloWorldCB.cs file, and execute the following command at the prompt:

```
csc /t:library /r:System.Web.dll HelloWorldCB.cs
```

This line asks the C# compiler (csc) to compile the HelloWorldCB.cs file into a library type assembly. This is designated using the /t or /target switch. The valid values for this switch are exe, winexe, library, or module. The exe option is for compiling console applications. The winexe option is for windows applications, and the module option is an advanced option that we won't be covering in this book. In addition, we need to reference the .NET Framework System.Web.dll assembly using the /r or /reference switch. This assembly contains a large portion of the code that we will need for developing ASP.NET pages and implements everything under the System.Web namespace. Referencing an assembly when compiling is not the same thing as including a namespace with the using directive. When we reference an assembly we are telling the compiler which other assemblies that it can examine for types used but not defined in our code. The using directive allows us to use types in a namespace without fully qualifying their names. Keep in mind that if you want to use classes that are in a namespace that is not in the DLL (or exe) you are building, you will have to reference them using the compiler options listed previously. Merely qualifying the name of a class or including the using alone will not allow your code to compile if the DLLs are not referenced.

Once you have executed the compiler command and it has compiled without error, a file named HelloWorldCB.dll will be created in the same directory. This is a .NET assembly file containing the class HelloWorldCB. This assembly file needs to be placed in the bin directory of the Web application. If you are still using the IIS default Web site, you may need to create a bin directory manually under inetpub\wwwroot. After doing so, move the HelloWorldCB.dll file into the bin directory.

Now we should be able to request the page from the Web browser. It should work exactly as the HelloWorld3 example. In addition, if you view the source of the rendered page, it should look very similar to the HelloWorld3 example.

That sure seemed like a lot of extra work to use code-behind, but as we'll soon see, Visual Studio .NET makes this whole process a piece of cake. But before we move on to that, let's examine the contents of the HelloWorldCB.cs file and introduce you to the Page class.

The Page Class

Every ASP.NET page is compiled into a class that inherits either directly or indirectly from the class System.Web.UI.Page. This class provides us with all of the base functionality that is required for ASP.NET to process a page on the server. It provides us with several events (discussed later in this section) that we can handle, as well as access to things like the Request and Response streams. The Page class is provided with the .NET Framework and is implemented in the assembly System.Web.dll. You can find this assembly and all of the other .NET Framework assemblies in the folder Winnt\ Microsoft.NET\Framework\v{version number}, where {version number} is the version of the framework that you have installed on your machine. These framework dlls are .NET assemblies, meaning that they contain Microsoft Intermediate Language (MSIL) code, not native x86 code. You can use a tool called ILDASM.exe to view .NET assemblies. Let's do this now and take a look at the System.Web.dll assembly.

Open up a command prompt, and execute the following command:

```
ildasm \Winnt\Microsoft.NET\Framework\v{version number}\System.Web.dll
```

On our machine, {version number} is 1.0.2609. Yours will be different, so you'll need to substitute your appropriate version number. This should start up the ILDASM utility, and you should see a screen similar to Figure 2.2.

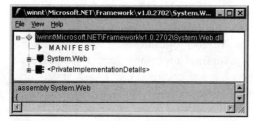

Figure 2.2   ILDASM view of System.Web.dll.

On the screen you can see that this assembly contains a namespace called System. Web and is represented in ILDASM as a node in the tree view with a shield-shaped icon. If you expand this node, you'll see that there are several other namespaces defined beneath System.Web. System.Web.UI is one of these namespaces. You'll also see many classes, enums, and interfaces that are defined in the System.Web namespace. Expand the System.Web.UI node of the tree view, and scroll down to the Page node. Expand this node, and you should see something similar to Figure 2.3.

There is quite a bit of information available to us here. We can see all of the methods, properties, events, and anything else that is defined and implemented in the Page class. For example, we can see that the Page class extends (inherits from) System.Web. UI.TemplateControl. We aren't going to go into the gory details of everything that is inside an assembly because it is beyond the scope of this book. We wanted to introduce you to the tool and give you a look at the internals of the System.Web.UI.Page class. You can experiment further with ILDASM if you wish. You don't have to worry about damaging anything, as ILDASM does not modify files in any way. It is a read-only tool. ILDASM might come in handy as a debugging tool if you are having problems using an assembly created by a third party. If you learn how to read MSIL, you could even see exactly what the code is doing.

Now let's revisit the code in the HellowWorldCB.cs file. We defined our Page class under the namespace Wiley.ASPNET because it is contained within the "namespace Wiley.ASPNET" code block. We've also used a few using directives to save us some typing.

```
using System;
using System.Web;
using System.Web.UI;
using System.Web.UI.WebControls;
```

Finally, we declare the class HelloWorldCB and declare its base class to be that of System.Web.UI.Page.

```
public class HelloWorldCB: System.Web.UI.Page
```

Inside the class definition, we defined a member of type System.Web.UI.WebControls. Label. Once again, we omitted the namespace prefix and defined the member variable as type Label because we imported the System.Web.UI.WebControls namespace with a using directive.

```
protected Label lblHelloWorld;
```

Notice that the member is named lblHelloWorld, which is the same ID that was assigned to the <asp:Label> control in the HelloWorldCB.aspx file. This allows ASP.NET to associate the two, and it allows you to programmatically access the lbl-HelloWorld control in the code-behind file. Another important thing to note is that nowhere in the HelloWorldCB.cs file do you have to create a new Label control and assign it to the lblHelloWorld member variable. Because this control was defined in the .aspx file, ASP.NET will create an instance of this control for us.

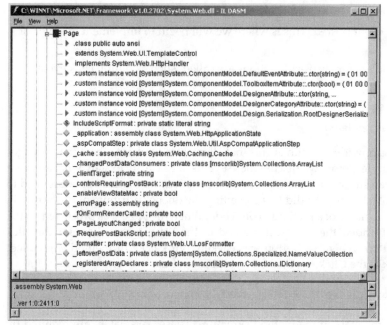

Figure 2.3   ILDASM view of the Page class.

The last thing that we define in the HelloWorldCB class is the method ClickedIt, which gets fired when the Submit button is clicked. The name of this method matches the value to which we set the onclick attribute of the button.

```
protected void ClickedIt(object sender, System.EventArgs e)
{
   lblHelloWorld.Text = ".NET Rules!";
}
```

Inside the method, we set the Text property of the lblHelloWorld member variable to the string ".NET Rules!". When the lblHelloWorld control is rendered, this text will be displayed.

Special Page Class Events

An ASP.NET page has a specific set of stages that it progresses through in its life cycle. Understanding these stages will go a long way to helping you understand how a page works and will help you greatly during debugging. Here is a high-level description of the stages in the page life cycle.

1. The page is initialized. This includes creating control instances and setting up event handlers.

2. The view state is processed, which populates the controls with data.

3. The Load event is fired. This is where we will begin to implement the logic of our page.

4. Event handlers for client-side actions are called, such as button click event handlers.

5. The view state is saved.

6. The page is rendered.

The Page class provides us with events that allow us to hook into the different stages of the page life cycle. Before we discuss these events, let's clarify exactly what an event is and how we can subscribe to it. In the previous section, we handled or subscribed to the click event of a button. We did this by setting the onclick attribute of the button in the .aspx file to the name of a method in our code. When the page was processed on the server, ASP.NET added the ClickedIt method to the list of subscribers for the click event of the button. When the button was clicked, our ClickedIt method was called. Let's take a look at the ClickedIt method signature again.

```
protected void ClickedIt(object sender, System.EventArgs e)
```

Notice the parameters in the method signature. These parameters are required by any method that wishes to subscribe to a click event. Every event defines a method signature that its subscribers must adhere to through the use of a *delegate*. A delegate is a special class that has a signature and can hold a reference to a method. It can hold a reference only to a method that matches its signature. To subscribe to the click event of a button we must use a System.EventHandler type delegate. This is the definition of System.EventHandler.

```
public delegate void EventHandler(
  object sender,
  EventArgs e
);
```

Our ClickedIt method matches the signature of EventHandler. We could subscribe our ClickedIt method to the click event of a button with the following C# code.

```
MyButton.Click += new System.EventHandler(ClickedIt);
```

With that line of code, we have created a new instance of System.EventHandler and given it a reference to our ClickedIt method. When used in this context, the += syntax takes on a special meaning that says add this EventHandler to the list of subscribers for the Click event. Likewise, we can remove an EventHandler from the list of subscribers by using the -= syntax as follows:

```
MyButton.Click -= new System.EventHandler(ClickedIt);
```

Now that we know how to subscribe to events and what delegates are, a couple of events of the Page class deserve special attention. If you are using in-line script and not code-behind, these events are prewired to special methods that you can define and take advantage of in your in-line script. If you are using code-behind, you're left to wire these events up yourself. Don't worry about the extra work of wiring up the events because Visual Studio .NET will do most of this for you.

> **NOTE** The @Page directive has an attribute called AutoEventWireup that can be set to true or false. This attribute is used to tell ASP.NET whether to automatically wire up the events of the Page class for us. When using code-behind, this attribute is usually set to false and the event wire-up is done manually or with the help of Visual Studio .NET. The default value is true, and if the AutoEventWireup attribute is omitted, as it normally will be when using in-line script, the Page class events will be auto-wired.

Let's take a look at the two most important events of the Page class and what each one should be used for.

Init

```
private void Page_Init(object sender, EventArgs e)
```

The Init event is the first event fired in a Page life cycle. It is during this event that ASP.NET creates all of the controls for the page. You will mainly use this event to wire up event handlers. If you are developing your pages with Visual Studio .NET, it will place event wire-ups for your controls inside the Page_Init method. It will also wire up a handler for the Load event here. To use this event, define a method called Page_Init with the EventHandler delegate signature, as follows:

```
{
   this.Load += new System.EventHandler(this.Page_Load);
}
```

Notice that we have wired up the Load event of the Page class to a method called Page_Load inside of the Page_Init method. This ensures that our handler for the Load event will be called. If you're using code-behind, you'll have to wire your Page_Init method to the Init event in the constructor of your code-behind class as follows:

```
public WebForm1()
{
   Page.Init += new System.EventHandler(Page_Init);
}
```

If you're using in-line script, this will be done for you.

One important thing to note about the Init event is that your page view state information cannot be accessed inside this method because it has not been loaded yet. This means that we can't do things such as validate values that a user may have entered on the page.

Load

The Load event is fired after the Init event. The main difference between the Load event and the Init event is the availability of the page view state. Unlike the Init event, the view state is available when the Load event is fired, so we can examine the values of controls and process the page as needed.

If you are using in-line script, the Page_Load method will be prewired to the Load event. The Page class defines a property called IsPostBack, which returns a Boolean true if the page is being requested on a postback or a Boolean false if the page is being requested by the client for the first time. Use this property to make sure certain code is executed only the first time the client requests the page—for example, retrieving data from a database and populating drop-down lists or tables. Because ASP.NET saves the state of the page, you don't have to obtain static data again from the database and repopulate the page on subsequent postbacks, as was the case with ASP. This makes the page execute a lot faster and doesn't use up valuable database and server resources when unnecessary.

A typical Page_Load method will be defined as follows:

```
private void Page_Load(object sender, System.EventArgs e)
{
    //Place any code that needs to be executed on every request here. This
    //could be things such as setting up a database connection that will
    //be used throughout the processing of the page.

    if(!IsPostBack)
    {
        //Place any code that needs to be executed only on first request
        //here. This would include things such as retrieving static data
        //from the database and populating drop-down lists or tables with
        //this data.
    }
    else
    {
        //Place any code that needs to execute only on a postback here.
        //This might include code that checks for some kind of user input
        //that wouldn't be available when the page Is first requested.
    }
}
```

Unload

The Unload event is fired when the page is unloaded from memory. It is a good place to take care of any clean-up for the page, such as closing any open database connections or releasing any other valuable resources. The Unload event is not prewired to any method, regardless of whether you use in-line script or code-behind. To use it, prewire it manually, just as we did with the Page_Load method previously.

OTHER PREWIRED EVENTS

There are four additional events that are prewired for you if you are using in-line script:

DataBinding. Prewired to Page_DataBind. Notifies the control to perform any DataBinding logic.

PreRender. Prewired to Page_PreRender. Used to perform any updates to controls just before the page is rendered.

Dispose. Prewired to Page_Dispose. Used to perform any page clean-up that is necessary.

Error. Prewired to Page_Error. This event is fired when an unhandled exception occurs in the processing of the page.

Although we won't be using these events right now you should be aware of the prewirings if you intend to use in-line script.

```
this.Unload += new System.EventHandler(this.Page_Unload);
```

Once again, Visual Studio .NET makes wiring up events like this a lot easier for you. You can double-click on an event name in the Visual Studio .NET property page, and it will create an event handler for you as well as wire it up to the event.

An Event Example

Let's rewrite the HelloWorld3 example to demonstrate the use of the Init and Load events. We'll use the Init event to wire up the click event handler for our button and the Load event to set the initial text of our Label control. Modify the HelloWorld3.aspx file as follows, and save it as HelloWorldEvents.aspx. The lines that need to be changed or added appear in bold:

```
<html>
  <head>
  </head>
  <body>
    <form method="post" runat="server">
      <asp:Label id=lblHelloWorld runat=Server />
      <br>
      <asp:Button id=btnSubmit text="Submit" runat=Server />
    </form>
  </body>
</html>

<script Language=C# runat=server>
```

```
void Page_Init(object sender, System.EventArgs e)
{
  //Wire up our Click event
  btnSubmit.Click += new System.EventHandler(ClickedIt);
}


void Page_Load(object sender, System.EventArgs e)
{
  if (!IsPostBack)
  {
    //Set the initial text of the label to Hello World
    lblHelloWorld.Text = "Hello World";
  }
}

void ClickedIt(object sender, System.EventArgs e)
{
  lblHelloWorld.Text = ".NET Rules!";
}


</script>
</html>
```

If you go to the new HelloWorldEvents.aspx page with your browser, it should work exactly as HelloWorld3.aspx. Let's look at what we changed and why it still works.

First, we eliminated the setting of the initial text of the label from the definition of the control by removing the Text attribute of <asp:Label> control lblHelloWorld. Notice that the text at the top still reads "Hello World" when the page is first requested. This text is set in the Page_Load method; we used the following code to set the Text property of the Label:

```
if (!IsPostBack)
{
  //Set the initial text of the label to Hello World
  lblHelloWorld.Text = "Hello World"
}
```

This code was placed inside the if statement so that it would execute only the first time the page is requested.

Next, we removed the onclick attribute of the <asp:Button> control and assigned the button an ID, btnSubmit. So, instead of prewiring the Click event of the button to the ClickedIt method inside the definition of the button, this is done in the Page_Init method with the following code:

```
void Page_Init(object sender, System.EventArgs e)
{
  //Wire up our Click event
  btnSubmit.Click += new System.EventHandler(ClickedIt);
}
```

This adds the ClickedIt method to the list of methods that will be called when the Click event of the btnSubmit button is fired.

This section should have given you a nice overview of the Page class. We'll cover it in further depth throughout the rest of the book. Chapter 5, "Creating More Advanced ASP.NET Pages," will show you how to write your own reusable Page class and give you several tips and tricks that will help simplify your pages and make them more efficient.

Now that we've seen how to develop ASP.NET pages with the use of a text editor, let's create the same application using Visual Studio .NET. You can see how the process is simplified for you.

Hello World with Visual Studio .NET

We're going to create our first project with Visual Studio .NET (from here on referred to as VS.NET) and take a look at all the functionality it offers. From this point on, we'll be using VS.NET for all of the ASP.NET development.

When you're ready, start up VS.NET. To get started, create a new project by bringing up the New Project dialog in one of several ways. You can click on the "New Project" button on the Start Page; select File, New, Project from the File Menu; or click on the New Project toolbar button. Once you have the New Project dialog open, select Visual C# Projects from the Project Types list on the left. Then select Web Application from the Templates list on the right, as shown in Figure 2.4.

Visual Studio .NET gives you a default project name of WebApplication1 and a default location of http://localhost, as seen in Figure 2.4. Change the project name to Chapter2, and click OK. After a few seconds of setup, the new project will be created and ready for work. Before we examine everything that's been included with the new project, notice that VS.NET also has created a new Virtual Directory in IIS with the same name as the project name and in the location that we specified in the New Project Dialog. In this case, the virtual directory is called Chapter2 and is located at in the virtual root directory of your Web server.

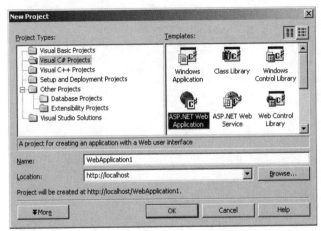

Figure 2.4 The new project dialog in Visual Studio .NET.

Now let's check out the project. Open up the Solution Explorer window, which is usually docked to the right side of VS.NET. Click on the Show All Files toolbar button at the top of the Solution Explorer window, and then expand all of the nodes of the tree view contained in the Solution Explorer. You should see something very similar to Figure 2.5.

Under the References node there are several assemblies that have been referenced for us by default. This makes all of the classes defined in these assemblies available for use within the application. VS.NET's intellisense feature should work with all of the classes defined in these assemblies. A bin directory also has been created for us. The bin directory is where VS.NET will place the project's assembly file, debug file, and any other non-.NET framework assemblies that we reference. Recall that ASP.NET will search the assemblies contained in the bin directory for any classes used in the code, including the code-behind Page classes.

You should also see a Global.asax file and its associated code-behind file, Global.asax.cs. The Global.asax file is used for handling special ASP.NET application events such as Application_Start and Session_Start. These are covered in detail in Chapter 5, and we'll see their uses there.

The Web.Config file is an XML file used for making overall application settings such as security and session state. We'll be covering what you can do with this file in Chapter 9, "Adding E-Commerce Essentials."

There is also a Chapter2.disco file. This is a Web services discovery file that is used to advertise any Web services that our Web site offers. We'll look at this in Chapter 7, "Web Services."

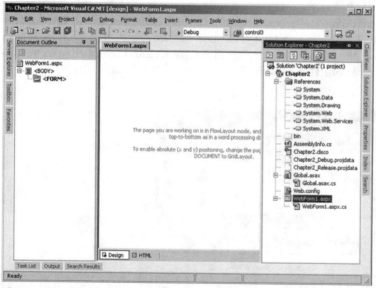

Figure 2.5 The Chapter2 project.

Finally, VS.NET has created one Web Form (another name for an ASP.NET page), called WebForm1.aspx, and its associated code-behind file, WebForm1.aspx.cs. VS.NET implements code-behind by default and takes care of a lot of the legwork that is required to use code-behind. Let's examine these two files. If you double-click the WebForm1.aspx file, VS.NET will open the Web Form in the Web Forms designer. In this view, you can drag and drop controls from the Toolbox onto the page. In addition to adding the control to the .aspx file, VS.NET will take make all of the necessary additions and changes to the associated code-behind file. Let's take a look at the actual code that is contained in the WebForm1.aspx file by clicking on the HTML button located at the bottom of the editor window.

The following @Page directive has been added to the top of the file:

```
<%@ Page language="c#" Codebehind="WebForm1.aspx.cs"
AutoEventWireup="false" Inherits="Chapter2.WebForm1" %>
```

The directive contains the following new attributes:

Language attribute.   Set to c# in this example. The language attribute defines the programming language used in all server code blocks on the ASP.NET page.

Codebehind attribute.   Set to the filename of the code-behind source file that was automatically created by VS.NET, in this case, WebForm1.aspx.cs. The Code-behind attribute is completely ignored by the ASP.NET runtime. It is used exclusively by VS.NET to keep track of which code-behind files go with which .aspx files. The WebForm1.aspx.cs code-behind file is located underneath the WebForm1.aspx node in the Solution Explorer tree view.

Inherits attribute.   Set to Chapter2.WebForm1 in this example. We saw the use of this attribute in our earlier code-behind example. The class that is referenced in this attribute must be derived directly or indirectly from the System.Web.UI.Page class. Let's take a look at our code-behind file, WebForm1.aspx.cs, and make sure that this is the case. Double-click the WebForm1.aspx.cs file in the Solution Explorer window to open it in the Source Editor. It should look similar to the following:

```
namespace Chapter2
{
    using System;
    using System.Collections;
    using System.ComponentModel;
    using System.Data;
    using System.Drawing;
    using System.Web;
    using System.Web.SessionState;
    using System.Web.UI;
    using System.Web.UI.WebControls;
    using System.Web.UI.HtmlControls;
```

```
/// <summary>
/// Summary description for WebForm1.
/// </summary>
public class WebForm1 : System.Web.UI.Page
{
  public WebForm1()
  {
    Page.Init += new System.EventHandler(Page_Init);
  }

  protected void Page_Load(object sender, System.EventArgs e)
  {
    // Put user code to initialize the page here
  }

  protected void Page_Init(object sender, EventArgs e)
  {
    //
    // CODEGEN: This call is required by the ASP+ Windows Form
    // Designer.
    //
    InitializeComponent();
  }

  #region Web Form Designer generated code
  /// <summary>
  /// Required method for Designer support - do not modify
  /// the contents of this method with the code editor.
  /// </summary>
  private void InitializeComponent()
  {
    this.Load += new System.EventHandler(this.Page_Load);
  }
  #endregion
  }
}
```

VS.NET has declared a default namespace that matches the name of the Web application. It also included several directives for the common namespaces that we'll use. Notice the declaration of the Page class, WebForm1. It is derived from the System.Web. UI.Page class.

The default constructor of the WebForm1 class wires up the Page_Init method to the Init event with this line of code.

```
Page.Init += new System.EventHandler(Page_Init);
```

Look familiar? This is precisely what we did manually in our earlier example.

The Page_Init method is implemented for us and makes a call to a method called InitializeComponent. InitializeComponent is a special method that is used by the VS.NET designer. It is contained within a #region block, which makes that entire area of code collapsible in the VS.NET source editor, as shown in Figure 2.6. Although there may be some circumstances in which you'll be forced to make changes in there, avoid messing with the code in the InitalizeComponent method unless it is absolutely necessary. It is possible that changes you might make in this method could be overwritten by the Web Form Designer or could confuse it in some way. Initially, the following code is the only code placed in InitializeComponent by the Web Form designer:

```
this.Load += new System.EventHandler(this.Page_Load);
```

This line wires up the Page_Load method to the Load event. VS.NET will add, delete, and edit code in the IntializeComponent method when you are using the Web Form designer. We'll see that in action shortly.

The Page_Load method has been implemented for us and is completely empty at this point.

Let's rewrite the Hello World application from scratch using VS.NET. The first thing that we need to do is drag and drop a Label control from the toolbox onto the form. To do this, switch back to the Design view of the Webform1.aspx file.

NOTE All of the helper windows (Toolbox, Solution Explorer, Properties window, and so on) can be docked at the left, right, or bottom edges of VS.NET. Once they are docked, they can be used in an auto-hide mode. When you need to use the window, you simply point to its tab located on the edge of the screen, and it will slide out for you to use. When you move the mouse cursor away from the window, it will retract itself back to the edge of the screen for you. You can also pin the window open by using the thumbtack icon located at the top of the helper window. When the window is pinned, it will stay open until you unpin it by pressing the thumbtack icon again.

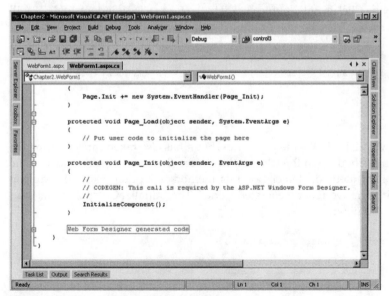

Figure 2.6 Our initial code-behind class.

Open the Toolbox window, docked at the left-hand side of VS.NET. Find the Label control, and drag it onto the design window. A Label control will be added to your form. You can drag the Label control to any area of the screen that you wish.

Next, change some properties of this Label control. Nearly everything that we'll need to change can be done with the Properties window. Right-click on the Label control, and select Properties from the context menu. The Properties window should appear. If the Properties window is docked and hidden, it will automatically slide out into view for you. Change the Text property to "Hello World" and the ID property to lblHelloWorld. When you're finished, click on the HTML button at the bottom of the Web Form designer window to see how VS.NET implemented the new Label control. You should see some code similar to the following:

```
<asp:Label runat="server">
  Hello World
</asp:Label>
```

The control has been assigned the ID of lblHelloWorld, and the runat attribute has been set to server. Instead of setting the Text attribute of the Label control, the Hello World text has been inserted between opening and closing <asp:Label> tags, which is exactly the same as setting the Text attribute. When the page is processed, the Label control will set the Text property to the value of the tag contents.

Now let's add a button to the page. Switch back to the Design view, and drag a button from the Toolbox onto the page. Once again, nearly everything that we'll need to change about the button can be done from the Properties window. Open the Properties window, and change Text property to "Submit" and the ID property to btnSubmit. Next we need to provide a handler for the Click event of the button. We can also do this from the Properties window. At the top of the Properties window, there is a lightning bolt icon. Click this icon to see a list of all of the available events for the Button control. Initially, we don't have any handlers for them because we haven't added any yet. To add a handler to the Click event, double-click it in the Properties window. VS.NET will open the WebForm1.aspx.cs file in the editor. The following btnSubmit_Click method has been added:

```
protected void btnSubmit_Click(object sender, System.EventArgs e)
{

}
```

Not only did VS.NET add the method for us, but it has also taken care of wiring the btnSumbit_Click method up to the Click event. To see this, you'll need to look at the InitializeComponent method. Remember, this method is hidden inside the #region marked as "Web Form Designer Generated Code". The InitializeComponent method should look like this now:

```
#region Web Form Designer generated code
/// <summary>
/// Required method for Designer support - do not modify
/// the contents of this method with the code editor.
```

```
/// </summary>
private void InitializeComponent()
{
  this.btnSubmit.Click += new System.EventHandler(this.btnSubmit_Click);
  this.Load += new System.EventHandler(this.Page_Load);
}
#endregion
```

Finally, we need to add the line of code to change the text of the lblHelloWorld control when the Submit button is clicked. Add the following line of code to the btnSubmit_Click method:

```
lblHelloWorld.Text = ".NET Rules!";
```

That is all of the code that we need to write. Because we're using code-behind, we now have to compile the project. To do this, select Build from the Build menu on the main menu bar. This is a whole lot easier than using the command-line compiler as we did in the earlier code-behind example. If your Build was successful, you'll see "Build succeeded" in the status bar at the bottom of the VS.NET window. You can also check out the Output or Task List windows to see if any errors were encountered and what they were.

If your build was successful, VS.NET will have placed the resulting Chapter2.dll and Chapter2.pdb files in the bin directory of your application. You can see this by looking in the bin folder in the Solution Explorer window. The Chapter2.dll file is a .NET assembly that contains the definition of the WebForm1 class and any other classes that we defined within the project. The .pdb file contains the debug symbols needed for debugging the project. By default, VS.NET will create a Debug version of the project. When you have completed your application, you should compile a Release version, which will be smaller and provide better performance. This can be done by selecting Build, Configuration from the menu bar, which displays the Configuration Manager dialog box, as seen in Figure 2.7. You can change the active configuration from Debug to Release with the drop-down box at the top of the dialog.

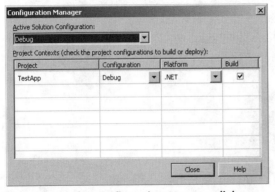

Figure 2.7 The Configuration Manager dialog.

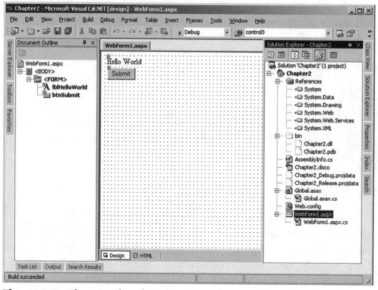

Figure 2.8   The completed project.

You should be able to navigate to your new WebForm1.aspx page with your browser, and it should work the same as the previous examples. If you've chosen to name everything as I have, then the URL of this new page should be http://localhost/Chapter2/Webform1.aspx.

A screenshot of what the project should look like when finished can be seen in Figure 2.8, and the complete source code for the WebForm1.aspx page can be seen in Listings 2.1 and 2.2.

```
<%@ Page language="c#" Codebehind="WebForm1.aspx.cs"
AutoEventWireup="false"
  Inherits="Chapter2.WebForm1" %>

<HTML>
  <HEAD>
    <meta name=vs_targetSchema content="Internet Explorer 5.0">
    <meta name="GENERATOR" Content="Microsoft Visual Studio 7.0">
    <meta name="CODE_LANGUAGE" Content="C#">
  </HEAD>
  <body MS_POSITIONING="GridLayout">
    <form method="post" runat="server">
      <asp:Label id=lblHelloWorld style="Z-INDEX: 101; LEFT: 8px;
        POSITION:absolute; TOP: 9px" runat="server">
        Hello World
      </asp:Label>
```

Listing 2.1   WebForm1.aspx

```
        <asp:Button id=btnSubmit style="Z-INDEX: 102; LEFT: 11px;
          POSITION: absolute; TOP: 38px" runat="server" Text="Submit">
        </asp:Button>
      </form>
    </body>
</HTML>
```

Listing 2.1   WebForm1.aspx (continued)

```
namespace Chapter2
{
  using System;
  using System.Collections;
  using System.ComponentModel;
  using System.Data;
  using System.Drawing;
  using System.Web;
  using System.Web.SessionState;
  using System.Web.UI;
  using System.Web.UI.WebControls;
  using System.Web.UI.HtmlControls;

  /// <summary>
  /// Summary description for WebForm1.
  /// </summary>
  public class WebForm1 : System.Web.UI.Page
  {
    protected System.Web.UI.WebControls.Label lblHelloWorld;
    protected System.Web.UI.WebControls.Button btnSubmit;
    private System.ComponentModel.IContainer components;

    public WebForm1()
    {
      Page.Init += new System.EventHandler(Page_Init);
    }

    protected void Page_Init(object sender, EventArgs e)
    {
      //
      // CODEGEN: This call is required by the ASP+ Windows Form
      // Designer.
      //
      InitializeComponent();
    }
```

Listing 2.2   WebForm1.aspx.cs

```
    #region Web Form Designer generated code
    /// <summary>
    /// Required method for Designer support - do not modify
    /// the contents of this method with the code editor.
    /// </summary>
    private void InitializeComponent()
    {
      this.components = new System.ComponentModel.Container();
      this.btnSubmit.Click += new
System.EventHandler(this.btnSubmit_Click);
      this.Load += new System.EventHandler(this.Page_Load);
    }
    #endregion

    private void Page_Load(object sender, System.EventArgs e)
    {

    }

    protected void btnSubmit_Click(object sender, System.EventArgs e)
    {
      lblHelloWorld.Text = ".NET Rules!";
    }
  }
}
```

Listing 2.2 WebForm1.aspx.cs (continued)

Wrapping Up the Chapter

In this chapter, we got a good taste of what an ASP.NET page is and how to develop one with and without VS.NET. We covered event handling and delegates and also discussed the System.Web.UI.Page class and its important events. We'll build on this foundation information in the next chapter as we discuss Server Controls in depth.

WHAT'S GOING ON IN THERE

We are going to cover some fairly advanced things in this section. Most of what we will cover here won't have any bearing on your ability to develop ASP.NET pages. If you are a beginner-level programmer you might just want to skip this section and go straight to Chapter 3. If you are really interested in what is going on behind the scenes to make ASP.NET work and where things are stored and cached on your machine, then read on.

We have already mentioned that a .NET assembly consists of Microsoft Intermediate Language (MSIL) and various meta data that makes the assembly self-describing. When we use code-behind, we must precompile our code into an assembly; however, the code in this assembly cannot be directly interpreted by the processor in the machine. It must first be just-in-time (JIT) compiled to x86 code by the .NET Framework before it can be used by the processor.

Earlier in this chapter we covered using in-line script on an .aspx page. Our preferred method is to use code-behind, but code-behind does not provide any performance advantages at runtime. Every ASP.NET page must be compiled the very first time it is requested, regardless of whether you use in-line script or code-behind. After this initial compilation is completed, the resulting x86 code is cached and subsequent requests for the page are executed using the compiled code. It is important to realize that any in-line script that you use on an ASP.NET page is not interpreted every time the page is requested, as was the case with ASP. It is compiled to x86 code, just as is the code-behind class. In fact, .NET code is not interpreted code, period, whether it be C#, VB.NET, or any other .NET-compliant language. Once a piece of code has been executed for the first time and therefore compiled to x86 code, the original MSIL code is not used again, unless something occurs that would require recompilation.

We already know that every ASP.NET page inherits from the Page class, but if you are using in-line script, how does this occur? The answer is that ASP.NET writes a C# class for you the first time the page is requested or whenever the page changes. It then compiles this C# class using the command-line compiler csc.exe. The resulting assembly .dll file is stored on the hard drive and then JITed to x86 code. The x86 code is cached in memory for reuse. You can actually take a look at the C# source file that ASP.NET creates. Let's look at an example.

We'll reuse our HelloWorld3.aspx page from earlier in the chapter. To make things a little easier, let's add the HelloWorld3.aspx page to our Chapter2 project. You can do this within VS.NET by opening the Chapter2 project and then choosing File, Add Existing Item from the menu bar. Once you've added the page to the project, request it with your Web browser. You'll probably notice that the page is somewhat slow on the first request, but subsequent requests are much faster. That's because the page had to be compiled on the first request.

Now let's examine the C# file that ASP.NET wrote for us for the HelloWorld3.aspx page. By default, these types of temporary files are stored in the following directory:

```
/Winnt/Microsoft.NET/Framework/v{version number}/Temporary ASP.NET
Files
```

This directory is configurable per Web application. If you'd prefer to have them placed in a different directory location, you can do so by setting the tempDirectory attribute of the <compilation> tag in the Web.config file for your application. We haven't talked about the Web.config file yet, but we wanted you to be aware that the temporary directory location is under your control.

Under the Temporary ASP.NET Files folder a new folder will be created for every ASP.NET application that runs on your Web server. Furthermore, there will be a strangely named folder under each application folder. It is in this folder that you will find all of the temporary files that ASP.NET creates for that particular application. The strange folder name is actually one of several hash codes used in a somewhat complex dependency-tracking

Continues

WHAT'S GOING ON IN THERE (CONTINUED)

scheme. The .cs file that was created for the HelloWorld3.aspx page will be located in this folder. The .cs file will also be named with a hash code. If you followed through the earlier examples, you should have three .cs files; open the one with the latest date.

We're not going to go through every detail of this file, as it is fairly complex, but we do want to point out that the class that is defined in this file inherits directly from **System.Web.UI.Page**.

```
public class HelloWorld3_aspx : System.Web.UI.Page,
System.Web.SessionState.IRequiresSessionState
```

The class has been named HelloWorld3_aspx, which is the same as the .aspx filename with an _aspx appended to it. In addition to inheriting from the Page class, it also inherits the IRequiresSessionState interface.

Near the top of the class declaration, you should be able to find the following line of code:

```
protected System.Web.UI.WebControls.Label lblHelloWorld;
```

This comes from the Label control that we added to the .aspx file. The Label control was assigned an ID of lblHelloWorld, which has been preserved. You should also see a declaration for the Button control that is on the page. We didn't give the Button control a specific ID, so ASP.NET has generated one for us. Our declaration looks like this:

```
protected System.Web.UI.WebControls.Button __control3;
```

We declared a method called ClickedIt within a <script> block on the page. If you search for ClickedIt in this .cs file, you will find that it has been added to the HelloWorld3_aspx class also.

There are several other files in this temporary directory. The .cmdline files contain the actual command-line arguments passed to csc.exe when a page is compiled. The .out files contain the results of the compilation, which would include any errors that occurred when the page was compiled. The .dll files are the MSIL assemblies created by the csc compilation. You can view these files with the ILDASM.exe tool, as was demonstrated earlier in the chapter in the Page Class section. Keep in mind that all of the files in these temporary directories are just that, temporary. Any changes you make to these files will eventually be overwritten.

How does all of this change if we are using code-behind? In fact, very little changes at all. Even if we are using code-behind, we can still have in-line script in the .aspx file, and if so, it will be handled exactly the same. The only real difference is that the generated class for a code-behind page does not inherit directly from the Page class. Instead, it inherits from the code-behind class, which inherits either directly or indirectly from the Page class. You can check this out for yourself by looking for the generated class for the WebForm1.aspx page that was created for Chapter2, which uses code-behind. The code-behind class name for this page was Chapter2.WebForm1. You can find the generated .cs file for this page in the same directory as the .cs file for the HelloWorld3 page. You should see the following class declaration in this file.

```
public class WebForm1_aspx : Chapter2.WebForm1,
System.Web.SessionState.IRequiresSessionState
```

Just as expected, the WebForm1_aspx class inherits directly from the code-behind class. It will include everything in the code-behind class, plus any in-line script that might be included in the .aspx file. You should also note that there are no declarations in the generated class for page control variables that were declared in the code-behind class. Any control variables that are declared in the code-behind class are instanced via the *new* keyword in the generated class. This is why we don't have to instance these variables ourselves in the code-behind class.

Server Controls

Now that we've covered the basics of building an ASP.NET page, it's time to examine all of the power that is provided with ASP.NET right off the shelf. ASP.NET provides many Server Controls that make page development much easier. Server Controls provide programmatic access to elements on the pages.

There are two types of Server Controls. *Web Server Controls* provide a level of abstraction from traditional HTML elements and make Web page development seem a lot like traditional windows application development. They do not necessarily render directly to a single HTML element and, in fact, some of them can render to a large number of HTML elements. This group of controls also includes *Validation Controls*, which make validating user input on the client or server side a whole lot easier than the methods that were needed with traditional ASP. *HTML Server Controls* map one-to-one to their HTML counterparts and provide an easy programming path for the experienced HTML developer.

We'll be covering most of the Server Controls that are included with ASP.NET off the shelf in this chapter. We'll analyze each control's important properties and methods and implement examples using them. In addition, we'll also learn the type of HTML that will be rendered by the controls and how it may differ depending on the type of browser the client is using. Before we start covering the controls, we'll discuss the topics of postback and Data Binding.

Postback

Before we begin this chapter, let's explain at a high level how ASP.NET gives the Web application programmer an event-driven programming model. We've already seen how easy it is to implement an event handler in Chapter 2, "Anatomy of an ASP.NET Page." This type of functionality was not nearly as easy to accomplish with traditional ASP. In our opinion, this is one of the best features of ASP.NET.

Postback is a term used to describe the action of a user submitting a page back to the Web server for processing. The client usually posts the page back to the server by clicking some type of button on the page. The HTML <form> element is what makes postback possible. We discussed the role of the <form> element in Chapter 2 in the *Introducing In-Line Script* section. In review, the *method* attribute of the <form> will typically be set to *post*. The *action* attribute will be set to the URL of a page or script to which the page should be posted. With ASP.NET, the action attribute will almost always be set to the URL of the page on which the <form> element resides. In other words, an ASP.NET page will post back to itself.

There are two most commonly used ways to post back or submit a form to the server. One method is through the use of the HTML <input type="submit"> or <input type="image"> elements, and the other is through the use of client-side script. The <input type="submit"> and <input type="image"> elements will always cause a postback of the <form> element that it resides in when it is clicked by the user. In the example code that follows, if the user clicks the Button1 button, the Form1 form will be submitted to the MyASPNETPage.aspx page.

```
<form method="post" runat="server" ID="Form1">
  <asp:Button id="Button1" runat="server" Text="Button 1"></asp:Button>
</form>
```

The rendered HTML:

```
<form name="Form1" method="post" action="MyASPNETPage.aspx" id="Form1">
  <input type="submit" name="Button1" value="Button 1" id="Button1" />
</form>
```

Recall from Chapter 2 that if the action attribute of the <form> element is not specified in the .aspx file, the default value is the name of the current page. This is why the action attribute of the <form> element in the rendered HTML is set to MyASPNET-Page.aspx. With ASP.NET, we can have a handler for the Click event of the Button1 button. So when the postback occurs, our Click event handler will be called. But what happens if we have two <input type="submit"> elements in the same form? How can we know which button was clicked when the page is submitted? The simplified answer is that when an <input type="submit"> button is clicked on a page, if the *name* attribute has been specified a name/value pair will be added to the form before it is submitted. ASP.NET can then determine which button has been clicked by examining the form object on the server for the existence of the name/value pair.

It is perfectly legal and commonplace to specify more than one <form> element on a standard ASP page. This is typically done to allow the page to be posted back to different pages or scripts depending on which form is submitted. In other words, you would typically set the action attribute of the separate <form> elements to different values. With ASP.NET, it is not necessary to have multiple <form> elements on a page, and, in fact, you will get a compile error if you have two <form> elements with the runat="server" attribute specified on the same page. Because ASP.NET gives us event handling, we can easily take different actions in our server code depending on how the user submitted the page without the use of multiple <form> elements in the .aspx file.

The other method of submitting a form is to call the submit() method of the form in client-side script. A script block to do this might look like the following (assuming the ID attribute of a <form> element on the page is set to form1):

```
<script language="javascript">
  function SubmitTheForm()
  {
    document.form1.submit();
  }
</script>
When a page has the need to submit itself when a user action is taken
other than clicking on an <input type="submit"> or <input type="image">
element, ASP.NET will render the following on the page (Again assuming
the ID attribute of the <form runat="server">  element on the page is
set to form1):<input type="hidden" name="__EVENTTARGET" value="" />
<input type="hidden" name="__EVENTARGUMENT" value="" />
<script language="javascript">
<!--
function __doPostBack(eventTarget, eventArgument)
{
  var theform = document.form1
  theform.__EVENTTARGET.value = eventTarget
  theform.__EVENTARGUMENT.value = eventArgument
  theform.submit()
}
// -->
</script>
```

ASP.NET will call the __doPostBack method when client-side events occur that the programmer has specified should cause a postback. For example, suppose we want our page to automatically be submitted when the user changes the selection in a list box. (We'll see a full example of how to do this in the *DropDownList* section later in this chapter.) The DropDownList control is the Web Server Control that we use for displaying list boxes. The DropDownList control will render to an HTML <select> element, which appears as a list box to the client. When the user changes the selection in the list box, the client-side *onchange* event of the <select> element is fired. The onchange event would be the appropriate place to call the __doPostBack function. The DropDownList control has a Boolean property called AutoPostBack. When set to true, any change in selection in the list box will cause the page to be posted back to the server. ASP.NET will render the <select> element to look similar to this:

```
<select name="DropDownList1" id="DropDownList1"
onchange="__doPostBack('DropDownList1','')" language="javascript">
```

The __doPostBack method is, in fact, called when the onchange event occurs if the AutoPostBack property of the DropDownList control is set to true. It passes the name of the <select> element as the first parameter to __doPostBack and nothing as the second parameter. Now look back at the __doPostBack method. The script in this method declares a variable called theform and sets it to document.form1.

```
var theform = document.form1
```

The values of the two <input type="hidden"> elements, __EVENTTARGET and __EVENTARGUMENT, are then set to the passed-in parameters eventTarget and eventArgument. __EVENTTARGET will always be set to the ID of the element that caused the form to be submitted. __EVENTARGUMENT is reserved for any extra information about the postback that needs to be submitted.

```
theform.__EVENTTARGET.value = eventTarget
theform.__EVENTARGUMENT.value = eventArgument
```

Last, the form is submitted by calling the submit() method.

```
theform.submit()
```

On the server side, ASP.NET will examine the __EVENTTARGET element on the form. If the form was submitted via the __doPostBack method, __EVENTTARGET will have a value. ASP.NET will use this value to determine which event handler needs to be called during post back.

This might seem fairly complicated to you, but the good news is you don't have to do any of it. ASP.NET does it all for us behind the scenes.

Data Binding

In its simplest form, Data Binding allows us to bind a property of a control to a data source, such as a field in a database. Each control will have its own unique way of displaying the bound data to the client. In the case of a Label control, it will display the data as a textual field on the page.

We can Data Bind a control on our page by writing a Data Binding expression within the declaration of a control in the .aspx file, or we can implement it in our code-behind class.

To Data Bind a control directly in the .aspx file we must use the <%# %> tags. Any code or expression that we place inside the <%# %> tags is referred to as a Data Binding Expression. You will typically use this method for nonlist type controls (controls that do not have multiple items), such as a Label, TextBox, or CheckBox. An example of Data Binding a control directly in the .aspx file can be seen in the *Label* section.

When Data Binding a list-type control, such as a DropDownList or CheckBoxList, you will normally do so by setting the *DataSource* property of the control to some type of data source. This can be done in the code-behind class or in a script block in the .aspx file. We'll see our first example of this type of Data Binding in the *ListBox Control* section.

All controls that have Data Binding capabilities implement a method called Data-Bind(). This method takes care of evaluating any Data Binding expressions in the .aspx file and/or processing any data source specified with the DataSource property. It is important to note that Data Binding Expressions and DataSource properties are not evaluated until the DataBind() method of the control with which they are associated is called. If the DataBind() method of the control is never called, no Data Binding will occur. Because the Page class is itself a control, it has an implementation of the DataBind() method. When the DataBind() method of any parent control is called, it in turn calls the DataBind() method of any children controls. Thus, if we call the DataBind() method of the Page class, all of the controls on our page will have their DataBind() methods called.

Web Server Controls

You've already been introduced to several of the Web Server Controls, such as <asp:Label> and <asp:Button>, in Chapter 2. Web Server Controls provide a type-safe object model to program against on the server. They do not map directly to HTML elements; instead they render HTML elements when a page is processed. This provides a level of abstraction from HTML elements, which makes them more powerful than the HTML Server Controls that we'll cover in a later section of this chapter. Because of the level of abstraction, a developer doesn't have to be an expert in HTML to develop ASP.NET pages. In addition, many of the Web Server Controls will render a combination of several different HTML elements to accomplish their task, but the developer needs to work with only one single Web Server Control.

One of the nicest things about Web Server Controls is their ability to detect browser capabilities and render HTML that will work and look best for each individual client. Initially, ASP.NET will detect either an UpLevel or DownLevel browser. *UpLevel browsers* are those that support HTML 4.0 and above, ECMAScript Version 1.2, the Microsoft Document Object Model (MSDOM), and Cascading Style Sheets (CSS). For the most part, the latest versions of Internet Explorer are the only browsers that qualify as UpLevel. *DownLevel browsers* are those that support only HTML 3.2 and backward. The Page class has a ClientTarget property that can be set to Auto, UpLevel, or Down-Level. If this property is set to Auto, ASP.NET will determine the browser's capabilities for you and render the most appropriate HTML. You can override this behavior by setting the ClientTarget property to either UpLevel or DownLevel, which forces ASP.NET to render either UpLevel or DownLevel HTML, respectively. The UpLevel setting can be used for intranet Web applications where the client browser is guaranteed to be a newer version of Internet Explorer.

TIP If you are developing a public Internet Web site, we recommend setting the ClientTarget property of all of your pages to DownLevel during the development process. Once your pages look good under this constraint, you can safely change the property to Auto and know that your pages will still look good for a DownLevel client.

All of the Web Server Controls are derived from System.Web.UI.WebControls. WebControl, which is in turn derived from System.Web.UI.Control. The Control class provides the bulk of the behind-the-scenes functionality for all of the Web Server Controls, such as Data Binding, View state, control containment, and basic events such as Init, Load, and Unload. The WebControl class expands on this mainly by adding style controlling properties such as BackColor, BorderStyle, Height, and Width. Each individual Web Server Control then expands on this further by adding properties and methods that make it a unique control. As we cover the controls, we'll point out the unique functionality that each one adds to the WebControl class. We'll also tell you a bit about the functionality provided by the base classes, Control and WebControl.

The sections that follow cover all of the Web Server Controls in detail and provide a few examples of how they can be used. Where appropriate, we'll show you which HTML elements are used to render the different controls and how it may differ from an UpLevel browser to a DownLevel browser.

Label

Probably the most basic of all of the Web Server Controls is the *Label control*. You've already seen how to use this control in Chapter 2, where we used the control to change some text on the page dynamically when a button was pressed. The text in a Label control cannot be edited by the user; it is read only. For this reason, you should use it for displaying dynamic read-only information on the page. The information could be dynamic in the fact that it is read in from a database or changed in response to a user action, among other things. Not only can the text of the Label control be changed dynamically, but the appearance of the text can also be changed. This includes characteristics ranging from the color and font of the text to whether the text is displayed at all, which is controlled by the Visible property.

If you just need to display some static text on the page that never needs to be changed, there is no need to use the Label control. You can just use HTML and save yourself a little processing overhead on the server when the page is rendered.

You might think that a Label control renders to an HTML <label> element, but this is not the case. (We'll see how the HTML <label> element is used when we cover the CheckBoxList and RadioButtonList controls later in this chapter.) In fact, the Label control renders to an HTML <span> element. This is true for UpLevel and DownLevel browsers, although the <span> element was not introduced until HTML 4.0. Browsers that do not support HTML 4.0 won't recognize the <span> element, but most browsers will let the tag pass through and will simply render any text contained within the <span> </span> tags. You'll run into problems with DownLevel browsers when you start getting fancy with the properties of the Label control. For instance, if you set a Label control to a particular height and width, it won't render as expected on a DownLevel browser. Let's look at this particular example and see why that is the case.

If we define an <asp:Label> on a page like this:

```
<asp:Label id=Label1 runat="server" Width="70px" Height="50px">
This is a label
</asp:Label>
```

it will render this HTML on an UpLevel browser:

Figure 3.1   Label control in an UpLevel browser.

```
<span id="Label1" style="height:50px;width:70px;">
This is a label
</span>
```

and it will look like the IE 6 screenshot shown in Figure 3.1.

The following HTML will be rendered for a DownLevel browser:

```
<span id="Label1">
This is a label
</span>
```

and it will look like the Opera 3.62 screenshot shown in Figure 3.2.

The difference is pretty obvious. The text of the Label control is too long to fit into the 70-pixel width constraint. In the UpLevel browser, the <span> element and its style attribute are supported, so the text is wrapped to stay within the width constraint. In the DownLevel browser, the style attribute is not even rendered because it wouldn't work anyway. The result is that a DownLevel browser doesn't wrap the text. This could be disastrous, depending on what you are trying to accomplish. A DownLevel browser will not honor any property that you assign to the Label control that will be rendered in the in-line style sheet of the <span> element. We'll see more examples like this in the sections to come; to avoid this, develop your pages with the ClientTarget property set to DownLevel, and change the ClientTarget propery to Auto when you release your application for testing.

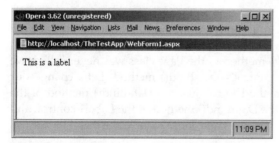

Figure 3.2   Label control in a DownLevel browser.

The Label control adds only one public property, *Text*, to the functionality of the WebControl base class. It does not add any public methods or events. We've already seen how to use this property in Chapter 2 to set the text that is displayed by the Label control. Now let's look at an example of Data Binding the Text property of a Label control.

Create a new ASP.NET Web application project called Chapter3. Add a new Web Form to the Chapter3 project using Visual Studio .NET. Call this new Web Form Label.aspx. If you want to save some typing you can download the entire Chapter3 project from the companion Web site. Drag a new Label control onto the form in design view, then switch to HTML view, and add the Text attribute to the <asp:Label> declaration as follows:

```
<asp:Label id=Label1 style="Z-INDEX: 101; LEFT: 10px; POSITION:
absolute;
TOP: 10px" runat="server" text="<%# DateTime.Now.ToString() %>">
</asp:Label>
```

The Data Binding Expression used here is DateTime.Now.ToString(), which will return the current date and time of the Web server as a string. Navigate to the page with your Web browser. You should see an empty page because the DataBind() method of the Label1 control was never called. Let's call the Label's DataBind() method in the Page_Load method of the code-behind class, like this:

```
protected void Page_Load(object sender, System.EventArgs e)
{
  // Put user code to initialize the page here
  Label1.DataBind();
}
```

Recompile the project, and view the page in your Web browser again. Now you should see the current date and time displayed on the page. Now add one more Data Binding Expression to the page, just below the <asp:Label> declaration, like this:

```
<asp:Label id=Label1 style="Z-INDEX: 101; LEFT: 10px; POSITION:
absolute;
TOP: 10px" runat="server" text="<%# DateTime.Now.ToString() %>">
</asp:Label>
<br>
<%# DateTime.Now.ToString() %>
```

Refresh the page in your browser. You might have thought that you would see the current date and time displayed twice on the page, but instead the output hasn't changed at all because the DataBind() method of the Page class was never called; we made an explicit call to the Label1 control's DataBind() method. Let's change our implementation of the Page_Load method to call just the DataBind() method of the page class. This should, in turn, call the DataBind() method of the Label1 control, and everything should work as expected. Change Page_Load to look like this.

```
protected void Page_Load(object sender, System.EventArgs e)
{
```

```
    // Put user code to initialize the page here
    this.DataBind();
}
```

Be sure to rebuild the project because you've made changes to the code-behind class, and then refresh the page again. If all went well, you should see the current date and time displayed twice as in Figure 3.3.

The text of a label control isn't the only property that can be Data Bound. In fact, any property with write access in any Web Server Control can be Data Bound. Just be careful to bind the property to the appropriate type. In the previous example, we were Data Binding the Text property, which expects a string. If we were Data Binding a property such as Visible, which expects a bool, then we would have to make sure our Data Binding Expression evaluated to a bool.

We encourage you to experiment more with the different properties of the Label control. Although it isn't a very exciting control, you'll find that you will use it very often.

Button

The *Button control* allows us to display a clickable button that will submit the page to the server and normally fire a click event handler. The Button control renders to an HTML <input type="submit"> element, so it will always submit the form back to the Web server when it is clicked. The Button control can be used in several different ways. We've already used a Button control to fire an event handler in several examples in Chapter 2. In those examples, we set this up either by setting the onclick attribute when we declared the button in the .aspx file or by adding an event handler in the code-behind C# class. Even if we don't create an event handler for the click event, the form will still be submitted when the button is pressed.

Because we've already covered the basics of the Button control in Chapter 2, let's take a look at some more advanced features. You may need to create some Button controls dynamically, perhaps in a list of some sort. In that case, you won't have the opportunity to create an onclick event handler for each individual button. You still need a way to determine which button was pressed so that you can take the appropriate action. The Button control provides the ability to do this via the *CommandName* and *CommandArgument* properties. Both of these properties are of type string. Let's look at a quick example that illustrates how to use them.

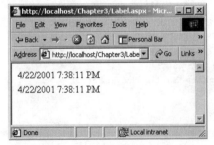

Figure 3.3 Data Binding a Label control.

Add a new Web Form to the Chapter3 project using VS.NET, and call it Button.aspx. Add a Label control and two Button controls to the form from the toolbox. Set the CommandName and CommandArgument properties of the two buttons to "Button1", "Button1Argument" and "Button2", "Button2Argument", respectively. Next, we need to provide a handler for the *Command* event. Just like the Click event, the Command event is fired when a button is clicked. The difference between the two is that the Command event delegate is passed a parameter of type CommandEventArgs, rather than EventArgs, which is passed to the Click event. You can see the difference in the code that follows.

```
private void Button_Command(object sender,
System.Web.UI.WebControls.CommandEventArgs e)
{
  //This Is a Command event handler
}


private void Button_Click(object sender, System.EventArgs e)
{
  //This Is a Click event handler
}
```

The CommandEventArgs parameter allows you to get at the CommandName and CommandArgument properties easily. Let's add a handler for the Command event of both of the buttons. We'll use the same method to handle both events. Inside that method we'll determine which button was pressed using the CommandName and CommandArgument parameters. The full source for this example can be seen in Listings 3.1 and 3.2, and a screen shot of the page after clicking Button 1 can be seen in Figure 3.4. You can also download both of these listings from the companion Web site.

```
<%@ Page language="c#" Codebehind="Button.aspx.cs"
AutoEventWireup="false"
Inherits="Chapter3.Button" %>
<HTML>
<HEAD>
  <meta name=vs_targetSchema content="Internet Explorer 5.0">
  <meta name="GENERATOR" Content="Microsoft Visual Studio 7.0">
  <meta name="CODE_LANGUAGE" Content="C#">
</HEAD>
<body MS_POSITIONING="GridLayout">
  <form method="post" runat="server">
    <asp:Label id="Label1" runat="server">Nothing Clicked</asp:Label>
    <br>
    <br>
    <asp:Button id=Button1 runat="server" Text="Button 1"
      commandname="Button1" commandargument="Button1Argument">
    </asp:Button>
    <p>
    </p>
```

Listing 3.1   Button.aspx

```
    <asp:Button id=Button2 runat="server" Text="Button 2"
      commandname="Button2" commandargument="Button2Argument">
    </asp:Button>
     
  </form>
</body>
</HTML>
```

Listing 3.1 Button.aspx (continued)

```
using System;
using System.Collections;
using System.ComponentModel;
using System.Data;
using System.Drawing;
using System.Web;
using System.Web.SessionState;
using System.Web.UI;
using System.Web.UI.WebControls;
using System.Web.UI.HtmlControls;

namespace Chapter3
{
  /// <summary>
  /// Summary description for Button.
  /// </summary>
  public class Button : System.Web.UI.Page
  {
    protected System.Web.UI.WebControls.Button Button2;
    protected System.Web.UI.WebControls.Button Button1;

    public Button()
    {
      Page.Init += new System.EventHandler(Page_Init);
    }

    protected void Page_Load(object sender, System.EventArgs e)
    {
    }

    protected void Page_Init(object sender, EventArgs e)
    {
      //
      // CODEGEN:This call is required by the ASP.NET Windows Form
      // Designer.
      //
```

Listing 3.2 Button.aspx.cs

```
            InitializeComponent();
    }


    #region Web Form Designer generated code
    /// <summary>
    /// Required method for Designer support - do not modify
    /// the contents of this method with the code editor.
    /// </summary>
    private void InitializeComponent()
    {
      this.Button1.Command += new

System.Web.UI.WebControls.CommandEventHandler(this.Button_Command);
      this.Button2.Command += new

System.Web.UI.WebControls.CommandEventHandler(this.Button_Command);
      this.Load += new System.EventHandler(this.Page_Load);
    }
    #endregion

    private void Button_Command(object sender,
      System.Web.UI.WebControls.CommandEventArgs e)
    {
      Label1.Text = "You clicked <b>" + e.CommandName +
        "</b> with an argument of <b>" + e.CommandArgument + "</b>";
}
  }
}
```

Listing 3.2   Button.aspx.cs (continued)

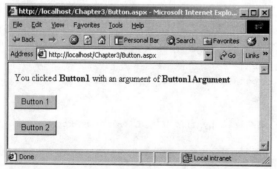

Figure 3.4   Handling the Command Event of a button.

As you can see in the Button_Command method in Listing 3.2, we access the CommandName and CommandArgument properties through the passed-in parameter e, which is of type CommandEventArgs.

When you are using a Button control on its own, you typically won't use the CommandName and CommandArgument properties. There is no need to because you can just handle the Click event of the Button; you already know which button is being clicked ahead of time because there is only one.

The Text property of the Button sets the text that is displayed on the face of the button. You can see that this property has been set for the two buttons in Listing 3.1. We could Data Bind this property just as we did in the Label example in the previous section.

That's about all there is to the Button control. In summary, the Button class extends the WebControl class by adding Text, CommandName, and CommandArgument properties. It also adds two events, Click and Command.

LinkButton

The *LinkButton control* provides the identical functionality as the Button control. The difference is that the LinkButton control renders to an <a> HTML element rather than an <input> element. When clicked, a LinkButton will submit the form just as a Button. It does so by setting the HREF attribute of the <a> element to call the __doPostBack function (covered in the *Postback* section earlier in the chapter), passing the ID of the control in as the eventTarget.

Create a new Web Form in your Chapter3 project, and call it LinkButton.aspx. Drop a LinkButton and a Label control on it from the toolbox. Set up a handler for the Click event of the LinkButton. In the handler, set the Text property of the Label control, just so you know the event has been handled. You should now have two controls on your .aspx page that look similar to this:

```
<asp:Label id="Label1" runat="server"></asp:Label>
<asp:LinkButton id=LinkButton1
runat="server">LinkButton</asp:LinkButton>
```

and an event handler like this:

```
private void LinkButton1_Click(object sender, System.EventArgs e)
{
  Label1.Text = "The LinkButton was clicked.<br>";
}
```

Request the page with your browser, and then view the source of the rendered page. You should see that the LinkButton was indeed rendered as an <a> element that looks like this:

```
<a id="LinkButton1"
href="javascript:__doPostBack('LinkButton1','')">LinkButton</a>
When the link is clicked, the javascript function __doPostBack will be
called, which submits the form. ASP.NET will then call the
LinkButton1_Click handler for us on the server.
```

Other than these client-side implementation details, the LinkButton behaves the same as a Button control.

Image

Fundamental to most Web pages is the ability to display images. The *Image control* displays images and changes them dynamically if we desire. It does not provide any events, so it will not respond to mouse clicks. The ImageButton class, covered in the next section, provides this ability.

The Image control renders to an HTML <img> element. The Image class inherits directly from WebControl and adds three fundamental properties. *AlternateText* sets the *alt* attribute of the <img> element and is the text that is displayed when the image is unavailable and as a tool tip when the mouse is hovered over the image. *ImageUrl* sets the *src* attribute of the <img> element and should contain the URL of the image to be displayed. *ImageAlign* sets the *align* attribute of the <img> element and is used to set how the image aligns on the page in relation to other elements.

Let's try an example with a little more substance to it to illustrate the use of the Image control. We'll create a rudimentary image viewer that allows the user to view image files located in a particular directory on the Web server. To do this, the contents of the specified directory are read using the *System.IO.Directory* class, and then ImageUrl property of an Image control is set on the page dynamically. The user will be allowed to navigate forward and backward through the images in the directory, using a couple of LinkButton controls. We'll handle the Click event of the two LinkButton controls to do this.

Getting a list of the files in a particular local directory is made easy with the System. IO.Directory class. The Directory class has a static method called GetFiles(string). It takes a directory path as a parameter and returns an array of strings that are the full pathnames of the files contained in the given directory.

```
string[] files = Directory.GetFiles(@"C:\images");
```

The preceding line of code would give us an array of filenames located in the C:\images directory.

To demonstrate some of the functionality available in the Request property of the Page class, we'll dynamically create the URL for the images rather than hard-coding the domain name and virtual directory. To do this we use the Page.Request.Url. GetLeftPart(UriPartial) method. This method returns a string representing different parts of the URL that was used to request the current page. UriPartial is an enumeration with three members, Scheme, Authority, and Path. *Scheme* will give the protocol segment of the URI such as "http://". *Authority* will give us the Scheme plus the Authority segment of the URI such as "http://localhost". *Path* will give us the full Path minus any trailers such as query parameters. So For the URL "http://localhost/ test.aspx?query=1", it would return http://localhost/test.aspx. We'll be calling GetLeftPart with the UriPartial.Authority parameter to give us the scheme and authority.

We'll also use the Page.Request.ApplicationPath property to get a string representing the virtual directory from which the page was requested. If the page was requested using the URL "http://localhost/Chapter3/Image.aspx", ApplicationPath will return "/Chapter3".

The example assumes that the folder containing the images we want to display will be located in the directory C:/inetpub/wwwroot/Chapter3/Images. You can change this if you wish.

If you are following along with the examples, add a new Web Form to your Chapter3 project called Image.aspx. The full source for the example can be seen in Listings 3.3 and 3.4. The working page can be seen in Figure 3.5.

```
<%@ Page language="c#" Codebehind="Image.aspx.cs"
AutoEventWireup="false"
  Inherits="Chapter3.Image" %>

<HTML>
  <HEAD>
    <meta content="Internet Explorer 5.0" name=vs_targetSchema>
    <meta content="Microsoft Visual Studio 7.0" name=GENERATOR>
    <meta content=C# name=CODE_LANGUAGE>
  </HEAD>
  <body MS_POSITIONING="GridLayout">
    <form method=post runat="server">
      <asp:linkbutton id=lnkPrevious Runat="server" NAME="lnkPrevious">
        Previous
      </asp:linkbutton>
        
      <asp:linkbutton id=lnkNext Runat="server" NAME="lnkNext">
        Next
      </asp:linkbutton>
      <p>
      </p>
      <asp:image id=Image1 runat="server" imagealign="Left">
      </asp:image>
    </form>
  </body>
</HTML>
```

Listing 3.3 Image.aspx

```
using System;
using System.Collections;
using System.ComponentModel;
using System.Data;
using System.Drawing;
using System.Web;
using System.Web.SessionState;
using System.Web.UI;
using System.Web.UI.WebControls;
using System.Web.UI.HtmlControls;
```

Listing 3.4 Image.aspx.cs

```csharp
using System.IO;

namespace Chapter3
{
  /// <summary>
  /// Summary description for Image.
  /// </summary>
  public class Image : System.Web.UI.Page
  {
    protected System.Web.UI.WebControls.LinkButton lnkPrevious;
    protected System.Web.UI.WebControls.LinkButton lnkNext;
    protected System.Web.UI.WebControls.Image Image1;

    private string[] m_arrImageNames;
    private string m_strImageDirectory =
      @"C:\inetpub\wwwroot\Chapter3\Images";

    public Image()
    {
      Page.Init += new System.EventHandler(Page_Init);
    }

    protected void Page_Load(object sender, System.EventArgs e)
    {
      if (!IsPostBack)
      {
        if (GetImages())
        {
          //Set the ImageUrl of Image1 to the first image that was found
          Image1.ImageUrl = GetImageURL(m_arrImageNames[0]);
        }
      }
    }

    protected void Page_Init(object sender, EventArgs e)
    {
      //
      //CODEGEN: This call is required by the ASP.NET Windows Form
      //Designer.
      //
      InitializeComponent();
    }

    #region Web Form Designer generated code
    /// <summary>
    /// Required method for Designer support - do not modify
    /// the contents of this method with the code editor.
    /// </summary>
```

Listing 3.4   Image.aspx.cs (continued)

```
private void InitializeComponent()
{
  this.lnkPrevious.Click +=
    new System.EventHandler(this.lnkPrevious_Click);
  this.lnkNext.Click += new System.EventHandler(this.lnkNext_Click);
  this.Load += new System.EventHandler(this.Page_Load);
}
#endregion

private void lnkPrevious_Click(object sender, System.EventArgs e)
{
  ChangeImage(-1);
}

private void lnkNext_Click(object sender, System.EventArgs e)
{
  ChangeImage(1);
}

private void ChangeImage(int intChange)
{
  //Get the list of Images
  if (GetImages())
  {
    //Find the image that we are currently displaying
    int x = 0;
    for (; x < m_arrImageNames.Length ; ++x)
    {
      //Is this the image that we are currently displaying?
      if (GetImageURL(m_arrImageNames[x]) == Image1.ImageUrl)
        break;
    }
    //Make sure we found the current image. If x is equal to the
    //length of the m_arrImageNames array then we did not.
    if (x == m_arrImageNames.Length)
    {
      //The image wasn't found, so just set Image1 to point to the
      //first image
      Image1.ImageUrl = GetImageURL(m_arrImageNames[0]);
    }
    else
    {
      //The image was found, so change the image
      x += intChange;
      //wrap to the end of the list if necessary
      if (x < 0)
        x = m_arrImageNames.Length - 1;
      //wrap to the beginning of the list if necessary
```

Listing 3.4 Image.aspx.cs (continued)

```
        if (x >= m_arrImageNames.Length)
          x = 0;

        //Set the ImageUrl and AlternateText to the URL for the new
        //image
        Image1.ImageUrl = GetImageURL(m_arrImageNames[x]);
        Image1.AlternateText = GetImageURL(m_arrImageNames[x]);
      }
    }
  }


  private bool GetImages()
  {
    //Get the image filenames
    m_arrImageNames = Directory.GetFiles(m_strImageDirectory);

    //Make sure there are images to display
    if (m_arrImageNames.Length == 0)
      return false;

    return true;
  }

  private string GetImageURL(string strImageFilePath)
  {
    //Request.Url.GetLeftPart(UriPartial.Authority) yields
    //"http://{domain name}"
    //Request.ApplicationPath yields "/{virtual directory}"
    return Request.Url.GetLeftPart(UriPartial.Authority) +
      Request.ApplicationPath + @"/Images/" +
      strImageFilePath.Substring(m_strImageDirectory.Length + 1);
  }
 }
}
```

Listing 3.4   Image.aspx.cs (continued)

In Listing 3.3, we've declared a couple of LinkButton controls and an Image control with an ID of Image1 all shown in bold.

All of the work is done in the code-behind class shown in Listing 3.4. Let's work through this code from top to bottom. We've added a using directive for the System.IO namespace, which is where the Directory class resides. You can also see that the Web Form designer added three members for the two LinkButton controls and the Image control. We then added a couple of our own private member variables. The first, m_arrImageNames, is a string array that we'll use to hold the array of filenames located in the image directory. We've hard-coded the image directory with the m_strImageDirectory member variable.

Figure 3.5   Image.aspx in action.

In the Page_Load method, we set the ImageUrl member of the Image1 control to the first image found in the directory. We've made sure to do this within an if (!IsPostBack) block so that this happens only the first time the page is requested by a particular client.

You can see that the designer has linked up the Click events of the two LinkButton controls to the methods lnkPrevious_Click and lnkNext_Click. Both of these methods simply make a call to the ChangeImage method, either passing a 1 for Next or a -1 for Previous.

The ChangeImage method gets the list of image filenames from the image directory. It then traverses through the array of filenames looking for the filename that matches the currently displayed image. Once we know the location in the array of the currently displayed image, we can move forward or backward in the list. A little code is also there to make sure that we wrap to the beginning or end of the list of images, if the user advances through all of the images in one direction or the other. Last, the ImageUrl and AlternateText properties of the Image1 control are set to the dynamically created URL of the appropriate image.

The GetImages method uses the Directory.GetFiles(string) method to fill the member m_arrImageNames with the filenames in the image directory.

The GetImageURL method creates a URL for a passed-in local image pathname. If we were going to run this example only on the local Web server, this wouldn't be necessary. We could just set the ImageUrl of the Image1 control to the local pathname, such as "C:\inetpub\wwwroot\Chapter3\Images\Image1.jpg". If the page is requested from another machine, obviously the images wouldn't be available on their C drive. We wanted the page to work, regardless of where it was requested from or on which Web server it was installed. To accomplish this, we used the URL that was used to request the Image.aspx page in the first place. From that URL we want to concatenate the scheme (which will be http://) plus the authority (which will be the domain name or IP address) plus the virtual directory (in this case, Chapter3). Then we can tack on the hard-coded "/Images" directory. The image filename is extracted from the passed-in full pathname using the Substring() method of the string class and is tacked on to the end of the URL.

ImageButton

The *ImageButton* control places an image that responds to mouse clicks on the page. The ImageButton class inherits from the Image class, which in turn inherits from the WebControl class. We get all of the functionality of the Image class, plus the Image-Button class implements all of the same functionality as a regular Button control.

The ImageButton control renders to an HTML <input type="image"> element. The only new functionality is with the Click event. ImageButton Click event handlers will receive an argument of type *ImageClickEventArgs*. ImageClickEventArgs has two public properties, *X* and *Y*, that provide the coordinates of the location where the image was clicked, which is then used to perform different actions, depending on where the image was clicked. A typical use is to designate certain areas of an image as hot spots and, when the user clicks within those areas, redirect them to an appropriate page.

For example, let's create a new Web Form called ImageButton.aspx in the Chapter3 project. Add the following controls inside the form tags of the .aspx file. Alternatively, you can add the controls to the form using the designer.

```
<asp:Label id=lblMessage runat="server" />
<p></p>
<asp:ImageButton id=btnImage runat="server"
  ImageUrl="Chapter3/Images/win2000.gif" />
```

The win2000.gif image was installed on our machine in the C:\inetpub\wwwroot directory by default. We copied it into the Images folder that we created for the example in the preceeding section. If you don't have that image, it is included in the Chapter3 project that can be downloaded from the companion Web site.

Add a handler for the Click event of the ImageButton and place the following line of code in the handler. Again, you can use the designer to create the Click handler for you.

```
lblMessage.Text =
  string.Format("You clicked the image at ({0}, {1})", e.X, e.Y);
```

Request the page with your browser and click on the image in multiple places. You should see a message containing the coordinates of where you clicked the image displayed at the top of the page. The coordinates given are relative only to the image itself, meaning that 0,0 is the upper-left corner of the image. You should see something similar to Figure 3.6.

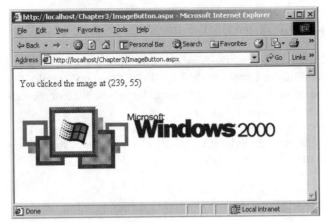

Figure 3.6   An Image button example.

HyperLink

Although the *HyperLink control* and the LinkButton control both take the appearance of hyperlinks and are both rendered as HTML anchor (<a>) elements, they are quite different in functionality. The HyperLink control does not provide any events other than the ones inherited from WebControl. It will not cause the page to be submitted back to the Web server, and there are no Click or Command events that you can handle on the server as you can with the LinkButton control. The HyperLink control simply provides the ability to link to another resource via the HTML <a> element. This control will provide a slight performance advantage over the LinkButton control when you need a simple link to another page. To use a LinkButton control for this purpose, a postback of the page is required and the click event handler must be processed. Inside the click event handler, code would be needed to redirect the client's browser to another page. This means that two requests to the Web server are needed. When using a HyperLink control, the client's browser is immediately redirected to the specified page, and only one request to the Web server is necessary.

The HyperLink control adds four additional properties to the base class WebControl: *Text*, *ImageUrl*, *NaviagteUrl*, and *Target*. Text is used to set the text that is displayed on the page for the hyperlink. ImageUrl is used to set an image that will be displayed as a hyperlink. If this property is set, the value in the Text property will be used as the alternate text for the image and also for the tool tip text when the mouse is hovered over the image. An exception to this is if the ToolTip property (inherited from the Web-Control class) is set; it will override the Text property, and its value will be displayed as the tool tip instead.

The NavigateUrl property is used to set the URL of the resource to link to when the hyperlink is clicked. Its value will be rendered to the HREF attribute of the <a> element.

The Target property will be rendered to the Target attribute of the <a> element. Target is used to specify the window or frame in which the linked resource should display. Its valid values are the same as the valid values for the Target attribute of the <a> element, which are _blank, _parent, _self, and _top.

When the ImageUrl property is used to display a hyperlink image, the HyperLink control will render an <img> element embedded in an <a> element. So for the following HyperLink control declaration:

```
<asp:HyperLink id=HyperLink1 runat="server"
  navigateurl="http://www.microsoft.com" target="_blank" Text="A
Picture"
    imageurl="Images/picture.jpg" tooltip="A tooltip for the picture">
```

this HTML will be rendered:

```
<a id="HyperLink1" title="A tooltip for the picture"
  href="http://www.microsoft.com" target="_blank">
  <img title="A tooltip for the picture"
    src="/Chapter3/Images/picture.jpg" alt="A Picture" border="0" />
</a>
```

Take a look at the screen shot shown in Figure 3.7. The image that was specified in the NavigateUrl property does not exist, so instead the alternate text is displayed. You can see that the alternate text for the image is "A Picture", which is the value of the Text property that we set. The tool tip of the image is "A tooltip for the picture", which is the value we assigned to the ToolTip property. Because we have set the Target property to _blank, when the image is clicked it will open a new browser window and navigate to www.microsoft.com.

Figure 3.7 The HyperLink control.

TextBox

The *TextBox* control provides the text entry ability on the Web page. It can be used in three different modes: *SingleLine*, *MultiLine*, or *Password*. The different modes are used by setting the *TextMode* property to the appropriate value. If it is used in SingleLine mode, it will render to an <input type="text"> element, which gives us a text box that will allow only a single line of text to be entered. In MultiLine mode it will render to a <textarea> element, which will allow multiple lines of text entry. In Password mode, it will render to an <input type="password"> element, which allows a single line of text to be entered, but the text is not displayed as the user enters it.

In addition to the TextMode property, the TextBox control also adds the *Columns*, *Rows*, *Wrap*, *MaxLength*, *ReadOnly*, *Text*, and *AutoPostBack* properties to the inherited WebControl class. It provides no additional methods and only one event, *TextChanged*.

The size of the text box is controlled through the Columns and Rows properties. Columns sets the width of the text box. If the TextBox control is used in SingleLine or Password modes, then the value of Columns is rendered to the *size* attribute of the <input> element. When in Multiline mode, it will be rendered to the *cols* attribute of the <textarea> element. The Rows property is applicable only when the TextBox control is used in MultiLine mode and sets the height of the text box or the number of rows of text that can be displayed in the text box at one time. The value of the Rows property renders directly to the *rows* attribute of the <textarea> element. The Wrap property is applicable only when in MultiLine mode as well. Its valid values are True and False. When Wrap is set to False, the *wrap* attribute of the <textarea> element will be set to off. When Wrap is set to True, which is the default, the wrap attribute of the <textarea> element will not be rendered at all because wrapping is enabled by default for the <textarea> element.

The MaxLength property is applicable only for the SingleLine and Password modes of the TextBox control. Quite simply, its value is rendered to the *maxlength* attribute of the <input> element and limits the number of characters that can be entered in the text box by the user.

The ReadOnly property renders to the *readonly* attribute of either the <input> or <textarea> elements. As you would expect, it leaves the text box in a noneditable state. If the ReadOnly property of the TextBox control is set to True, then the readonly attribute will be rendered with a value of readonly. If the ReadOnly property is set to False, then the readonly attribute will not be rendered at all.

The Text property provides programmatic access to the contents of the text box. It can be used to set the text that is displayed in the text box initially, such as a prompt of some sort, and to retrieve the text entered by the client.

The TextChanged event is fired on the server when the form is submitted if and only if the client has made changes to the text. This event could be handled to do some sort of complex validation of the text entered by the client or anything else that is necessary.

When set to True, the AutoPostBack property automatically causes the page to be posted to the server whenever focus leaves the text box and the client has made changes to the text. You would typically use the AutoPostBack property in conjunction with handling the TextChanged event. Just as the Click event of the LinkButton control was implemented, the AutoPostBack mechanism is implemented on the client with a JavaScript function called __doPostBack(). The *onchange* event of the <input> or <textarea> element is set to call this function. Just as with the LinkButton control, __doPostBack will post the page back to the server. If you have handled the TextChanged event, your event handler will be called when the page is posted.

Let's look at an example that uses three different TextBox controls to demonstrate some capabilities. Create a new Web Form in the Chapter3 project called TextBox.aspx. Add the following controls inside the <form> tags in the TextBox.aspx file:

```
<asp:Label id="Label1" runat="server"></asp:Label>
<br>
SingleLine<br>
<asp:textbox id=txtSingleLine runat="server" maxlength="20"
columns="25">
</asp:textbox>
<p></p>
Password<br>
<asp:textbox id="txtPassword" runat="server" maxlength="20" columns="25"
  textmode="Password">
</asp:textbox>
<p></p>
MultiLine<br>
<asp:textbox id="txtMultiLine" runat="server" columns="50"
  textmode="MultiLine" rows="3" wrap="False" autopostback="True">
</asp:textbox>
<p></p>
<asp:Button id=btnSubmit runat="server" Text="Submit">
</asp:Button>
```

Add the following code to the TextBox.aspx.cs file:

```
protected void Page_Load(object sender, System.EventArgs e)
{
  if (IsPostBack)
  {
    Label1.Text = "Page_Load was called via a post back.<br>";  }
}
```

Wire up the TextChanged event handlers for all three TextBox controls either via the Properties window in design view or by adding the code manually in the Initialize-Component() method. Code the handlers like this:

```
private void txtSingleLine_TextChanged(object sender, System.EventArgs e)
{
  Label1.Text += "The Single Line text was changed.<br>";}

private void txtPassword_TextChanged(object sender, System.EventArgs e)
{
  Label1.Text += "The Password text was changed.<br>";}
```

```
private void txtMultiLine_TextChanged(object sender, System.EventArgs e)
{
   Label1.Text += "The MultiLine text was changed.<br>";}
```

Compile the project, and request it in your browser. Enter some text in all three text boxes. Don't click the Submit button, but when you've finished entering text in the MultiLine text box, click back on the SingleLine text box. Notice that the form is submitted, even though we never clicked the Submit button. This is because we set that AutoPostBack property to True for the MultiLine TextBox control. The page should now look like the screen shot in Figure 3.8.

Examining the text that is displayed at the top of the page, you can see that the Page_Load method did get called when the page was posted back to the server. After the Page_Load method is called, the TextChanged event handlers for all three TextBox controls were called.

The state of the SingleLine and MultiLine text boxes were maintained, as we can still see the text that we entered in them. There is no text in the Password text box. For security reasons, state is not maintained between page calls when the TextBox is used in Password mode. Because of this, the text of the Password text box has changed or been cleared out for us. You should keep this in mind when you are handling the TextChanged event of a TextBox in Password mode. The TextChanged event for the Password TextBox was fired when the page was submitted for the first time because we changed the text ourselves. Because ASP.NET has changed the text contained in this text box when the page was submitted, the TextChanged event will be fired again when the page is submitted a second time. To illustrate this, click the Submit button, without making any changes to any of the text boxes. You should see that the TextChanged event for the Password box is fired again. If you click the Submit button one more time without changing anything, none of the TextChanged events is fired.

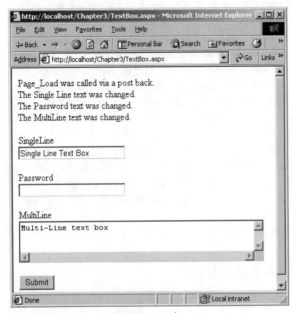

Figure 3.8 The TextBox control.

Note that you cannot enter more than 20 characters in the SingleLine text box because we set the MaxLength property to 20. The MultiLine text box is three rows in height because we set the Rows property to 3, and because we set the Wrap property of this control to False, the text will not wrap and we have been given a horizontal scroll bar.

CheckBox

The *CheckBox* control, as you would expect, provides check box entry ability. The CheckBox control renders to an HTML <input type="checkbox"> element along with an HTML <label> element wrapped up inside a <span> element. This is the first control that we've seen that actually renders to more than one HTML element. The typical rendered HTML for a CheckBox control looks like this:

```
<span>
  <input id="CheckBox1" type="checkbox" name="CheckBox1" />
  <label for="CheckBox1">Selection 1</label>
</span>
```

The <label> element renders the text that is displayed along with the <input> element. In addition, the <label> element's *for* attribute is set to the ID of the <input> element. This allows the user to click on the text of the <label> element as well as click on the check box itself to check or uncheck it. Keep in mind that the <label> element was not introduced until HTML 4.0. It will be rendered to, but ignored by DownLevel browsers, so that means you won't be able to click on the text for checking and unchecking in a browser that doesn't fully support HTML 4.0. The text that is contained inside the <label> tags will still be displayed, however.

The CheckBox control adds the *Checked*, *Text*, *TextAlign*, and *AutoPostBack* properties to the inherited WebControl class. In addition, it adds one event, *CheckedChanged*. The Checked property is of type bool and can be used to determine the state of the check box, checked or unchecked. It can also be used to set the state of the check box programmatically. The Text property simply sets the text that is displayed alongside the check box. The TextAlign property has two valid values, *Left* and *Right*. It determines whether the text set with the Text property is displayed on the left- or right-hand side of the check box. The AutoPostBack property provides the same functionality that it did with the TextBox control. Whenever the state of the check box is changed, the form will automatically be posted back to the server, and the CheckedChanged event will be fired. If you have provided a handler for this event, that handler will be called for you.

Let's run through a quick example. Create a new Web Form in your Chapter3 project called CheckBox.aspx. Add the following to the .aspx file inside the <form> tags:

```
<asp:Label id=Label1 runat="server" />
<p></p>
<asp:CheckBox id=CheckBox1 runat="server" text="Selection 1"
  textalign="Left" AutoPostBack=true />
```

Provide a handler for the CheckedChanged event, and add the following code to your handler:

```
Label1.Text = string.Format("Selection 1 is {0}",
    CheckBox1.Checked ? "checked" : "not checked");
```

If you or the Web Form designer haven't done so already, be sure to add member variables for the Label and CheckBox controls in your code-behind class. Compile the project and browse to the new page with your browser. It should look similar to the screenshot shown in Figure 3.9. Because we have set the AutoPostBack property to true, the form is submitted every time we change the state of the check box and the CheckedChanged event is fired for us. The code we added to the handler simply changes the text of the Label control to inform us of the state of the CheckBox control.

RadioButton

The *RadioButton* control inherits directly from CheckBox. As you would expect, its behavior and programmability are very similar to the CheckBox. The RadioButton control renders to an HTML <input type="radio"> element. Just as with the CheckBox control, a <label> element is also rendered with each <input> element inside of a <span>.

RadioButton adds only one property to the inherited CheckBox class, *GroupName*. GroupName renders directly to the *name* attribute of the <input> element. Any <input type="radio"> elements on an HTML page that have the same name attribute value are considered to be in a group and have mutually exclusive selection capabilities. Therefore, if you have several RadioButton controls on a page and set all of their GroupName properties to the same value, only one of the radio buttons in the group will be selected at any one time.

Because this is the only functional difference between a CheckBox and RadioButton control, let's look at a very simple example to see this in action. Create a new Web Form in your Chapter3 project called RadioButton.aspx, and add the following inside the <form> tags.

Figure 3.9 The CheckBox control.

```
<asp:RadioButton id=RadioButton1 runat="server"
  groupname="RadioButtonGroup" text="Selection 1" />
<br>
<asp:RadioButton id=Radiobutton2 runat="server"
  groupname="RadioButtonGroup" text="Selection 2" />
<br>
<asp:RadioButton id=Radiobutton3 runat="server"
  groupname="RadioButtonGroup" text="Selection 3" />
```

The resulting page should look like Figure 3.10. If you click on the radio buttons, you'll find that only one can be selected at a time.

DropDownList

The *DropDownList* control provides us with a list box UI element. It inherits directly from the *ListControl* class. The *ListControl* class serves as a base class from which other specific list control classes are developed. You probably won't use the ListControl object directly, unless you are writing your own list control that inherits from the List-Control class. Instead, you'll be using one of DropDownList, ListBox, CheckBoxList, or RadioButtonList. We'll cover the majority of the common functionality that the List-Control class provides each of these controls in this section. The ListControl is used to store and display name/value pairs. It will be used only for displaying single field items. Each item has a text name for displaying in the list and may have an underlying text value that is usually used programmatically. All of the items of the ListControl are stored in a ListItemCollection accessible via the *Items* property. The ListItemCollection is a collection of ListItem objects. Each ListItem object has a *Text, Value,* and a Boolean *Selected* property that can be used to determine if an item is selected or to select it programatically. We can create ListItem objects and insert them into the Items collection of the ListControl manually, or we can Data Bind to various data sources and let the List-Control populate the Items collection for us.

The DropDownList control renders to an HTML <select> element, which appears as a drop-down list as long as the *size* attribute either is not specified or is not given a value greater than 1. The DropDownList control chooses not to specify the size attribute at all. In addition, because the DropDownList does not support multiple selections, it will never set the *multiple* attribute of the <select> element. This also prevents the <select> element from displaying as anything other than a drop-down list. The items in the DropDownList will render as HTML <option> elements inside the <select> element. This is true for all controls that inherit from ListControl. In addition, if an item is selected, the associated <option> element will have its *selected* attribute set.

The ListControl provides one special event, *SelectedIndexChanged*. This event is fired whenever the form is posted back to the server and the selected item of a ListControl based object has changed.

The *SelectedIndex* property retrieves the index of the currently selected item in the DropDownList. It also sets the currently selected item, whereas the *SelectedItem* property returns the actual ListItem object associated with the selected item. In controls that allow multiple selections such as the RadioButtonList and ListBox, the SelectedIndex property will return the index of the item that has the lowest ordinal value. Similarly, the SelectedItem property will return the selected item that has the lowest ordinal value.

Figure 3.10 The RadioButton control.

The ListControl also provides the *AutoPostBack* property. As with the TextBox control, when this property is set to true, the form will automatically post back to the server when the selected item is changed. Once again, the automatic postback is implemented using the __doPostBack JavaScript function.

Now let's take a look at a simple example with the DropDownList. In this example, we will add items manually at design time within the .aspx page. In addition, we'll handle the SelectedIndexChanged event in our code-behind class.

Create a new Web Form in your Chapter 3 project called DropDownList.aspx. Add a single DropDownList control to the form, along with a single Label control similar to this.

```
<asp:Label id=Label1 runat="server" />
<p></p>
<asp:DropDownList id=DropDownList1 runat="server" autopostback="True"
  SelectedIndexChanged="DropDownList1_SelectedIndexChanged">
  <asp:ListItem>Selection 1</asp:ListItem>
  <asp:ListItem>Selection 2</asp:ListItem>
  <asp:ListItem>Selection 3</asp:ListItem>
  <asp:ListItem>Selection 4</asp:ListItem>
  <asp:ListItem>Selection 5</asp:ListItem>
</asp:DropDownList>
```

As you can see, adding items at design time is simply a matter of declaring a series of <asp:ListItem> controls inside the <asp:DropDownList> tags. This is the case for any control that inherits from ListControl, such as ListBox, CheckBoxList, and RadioButtonList.

You'll also need to add the DropDownList1_SelectedIndexChanged method handler to the code-behind file as follows.

```
protected void DropDownList1_SelectedIndexChanged(object sender,
  System.EventArgs e)
{
  Label1.Text = string.Format("The text of the item you selected is
{0}",
  DropDownList1.SelectedItem.Text);
}
```

If you navigate to this page with your browser and change the selection in the list box, you should see something similar to Figure 3.11. The HTML that is rendered for the <select> element will look something like this.

```
<select name="DropDownList1" id="DropDownList1"
  onchange="javascript:__doPostBack('DropDownList1','')">
  <option value="Selection 1">Selection 1</option>
  <option value="Selection 2">Selection 2</option>
  <option selected="selected" value="Selection 3">Selection 3</option>
  <option value="Selection 4">Selection 4</option>
  <option value="Selection 5">Selection 5</option>
</select>
```

The form is automatically submitted whenever the selection changes because we set the AutoPostBack property to true. In the SelectedIndexChanged handler, we were able to access the item that is currently selected using the SelectedItem property of the DropDownList.

When using DataBinding, it is necessary to specify the data source to bind to using the *DataSource* property. The ListControl then creates a ListItem for every item in the data source and inserts it into the Items collection. When creating the ListItem objects, by default the Text and Value properties are assigned whatever is returned by the ToString() method of the items in the data source. Usually this isn't what you want. Unless the ToString() method of the objects in the data source has been overridden and provided a meaningful value, the ToString() method of the base class will be called. If the base class is of type *object*, the ToString() method returns the fully qualified name of the class. To avoid these problems, we recommend that you always provide a specific value for the *DataTextField* and *DataValueField* properties of the ListControl. These two properties determine which fields of the items in your specified data source are assigned to the Text and Value properties of the ListItem objects. If we had a collection of the following object type:

```
public class CTestObject
{
  public string m_strName
  public int m_intValue;

  public string Name
  {
    get { return m_strName; }
    set { m_strName = value; }
  }

  public int Value
  {
    get { return m_intValue; }
    set { m_intValue = value; }
  }
}
```

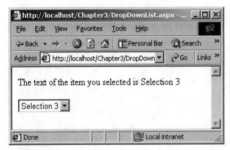

Figure 3.11   DropDownList with design time added items.

we could bind to it like this:

```
//Create an array of CTestObjects
CTestObject[] TestObjectArray = new CTestObject[5];

//Fill the array with CTestObject objects
for (int x = 0 ; x < 5 ; ++x)
{
  TestObjectArray[x] = new CTestObject();
  TestObjectArray[x].Value = x;
  TestObjectArray[x].Name = "Object " + x.ToString();
}

//Assume we are using a DropDownList that inherits from ListControl
DropDownList1.DataSource = TestObjectArray;
DropDownList1.DataValueField = "Value";
DropDownList1.DataTextField = "Name";
//Bind the list
DropDownList1.DataBind();
```

This would look like Figure 3.12. If we had neglected to set the DataValueField and DataTextField properties, it would look similar to Figure 3.13.

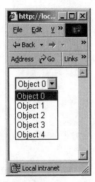

Figure 3.12   DropDownList with DataValueField and DataTextField set.

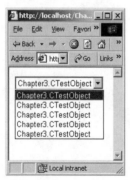

Figure 3.13   A DropDownList without specifying DataValueField and DataTextField.

The DataTextFormatString property of the ListControl allows you to format the DataTextField. In most cases, you won't be creating your data sources manually, as we did in the previous example. You'll be retrieving collections from a database or some other data store. Perhaps the field that you want to display for the ListControl is of type decimal and contains currency values. It would be nice to be able to display those values with a "$" tacked on to the beginning and to make sure that they are rounded to two decimal places. The DataTextFormatString provides this ability. You can set DataTextFormatString to any valid .NET Format String. (A throrough discussion of format strings can be found in a document titled "Formatting Strings" in the MSDN library.) In the previous example, if we set DataTextField = "Value", we could ensure that those values were displayed in a currency format by setting the DataTextFormatString as follows:

```
DropDownList1.DataTextFormatString = "{0:c}";
```

The DropDownList now looks like Figure 3.14.

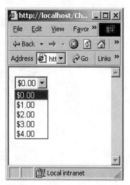

Figure 3.14   A DropDownList using DataTextFormatString.

ListBox

The *ListBox* control provides us with a list box UI element, which can be set to a specific height and width and contain multiple items in a list. The ListBox control also inherits directly from ListControl. The ListBox adds two properties to those supplied by the ListControl class: *Rows* and *SelectionMode*. Rows simply allows you to set the height in characters of the list box that is displayed and must be 1 or greater. SelectionMode can be set to either Single or Multiple. When set to Single, only one item in the list box can be selected at one time. When set to Multiple, several items can be selected by the user at once.

The ListBox control also renders to an HTML <select> element; however, a ListBox control will always specify the *size* attribute of the <select> element because the Rows property renders directly to the size attribute of the <select> element and, as mentioned previously, its value can be no less than 1. If the SelectionMode property is set to Multiple, the *multiple* attribute of the <select> element will be set; otherwise, the multiple attribute will not be rendered at all. In effect, this means that if we declare a ListBox control with a SelectionMode of Single and a Rows value of 1, it will indeed render as a drop-down list on the Web page. The resulting HTML in this case would look similar to the following:

```
<select name="ListBox1" id="ListBox1" size="1">
  <option value="Selection 1">Selection 1</option>
</select>
```

The ListBox control, as well as the CheckBoxList (covered in the next section), supports multiple item selection; however, the ListControl class does not provide a simple mechanism for determining which items are selected. The SelectedItem property will return only the lowest-ordinal selected item, not all items that are selected. Because of this, if you want to determine which items are selected, you will need to check every item in the list to see if its Selected property is set to true. Let's take a look at an example of how to do this.

Create a new Web Form in your Chapter3 project, and call it ListBox.aspx. Add a single Label control and a single ListBox control to the form, such as this.

```
<asp:label id=Label1 runat="server"></asp:label>
<p></p>
<asp:ListBox id=ListBox1 runat="server" AutoPostBack=true
  SelectionMode="Multiple">
</asp:ListBox>
```

Let's go back to using Data Binding again and declare the CTestObject class in the code-behind file. Refer back to the ListControl section for the implementation of the CTestObject class. Once you've added the CTestObject class to the ListBox.aspx.cs code-behind file, add the following code to the Page_Load method.

```
if (!IsPostBack)
{
  CTestObject[] TestObjectArray = new CTestObject[5];
```

```
for (int x = 0 ; x < 5 ; ++x)
{
  TestObjectArray[x] = new CTestObject();
  TestObjectArray[x].Name = "Object " + x.ToString();
  TestObjectArray[x].Value = x;
}

ListBox1.DataSource = TestObjectArray;
ListBox1.DataTextField = "Name";
ListBox1.DataValueField = "Value";
ListBox1.DataBind();
}
```

NOTE We'll be using the CTestObject class and the preceding Page_Load code in the examples in the CheckBoxList and RadioButtonList sections also. The only thing that will change is the name of the control whose DataSource, DataTextField, DataValueField, and DataBind properties and methods are set or called.

We'll also need to handle the SelectedIndexChanged event for the ListBox1 control. Place the following source code in the handler that you create.

```
//Clear any text that exists in Label1
Label1.Text = string.Empty;

//Iterate through all of the items in the ListBox checking to see if
//each item is selected
foreach (ListItem item in ListBox1.Items)
{
  if (item.Selected)
  {
    Label1.Text += string.Format("{0} is selected<br>", item.Text);
  }
}
```

If you compile this and browse to the page with your browser, it should look similar to Figure 3.15. You can select multiple items in the list by holding down either the SHIFT or CTRL keys. The form should automatically submit itself each time the selection is changed and call your SelectedIndexChanged event handler.

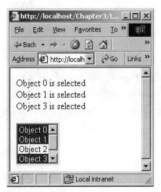

Figure 3.15   ListBox control that supports multiple selections.

CheckBoxList

The *CheckBoxList* control adds the power and convenience of Data Binding to the CheckBox control to a multiple-item data source. If you have a dynamically changing list of items that need to be displayed as check box input elements, then the Check-BoxList is your answer. The CheckBoxList renders its check boxes exactly as did the CheckBox control. Each <span>, <input type="checkbox">, <label> set that make up an individual check box are rendered inside of an HTML <table> or are entirely encapsulated in an HTML <span> element. Whether the check boxes are contained inside of a <table> or <span> is directly controlled by the *RepeatLayout* property. The valid values for this property are *Table* and *Flow*. When set to Table, the check boxes will be rendered in a table format. When set to Flow, the check boxes will be rendered inside a <span> element. Because the <span> element is typically not supported in a DownLevel browser, it's probably best to stick with Table.

The *RepeatDirection* property allows you to specify whether the check boxes will render in a horizontal list across the page or in a vertical list down the page. The valid values for this property are *Horizontal* and *Vertical*, with Vertical being the default value. Keep in mind that the CheckBoxList control will render all of the items in its Items collection. If you have set RepeatDirection to Horizontal and have five items to display but only three will fit in the horizontal width available, the items will wrap to the next line. The width available might be limited by setting the Width property to some value, or it might simply be limited by screen real estate. In either case, once the available width has been utilized, further items will wrap to the next line.

The *RepeatColumns* property is used to specify the number of horizontal columns that the control should attempt to render. If RepeatDirection is set to Horizontal, the value of RepeatColumns would be used to specify when the list should wrap to the next line. This is accomplished with a simple HTML <br> element when RepeatLayout is set to Flow and established with a new row or <tr> element when RepeatLayout is set to Table. For a CheckBox control with four items, RepeatLayout of Flow, Repeat-Direction of Horizontal, and RepeatColumns of 2, the rendered HTML would look similar to the following:

```
<span id="CheckBoxList1">
  <span>
    <input id="CheckBoxList1_0" type="checkbox" name="CheckBoxList1:0"/>
    <label for="CheckBoxList1_0">Object 0</label>
  </span>
  <span>
    <input id="CheckBoxList1_1" type="checkbox" name="CheckBoxList1:1"/>
    <label for="CheckBoxList1_1">Object 1</label>
  </span>
  <br>
  <span>
    <input id="CheckBoxList1_2" type="checkbox" name="CheckBoxList1:2"/>
    <label for="CheckBoxList1_2">Object 2</label>
  </span>
  <span>
    <input id="CheckBoxList1_3" type="checkbox" name="CheckBoxList1:3"/>
    <label for="CheckBoxList1_3">Object 3</label>
  </span>
  <br>
</span>
```

As you can see, a <br> element is used to wrap the check box list to the next horizontal line of the page after the second check box is rendered. If we take the same example again but this time set RepeatLayout to Table, HTML similar to the following would be rendered:

```
<table id="CheckBoxList1" border="0">
  <tr>
    <td>
      <span>
        <input id="CheckBoxList1_0" type="checkbox"
          name="CheckBoxList1:0"/>
        <label for="CheckBoxList1_0">Object 0</label>
      </span>
    </td>
    <td>
      <span>
        <input id="CheckBoxList1_1" type="checkbox"
```

```
          name="CheckBoxList1:1"/>
        <label for="CheckBoxList1_1">Object 1</label>
      </span>
    </td>
  </tr>
  <tr>
    <td>
      <span>
        <input id="CheckBoxList1_2" type="checkbox"
          name="CheckBoxList1:2"/>
        <label for="CheckBoxList1_2">Object 2</label>
      </span>
    </td>
    <td>
      <span>
        <input id="CheckBoxList1_3" type="checkbox"
          name="CheckBoxList1:3"/>
        <label for="CheckBoxList1_3">Object 3</label>
      </span>
    </td>
  </tr>
</table>
```

Here, the RepeatColumns value of 2 is implemented by allowing only two check boxes to be rendered inside of each table row <tr> element. In both cases, the resulting page would look similar to Figure 3.16.

The RepeatColumns property causes some fairly obvious results when the Repeat-Direction is Horizontal; however, when RepeatDirection is Vertical, the results might not be what you would expect. Let's look at a couple of examples. If we have a Check-BoxList with four items, RepeatDirection of Vertical, RepeatColumns of 4, and Repeat-Layout of either Table or Flow, the page will look similar to Figure 3.17; however, if RepeatColumns is set to 3, we end up with something similar to Figure 3.18.

Figure 3.16 Horizontal CheckBoxList with two columns.

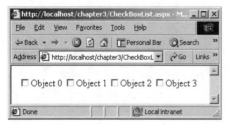

Figure 3.17   Vertical CheckBoxList with four columns.

When RepeatColumns is 4, the results are what you would expect; all four items are rendered in separate columns. When RepeatColumns is 3, the items are rendered only to two separate columns. Because we have four items in the list, we have enough items to render to three columns. That would mean, though, that one column would have two items, whereas the other two would have only one item. That wouldn't look nearly as nice as what you see in Figure 3.18. The CheckBoxList will intelligently come up with a number of columns that renders as symmetrically as possible for the number of items that you have in the list. This may or may not be what you want. If you need a greater degree of freedom and control in the layout of your check boxes, you might want to consider using the CheckBox control itself, rather than the CheckBoxList.

The CheckBoxList also implements the *CellPadding* and *CellSpacing* properties. These are applicable only when RepeatLayout is set to Table and they render directly to the cellpadding and cellspacing attributes of the HTML <table> element that will contain all of the check boxes. CellPadding sets the distance between the border of each cell and its contents, while CellSpacing sets the distance between each cell in the table.

The *TextAlign* property is also implemented and has the same affect that it does with the CheckBox control. It simply determines which side the text of a check box will be rendered on, left or right.

The CheckBoxList supports multiple selections just as the ListBox. To determine which items are selected programmatically, you will have to iterate through the Items collection and check each ListItem control individually, just as we did in the ListBox control example.

Figure 3.18   Vertical CheckBoxList with three columns.

RadioButtonList

The *RadioButtonList* is completely identical to the CheckBoxList with the exceptions that radio buttons are rendered on the page rather than check boxes and multiple selections are not allowed. All of the <input type="radio> elements that are rendered will have their *name* attribute set to the name that you assign to the RadioButtonList control. Therefore, all of the radio buttons will be in the same group, and this will force single selection availability. Other than that, there isn't anything new to cover with the RadioButtonList; the rest of the behavior is the same as the CheckBoxList control.

Panel

The *Panel* control has several different uses. First and foremost, you will use it as a container for other controls. This allows you to easily hide or show groups of related controls programmatically. If you set the *Visible* property of a Panel control to False, all of the controls contained within it will also be invisible. Likewise, if you set the *Enabled* property of the Panel control to False, all of the contained controls will also be disabled.

The Panel control adds three properties to the inherited WebControl class. *BackImageUrl* can be set to the URL of an image file that you wish to display as the background of the Panel. If the image is smaller than the size of the Panel, the image will be tiled to fill up the leftover space. *HorizontalAlign* provides the ability to specify how controls contained within the Panel control should be aligned. Valid values for this property are NotSet (the default), Left, Right, Center, and Justify. The *Wrap* property can be either True or False and designates whether we want to allow the Panel control to wrap its contents to the next line if the width of the Panel has been exceeded.

The Panel will render to an HTML <div> element on an UpLevel browser, and any contained controls will be rendered within the <div> element. In a DownLevel browser it will render to an HTML <table> element, and all of the contained controls will be rendered into the first row and cell of the table. The difference between the DownLevel and UpLevel browser in this case is quite significant. If you're not careful, you can get yourself into big trouble with the Panel control with consistency in the look of your page between a DownLevel and UpLevel browser. We'll see an example of this later in this section. Let's create a quick example page that demonstrates the show/hide type functionality of the Panel control as well as some caveats between UpLevel and DownLevel browser representation of the Panel control. Add a new Web Form to the Chapter3 project, and call it Panel.aspx. Add the following inside the form tags in the .aspx file:

```
<asp:CheckBox id=CheckBox1 runat="server" Text="Hide Panel"
  AutoPostBack=true />
<p></p>
<asp:Panel id=Panel1 runat="server" width="150px" height="90px"
  wrap="False" horizontalalign="Right">
  <asp:Label id=Label1 runat="server"
    Text="A Label that is just way too long" />
  <asp:TextBox id=TextBox1 runat="server" />
  <p></p>
  <asp:Button id=Button1 runat="server" Text="A Button" />
</asp:Panel>
```

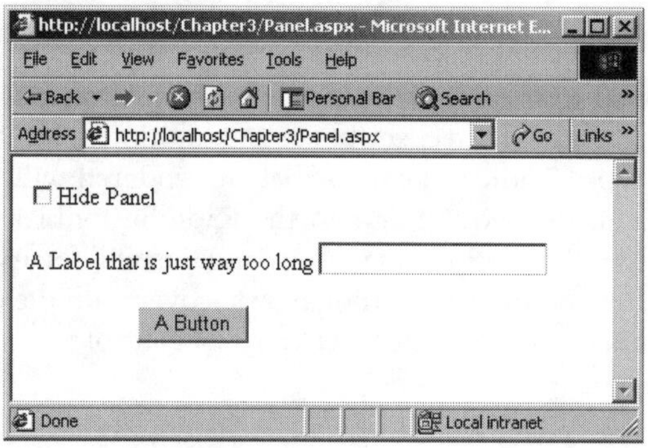

Figure 3.19 A visible panel.

As you can see, adding controls to a Panel at design time is as simple as declaring them inside of the <asp:Panel> opening and closing tags. We need to handle the CheckedChanged event of the CheckBox1 control, so add a handler for this event, and include the following code in the handler.

```
if (CheckBox1.Checked)
  Panel1.Visible = false;
else
  Panel1.Visible = true;
```

When the check box is selected and deselected, the form will automatically be posted to the server. The code in the handler will simply change the Visible property to True or False, depending on the checked state of the CheckBox control. Figure 3.19 shows the page with the Panel visible, and Figure 3.20 shows the page with the Panel invisible in Internet Explorer 6.0.

IE 6.0 is an UpLevel browser, so the Panel control was rendered to an HTML <div> element. We set the Width of the Panel control to 150px, which is not wide enough to accommodate the Label control and the TextBox control on the same horizontal line. We set the Wrap property to False. In an UpLevel browser this prevents the contents from being wrapped to the next line even if they exceed the Width that we have specified for the Panel control. As you can see in Figure 3.19, the Label and TextBox controls are rendered on the same line. We also set the HorizontalAlign property to Right. The Button control has been justified to the right edge of our original 150px width specification. This may or may not be what you want; in this case, it doesn't look good because we don't allow the Panel to automatically wrap for us.

Now take a look at what this page looks like in a DownLevel browser such as Opera 3.62, as shown in Figure 3.21. That's quite a difference. The Panel is all the way over on the right edge of the screen, and although we set Wrap to False, the contents have been wrapped anyway. Let's look at the rendered HTML and see why this is happening.

```
<table id="Panel1" align="Right" nowrap="nowrap" cellpadding="0"
cellspacing="0"
  border="0" height="90" width="150">
  <tr>
```

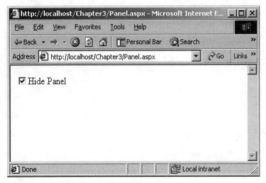

Figure 3.20 An invisible panel.

```
<td align="Right">
  <span id="Label1">A Label that is just way too long</span>
  <input name="TextBox1" type="text" id="TextBox1" />
  <P></P>
  <input type="submit" name="Button1" value="A Button" id="Button1" />
</td>
  </tr>
</table>
```

The problem is that the *align* and *nowrap* properties have been set on the <table> element itself. The nowrap attribute has not been set on the <td> element within the table, and that is why the contents of the cell are not wrapping as we specified. If the align and nowrap settings were removed from the <table> element and both placed on the <td> element within the table, the DownLevel version of the Panel would look nearly identical to the UpLevel version. Perhaps this will be changed in the future, but for now this is the way it works. Consequently you need to be careful using the Panel control when you are targeting a broad range of browser clients.

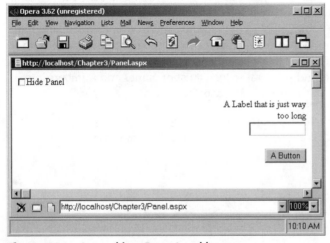

Figure 3.21 A panel in a DownLevel browser.

Controls can also be added to the Panel dynamically at runtime. The Panel control has a *Controls* property, which is a collection of all of its child controls. To add controls at runtime, the Add() method of the Controls property can be called and passed the control that needs to be added. So, for example, we could add five Label controls to a Panel with code like this.

```
for (int x = 0 ; x < 5 ; ++x)
{
  //Create the Label
  Label lblDynamicLabel = new Label():
  lblDynamicLabel.Text = "Label " + x.ToString();
  //Add the Label to the Panel
  Panel1.Controls.Add(lblDynamicLabel);
}
```

We'll see several more examples of uses for the Panel control throughout the remainder of the book.

Table, TableRow, and TableCell

Most ASP applications use a table at one point or another, due to the fact that it is such a good way to show formatted data in a customized layout. In ASP.NET, you can create your tables on the server using the TableRow and TableCell objects.

The simplest way to create a table and fill it dynamically is to use the asp:Table control in your aspx file. There are also the asp:TableRow and asp:TableCell server controls. Using these in your aspx files at design time creates a fixed number of rows and tables, to be generated on the server, and allows you to add content to them dynamically. In most cases, however, a program needs to output an unknown amount of data into a table for display purposes. Using just the asp:Table tag in the aspx file and creating TableRows and TableCells in the server code allows us to position and size the table at design time, but fill it in at runtime. Note that when using this technique, nowhere do you include any <tr> or <td> tags yourself. Now that you have a shell table being generated on the server by ASP.NET, you can create rows and cells for it dynamically by using the TableRow and TableCell objects, respectively. We won't explain anything about table programming in HTML because you probably are quite familiar with it already. Let's just dive right into a table using these objects.

Take, for example, a table, and we want to load a list of names and numbers into it. Let's first create the table in the aspx file using asp:Table:

```
<%@ Page language="c#" Codebehind="TableCellTableRow.aspx.cs"
    AutoEventWireup="false" Inherits="Ch03.TableCellTableRow" %>

<html>
  <head>
    <meta name="GENERATOR" Content="Microsoft Visual Studio 7.0">
    <meta name="CODE_LANGUAGE" Content="C#">
  </head>
  <body>
```

```
    <form method="post" runat="server">
      <asp:table id=table1
        runat=server
        border=1
        cellspacing=0
        cellpadding=0>
        </asp:table>
    </form>
  </body>
</html>
```

Notice that we just included the asp:Table control, but we left it empty of any rows or cells. In this table declaration, we can modify its styles, borders, color, placement, and more. Now we fill in the table in server code with something like this:

```
TableCell cell = new TableCell();
cell.Text = "Hello";
TableRow row = new TableRow();
row.Cells.Add(cell);
tablevariable.Rows.Add(row);
```

It is very simple and works like many of the grids or tables you may have used in the rich client world. To try this sample, create a new WebForm called TableCell-TableRow.aspx, and use the code in Listing 3.5 for the code-behind class. The most relevant lines of code are in bold. You can see this page in action in Figure 3.22.

```
namespace Ch03
{
    using System;
    using System.Collections;
    using System.ComponentModel;
    using System.Data;
    using System.Drawing;
    using System.Web;
    using System.Web.SessionState;
    using System.Web.UI;
    using System.Web.UI.WebControls;
    using System.Web.UI.HtmlControls;


    /// <summary>
    ///              Summary description for TableCellTableRow.
    /// </summary>
    public class TableCellTableRow : System.Web.UI.Page
    {
        //Create a server variable for the table.
        protected System.Web.UI.WebControls.Table table1;

        public TableCellTableRow()
```

Listing 3.5 Dynamically creating an HTML table

```
    {
        Page.Init += new System.EventHandler(Page_Init);
    }

    protected void Page_Load(object sender, System.EventArgs e)
    {
        //Create a new row.
        TableRow row = new TableRow();

        //Create the first cell, add it to the row.
        TableCell cell = new TableCell();
        cell.Text = "Joe";
        row.Cells.Add(cell);

        //Create the second cell, add it to the row.
        cell = new TableCell();
        cell.Text = "555-4875";
        row.Cells.Add(cell);

        //Add the completed row to the table.
        table1.Rows.Add(row);
    }

    protected void Page_Init(object sender, EventArgs e)
    {
        InitializeComponent();
    }

    private void InitializeComponent()
    {
        this.Load += new System.EventHandler(this.Page_Load);
    }
    }
}
```

Listing 3.5   Dynamically creating an HTML table (continued)

See how easy it is to create the table row? This creates the correct HTML to be sent to the browser for a table, with correct <tr> and <td> tags. This is so much nicer than doing it the ASP way, with server script code peppered throughout the HTML to produce the desired table. Notice that just as when programming any server control, there has to be a valid variable representing the object in the class, or else you would have nothing to program to. If you use the WebForm editor in Visual Studio .NET to drag and drop a table onto your page, the table variable will be put into your code for you. It is possible, though, to just type the asp:table code into the asp file yourself and then add the variable to the code-behind class manually. Remember that the system uses the directive at the top of all Visual Studio .NET-created WebForms to link the actual variable with the UI control and instantiate it for you. That is why there is no code that creates a new table explicitly, at least none that we can see. If you do insert the table and its variable manually, do make the variable have a class scope as well as a protected access level, or the system won't correctly perform this link for you.

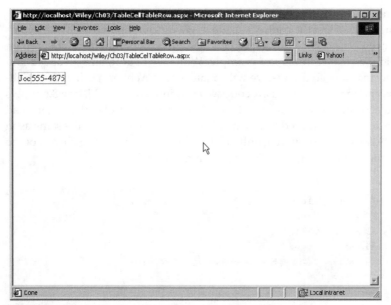

Figure 3.22   A simple table with a row and a cell.

As for using the controls themselves, let's look at some of the important properties. The actual Table object itself contains many properties, mostly used for look and feel. You can set the cellspacing, border, a cascading style sheet style, or width on the server in code. We won't go into detail here about these things because we all have used tables in HTML many times before. Note that you can still set some of these properties in the aspx file as well; this would allow you to make simple changes without recompiling; however, there is not a lot to do with Table functionally. Most of the good stuff lies in the TableRow and TableCell. The TableRow has many properties, like the Table object, for defining the look and feel of the resulting row. Because you would likely not have one of these defined in your aspx given that their power is in using them dynamically, you will usually set these types of properties in server code. Possibly the most important property is the Cells collection. This represents the cells in the row, or the <td> tags. We have used the TableRow many times, and it is a great and powerful tool, but we rarely do anything with it other than fill its Cells collection with TableCells. The TableCell has the same type of UI-related properties, but it also has the vital text element as well. This is where the actual visible text in the table gets set. The text you set here is the same as if you were to do something like this in HTML: <td>Hello World</td>. In many cases, you get long mileage out of a table simply by creating TableCells, setting their text, adding them to the Cells collections of TableRows, and adding the rows to a table.

Now let's take things a little further. Remember when we said that setting the Text property of the TableCell was the main way of creating the visible text in a table? It is, but there is another way as well. Because we all know the TableCell is essentially the object representing the <td> tag in your table, we can add anything we want to it. In HTML, don't we commonly (probably more often than not) add more than just text to a <td>? Well, the TableCell is a container control, and thus it has the Controls collection, which is made up of just the controls inside it. We can add other things like hyperlinks, pictures, even other tables to TableCells. Let's add a hyperlink to a table cell on the number field we created in the last example. While we're at it, let's go ahead and add some nice formatting. To do this, we will create a new WebForm called TableCell-Hyperlink.aspx, and in its place the aspx code we used in Listing 3.5. Listing 3.6 shows the code-behind class in which we'll add a HyperLink server control to the cell, instead of just setting its text. We won't redo the aspx file because it will remain the same as in the last sample. Also, we are providing only the Page_Load code because the rest of the code has not changed either. Figure 3.23 shows this example in action.

```
protected void Page_Load(object sender, System.EventArgs e)
{
    //Modify the tables look
    table1.CellPadding = 2;
    table1.HorizontalAlign = HorizontalAlign.Center;
    table1.BorderWidth = 2;
    table1.BorderStyle = BorderStyle.Outset;

    //Like before, create the row and cells.
    TableRow row = new TableRow();
    row.BackColor = Color.Azure;

    //Create the first cell, add it to the row.
    TableCell cell = new TableCell();
    cell.Text = "Joe";
    cell.Width = Unit.Pixel(100);
    row.Cells.Add(cell);

    //Create the second cell, add it to the row.
    cell = new TableCell();
    cell.Width = Unit.Pixel(100);

    //Create a link, add it to the cell
    string n = "555-4875";
    HyperLink link = new HyperLink();
    link.Text = n;
    link.NavigateUrl = string.Format("number.aspx?number={0}",
        Server.UrlEncode(n));

    cell.Controls.Add(link);
    row.Cells.Add(cell);

    //Add the completed row to the table.
    table1.Rows.Add(row);
}
```

Listing 3.6 Creating an HTML table with more complex contents

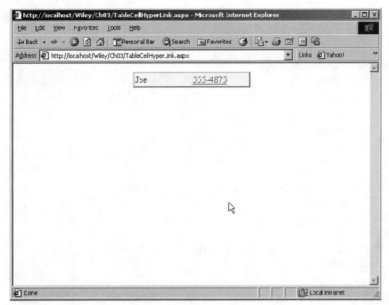

Figure 3.23   A table with a hyperlink.

For the formatting, we simply set some properties on the correct controls. The table is where you define cellpadding, alignment, and the outer border; the row is fine for defining a color, and the cells get their own explicit widths. We also could have set the cellpadding, cellspacing, and background color properties directly on the asp:Table object in the aspx file instead, which would have worked as well. For the hyperlink, we created a new HyperLink object, set its properties, and added it to the collection of controls in the cell. Instead of using the HyperLink, we could have written the <a> code into the cell, as follows:

```
cell.Text = string.Format("<a href=number.aspx?={0}>{1}</a>",
    Server,UrlEncode(n), n);
```

That would accomplish the same result, but without the object-oriented code. Now let's go another step and add a button to a table cell, which will have a handler attached to it when we create the object. Again, the aspx and other C# code remains the same as the preceding code; however, this time we are sans the nice formatting. This time, create a TableCellButton.aspx, and use the Page_Load from Listing 3.7 in the code-behind class. This can be seen in Figure 3.24.

```
protected void Page_Load(object sender, System.EventArgs e)
{
    //Like before, create the row and cells.
    TableRow row = new TableRow();
```

Listing 3.7   An HTML table containing server controls

```
    //Create the first cell, add it to the row.
    TableCell cell = new TableCell();
    cell.Text = "Joe";
    cell.Width = Unit.Pixel(100);
    row.Cells.Add(cell);

    //Create the second cell, add it to the row.
    cell = new TableCell();
    cell.Width = Unit.Pixel(100);


    //Create a button, add it to the cell
    string n = "555-4875";
    Button btn = new Button();
    btn.Text = n;
    btn.Click += new System.EventHandler(this.btn_Click);
    cell.Controls.Add(btn);
    row.Cells.Add(cell);

    //Add the completed row to the table.
    table1.Rows.Add(row);
}

protected void btn_Click(object sender, EventArgs e)
{
    Response.Write("Clicked the button<br>");
}
```

Listing 3.7   An HTML table containing server controls (continued)

That's great, but if we have more than one dynamically created button on the page, how do we know which button was clicked? For this let's resort to a custom button class that extends a regular button to have a variable to hold a number. In this example, we will use a public member variable, for simplicity. In a real-world application, you may want to use a public property instead. When the user clicks this button, we can perform a cast in the handler to see what the number is for the clicked button. Create a WebForm called TableCellMyButton.aspx, and again use the same aspx file as before. This time include the entire source in Listing 3.8 in the code-behind class, as opposed to just the Page_Load. This contains the definition of the new button class. Also, we added two rows to the table, so you can better see the new button class in action.

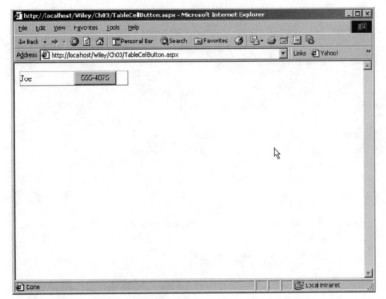

Figure 3.24   A table with a button.

```
namespace Ch03
{
    using System;
    using System.Collections;
    using System.ComponentModel;
    using System.Data;
    using System.Drawing;
    using System.Web;
    using System.Web.SessionState;
    using System.Web.UI;
    using System.Web.UI.WebControls;
    using System.Web.UI.HtmlControls;

    public class TableCellMyButton : System.Web.UI.Page
    {
        protected System.Web.UI.WebControls.Table table1;


        public TableCellMyButton()
        {
            Page.Init += new System.EventHandler(Page_Init);
```

Listing 3.8   An HTML table containing custom server controls

```
        }

        protected void Page_Load(object sender, System.EventArgs e)
        {
            //Like before, create the row and cells.
            TableRow row = new TableRow();

            //Create the first cell, add it to the row.
            TableCell cell = new TableCell();
            cell.Text = "Joe";
            cell.Width = Unit.Pixel(100);
            row.Cells.Add(cell);

            //Create the second cell, add it to the row.
            cell = new TableCell();
            cell.Width = Unit.Pixel(100);

            //Create a button, add it to the cell
            string n = "555-4875";
            MyButton btn = new MyButton();
            btn.Text = "Click Me";
            btn.number = n;
            btn.Click += new System.EventHandler(this.btn_Click);
            cell.Controls.Add(btn);
            row.Cells.Add(cell);

            //Add the completed row to the table.
            table1.Rows.Add(row);

            //Create another row and cells.
            row = new TableRow();

            cell = new TableCell();
            cell.Text = "Mary";
            cell.Width = Unit.Pixel(100);
            row.Cells.Add(cell);

            cell = new TableCell();
            cell.Width = Unit.Pixel(100);

            n = "725-1443";
            btn = new MyButton();
            btn.Text = "Click Me";
            btn.number = n;
            btn.Click += new System.EventHandler(this.btn_Click);
            cell.Controls.Add(btn);
            row.Cells.Add(cell);

            //Add the second row to the table.
```

Listing 3.8   An HTML table containing custom server controls (continued)

```
                table1.Rows.Add(row);
        }

        protected void btn_Click(object sender, EventArgs e)
        {
            //Cast out the sender to a MyButton, and get number.
            Response.Write(string.Format("Clicked number {0}<br>",
                ((MyButton)sender).number));
        }

        protected void Page_Init(object sender, EventArgs e)
        {
            InitializeComponent();
        }

        private void InitializeComponent()
        {
            this.Load += new System.EventHandler(this.Page_Load);
        }
    }

    //My custom button
    public class MyButton : Button
    {
        public MyButton() : base() {}
        public string number;
    }
}
```

Listing 3.8   An HTML table containing custom server controls (continued)

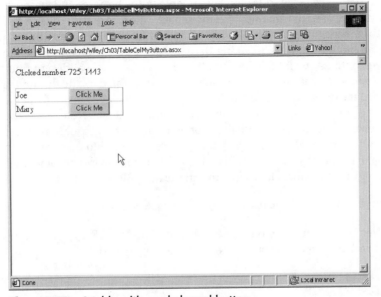

Figure 3.25   A table with a subclassed button.

You can see how great it is to have object-oriented access to table programming. There is one important caveat about adding controls dynamically to a table, or any other control or page, as we have just done. If the code to load the table in Listing 3.8 were inside the !IsPostBack, meaning run only the first time a user hits the page, you will encounter a tricky problem. If View state is enabled, which it is by default, the page will be reloaded by View state instead of code processing, if the table code is done only on a nonpostback request. This is fine in other cases where the controls are defined in the aspx page, but here we have created the controls in code only; they don't exist in the aspx file at all. In this case the page will be blank on all subsequent page hits by a user. The <table> will still be in the HTML code on the browser because it was defined in the aspx file and created every time the page is sent. But the page is blank because there are no cells in the table. If you had a complex page with other UI items showing up, and only some small portion of the page not being created on a PostBack, it may slip into production that way. To remedy this, just don't create controls dynamically in a !IsPostBack section, but create them on every request. That will ensure that they are always there.

DataGrid

The *DataGrid* object is a super powerful tool for creating formatted output of data in a grid- or table-like view. It differs from the asp:Table control in that it is geared for uniform row/column data, which has the same layout on every row. This is not a limitation, however, because it is a common task to display rows of the same type in a table layout. There are also some related advanced controls called the Repeater and DataList. Those controls, however, are fairly advanced, so we will introduce them in Chapter 5, "Creating More Advanced ASP.NET Pages," when we can bind them to real data. The DataGrid control will also be covered in more detail there, but for now let's go through the basics of this control.

The DataGrid is specifically designed for laying out, displaying, and allowing interaction with bound data. The DataGrid renders to a table in the browser and supports the same UI that you are used to using with HTML tables. This means that you can format a DataGrid to look any way you like, within the robust formatting capabilities of a table. DataGrids are bound controls, meaning they require a data source to which to bind and get their contents at runtime. You don't add rows to a table at design time, although you can add static columns. All rows in the grid are created on the fly and are based on the data in the data source. The data that is actually displayed textually in the grid comes from the public properties of each object in the data source. Note that if you have a data source with objects that expose their contents only through public member variables (and not through public properties), the grid will not bind to them properly. Use properties on objects that you know will be loaded into a DataGrid at some time. A DataGrid in its most simple form looks like this in the aspx file:

```
<asp:DataGrid Id=DataGrid1 runat="Server"></asp:DataGrid>
```

which is no different from using any other type of control in ASP.NET. In your code-behind code, you will use something similar to the following to load it:

```
DataGrid1.DataSource = ds;
DataGrid1.DataBind();
```

This is also very simple in its basic form. For our first example of a very basic Data-Grid, we will need something to bind to. We will use a framework-provided data structure and load it with a bit of simple data just before the bind occurs. Keep in mind that the DataGrid's home turf is in the database arena, where there is very often a need to show data that is row/column based. We'll use the DataGrid heavily throughout the book, especially when we start to access relational data in Chapter 4, "Database Access," and Chapter 5. Don't worry that you don't learn the whole control in this section; it is a large control, and its discussion spans many parts of the book. For this example, create a new WebForm called DataGrid.aspx, and either drag a DataGrid from the Toolbox onto your form or enter the bold code from Listing 3.9. Remember that if you create a control in your aspx code manually, you will also have to create its variable declaration in the code-behind class manually. Calling DataBind in this case is just like calling it in the server controls at the beginning of the chapter. In this case, we are binding the DataGrid to an ArrayList. You can see this page in Figure 3.26.

```
<%@ Page language="c#" Codebehind="DataGrid.aspx.cs"
AutoEventWireup="false"
    Inherits="Ch03.DataGrid" %>

<HTML>
    <HEAD>
        <meta name="GENERATOR" Content="Microsoft Visual Studio 7.0">
        <meta name="CODE_LANGUAGE" Content="C#">
    </HEAD>

    <body>
        <form method="post" runat="server">
            <asp:DataGrid id=DataGrid1 runat="server">
            </asp:DataGrid>
        </form>
    </body>
</HTML>

namespace Ch03
{
    using System;
    using System.Collections;
    using System.ComponentModel;
    using System.Data;
    using System.Drawing;
    using System.Web;
    using System.Web.SessionState;
    using System.Web.UI;
    using System.Web.UI.WebControls;
    using System.Web.UI.HtmlControls;

    public class DataGrid : System.Web.UI.Page
```

Listing 3.9 A simple DataGrid

```
{
    protected System.Web.UI.WebControls.DataGrid DataGrid1;

    public DataGrid()
    {
        Page.Init += new System.EventHandler(Page_Init);
    }

    protected void Page_Init(object sender, EventArgs e)
    {
        InitializeComponent();
    }

    private void InitializeComponent()
    {
        this.Load += new System.EventHandler(this.Page_Load);
    }

    private void Page_Load(object sender, System.EventArgs e)
    {
        //Create something to use as a data_source
        ArrayList arr = new ArrayList();
        arr.Add("Joe Smealy");
        arr.Add("Tom Blankensmith");
        arr.Add("Mary James");

        //Setup and perform the bind
        DataGrid1.DataSource = arr;
        DataGrid1.DataBind();
    }
}
}
```

Listing 3.9   A simple DataGrid (continued)

We mentioned before that objects in the data source must have public properties in order for the DataGrid to bind to them properly. If there are no public properties in the objects that the DataGrid is attempting to load via a Databind call, the DataGrid will attempt to call ToString on each one. The ToString method in this case returns the string itself because the data source array contains objects of type string. Next, we will create a small custom object, with some public properties, and bind to a data source full of them. Create a WebForm called DataGridCustomObjectBind, and use the same aspx code as in the previous example. In the code-behind class, use the Page_Load code shown in Listing 3.10. The rest of the code-behind code is not shown because it is the same as in the previous example. Included in the same listing is the custom class we created to bind with. We declared the class in the same file as the code-behind, but it could also be in its own .cs class file if that suits your needs better. You can see this example in Figure 3.27.

```
...
protected void Page_Load(object sender, System.EventArgs e)
{
    //Create datasource
    ArrayList arr = new ArrayList();
    arr.Add(new MyPerson("Smealy", "Joe", "584-47-8747"));
    arr.Add(new MyPerson("Tom", "Blankensmith", "563-45-5514"));
    arr.Add(new MyPerson("Mary", "James", "554-54-5587"));

    DataGrid1.DataSource = arr;
    DataGrid1.DataBind();
}
...

public class MyPerson
{
    private string m_LastName;
    private string m_FirstName;
    private string m_SSN;

    public MyPerson(string FirstName, string LastName, string SSN)
    {
        m_LastName = LastName;
        m_FirstName = FirstName;
        m_SSN = SSN;
    }

    public string LastName
    {
        set { m_LastName = value; }
        get { return m_LastName; }
    }

    public string FirstName
    {
        set { m_FirstName = value; }
        get { return m_FirstName; }
    }

    public string SSN
    {
        set { m_SSN = value; }
        get { return m_SSN; }
    }
}
```

Listing 3.10 A simple custom class to use as data source items

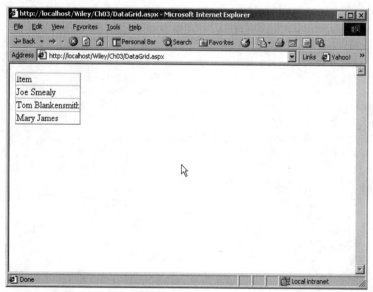

Figure 3.26   A simple DataGrid.

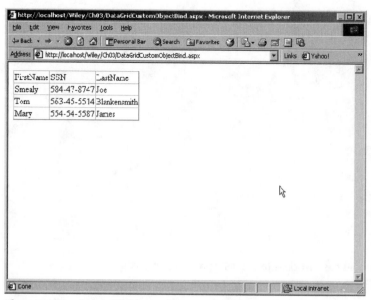

Figure 3.27   A DataGrid bound to custom objects.

Now let's move onto customizing the DataGrid somewhat. In the Listing 3.10 example, the DataGrid used property indexers to look at each public property of the objects in the data source. For each one it found, it created a column header from the name of the property and the cells from the value of each property. Each row in the DataGrid represents one object in the data source. In this case, this was automatic because the DataGrid has a property called AutoGenerateColumns, which is set to true by default. For the next example, let's turn off this property and create the aspx code needed to load specific data from the data source. Create a WebForm called DataGridBound-Column, and use the same code-behind class as in Listing 3.10, without the MyPerson class. That the code in the code-behind class merely creates or opens the data source and calls bind means that we can change layout and column characteristics of your DataGrid solely in the aspx file without having to recompile. The code that creates the specific column bindings is shown in bold in Listing 3.11. We use the asp:Bound-Column control, which must be used within the context of the DataGrid. These lines are telling the DataGrid to look for the property named in the DataField element, give it a column header and a width, and load its value into the cell. The DataGrid faithfully does this, and the results appear in Figure 3.28.

```
<%@ Page language="c#" Codebehind="DataGridBoundColumns.aspx.cs"
AutoEventWireup="false" Inherits="Ch03.DataGridBoundColumns" %>

<html>
    <head>
        <meta name="GENERATOR" Content="Microsoft Visual Studio 7.0">
        <meta name="CODE_LANGUAGE" Content="C#">
    </head>
    <body>
        <form method="post" runat="server">
            <asp:DataGrid id=DataGrid1 runat="server"
                AutoGenerateColumns=False>

                <Columns>
                    <asp:BoundColumn DataField=LastName
                        HeaderText="Last Name" ItemStyle-Width=200px>
                    </asp:BoundColumn>

                    <asp:BoundColumn DataField=FirstName
                        HeaderText="First Name" ItemStyle-Width=200px>
                    </asp:BoundColumn>

                    <asp:BoundColumn DataField=SSN
                        HeaderText="Social" ItemStyle-Width=100px>
                    </asp:BoundColumn>
                </Columns>
            </asp:DataGrid>
        </form>
    </body>
</html>
```

Listing 3.11 A DataGrid with user-specified column bindings

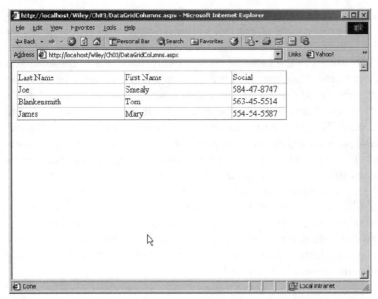

Figure 3.28 A DataGrid with user-specified column bindings.

Now let's add a button to each row, so the user can actually interact with the Data-Grid. The code is similar to Listing 3.11, except that we must change the Last Name column binding from a BoundColumn to a ButtonColumn. Create a new WebForm called DataGridButtonColumns, and enter the code-behind class code from Listing 3.11. Next, add the button handler by adding an ItemCommand handler for the DataGrid in the code-behind class. Again, this is just like other controls, in that you can double-click the event you want in Visual Studio .NET and it will create the handler for you. Note that although the column is called a ButtonColumn, it looks like a hyperlink. You can set the ButtonType property to render either a link or a button. Either way, the click on this item in the browser causes the JavaScript form submittal code to run and go back to the server. The important thing to remember is that like all server controls in ASP.NET, the handler code runs on the server. So, what function gets called? In this case, we are going to handle the ItemCommand handler on the DataGrid and not the ButtonColumn itself. ButtonColumns don't even have events. The reason for this is that events for controls inside of a DataGrid are bubbled up to the DataGrid itself. The DataGrid then fires these events. Now that we have added the ButtonColumn, we have something to cause the firing of the event. Listing 3.12 shows us the code, and Figure 3.29 shows us the WebForm in action.

```
<%@ Page language="c#" Codebehind="DataGridButtonColumns.aspx.cs"
    AutoEventWireup="false" Inherits="Ch03.DataGridButtonColumns" %>

<HTML>
    <HEAD>
```

Listing 3.12 A DataGrid with a button column

```
            <meta name="GENERATOR" Content="Microsoft Visual Studio 7.0">
            <meta name="CODE_LANGUAGE" Content="C#">
        </HEAD>
        <body>
            <form method="post" runat="server">
                <asp:DataGrid id=DataGrid1 runat="server"
                    AutoGenerateColumns=False>

                    <Columns>
                        <asp:ButtonColumn ButtonType=LinkButton
                            DataTextField=LastName HeaderText="Last Name"
                            ItemStyle-Width=200px>
                        </asp:ButtonColumn>

                        <asp:BoundColumn DataField=FirstName
                            HeaderText="First Name" ItemStyle-Width=200px>
                        </asp:BoundColumn>

                        <asp:BoundColumn DataField=SSN HeaderText="Social"
                            ItemStyle-Width=100px>
                        </asp:BoundColumn>
                    </Columns>
                </asp:DataGrid>
            </form>
        </body>
</HTML>

namespace Ch03
{
    using System;
    using System.Collections;
    using System.ComponentModel;
    using System.Data;
    using System.Drawing;
    using System.Web;
    using System.Web.SessionState;
    using System.Web.UI;
    using System.Web.UI.WebControls;
    using System.Web.UI.HtmlControls;

    public class DataGridButtonColumns : System.Web.UI.Page
    {
        protected System.Web.UI.WebControls.DataGrid DataGrid1;

        public DataGridButtonColumns()
        {
            Page.Init += new System.EventHandler(Page_Init);
        }

        protected void Page_Init(object sender, EventArgs e)
```

Listing 3.12   A DataGrid with a button column (continued)

```
        {
            InitializeComponent();
        }

    private void InitializeComponent()
    {
        this.DataGrid1.ItemCommand += new
            System.Web.UI.WebControls.DataGridCommandEventHandler(
            this.DataGrid1_ItemCommand);
        this.Load += new System.EventHandler(this.Page_Load);
    }

    private void Page_Load(object sender, System.EventArgs e)
    {
        //Create datasource
        ArrayList arr = new ArrayList();
        arr.Add(new MyPerson("Smealy", "Joe", "584-47-8747"));
        arr.Add(new MyPerson("Tom", "Blankensmith", "563-45-5514"));
        arr.Add(new MyPerson("Mary", "James", "554-54-5587"));

        DataGrid1.DataSource = arr;
        DataGrid1.DataBind();
    }

    protected void DataGrid1_ItemCommand(object source,
        System.Web.UI.WebControls.DataGridCommandEventArgs e)
    {
        //Show which item we clicked.
        Response.Write("Item Command on " + e.Item.Cells[1].Text);
    }
    }
}
```

Listing 3.12   A DataGrid with a button column (continued)

In the arguments to the ItemCommand handler, we have access to the actual row item that was clicked. We can interrogate this argument for contents from the cells on that row, but there is actually a better way of handling the ItemCommand event. We can set the CommandName property in the aspx page on the ButtonColumn to whatever we would like. Then in the handler, this property is available in the EventArgs argument. We can then check to see which ButtonColumn the user clicked, as well as information from the cells on that particular row. This makes it very easy to have a DataGrid with two hyperlink columns, each to perform a different action.

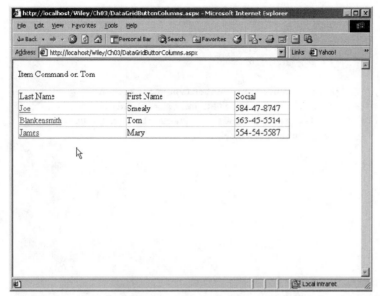

Figure 3.29   A DataGrid with a button columns in action.

```
<%@ Page language="c#"
Codebehind="DataGridButtonColumnsCommandName.aspx.cs"
AutoEventWireup="false" Inherits="Ch03.DataGridButtonColumnsCommandName"
%>
<HTML>
    <HEAD>
        <meta name="GENERATOR" Content="Microsoft Visual Studio 7.0">
        <meta name="CODE_LANGUAGE" Content="C#">
    </HEAD>
    <body>
        <form method="post" runat="server">
            <asp:DataGrid id=DataGrid1 runat="server"
                AutoGenerateColumns=False>

                <Columns>
                    <asp:ButtonColumn ButtonType=LinkButton
                        CommandName=HitLastName DataTextField=LastName
                        HeaderText="Last Name" ItemStyle-Width=200px>
                    </asp:ButtonColumn>
```

Listing 3.13   Using CommandName in a DataGrid column

```
                      <asp:BoundColumn DataField=FirstName
                          HeaderText="First
                          Name" ItemStyle-Width=200px>
                      </asp:BoundColumn>

                      <asp:ButtonColumn ButtonType=LinkButton
                          CommandName=HtiSSN DataTextField=SSN
                          HeaderText="Social" ItemStyle-Width=200px>
                      </asp:ButtonColumn>
                  </Columns>
              </asp:DataGrid>
          </form>
      </body>
  </HTML>


  namespace Ch03
  {
      using System;
      using System.Collections;
      using System.ComponentModel;
      using System.Data;
      using System.Drawing;
      using System.Web;
      using System.Web.SessionState;
      using System.Web.UI;
      using System.Web.UI.WebControls;
      using System.Web.UI.HtmlControls;

      public class DataGridButtonColumnsCommandName : System.Web.UI.Page
      {
          protected System.Web.UI.WebControls.DataGrid DataGrid1;

          public DataGridButtonColumnsCommandName()
          {
              Page.Init += new System.EventHandler(Page_Init);
          }

          protected void Page_Init(object sender, EventArgs e)
          {
              InitializeComponent();
          }

          private void InitializeComponent()
          {
              this.DataGrid1.ItemCommand += new
              System.Web.UI.WebControls.DataGridCommandEventHandler(
                  this.DataGrid1_ItemCommand);
              this.Load += new System.EventHandler(this.Page_Load);
```

Listing 3.13   Using CommandName in a DataGrid column (continued)

```
        }

        private void Page_Load(object sender, System.EventArgs e)
        {
            //Create data source
            ArrayList arr = new ArrayList();
            arr.Add(new MyPerson("Smealy", "Joe", "584-47-8747"));
            arr.Add(new MyPerson("Tom", "Blankensmith", "563-45-5514"));
            arr.Add(new MyPerson("Mary", "James", "554-54-5587"));

            DataGrid1.DataSource = arr;
            DataGrid1.DataBind();
        }

        protected void DataGrid1_ItemCommand(object source,
            System.Web.UI.WebControls.DataGridCommandEventArgs e)
        {
            Response.Write(string.Format("{0} on {1}", e.CommandName,
                e.Item.Cells[1].Text));
        }
    }
}
```

Listing 3.13 Using CommandName in a DataGrid column (continued)

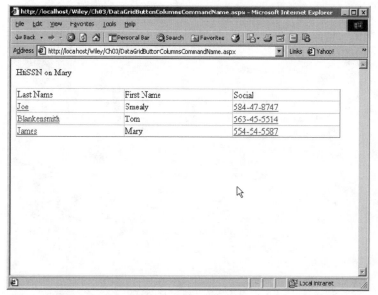

Figure 3.30 Using a CommandName in a DataGrid in action.

In Listing 3.13 we found out which ButtonColumn was clicked by its Command-Name, which is part of the DataGridCommandEventArgs parameter of the Item-Command handler. Refer to Figure 3.30 to see it in action.

All of these features are great, but it is still somewhat cumbersome to get particular data from the rows when you select one by clicking a ButtonColumn link. Sure, we have been able to pull some data by looking directly in the cells of the selected item, but that is a less-than-perfect method. What if you rearrange the columns in the aspx file or have new columns in the data source because your database changed? Your code would not be correct if the indices were out of sync when indexing a cell in a row. A better way to do it is with the DataKeyField property. This is a place in each row into which you can store any bound data property from the data source. It is not related with a column, or even visible. This is a perfect place to put a record ID for a database, or any kind of key information that would allow you to look up more information. For the next example, create a WebForm called DataGridKeyField and include the Data-Grid from Listing 3.14 in it. We will bind to a collection of MyPerson objects again, but this time we use the ID field of the MyPerson class to insert into the DataKeyField of each row in the DataGrid. Then, when we are back on the server handling an event that occurs because of clicking a ButtonColumn link, we can get this value and look up the real MyPerson.

```
<%@ Page language="c#" Codebehind="DataGridKeyField.aspx.cs"
AutoEventWireup="false" Inherits="Ch03.DataGridKeyField" %>

<HTML>
    <HEAD>
        <meta name="GENERATOR" Content="Microsoft Visual Studio 7.0">
        <meta name="CODE_LANGUAGE" Content="C#">
    </HEAD>
    <body>
        <form method="post" runat="server">
            <asp:DataGrid id=DataGrid1 runat="server"
                AutoGenerateColumns=False DataKeyField="PersonID">

                <Columns>
                    <asp:ButtonColumn ButtonType=LinkButton
                        CommandName=Select DataTextField=LastName
                        HeaderText="Last Name" ItemStyle-Width=200px>
                    </asp:ButtonColumn>

                    <asp:BoundColumn DataField=FirstName
                        HeaderText="First Name" ItemStyle-Width=200px>
                    </asp:BoundColumn>

                    <asp:BoundColumn DataField=SSN HeaderText="Social"
                        ItemStyle-Width=200px>
                    </asp:BoundColumn>
                </Columns>

                <SelectedItemStyle BackColor="Navy" ForeColor="White">
```

Listing 3.14 Using the DataKeyField in a DataGrid

```
                        </SelectedItemStyle>
                    </asp:DataGrid>
                </form>
            </body>
</HTML>

namespace Ch03
{
    using System;
    using System.Collections;
    using System.ComponentModel;
    using System.Data;
    using System.Drawing;
    using System.Web;
    using System.Web.SessionState;
    using System.Web.UI;
    using System.Web.UI.WebControls;
    using System.Web.UI.HtmlControls;

    public class DataGridKeyField : System.Web.UI.Page
    {
        protected System.Web.UI.WebControls.DataGrid DataGrid1;

        public DataGridKeyField()
        {
            Page.Init += new System.EventHandler(Page_Init);
        }

        protected void Page_Init(object sender, EventArgs e)
        {
            InitializeComponent();
        }

        private void InitializeComponent()
        {
            this.DataGrid1.SelectedIndexChanged += new
System.EventHandler(
                this.DataGrid1_SelectedIndexChanged);
            this.Load += new System.EventHandler(this.Page_Load);

        }

        private void Page_Load(object sender, System.EventArgs e)
        {
            //Create datasource
            ArrayList arr = new ArrayList();
            arr.Add(new MyPerson("Smealy", "Joe", "584-47-8747",
                "1477485"));
            arr.Add(new MyPerson("Tom", "Blankensmith", "563-45-5514",
                "5447869"));
```

Listing 3.14 Using the DataKeyField in a DataGrid (continued)

```
        arr.Add(new MyPerson("Mary", "James", "554-54-5587",
            "3254785"));

        DataGrid1.DataSource = arr;
        DataGrid1.DataBind();
    }

    protected void DataGrid1_SelectedIndexChanged(object source,
        System.EventArgs e)
    {
        int i = DataGrid1.SelectedIndex;
        Response.Write(string.Format("Key selected {0}",
            DataGrid1.DataKeys[i].ToString()));
    }
  }
}
```

Listing 3.14   Using the DataKeyField in a DataGrid (continued)

In this example, we accomplished our goal of getting information related to a single row in the DataGrid, and we saw a few new things. First, the ButtonColumn CommandName changed from one we made up to "Select," which is unique to ASP.NET. When the server sees this CommandName, it will select the correct row by both changing its look and reflecting these changes in the SelectedIndex and SelectedItem properties of the DataGrid. These properties can be used just like the respective ones in a rich client application where you would be looking at the selected index of a ListView, for example. The change in the UI is made because the SelectedItemStyle attributes were set up on the table in the aspx file. Whatever this is set to, with all of its UI properties, is how the selected grid item will look as soon as the page returns from the click handler. Also, in this example we varied from the ItemCommand to the SelectedIndexChanged event. But the important part is that we modified the DataGrid in the aspx file to have a DataKeyField property set to PersonID. This makes the DataGrid load the PersonID property value from each of the MyPerson objects in the data source into each row, along with the other columns we selected to show. This is similar to the item data pointer in an MFC CListView control or the key property on items in a VB6 list control. It allows you to store some data along with the row, yet not have to see it. In a real-world application, you would take this key data and look up the detail record for the corresponding record in the grid, for example. You can see the code in action in Figure 3.31.

To wrap up this section, we will create one final DataGrid that makes use of a few formatting techniques, that shows off how nice a fully formatted DataGrid can look. There are many more aspects to the DataGrid, however, and they will be covered throughout the book. Later on, we will look at editing rows in a DataGrid, as well as handling events that occur as the DataGrid is being created by the system and being able to influence its creation on the fly. Create a WebForm called DataGridFormatted, and include the DataGrid shown in Listing 3.15. Again, we use the MyPerson class for the data items, so include the MyPerson declaration from Listing 3.10 in your code. Figure 3.32 shows the formatted DataGrid in action.

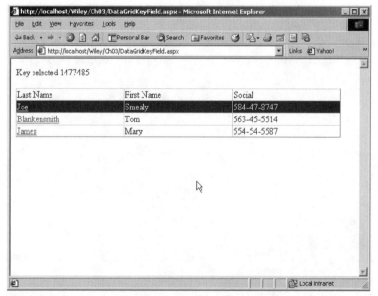

Figure 3.31   A DataGrid with a DataKeyField in action.

```
<%@ Page language="c#" Codebehind="DataGridFormatted.aspx.cs"
AutoEventWireup="false" Inherits="Ch03.DataGridFormatted" %>

<HTML>
    <HEAD>
        <meta name="GENERATOR" Content="Microsoft Visual Studio 7.0">
        <meta name="CODE_LANGUAGE" Content="C#">
    </HEAD>
    <body>
        <form method="post" runat="server">
            <asp:DataGrid id=DataGrid1 runat="server"
                AutoGenerateColumns=False
                borderstyle="None"
                cellpadding="2"
                backcolor="White"
                borderwidth="1px"
                Font-Name="Verdana"
                Font-Size="9pt"
                bordercolor="#CC9966">

                <FooterStyle ForeColor="#330099" BackColor="#FFFFCC">
                </FooterStyle>

                <ItemStyle ForeColor="Black" BackColor="White">
                </ItemStyle>

                <AlternatingItemStyle ForeColor="Black"
```

Listing 3.15   A nicely formatted DataGrid

```
                        BackColor="WhiteSmoke">
            </AlternatingItemStyle>

            <SelectedItemStyle Font-Bold="True" ForeColor="#663399"
                BackColor="#FFCC66">
            </SelectedItemStyle>

            <HeaderStyle Font-Bold="True" ForeColor="#FFFFCC"
                BackColor="#990000">
            </HeaderStyle>

            <Columns>
                <asp:ButtonColumn Text="Select" HeaderText="Select"
                    CommandName="Select">
                    <ItemStyle Width="40px">
                    </ItemStyle>
                </asp:ButtonColumn>

                <asp:TemplateColumn HeaderText="Name" ItemStyle-
                    Width=300px>
                    <ItemTemplate>
                        <asp:Label Runat=server Text='<%#
                            string.Format("{0}, {1}",

((MyPerson)Container.DataItem).LastName,

((MyPerson)Container.DataItem).FirstName)
                            %>'
                            ID="Hyperlink1" NAME="Hyperlink1">
                        </asp:Label>
                    </ItemTemplate>
                </asp:TemplateColumn>

                <asp:BoundColumn DataField="SSN"
                    HeaderText="Social">
                    <ItemStyle Width="200px">
                    </ItemStyle>
                </asp:BoundColumn>

                <asp:TemplateColumn HeaderText="Lookup" ItemStyle-
                    Width=40px>
                    <ItemTemplate>
                        <asp:HyperLink Runat=server Text="Lookup"
                            NavigateUrl='<%#
                            string.Format("lookup.aspx?id={0}",
                                Server.UrlEncode(

((MyPerson)Container.DataItem).PersonID)
                            ) %>'>
```

Listing 3.15 A nicely formatted DataGrid (continued)

```
                               </asp:HyperLink>
                          </ItemTemplate>
                     </asp:TemplateColumn>

                 </Columns>
            </asp:DataGrid>
        </form>
    </body>
</HTML>

namespace Ch03
{
    using System;
    using System.Collections;
    using System.ComponentModel;
    using System.Data;
    using System.Drawing;
    using System.Web;
    using System.Web.SessionState;
    using System.Web.UI;
    using System.Web.UI.WebControls;
    using System.Web.UI.HtmlControls;

    public class DataGridFormatted : System.Web.UI.Page
    {
        protected System.Web.UI.WebControls.DataGrid DataGrid1;

        public DataGridFormatted()
        {
            Page.Init += new System.EventHandler(Page_Init);
        }


        protected void Page_Init(object sender, EventArgs e)
        {
            InitializeComponent();
        }

        private void InitializeComponent()
        {
            this.Load += new System.EventHandler(this.Page_Load);
        }


        private void Page_Load(object sender, System.EventArgs e)
        {
            LoadDataGrid();
        }
```

Listing 3.15   A nicely formatted DataGrid (continued)

```
              private void LoadDataGrid()
              {
                  System.Collections.ArrayList arr = new
                      System.Collections.ArrayList();

                  arr.Add(new Ch03.MyPerson("Smealy", "Joe", "584-47-8747",
                      "605148"));

                  arr.Add(new Ch03.MyPerson("Tom", "Blankensmith",
                      "563-45-5514", "114700"));

                  arr.Add(new Ch03.MyPerson("Mary", "James", "554-54-5587",
                      "159986"));

                  arr.Add(new Ch03.MyPerson("Sally", "Weller", "593-16-3714",
                      "325448"));

                  arr.Add(new Ch03.MyPerson("Gerald", "Johns", "587-55-9025",
                      "222598"));

                  arr.Add(new Ch03.MyPerson("Gary", "Miller", "594-57-6249",
                      "121548"));

                  arr.Add(new Ch03.MyPerson("Nancy", "Becker", "595-3665",
                      "958746"));

                  arr.Add(new Ch03.MyPerson("Timothy", "Stevens", "523-4458",
                      "148756"));

                  arr.Add(new Ch03.MyPerson("Sarah", "Lawrence", "596-4144",
                      "418756"));

                  this.DataGrid1.DataSource = arr;
                  this.DataGrid1.DataBind();
              }
          }
      }
```

Listing 3.15   A nicely formatted DataGrid (continued)

In this example, we see many of the formatting enhancements you can do with the DataGrid. First, we have the ItemStyle, AlternatingItemStyle, HeaderStyle, Footer-Style, and SelectedItemStyle. These are subelements of the grid to allow you to change the look of different types of rows. With these you can control the font, color, bold, or background, or you can set a row to a CSS style. We won't go into the syntax of setting these up because the VS.NET IDE will do a nice job for you using the DataGrid Auto-Format and DataGrid Property Builder features. We personally use a combination of these tools mixed with hand editing the aspx. Try some experiments using these features to set the look of your DataGrid, and then go into the aspx code manually to see exactly how the code was generated.

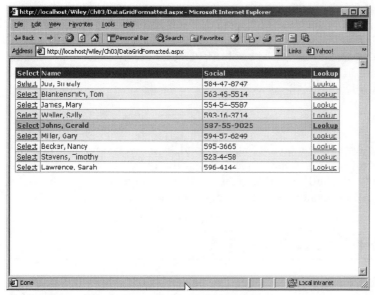

Figure 3.32   A nicely formatted DataGrid in action.

Another new aspect was added in Listing 3.15: the TemplateColumn, which again can be added using the Property Builder applet of Visual Studio .NET. This allows you to add most any controls you want to the cells in the DataGrid. Recall that the cells in a DataGrid are merely <td> table elements once they reach the browser, and they can contain whatever other HTML you want. In this example, we added some server controls with in-line script. In the first TemplateColumn, we will use an asp:Label to render the MyPerson name formatted as LastName, FirstName. When performing complex customizing like this, we resort to in-line scripting, which was explained in Chapter 2. Here is a quick rehash as it applies to this example.

The ((MyPerson)Container.DataItem).PersonID) line represents the DataItem from the DataGrid. Think of this as the actual object within the data source to which we are binding, although it does need to be cast out accordingly. In this case, the DataItem is actually the MyPerson for the current DataGrid row item. We can see that by casting, we are able to get at the properties of the data source objects in their native form. Then, we use the frameworks string class to format the contents, which will return a string to the DataGrid to render in the label. In actuality, we are binding a Label control to one of the bound pieces of data in its container. This technique is also used to set up the asp:HyperLink, which is in the last column, and links to another (nonexistent) page with the MyPerson PersonID as a parameter. It is true that the business logic probably could be done just the same by setting up a ButtonColumn, looking at the ID on the server from the DataKeyField, building the new URL in code, and redirecting to it. We wanted to show you a different option. Besides, it does save at least one trip to the server by having just a hyperlink on the client. As you can see, the TemplateColumns, ButtonColumns, and BoundColumns can live happily together in one DataGrid. Just remember that when using other server controls inside a TemplateColumn, they still must have the runat=server attribute set, just as if they were being used anywhere else. Also, if the objects in your data source are not in the same namespace as your page, you will have to include their namespace in the aspx file as well. This has to be done so that the cast applied to the DataItems can be resolved. You cannot rely on having the using <namespace> clause in your code-behind file; you must include something like the following at the top of the aspx file as well:

```
<%@ Import Namespace="MyPersonNameSpace" %>
```

This section was just a primer on the DataGrid, and, as stated before, we will revisit this control again in Chapters 4 and 5. We feel that the DataGrid is one of the best server controls in the standard suite, due to the fact that it is so common to need to display rows of data in this manner and the ease of use of the control itself.

HTML Server Controls

Any HTML element on an ASP.NET page can be converted into an HTML Server Control. The only action that is required to turn an HTML element into an HTML Server Control is to add the runat attribute of the HTML element and set it to "server". We have been using an HtmlForm control in nearly every example that we've covered in the book thus far. Either we added it manually, or the Web Form designer did it for us. It looks like this:

```
<form method="post" runat="server">
```

When the page is processed on the server, ASP.NET creates an instance of the Html-Form class to represent the form and provide us with programmatic access to it. By adding the runat="server" attribute, we can turn any HTML element into an HTML Server Control on the server. For instance, to make a <span> HTML element an HTML Server Control, we can just declare it like this:

```
<span id=Span1 runat="server"></span>
```

This ability gives a programmer who wants to stick with traditional HTML syntax the same server-side programmatic access to controls as is provided by the Web Server Controls. There are specific .NET Framework-provided classes that are used to represent many of the HTML Server Controls, such as HtmlForm to represent a <form> element and HtmlAnchor to represent an <a> element. A class does not exist, however, for every HTML element that exists. This problem is alleviated by the use of the Html-GenericControl, covered later in this chapter. By using HTML Server Controls, you circumvent ASP.NET's ability to determine the client browser capabilities and render HTML that will work best for that particular client. Because you are explicitly stating which HTML elements you want to use, your page may not work on an older Down-Level browser if you use elements that it doesn't support. Other than the HtmlForm, we won't be using HTML Server Controls too often in this book; however, we will cover a few of the more important points about HTML Server Controls in the sections that follow.

All HTML Server Controls derive indirectly from the HtmlControl class. The Html-Control class derives directly from the Control class, just as did the WebControl class from which all Web Server Controls inherit. That means that we get a lot of the same base functionality that Web Controls provide, such as Data Binding, View state, control containment, and basic events such as Init, Load, and Unload. The .NET Framework provides three classes that derive directly from HtmlControl. They are *HtmlContainer-Control*, *HtmlImage*, and *HtmlInputControl*. All of the HTML Server Controls that are provided derive from either HtmlContainerControl or HtmlInputControl. HtmlImage is a control that you will use directly.

HTML Server Controls that must have a closing tag will be derived from Html-ContainerControl. The HtmlContainerControl class adds two properties to the inherited HtmlControl class, *InnerHtml* and *InnerText*. These two properties are used to set the contents that are rendered between the opening and closing tags of the HTML element. InnerText provides automatic HTML encoding and decoding, while InnerHtml does not.

The HtmlInputControl class provides the base functionality for all HTML <input> elements. Its *Type* property specifies which type of <input> element it is, such as text, radio, or check box.

For the most part, you will find that any properties of the HTML Server Controls beyond those provided by their base class will have the same name as the attributes of the HTML element to which they render. For example, the HtmlAnchor class has properties such as HRef, Name, and Title, which are the same as the corresponding attributes for the HTML <a> element. In addition, most of the HTML Server Controls that allow user interaction add a server-side event. The name of the event will be either *ServerClick* or *ServerChange*, depending on whether it is a clickable element, such as a button or hyperlink, or a data entry element, such as a text box or drop-down list.

Table 3.1 lists all of the HTML Server Controls and the classes from which they derive.

Table 3.1 HTML Server Controls

CONTROLS DERIVED FROM HTMLCONTAINER	CONTROLS DERIVED HTMLINPUTCONTROL	CONTROLS DERIVED FROM HTMLIMAGE
HtmlAnchor	HtmlInputButton	(no derived controls)
HtmlButton	HtmlInputCheckBox	
HtmlForm	HtmlInputFile	
HtmlGenericControl	HtmlInputHidden	
HtmlSelect	HtmlInputImage	
HtmlTable	HtmlInputRadioButton	
HtmlTableCell	HtmlInputText	
HtmlTableRow		
HtmlTextArea		

Obviously, many HTML elements are missing. For example, there is no specific control for the <span> element. As shown earlier, we can still turn a <span> element into an HTML Server Control by adding the runat="server" attribute, but what object is used to represent that element on the server side and provide access to it? This is where the HtmlGenericControl comes in. It is the object used for programmatic access to any element that does not have a specific class implementation provided by the .NET Framework. Let's look at an example of how we can use this to access a <span> element and change its contents and attributes dynamically.

Create a new Web Form in your Chapter3 project, and call it span.aspx. Add the following inside the <form> tags:

```
<span id=Span1 runat="server"></span>
<p></p>
<input type=submit Value="Change To Red" id=Submit1 name=Submit1
  runat="server">
```

This code just declared two HTML Server Controls, simply by including the runat="server" attribute. To access these elements in the code-behind class, we need to declare HtmlGenericControl for the <span> element and HtmlInputButton for the <input type=submit> element.

```
protected System.Web.UI.HtmlControls.HtmlGenericControl Span1;
protected System.Web.UI.HtmlControls.HtmlInputButton Submit1;
```

Now we can access these two elements on the server side through these member variables. Add the following code to the Page_Load method:

```
if (!IsPostBack)
{
  Span1.InnerHtml = "This is a span element<br>with a line break";
}
```

This will set the text that is rendered inside of the <span> tags. We have set the text using the InnerHtml property to demonstrate that it does not provide HTML encoding. This means that an actual <br> element will be rendered inside the <span> tags and therefore a line break will occur, as shown in Figure 3.33. If we had set the InnerText property instead, the page would look like Figure 3.34 and the actual text that is rendered inside the <span> tags would be HTML encoded as follows.

```
This is a span element&lt;br&gt;with a line break
```

Figure 3.33   Setting the text of a span element with InnerHtml.

Next, we need to wire up a handler for the ServerClick event of the <input type= submit> element. This can be done in either the Page_Init or InitializeComponent methods like this:

```
this.Submit1.ServerClick += new
   System.EventHandler(this.Submit1_ServerClick);
```

Then, of course, we need to provide the handler as follows:

```
private void Submit1_ServerClick(object sender, System.EventArgs e)
{
  //Change the color of the span element and the text of the submit
button
  if (Span1.Style["color"] == "red")
  {
    //Clear the style-color attribute
    Span1.Style["color"] = "";
    //Change the text of the button
    Submit1.Value = "Change to red";
  }
  else
  {
    //Clear the style-color attribute
    Span1.Style["color"] = "red";
    //Change the text of the button
    Submit1.Value = "Change to normal";
  }
}
```

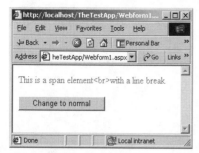

Figure 3.34   Setting the text of a span element with InnerText.

This code checks to see if the color of the text in the <span> element is red. If it's not, the color is set to red. We can access all of the attributes of the *style* associated with the <span> element using the *Style* property of the HtmlGenericControl. As you can see, this is how we check and set the color of the <span> text. In addition, we also change the text displayed on the button. This is done easily through the *Value* property of the HtmlInputButton control.

As we mentioned earlier, we won't be using the HTML Server Controls too often in this book, but this should give you a general idea of their capabilities. In most cases, you are better off to use the supplied Web Server Controls.

Validation Controls

A task that every good programmer must do is validating user input. In a typical Windows application, validation is not very difficult. All of the controls on a form can be validated when the user presses some sort of OK button, or validation can take place on each specific control as the user is entering the data. In ASP, user input validation was not a straightforward or clean task. Unless you wrote some sort of client-side script or DHTML, validation had to take place when the form was submitted to the server. Usually this validation was handled manually with a script that was called at the beginning of page processing. A simple validation, such as a required field, had to be checked for manually and an error message generated manually as well. ASP.NET has addressed this mundane task with validation controls.

Validation controls can be defined in the .aspx file just as Web Server or HTML Server Controls. There are several Validation Controls for performing the more common types of validation, such as a required field. In addition, a custom validator gives you complete control over the validation that occurs. In a nutshell, you choose the type of Validation Control that you need and wire it to a specific input control on your page. When the page is submitted the Validation Control will validate the input control to which it is assigned. If the Validation Control detects an invalid entry, an error message is usually displayed in one of several ways. The validation always occurs on the server side when the page is submitted; however, validation can also occur on the client side if the client browser supports DHTML. This eliminates the need for the round trip to the server and speeds up the data-entry process. Validation will still occur on the server side, even if validation has already taken place on the client side.

You can assign as many Validation Controls to one input control as necessary. This allows you not only to mark a field as required, but also to make sure that whatever the user enters is the type of information that you expect. It is important to know that the RequiredFieldValidator control, covered in the following section, is the only control that enforces required entry. The other Validation Controls will always validate to true if the user does not enter anything into the field being validated. In other words, they don't do anything unless there is some input to validate.

All of the Validation Controls derive directly from the BaseValidator class, which in turn is derived from the Label class. The BaseValidator class defines a property called *ControlToValidate*, which is set to the ID of the input control that is to be validated. The *IsValid* property is a Boolean property that can be checked programmatically to determine if the input was valid or invalid. In addition, this property can be set programmatically to force the Validation Control to whatever state we choose. In addition, we can force validation to occur on the server side at any time by calling the *Validate* method. This causes validation to occur and will update the *IsValid* property appropriately. The Page class itself defines an IsValid property. This property provides a quick and easy way to see if all of the controls on the page are valid or if there are errors. If any of the Validation Controls on the page are not valid, the Page class IsValid property will be set to False.

There are a few more properties of the BaseValidator class. The *Display* property determines whether the validator control reserves space on the page to display its error message, even when the error message is not visible. It can be set to either *Static* or *Dynamic*. When set to Static (the default), the Validation Control will occupy enough space to accommodate its error message, even when the error message is not visible. This prevents other controls from shifting on the page when the validator control displays its error message. In contrast, the Dynamic setting does not reserve space for the error message when it is not visible. Therefore, it's possible that other controls on the page might be shifted when the error message is displayed.

The *EnableClientScript* property is of type bool and allows us to turn off client-side validation for a specific Validation Control. This property is set to True by default. If it is set to False, no client-side script will be generated for client-side validation, regardless of whether the client supports DHTML.

RequiredFieldValidator

Before we go any further, let's look at a simple case of checking for a required field and get our feet wet with the Validation Controls. Create a new Web Form in your Chapter3 project, and call it ValidationControls.aspx. You can download the code for this page from the companion Web site. Add the following inside the <form> tags.

```
Vehicle Year: 
<asp:TextBox id=txtVehicleYear runat="server"></asp:TextBox>
<asp:RequiredFieldValidator id=vldVehicleYearReqd runat="server"
  ErrorMessage="Vehicle Year is a required field"
  controltovalidate="txtVehicleYear">
```

```
</asp:RequiredFieldValidator>
<P></P>
<asp:Button id=Button1 runat="server" Text="Submit">
</asp:Button>
```

This example is fairly straightforward. We have defined a *RequiredFieldValidator* control and set the ControlToValidate property to the ID of txtVehicleYear. As you might have guessed, the RequiredFieldValidator control is used to force required entry of a field on the page. If you navigate to this page and click the Submit button without typing anything in the text box, you should see something like Figure 3.35. An error message should be displayed next to the control with the text that we specified in the *ErrorMessage* property of the RequiredFieldValidator control. If you are using a browser that supports DHTML, you will notice that the error message is displayed without a round trip to the server. If your browser doesn't support DHTML, the error message will still be displayed, but only after a round trip to the server, where the validation will occur.

Let's take a look at the difference between the HTML source rendered for a DHTML and non-DHTML browser and see how client-side validation is implemented. First, let's look at the DHTML case. The rendered HTML for the required field example should look similar to Listing 3.5. The first thing to notice is the declaration of the <form> tag. The onsubmit attribute of the <form> element has been set to Validator-OnSubmit(), so just before the form is posted to the server, this JavaScript function will be called. After the <form> declaration we see that a JavaScript source file has been included called WebUIValidation.js. This file is installed with the framework and placed under the inetpub\wwwroot_aspx directory of your Web server. It contains the JavaScript code for implementing client-side evaluation for all of the Validation Controls. Immediately after the declaration of the <input> element, a <span> element has been rendered for the RequiredFieldValidator control. The controltovalidate and errormessage attributes are exactly as we defined for the same named attributes of the RequiredFieldValidator. In addition, an attribute named *evaluationfunction* is set to RequiredFieldValidatorEvaluateIsValid. This is a JavaScript function that is defined in the file WebUIValidation.js. The style of the <span> element has been set, and the visibility has been set to hidden. This is why we don't see the error message when the page is loaded initially.

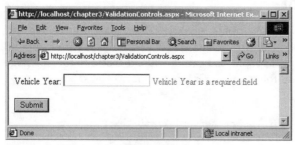

Figure 3.35   RequiredFieldValidator.

In the <script> blocks defined at the bottom of the source an array called Page_Validators is defined. All of the Validation Controls that you have defined in your page will be added to this array. In this case, we have only one, txtVehicleYearReqd. This array is used by several of the JavaScript functions in the WebUIValidation.js file. Further down we see some script that verifies the existence of the correct version of the WebUIValidation.js file.

Finally, the ValidatorOnSubmit function is defined, which calls the Validator-CommonOnSubmit function. ValidatorCommonOnSubmit is defined in the WebUI-Validation.js file and basically loops through all of the Validation Controls in the Page_Validators array, executes the appropriate evaluation function for each of them, and, if necessary, displays error messages for controls that do not have valid entries. We're not going to go any further into the implementation details of the WebUIValidation.js file. You can open it up and take a look at it yourself if you're interested in the specifics of how it works.

```html
<HTML>
  <HEAD>
    <meta name="GENERATOR" Content="Microsoft Visual Studio 7.0">
    <meta name="CODE_LANGUAGE" Content="C#">
    <meta name=vs_defaultClientScript content="JScript">
    <meta name=vs_targetSchema content="Internet Explorer 5.0">
  </HEAD>
  <body ms_positioning="GridLayout">
    <form name="RequiredFieldValidator" method="post"
      action="RequiredFieldValidator.aspx" language="javascript"
      onsubmit="ValidatorOnSubmit();" id="RequiredFieldValidator">

        <input type="hidden" name="__VIEWSTATE"
          value="dDwtMjA3MzEyODU5NTs7Pg==" />

        <script language="javascript"
          src="/_aspx/1.0.2728/script/WebUIValidation.js">
        </script>

        Vehicle Year: 
        <input name="txtVehicleYear" type="text" value="fdas"
          id="txtVehicleYear" />
        <span id="vldVehicleYearReqd" controltovalidate="txtVehicleYear"
          errormessage="Vehicle Year is a required field"
          evaluationfunction="RequiredFieldValidatorEvaluateIsValid"
          initialvalue="" style="color:Red;visibility:hidden;">
          Vehicle Year is a required field
        </span>
        <P></P>
        <input type="submit" name="Button1" value="Submit" id="Button1"
/>
```

Listing 3.16   RequiredFieldValidator in action

```
<script language="javascript">
<!--
  var Page_Validators =  new Array(document.all["vldVehicleYearReqd"]);
// -->
</script>

<script language="javascript">
<!--
var Page_ValidationActive = false;
if (typeof(Page_ValidationVer) == "undefined")
  alert("Unable to find script library WebUIValidation.js.");
else if (Page_ValidationVer != "119")
  alert("This page uses an incorrect version of WebUIValidation.js. The
  page expects version 119. The script library is " + Page_ValidationVer
  + ".");
else
  ValidatorOnLoad();

function ValidatorOnSubmit() {
  if (Page_ValidationActive) {
    ValidatorCommonOnSubmit();
  }
}
// -->
</script>
    </form>
  </body>
</HTML>
```

Listing 3.16   RequiredFieldValidator in action (continued)

For the non-DHTML browser, no client-side evaluation can occur, so no JavaScript is rendered. In fact, nothing at all is rendered for the RequiredFieldValidator control. When the page is submitted back to the server all of the Validation Controls will fire and appropriate error messages will be rendered if necessary and sent back to the client.

RegularExpressionValidator

The RegularExpressionValidator checks for a specific pattern of entry in an input control. Regular expressions are a type of pattern-matching notation that allows us to specify a particular pattern or patterns of text to search for within a string. We can specify the regular expression that should be used by the RegularExpressionValidator through the ValidationExpression property. If the input doesn't match the pattern specified, the validator control will be invalid. ValidationExpression is the only member that the RegularExpressionValidator class adds to the BaseValidator class.

NOTE We're not going to cover the regular expression syntax in this book, but you can find all the information that you need about it in the MSDN library. An important thing to note is that when the RegularExpressionValidator runs on the client side for a DHTML-compliant browser, the regular expression syntax used is that of JavaScript. On the server side, the Regex regular expression syntax is used. For this reason, it is possible to have different validation on the client and server sides. Microsoft recommends that you use the JavaScript syntax, which is a subset of the Regex syntax, to prevent differences in validation on the client and server sides. The following documents can get you on the right path for writing regular expressions.

Javascript

```
http://msdn.microsoft.com/library/periodic/period99/valid.htm
```

Regex

```
http://msdn.microsoft.com/library/default.asp?url=/library/
en-us/cpguidnf/html/cpconcomregularexpressions.asp
```

Let's add a RegularExpressionValidator to the previous example. We want the user to enter a four-digit year into our Vehicle Year field. We've already added a Required-FieldValidator, which will enforce an entry of some sort. Add the following right below the RequiredFieldValidator declaration in the ValidatorControls.aspx file.

```
<asp:RegularExpressionValidator id=vldVehicleYearReg runat="server"
   ErrorMessage="Please enter a four-digit year"
   validationexpression="\d\d\d\d" controltovalidate="txtVehicleYear">
</asp:RegularExpressionValidator>
```

Now if you browse to the page, you will get an error message if you enter anything other than four digits. You will still get the original RequiredFieldValidator error message if you submit the form without entering anything in the Vehicle Year field. You probably noticed a problem with the way the error message for the RegularExpressionValidator is displayed. The error message is shifted over to the far right side of the page away from the Vehicle Year field that it applies to, as shown in Figure 3.36. This is because the Display property of the RequiredFieldValidator is set to Static. Even though its error message is not being displayed, the space is still reserved. We could eliminate this problem by changing the Display property to Dynamic, but this could cause other controls on the page to shift undesirably when the message is displayed. The more common thing to do is to display all error messages for the page in one common place. In addition, the fields in error are usually marked in some way to signify that they require attention. Displaying the error messages in one common place is easily implemented with the ValidationSummary control.

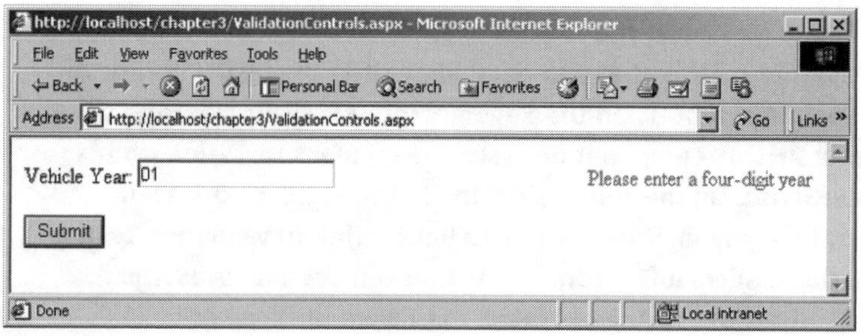

Figure 3.36 A Shifted Error Message.

ValidationSummary

The *ValidationSummary* control's sole purpose is to display the error messages of all Validation Controls on a page in one common place. You can customize the way that the error messages are displayed. Normally, you should need only one Validation-Summary control on a particular page. Simply define it in the .aspx file, and set properties to control the way that it is displayed.

The ValidationSummary class inherits directly from WebControl, not BaseValidator. Because it isn't doing any validation itself, that wouldn't be necessary. The *Display-Mode* property is used to control the format in which the error messages are displayed. Its valid values are *List*, *BulletList*, and *SingleParagraph*. List places each error message on a separate line. BulletList, as the name implies, displays the messages in a bulleted list. SingleParagraph causes all of the messages to flow together in one section. There is also a *HeaderText* property, which sets some text that will be displayed just prior to the error messages when one or more errors occur.

The error messages that are displayed by the ValidationSummary control can be displayed in one of two different ways or both. They can be displayed on the page itself in either UpLevel or DownLevel browsers. In addition to this, an UpLevel browser will be able to display the error messages in a pop-up window. You can specify which methods you want with the *ShowSummary* and *ShowMessageBox* properties. Both of these properties are of type bool. If the ShowSummary property is set to True, error messages will be displayed as part of the page in the location of the ValidationSummary control. If the ShowMessageBox property is set to True, error messages will be displayed in a pop-up window. You can set both of these properties to True if you like. In an UpLevel browser, the user will see the pop-up window and the error message summary on the page. In a DownLevel browser, the user would not see the pop-up window.

Let's rework the ValidationControl.aspx page to use a ValidationSummary control. Add the following immediately after the <form> tag:

```
<asp:validationsummary id=ValidationSummary1 runat="server"
  displaymode="BulletList"
  headertext="The following errors were encountered:">
</asp:validationsummary>
```

Figure 3.37   Required field error.

Rather than display the error message next to the control and in the ValidationSummary control, let's make a simple asterisk appear next to the control when it is invalid. If we set the *Text* property of the Validation Controls to "*", this is the text that will appear at the location of the Validation Control when it is invalid. If the Text property is set to anything other than an empty string, its value will be displayed in the location of the Validation Control rather than the value of the ErrorMessage property. The text of the ErrorMessage property will still be used for display in the ValidationSummary control. Having said that, add the Text attribute to both the RequiredFieldValidator and the RegularExpressionValidator and set it to "*". In addition, set the Display attribute of each control to Dynamic. This will prevent the asterisk from shifting around on us. Now when the page is submitted, it should look like Figures 3.37 and 3.38 when errors occur.

We recommend utilizing the ValidationSummary whenever possible. If you are designing pages that require a lot of user input and therefore a lot of validation and possible error messages, it provides a lot of functionality with very little effort.

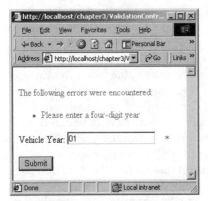

Figure 3.38   Four digits required error.

RangeValidator

The RangeValidator verifies that an entered value is between a specified maximum and minimum value. The type of data that you are comparing is specified using the *Type* property. The valid values are String, Integer, Double, Date, and Currency. The text of the control to be validated is converted to the specified type before validation occurs. If the conversion fails then the control will be invalid. This could happen, for example, if you set the Type property to Integer, but the user typed in some nonnumeric characters. The minimum and maximum values are specified with the *MinimumValue* and *MaximumValue* properties.

Let's add a RangeValidator to the ValidationControls.aspx page to verify that the user has entered a year between 1950 and 2001. Add the following immediately after the RegularExpressionValidator:

```
<asp:RangeValidator id=vldVehicleYearRng runat="server"
  ErrorMessage="Please enter a year between 1950 and 2001" Text="*"
  Display=Dynamic controltovalidate="txtVehicleYear" maximumvalue="2001"
  minimumvalue="1950" type="Integer">
</asp:RangeValidator>
```

Now if we enter a year that is not greater than or equal to 1950 and less than or equal to 2001, the RangeValidator will be invalid, and its error message will be displayed. It will also be invalid if anything other than numerical text is entered.

CompareValidator

The *CompareValidator* can be used to compare the contents of one input control to the contents of another or to some static value. Comparing to the contents of another input control can be useful in many situations. For example, if we are asking the user to create a password, we will probably ask the user to enter it twice in two separate text boxes. We could use the CompareValidator on the second text box and specify that the contents of the second text box must be equal to the contents of the first.

If you wish to compare to another input control, specify that control's name in the *ControlToCompare* property. Just as with the RangeValidator, you can specify the type of data that you expect to be comparing with the Type property; again, the valid values are String, Integer, Double, Date, and Currency. The *Operator* property is where we specify what type of comparison to perform. The valid values are Equal (the default), *NotEqual, GreaterThan, GreaterThanEqual, LessThan, LessThanEqual,* and *DataTypeCheck.* The CompareValidator can also be used to compare to a set value using the *ValueToCompare* property. You can't use both the ControlToCompare and ValueToCompare properties simultaneously. If you do, the ControlToCompare will be the only one used. The value that you set in the ValueToCompare property doesn't have to be determined at design time. It could be something that is determined at runtime, possibly read in from a database, which provides a great amount of flexibility and functionality.

Let's create a new example to demonstrate the use of this control. We'll create a page that asks the user to enter a desired User ID and password. If everything checks out well, a success message will be displayed along with a link to restart the sample. Create a new Web Form in your Chapter3 project called ValidationControls2.aspx. Enter the following inside the <form> tags.

```
<asp:validationsummary id=ValidationSummary1 runat="server"
  displaymode="BulletList"
  headertext="The following errors were encountered:">
</asp:validationsummary>
<br>
Enter your desired User ID and Password below:
<p></p>
<asp:Label runat="server" width=100 Text="User ID:"></asp:Label>
<asp:textbox id="txtUserID" runat="server"></asp:textbox>
<br>
<asp:Label runat="server" width=100 Text="Password:"></asp:Label>
<asp:textbox id="txtPassword" runat="server"
  TextMode=Password>
</asp:textbox>
<br>
<asp:Label runat="server" width=100 Text="Verify:"></asp:Label>
<asp:textbox id="txtVerifyPassword" runat="server"
  TextMode=Password>
</asp:textbox>
<asp:CompareValidator id="vldVerifyPasswordCmp" Runat="server"
  ErrorMessage="The password you entered does not verify with itself.
  Please re-enter your password." Text="*" Display=Dynamic
  controltovalidate="txtVerifyPassword" type="String"
  controltocompare="txtPassword">
</asp:CompareValidator>
<p></p>
<asp:button id=Button1 runat="server" Text="Submit"></asp:button>
```

We've left out any other Validation Controls that would more than likely be necessary if this were a real application, just to keep things simple. For example, all three fields would probably need RequiredFieldValidators, and we would probably want User Ids and passwords to be a certain number of characters. We did, however, make use of the ValidationSummary control. Create a handler for the Button1 Click event and place the following code in the handler.

```
Response.Write(string.Format("Successfully created User ID <b>{0}</b> "
+
  "with password <b>{1}</b><p></p>", txtUserID.Text, txtPassword.Text));
Response.Write("Click <a href=ValidationControls2.aspx>here</a> to try "
+
  "again.");
Response.End();
```

Compile the project, and view the page in your browser. As long as you enter the same text in the Password and Verify fields, the form will validate and submit to the server where the Button1 Click event handler will be called. The handler simply writes out a success message and creates a hyperlink back to the same page again. We added this only to make it easier for you to play around with the sample. Obviously, if the user has successfully created a User ID, there's no need for him or her to go back to the page again.

CustomValidator

The CustomValidator provides the ability to take the entire validation process into your own hands. You can write your own validation function to run on the server and the client. When a page is submitted the *ServerValidate* event of any CustomValidator controls is fired at the same time that all other Validation Controls are verified. To provide server-side validation for a CustomValidator, you simply provide a handler for the ServerValidate event. The handler delegate must take the following form:

```
void HandlerName (object source, ServerValidateEventArgs args)
```

The ServerValidateEventArgs parameter has two properties. *Value* is the value of the input control to which the CustomValidator is assigned. This would be the value on which you would perform your validation. The *IsValid* property of ServerValidate-EventArgs should be set to True or False to signify success or failure.

In most cases, the CustomValidator will be used for server-side validation only. One particular use would be when validation of a particular input requires checking something in the database. For instance, in the example in the preceding section, we might want to verify that the User ID entered by the user isn't already taken by another user. Because we don't have a list of all users in our database on the client side, client-side validation isn't possible or at least not practical. In the case that we do need to perform custom client-side validation, a function must be written in a language that will run on a client-side browser. This will probably be JavaScript or VBScript. The function will need to accept two parameters just as did the ServerValidate event handler. Last, we will need to supply the CustomValidator the name of the function via the *ClientValidationFunction* property. As long as the client is an UpLevel browser, the validation will take place on the client side. Remember that your server-side validation function will also be called when the page is submitted back to the server, so it's important that these two functions perform the same validation.

Let's expand on the ValidationControls2.aspx page and use a CustomValidator to verify the User ID that has been entered. Because we haven't covered database access yet, we'll just hard-code a few User IDs into the validation functions and make sure that the user hasn't entered one of those. Add the following immediately after the TextBox txtUserID declaration in the ValidationControls2.aspx file:

```
<asp:CustomValidator id=vldUserIDCstm Runat="server"
  ErrorMessage="The User ID you have entered is already in use" Text="*"
  Display=Dynamic controltovalidate="txtUserID">
</asp:CustomValidator>
```

We'll need to provide a handler for the ServerValidate event in the code-behind class like this:

```
private void vldUserIDCstm_ServerValidate(object source,
  System.Web.UI.WebControls.ServerValidateEventArgs args)
{
  if (args.Value == "JoeHealy" || args.Value == "SpikePierson" ||
    args.Value == "AndyJohnston")
```

```
  {
    args.IsValid = false;
  }
  else
  {
    args.IsValid = true;
  }
}
```

This simply checks the Value property of the ServerValidateEventArgs parameter. If it is equal to one of the hard-coded names, the IsValid property is set to False; otherwise, the IsValid property is set to True.

The last thing we need to do is modify the Button1 Click event handler to check the Page class IsValid property. If the page is not valid, then we should just return and allow the Validation Controls to display their error messages. We can accomplish this by wrapping all of the existing code in the Button1 Click event handler inside of an if statement like this.

```
if (Page.IsValid)
{
...
}
```

Now if you view the page and enter one of the hard-coded User IDs, you should see an error message stating that the User ID is already in use. If you enter anything else for the User ID, the page should work just as it did before. Also notice that because we didn't supply a client-side validation function, the error asterisk is not displayed next to the User ID text box until the page is posted back to the server. Let's supply a client-side VBScript function and see if this changes. Add the following script to the bottom of the ValidationControls2.aspx file:

```
<script language=vbscript>
function vldUserIDCstm_ClientValidate(source, args)
  If (args.Value = "JoeHealy" Or args.Value = "SpikePierson" Or
      args.Value = "AndyJohnston") Then
    args.IsValid=false
  Else
    args.IsValid=true
  End If
end function
</script>
```

Set the ClientValidationFunction property of the CustomValidator to the name of this function. The entire declaration of the CustomValidator should now be like this:

```
<asp:CustomValidator id=vldUserIDCstm Runat="server"
  ErrorMessage="The User ID you have entered is already in use" Text="*"
  Display=Dynamic controltovalidate="txtUserID"
  clientvalidationfunction="vldUserIDCstm_ClientValidate">
</asp:CustomValidator>
```

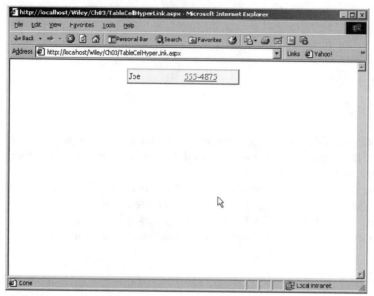

Figure 3.39   ValidationControls2.

After making these changes, if you type in one of the hard-coded User IDs, you will notice that the * that we supplied in the Text property shows up next to the input control as soon as the control loses focus and without posting back to the Web server. That is your client-side validation function in action. A screen shot of the Validation-Controls2 example can be seen in Figure 3.39.

Wrapping Up the Chapter

We have covered a lot of ground in this chapter and learned all about the Server Controls that come with ASP.NET. Server Controls are one of the most powerful features of ASP.NET. You will be using them constantly, and the more you use them, the more powerful you will realize they are. With ASP.NET, making complex Web pages doesn't have to be a complex programming task anymore.

In the next chapter, we will learn how easy database access is with the .NET Framework. As we learn how to access data, we will bind some of the controls that we covered in this chapter to dynamic data from a database.

Database Access

In this chapter we'll introduce database access via ADO.NET. We'll cover error handling under the .NET framework first because we have to be prepared for unpredictable errors when accessing a database. Then we'll dig into ADO.NET and find out how easy it is to access data with Microsoft's newest data access object model. Many of the database access examples in this chapter will utilize the DataGrid Server Control, which was covered in Chapter 3, "Server Controls." All of the examples will utilize error handling to help get you into the habit of including it in your code. The examples and concepts provided in this chapter will serve as a foundation building block in the automobile parts application that we'll begin building in Chapter 6, "Applying What We've Learned So Far."

Error Handling

Error handling is probably the most overlooked and set-aside task by application programmers. This is a problem that is common in classic ASP applications due to the poor error-handling capabilities of the scripting languages. Often, programmers sit down to write a particular piece of code with the idea that they are just testing things or figuring out how to solve a particular problem. No error handling is added to this code to shave time off the "testing" process. The problem is, often this test code makes it into production applications. This problem is compounded when you are programming for the

Web because you may not know who your users are or have any way of getting feedback from them if there are errors in your application that have squeaked past the testing process. You could still log errors in some fashion, but user feedback is very important in determining how to reproduce errors. Fortunately, the .NET Framework provides us with a very robust error-handling mechanism. It can provide a great deal of information that can be logged when errors occur and assist in tracking problems down and resolving them. For the most part, exception handling is quick and easy, so do yourself and others a favor and include it the first time around.

Exceptions are defined as anything that occurs during program execution that is unexpected under normal circumstances. Exceptions can occur on any line of code, as the .NET runtime itself will throw exceptions if it detects abnormal or unrecoverable conditions. For example, let's assume that we have a section of code in which we will *try* to make a connection to a SQL Server database, which is expected to always be available. If the database is unavailable or the network is down, no connection can be made and ADO.NET will *throw* an exception. Because we know this exception can occur, as programmers we are responsible for providing a way to *catch* the exception and handle it gracefully. *Finally*, we need to clean up and free any resources as necessary. I have italicized the words *try, throw, catch,* and *finally*, as they are C# keywords for structured exception handling, which we cover later in this chapter.

The .NET Base Class Library (BCL) defines a class called *Exception*. This is the base class used by the runtime to create and throw exceptions when they occur. The Exception class defines several properties, but the two most important ones are *Message* and *StackTrace*. Message contains a description of the actual exception that occurred and the probable causes. StackTrace provides a list of all method calls that were on the stack when the error occurred, effectively giving us the path of execution that resulted in the error. If debug information is available, it can even provide us with the source code file and line number where the error occurred. Many specific exceptions are defined in the BCL, all of which derive from the Exception class. For instance, there is a SQLException class that will be used to throw any exceptions that occur within a SQL Server database. These specific exception classes are important, as they provide a way to selectively catch specific exceptions and take appropriate actions when they occur, rather than catching all exceptions and taking the same action regardless of the cause of the exception.

Whenever a section of code is written that has the potential to cause an exception, it should be wrapped up inside of a try block, like this:

```
try
{
   //...code that might cause an exception
}
```

One or more catch blocks must immediately follow the try block. You should provide catch blocks for specific types of exceptions if possible, as well as a general exception catch block for anything that might slip through the cracks. Be sure to include the specific exception catch blocks first because they are evaluated in inner to outer order. In the case of database access, you might do something like this:

```
try
{
    //...code that might cause a database exception
}
catch(SQLException e)
{
    //...handle the database exception
}
catch(Exception e)
{
    //...handle any other exceptions
}
```

The catch blocks are defined similarly to a class method. They usually take one argument derived from Exception. A catch block can also be defined without any parameters at all, in which case it will catch any type of exception, just as the last catch handler in the preceding code. Whether to use one over the other depends on where you intend to actually handle and address the exception. If you don't intend to use the information that is available in the Exception object in your catch block, then use the parameter-less catch block.

What happens if an exception occurs within a method call and it is not wrapped up in a try/catch block? The framework will begin unwinding the call stack until it finds a catch block that can handle the exception. If none are found, this is called an unhandled exception, and the runtime will catch the exception and display an error message. This is definitely not what you want to happen because the error message is definitely not an end-user-friendly one. You are much better off ensuring that you catch all of your own exceptions so that you can either recover from them or display a friendly error message to your users.

You might also want to rethrow the exception and let a catch block that is defined somewhere further up the call stack handle it. Even with the parameter-less catch handler you can still rethrow the current exception, like this:

```
try
{
    //...code that might cause an exception
}
catch
{
    throw;
}
```

The throw keyword can be used entirely by itself as in the preceding example, in which case the current exception object is rethrown and will be handled, we hope, by some outer catch block. The throw keyword can also be used to throw a new exception. As an example, let's assume that we have defined a method in an object, which takes one parameter. If the caller of the method passes in a null parameter, we might want to throw an ArgumentNullException, as shown here:

```
public void MyMethod(MyObject param1)
{
  if (param1 == null)
  {
    throw(new ArgumentNullException("param1");
  }

  //...process normally
}
```

Notice that we had to use the *new* keyword to create the ArgumentNullException object and that we passed in the name of the parameter that was null to the constructor. The object that called this method has a catch block that will catch it and handle it gracefully, we hope.

The last thing that we want to cover about exception handling is the finally block. When unexpected errors occur and exceptions are thrown, valuable resources may still be in use and need to be released back to the system. Perhaps you have included code to clean up these resources somewhere inside your method, but if an exception is thrown and execution is passed to a catch block, that cleanup code may never get a chance to execute. Code that you include in a finally block will always be called, regardless of whether an exception occurs. Therefore, this is the perfect place to free resources and perform any necessary clean-up. The finally block should be defined immediately following your last catch block. Here is an example of how you might use the finally block:

```
public void MyDatabaseMethod()
{
  try
  {
    //...Create and Open a database connection
    //...Use the database connection
  }
  catch(SQLException e)
  {
    //...handle the database exception
  }
  catch(Exception e)
  {
    //...handle any other exceptions
  }
  finally
  {
    //...Close the database connection
  }
}
```

Because we've created and opened a database connection inside of this method, we need to make sure we close the connection before the method returns. Because the finally block will execute regardless of whether an exception is thrown, our method will always close the connection.

We've covered the basics of exception handling with C#. There are a few more tips and tricks that you'll see throughout the rest of the book concerning exception handling as we use the concepts discussed in this section when we build the example applications later in the book. This should be enough to get your feet wet and avoid any confusion as we move on to database access in the next section.

Database Access Using ADO.NET

There is enough information to cover about ADO.NET to constitute a separate book on the subject. As a matter of fact, there are books dedicated to the subject already on the shelves. Having said that, we're going to cover the basics of ADO.NET as they apply to Web application programming tasks and database access. If you're interested in learning more about ADO.NET, you should pick up a copy of *Programming ADO.NET* by Richard Hundhausen and Steven Borg (John Wiley & Sons, 2002).

ADO.NET was built with the Internet and distributing computing at the forefront, and it uses XML to transmit data; so any application that can read XML can work with the data provided through ADO.NET. With ADO, data was accessed through the use of the *Recordset* object. The Recordset allowed the view of only one table at a time. If you needed to access data from several tables in the database a JOIN query was necessary so that all of the required data was part of the same Recordset. Navigation through the records in the Recordset was done by calling the MoveNext() and MovePrevious() methods. ADO.NET provides two objects for accessing data, the *DataReader* and the *DataSet*.

The DataReader provides forward-only, always connected access to the database, which means a connection to the database is maintained as long as the DataReader is open. Like the Recordset, the DataReader allows only one table to be accessed at a time, and navigation through records is done by calling the Read() method. As opposed to the ADO Recordset, the DataSet can store multiple tables, their schema, relationships, and constraints. In other words, it can be viewed as an in-memory representation of the database. The DataSet object has a collection of *DataTable* objects, which in turn have a collection of *DataRow* objects. This makes navigation through records extremely flexible and easy because you can access the data in these collections just as you would any other collection in C#. You might use the foreach statement to traverse through all of the DataRows in a DataTable, or you can access particular rows via ordinal or primary key. ADO.NET DataSets also provide a completely disconnected view of the data, which means that no connection is maintained to the database. As a matter of fact, the DataSet object doesn't know anything about the data source from which it gets its data. DataSets communicate with a data source through the use of a DataAdapter object, which will open and close connections to the database as needed. The fact that the DataSet object is unaware of its data source makes it very generic and robust enough to use with many types of data sources. You can load a DataSet with data from any type of source, or even create a database schema and populate a DataSet with data manually.

In addition, ADO.NET DataSets provide a performance advantage over ADO Recordsets for disconnected applications. Disconnected data access was provided in ADO through the use of disconnected Recordsets. Transmitting these disconnected Recordsets across the network required the overhead of COM marshalling, which also placed a restriction on the data types that could be used. In addition, most firewalls are not configured to allow requests such as COM marshalling to pass through, which can make the disconnected Recordset unusable in many applications. Transmitting an ADO.NET DataSet across the network is done by transmitting an XML stream. Not only does this remove the restriction on data types and the overhead of COM marhsalling, but XML streams will easily pass through the typical firewall. The DataSet has also been designed to read and write XML with ease.

While the DataSet is clearly a very powerful tool for database access, its inherent disconnected nature and many of its capabilities apply more to long-running client/server type applications. In these types of applications, it makes sense to hold a cached, disconnected DataSet in memory, manipulate that data, and then reconcile the changes with the database when appropriate. Because the DataSet is disconnected, valuable database resources are not held, which provides for greater scalability. Web applications themselves are connectionless, though. In general, a page is requested, data is retrieved from the database, the data is formatted into HTML and returned to the client browser, and the connection to the database is closed and possibly made available for reuse by a new client. For this scenario, what we need is an extremely fast and efficient way to retrieve data from the database in a read-only, forward-only manner. This is where the SqlDataReader and OleDbDataReader objects are handy. These objects are designed to provide the fastest access to your data. They are not as robust as the DataSet object, as they do not handle multiple tables, relations, or schema. In a Web scenario where data is requested and input only for the duration of a page request and does not maintain the DataSet between client requests, the robust features of the DataSet become a moot point. What you want with a Web application is speed, and the use of the SqlDataReader object along with SQL Server stored procedures will provide maximum data access speed.

Let's take a look at the architectural design of ADO.NET. Whenever you are accessing data, you will need to reference the System.Data namespace. This namespace contains all of the classes and interfaces that provide the foundation of ADO.NET. It is in this namespace that the DataSet and all of its associated classes can be found. The initial release of the .NET framework provides two managed providers for accessing data. The first is a SQL Server manager provider whose associated classes can be found in the System.Data.SqlClient namespace. The second is an OLE DB provider for accessing any OLE DB-compliant data source; its associated classes can be found in the System.Data.OleDb namespace. The classes within these two managed provider namespaces provide the ability to work with their specific data sources. The SQL Server managed provider provides the fastest, most efficient access to a SQL Server database. The OLE DB provider is there to provide access to all other data sources that support OLE DB, which is a lot. In the future, we hope to see new managed providers that will give us more efficient access to specific data sources. Database vendors will have the ability to write managed providers for their database products, and we hope that companies like Oracle and IBM will do just that.

NOTE At the time this book was written, Microsoft had provided a Beta version of an ODBC Managed Provider, so check the Microsoft Web site for further information on that.

The managed providers are the means of connecting to and communicating with the data sources. Several of the classes found within the managed providers are created by implementing interfaces that are defined in the System.Data namespace. For example, the System.Data.SqlClient.SqlConnection and System.Data.OleDb.OleDbConnection classes both implement the System.Data.IDbConnection interface. It is through implementing these common interfaces that the managed providers will maintain a consistent implementation. This is nice for the programmer because it minimizes the amount of work that will need to be done to switch from one managed provider to another. Let's say that you develop an application that communicates with an Oracle database. You would have to use the OLE DB managed provider currently, but later when someone creates an Oracle managed provider, you should be able to easily modify your code to switch to the new provider. Because both providers will support the same base methods and properties, for the most part you will need to change only the class names from the OleDb namespace classes to the classes in the new managed provider namespace.

Take a look at Figure 4.1 to see a conceptual view of how ADO.NET is designed. Notice again that the DataSet is not part of a managed provider because it is not tied to any particular data source. The DataReader, though, is implemented by the managed providers. In the case of the SqlDataReader, it has been designed to work specifically with SQL Server, and the OleDbDataReader has been designed to work with any OLE DB-compliant database. The classes within the SqlClient managed provider have all been written to work specifically with Microsoft SQL Server. Although you can access a SQL Server database by using the classes provided in the OleDb managed provider, the SqlClient managed provider will always provide you with greater performance and flexibility when dealing with a SQL Server database. Every managed provider will implement a Connection class for establishing connections to the data source and a Command class for executing commands on the data source. In addition, a DataReader class will be provided, and a DataAdapter class will be implemented to allow the use of the DataSet class with the data source. An Exception class will exist to provide detailed information whenever an error occurs within the data source. Last, if the data source supports transactions a Transaction class will be provided.

Without further ado, let's get to the basics of how to access some data. First, we're going to need some sort of data source. For the majority of examples in this book, we will be using MSDE (Microsoft Data Engine). A version of MSDE is provided with the .NET Framework SDK, or you can download a free version from the Microsoft Web site. A link to the download location for MSDE is provided on the companion Web site. MSDE is a fully compatible SQL Server database engine. It is an excellent database to use for developing an application that will run on SQL Server when released. It can also be used in production for small-scale systems, and it provides an easy upgrade path to the power of a full SQL Server 2000 database engine. For the examples in this section of the book, we use the ever-popular Northwind database, which is installed by default. In later chapters of the book, we'll build our own database for use with our car parts business. Because we will primarily be using MSDE in this book, most of the data access examples and code will use the SQL Server managed provider. We will show some examples of how to use the OLE DB provider to connect a Microsoft Access database; however, you will find that the classes and methods are nearly identical. Because of this, we mainly focus on the SQL Server managed provider to avoid any confusion. So, get MSDE installed, and let's start accessing some data.

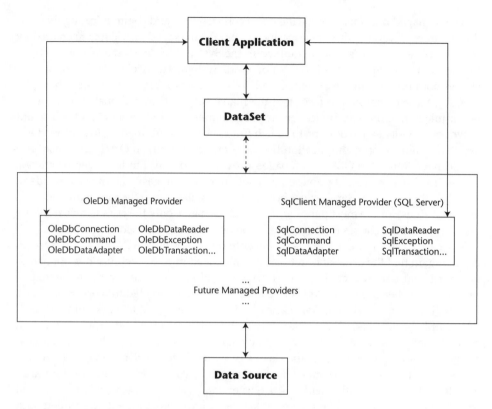

Figure 4.1   ADO.NET architecture.

Connection

As with ADO, the Connection object is your means for establishing communication with a data source. The SQL Server managed provider implementation is named *Sql-Connection*, and the OLE DB version is *OleDbConnection*. As mentioned earlier, both of these classes implement the System.Data.IDbConnection interface.

The *ConnectionString* property is used to tell the Connection object which database to connect to and with what options. The ConnectionString for the OLE DB provider is in the same format as the current OLE DB connection strings used with ADO. The ConnectionString for the SQL Server provider is similar to the OLE DB format, but it has some extra SQL Server specific options, some that we will be covering shortly. When the ConnectionString property is set, it is immediately parsed and checked for errors. Any properties of the Connection object that have corresponding connection string values will be updated to reflect the value passed in via the connection string. For example, the Connection objects have a *ConnectionTimeout* property that can be updated by setting the *Connection Timeout* name/value pair in the ConnectionString. Incidentally, the ConnectionTimeout property is used to set the amount of time in seconds to wait for a connection to be established to the database before giving up and generating an error. In its simplest form, your connection strings will look something like this.

```
@"Data Source=(local)\NetSDK;Initial Catalog=Northwind;
  User ID=sa;pwd=;"
```

The Data Source is the name or the network address of the SQL Server instance to which you wish to connect. When we installed the version of MSDE that ships with the SDK samples, it created an MSDE instance with the name local\NetSDK, so that's the instance name that we used. Also, notice the backslash in the name. To avoid any compiler errors, we included the @ symbol before the opening quote of the string, which tells the C# compiler to treat it as a verbatim string and ignore any escape sequences. Alternatively, we could have specified the Data Source as local \\NetSDK to achieve the same result. Specify which database within the data source to which you wish to connect in the Initial Catalog value. Finally, the User ID and pwd or password values are used to log in to the database. Note that if we were using the OLE DB provider to connect to an OLE DB data source we would also need to specify the Provider value in the connection string.

The *Database* and *State* properties are both read-only. Database will give us the name of the database to which the connection will connect if it is currently closed, or the name of the database with which the connection is associated if it is already open. The State property is used to retrieve the current state of the connection. Its valid values are the System.Data.ConnectionState enumeration values: Broken, Closed, Connecting, Executing, Fetching, and Open.

To open a connection, simply call the *Open()* method, which will attempt to connect with the settings specified in the ConnectionString property for the specified ConnectionTimeout interval. If a connection is successfully established, no exceptions will be thrown and the connection is ready for use. If a connection cannot be established within the timeout period, a SqlException will be thrown. In addition, an Exception will also be thrown if the connection is already opened and the Open() method is called. It is extremely important to wrap up all of your database access code inside of a try block with appropriate catch handlers. The ADO.NET class methods will not return error codes, but if an error occurs Exceptions will always be thrown. For this reason, you should always be prepared to catch and handle database exceptions.

When you are finished with the connection, remember to call the *Close()* method to close the connection and free up valuable server resources. Calling the Close() method when the connection is already closed is not a problem, and no exceptions will be thrown.

Command, DataAdapter, and DataSet

As mentioned earlier in the chapter, the DataSet is unaware of its data source. The DataSet retrieves, inserts, and updates data through the use of a DataAdapter. The managed provider that you are using will supply a DataAdapter class. The *SqlDataAdapter* is supplied by the SqlClient managed provider, and the *OleDbDataAdapter* is supplied by the OleDb managed provider. The DataAdapter classes have four properties called *SelectCommand*, *UpdateCommand*, *InsertCommand*, and *DeleteCommand*. If you are using a SqlDataAdapter these properties are of type *SqlCommand*; for an OleDbDataAdapter they are of type *OleDbCommand*.

Let's look at the Command objects. The *CommandText* property is used to set the text of the command to execute on the data source. The *CommandType* property tells the Command object how to treat the text in the CommandText property. Its valid values come from the *System.Data.CommandType* enumeration and are *StoredProcedure*, *TableDirect*, and *Text* (the default). (Note that the TableDirect type is not supported by the SQL Server managed provider.) The Command object also has a *Connection* property, which should be set with the appropriate connection type of either SqlConnection or OleDbConnection. If you are using a stored procedure or parameterized query, you can set the parameters using the *Parameters* collection, which is a collection of either SqlParameter or OleDbParameter objects.

Let's walk through a general example of how data is accessed through the DataSet. The first thing we need to do is create four command objects and assign them to each of the four properties of the DataAdapter: SelectCommand, UpdateCommand, InsertCommand, and DeleteCommand. We need to supply only Command objects for the types of data access that we intend to perform. If you will never be deleting data, there is no need to specify a Command object for the DeleteCommand property. Each of these Command objects should have a Connection object associated with it; it can, and in most cases will be, the same Connection object. To fill the DataSet with data, we call the *Fill()* method of the DataAdapter and pass the DataSet as a parameter. Now we can work with the data in the DataSet. We can read the data and insert, update, or delete rows. The DataSet will mark the modified rows as new, updated, or deleted. When we are ready to send our changes back to the data source, we call the *Update()* method of the DataAdapter, again passing the DataSet as a parameter. The DataAdapter will examine the DataSet, calling the UpdateCommand for any modified rows, the InsertCommand for any new rows, and the DeleteCommand for any deleted rows.

Let's work through a simple example of retrieving data using the DataSet. Create a new Web Form in the Chapter4 project and call it EmployeesWithSql.aspx. The code for this page can be downloaded from the companion Web site. We'll use the SQL Server managed provider to retrieve the employees in the Employees table of the Northwind database in our MSDE installation. Add a single Label control on the page called Label1, and then add the following code to the Page_Load method of the code-behind class:

```
private void Page_Load(object sender, System.EventArgs e)
{
  //Create the Connection
  SqlConnection conn =
    new SqlConnection(@"Data Source=(local)\NetSDK;Initial
Catalog=Northwind;User ID=sa;pwd=;");

  //Create the Command, passing in the SQL statement and the Connection
  SqlCommand cmd = new SqlCommand("Select * FROM Employees", conn);

  //Create a SqlAdapter object
  SqlDataAdapter adp = new SqlDataAdapter();
```

```
    //Set the SelectCommand to our newly created SqlCommand object
    adp.SelectCommand = cmd;

    //Create a DataSet object
    DataSet ds = new DataSet();
    //Create an Employees table in the DataSet and fill it with the data
    //collected from SelectCommand of the SqlDataAdapter
    adp.Fill(ds, "Employees");

    //Iterate through the Rows collection of the Employees table
    foreach (DataRow dr in ds.Tables["Employees"].Rows)
    {
      Label1.Text += string.Format("{0} {1}<br>", dr["FirstName"],
        dr["LastName"]);
    }
}
```

There should already be a reference to the System.Data namespace added for you if you created your Web Form with Visual Studio .NET. You will need to add a using statement to the top of your code-behind file to the System.Data.SqlClient namespace, like this:

```
using System.Data.SqlClient;
```

This example is shown in Figure 4.2. Let's walk through the code and see what we've done. First we created a SqlConnection object, just as we did in the preceding section. Then we created a SqlCommand object passing in the command text and the SqlConnection object as parameters to the constructor.

```
//Create the Command, passing in the SQL statement and the Connection
SqlCommand cmd = new SqlCommand("Select * FROM Employees", conn);
```

Figure 4.2 EmployeesWithSql.aspx.

We could have created the SqlCommand with the default parameter less constructor and used the CommandText and Connection properties to set these things, but passing them into the constructor is cleaner and requires less code. Also, notice that we did not execute the Open() method of the SqlConnection object. If the SqlCommand object is given a closed SqlConnection, it will open it when it is needed and close it when it has finished with it. If the SqlCommand object is given an open SqlConnection, it will not close it when it is finished. This is a nice feature; later on we will be making multiple calls to the database and will open a SqlConnection one time and use it for the duration of the page processing without having to close and reopen it multiple times. Next, we created a SqlAdapter object and then set the SelectCommand property to the newly created SqlCommand object.

```
//Create a SqlAdapter object
SqlDataAdapter adp = new SqlDataAdapter();
//Set the SelectCommand to our newly created SqlCommand object
adp.SelectCommand = cmd;
```

We then created a DataSet and filled it using the SqlAdapter.Fill() method. The Fill() method of the SqlAdapter uses the SqlCommand object assigned to the SelectCommand property to retrieve the data from the database. The Fill() method has several overloads, but the one we've chosen to use takes two parameters. The first is the DataSet object, which should be filled with the data, and the second parameter is a string that will be the name of the table created in the DataSet object to hold the data.

```
//Create a DataSet object
DataSet ds = new DataSet();
//Create an Employees table in the DataSet and fill it with the data
//collected from SelectCommand of the SqlDataAdapter
adp.Fill(ds, "Employees");
```

The *DataTable* class represents tables in a DataSet object. When the Employees table was created, an instance of the DataTable class was created and added to the *Tables* collection of the DataSet object. The DataTable class is fairly complex and allows you to do things such as add constraints and manipulate column properties. We won't be covering any advanced features of the DataTable in this book. The DataTable contains a collection of *DataRow* objects, which is accessible via the *Rows* property. We can iterate through the Rows collection and access the values in the columns of each row through the DataRow object's indexer [ ] by supplying either a column integer ordinal value or a string value representing the name of the column. This is exactly what has been done in the example and for each DataRow the FirstName and LastName of each Employee is printed out.

We can easily change this example to work with the Access database, Northwind.mdb, using the OLE DB managed provider. To do so, first change the using statement from System.Data.SqlClient to System.Data.OleDb. Then make the following highlighted changes to the previous example code. This code is also available from the companion Web site and is called EmployeesWithOleDb.aspx.

```
private void Page_Load(object sender, System.EventArgs e)
{
  //Create the Connection
  OleDbConnection conn =
    new OleDbConnection(@"Provider=Microsoft.JET.OLEDB.4.0;Data
Source=C:\Program Files\Microsoft Office\Office\Samples\Northwind.mdb");

  //Create the Command, passing in the SQL statement and the Connection
  OleDbCommand cmd = new OleDbCommand("Select * FROM Employees", conn);

  //Create an OleDbAdapter object
  OleDbDataAdapter adp = new OleDbDataAdapter();
  //Set the SelectCommand to our newly created OleDbCommand object
  adp.SelectCommand = cmd;

  //Create a DataSet object
  DataSet ds = new DataSet();
  //Create an Employees table in the DataSet and fill it with the data
  //collected from SelectCommand of the OleDbDataAdapter
  adp.Fill(ds, "Employees");

  //Iterate through the Rows collection of the Employees table
  foreach (DataRow dr in ds.Tables["Employees"].Rows)
  {
    Label1.Text += string.Format("{0} {1}<br>", dr["FirstName"],
      dr["LastName"]);
  }
}
```

All we had to do was modify the class names from the classes in the System.Data.
SqlClient namespace to the corresponding classes in the System.Data.OleDb namespace as well as modify the connection string. The rest of the code remains the same,
particularly any code that uses the DataSet object because it works the same regardless
of the data source being used.

Now let's modify this example once again and bind a DataGrid to the Employees
table of the DataSet, rather than print out the results using a Label control. We'll go
back to using the SQL managed provider for this example. Create a new Web form
called EmployeesWithDataGrid.aspx and add a DataGrid to the .aspx file as follows:

```
<asp:DataGrid id=EmployeeGrid runat="server" AutoGenerateColumns=False>
  <Columns>
    <asp:TemplateColumn HeaderText="Employee Name">
      <ItemTemplate><%# string.Format("{0} {1}",
        ((DataRowView)(Container.DataItem))["FirstName"],
        ((DataRowView)(Container.DataItem))["LastName"]) %>
      </ItemTemplate>
    </asp:TemplateColumn>
  </Columns>
</asp:DataGrid>
```

Here we use a Template Column to combine the FirstName and LastName fields of the Employees table into one displayed column on the DataGrid. The Container. DataItem had to be cast to a DataRowView class, which is defined in the System.Data namespace, to allow the use of the column indexer. You will need to import the System.Data namespace using the @Import directive in the .aspx file like this:

```
<%@ Import namespace="System.Data" %>
```

Add the following code to the Page_Load method of the code-behind class :

```
private void Page_Load(object sender, System.EventArgs e)
{
  //Create a SqlAdapter object
  SqlDataAdapter adp = new SqlDataAdapter("Select * FROM Employees",
    @"Data Source=(local)\NetSDK;Initial Catalog=Northwind;User
ID=sa;pwd=;");

  //Create a DataSet object
  DataSet ds = new DataSet();
  //Create an Employees table in the DataSet and fill it with the data
  //collected from SelectCommand of the SqlDataAdapter
  adp.Fill(ds, "Employees");

  EmployeeGrid.DataSource = ds.Tables["Employees"].DefaultView;
  EmployeeGrid.DataBind();
}
```

Notice that we have opted not to create the SqlCommand and SqlConnection objects specifically in this code, but rather have passed in the command text and the connection string as parameters to one of the overloaded SqlAdapter constructors, which will create them for us. It makes the code a little simpler, but it doesn't provide the ability to reuse the SqlConnection for other things. A SqlConnection will be created for us, opened, used, and then closed.

We set the DataSource of the DataGrid to the *DefaultView* of the Employees table in the DataSet. The DefaultView property gives us a *DataView* object. The DataView is used to provide a view or a subset of the data in a DataTable; by default all of the rows of the DataTable are returned. You can filter which rows are returned with a DataView by setting the *RowFilter* property of the DataView with a filter string such as

```
FirstName = "Nancy"
```

For this example, we just bind to the default implementation of DefaultView, which gives us all of the rows in the Employees table. The last thing we have to do is call the *DataBind()* method of the DataGrid. Note that we could also call the DataBind() method of the Page class, which will call DataBind() for all of its child controls. The DataGrid can be seen in Figure 4.3.

Figure 4.3 Employees with a DataGrid.

Now let's go through an example that allows us to update, add, and delete data using the DataSet and the SqlDataAdapter. We'll have to supply SqlCommand objects for the SelectCommand, UpdateCommand, InsertCommand, and DeleteCommand properties of the SqlDataAdapter to achieve this. Once again, we'll use a DataGrid to display the data, but we'll add a couple of button columns to allow us to select and delete rows. We won't be using the in-place editing features of the DataGrid for this example, but there will be examples of this provided later in the book. We'll use some text boxes to allow us to edit existing employees and add new ones. We've included the entire source for the page called EmployeesUpdateable.aspx, in Listings 4.1 and 4.2. Note that this is not the most elegant, preferable, or efficient way to implement this functionality, but it will demonstrate some more details of the DataSet. You'll also see a few very good reasons why the DataSet isn't usually the best choice for use in a Web application.

```
<%@ Page language="c#" Codebehind="EmployeesUpdateable.aspx.cs"
  AutoEventWireup="false" Inherits="Chapter4.EmployeesUpdateable" %>
<%@ Import namespace="System.Data" %>

<HTML>
  <HEAD>
    <meta name="GENERATOR" Content="Microsoft Visual Studio 7.0">
    <meta name="CODE_LANGUAGE" Content="C#">
    <meta name=vs_defaultClientScript content="JScript">
    <meta name=vs_targetSchema content="Internet Explorer 5.0">
  </HEAD>
  <body>
```

Listing 4.1 EmployeesUpdateable.aspx

```
<form id="EmployeesUpdatable" method="post" runat="server">
  <table>
    <tr>
      <td>
        <b>First Name</b>
        <br>
        <asp:TextBox id=txtFirstNameAdd runat="server">
        </asp:TextBox>
      </td>
      <td>
        <b>Last Name</b>
        <br>
        <asp:TextBox id=txtLastNameAdd runat="server">
        </asp:TextBox>
      </td>
      <td>
        <br>
        <asp:Button id=btnEmployeeAdd text="Add" width=100
          runat="server">
        </asp:Button>
      </td>
    </tr>
    <tr>
      <td>
        <b>First Name</b>
        <br>
        <asp:TextBox id=txtFirstNameEdit enabled=False
          runat="server">
        </asp:TextBox>
      </td>
      <td>
        <b>Last Name</b>
        <br>
        <asp:TextBox id=txtLastNameEdit enabled=False
          runat="server">
        </asp:TextBox>
      </td>
      <td>
        <br>
        <asp:Button id=btnEmployeeUpdate text="Update" width=100
          enabled=False runat="server">
        </asp:Button>
      </td>
    </tr>
  </table>
  <P></P>
  <asp:datagrid id=EmployeeGrid runat="server"
    AutoGenerateColumns="False" >
```

Listing 4.1 EmployeesUpdateable.aspx (continued)

```
        <Columns>
          <asp:ButtonColumn Text="Select" HeaderText="Select"
            CommandName="Select">
          </asp:ButtonColumn>
          <asp:ButtonColumn Text="Delete" HeaderText="Delete"
            CommandName="Delete">
          </asp:ButtonColumn>
          <asp:TemplateColumn HeaderText="Employee Name">
            <ItemTemplate><%# string.Format("{0} {1}",
              ((DataRowView)(Container.DataItem))["FirstName"],
              ((DataRowView)(Container.DataItem))["LastName"]) %>
            </ItemTemplate>
          </asp:TemplateColumn>
        </Columns>
      </asp:datagrid>
    </form>
  </body>
</HTML>
```

Listing 4.1 EmployeesUpdateable.aspx (continued)

```
using System;
using System.Collections;
using System.ComponentModel;
using System.Data;
using System.Data.SqlClient;
using System.Drawing;
using System.Web;
using System.Web.SessionState;
using System.Web.UI;
using System.Web.UI.WebControls;
using System.Web.UI.HtmlControls;

namespace Chapter4
{
  /// <summary>
  /// Summary description for EmployeesUpdatable.
  /// </summary>
  public class EmployeesUpdateable : System.Web.UI.Page
  {
    private DataSet ds;
    private SqlDataAdapter adp;
    protected System.Web.UI.WebControls.TextBox txtFirstNameAdd;
    protected System.Web.UI.WebControls.TextBox txtLastNameAdd;
    protected System.Web.UI.WebControls.Button btnEmployeeAdd;
```

Listing 4.2 EmployeesUpdateable.aspx.cs

```
      protected System.Web.UI.WebControls.TextBox txtFirstNameEdit;
      protected System.Web.UI.WebControls.TextBox txtLastNameEdit;
      protected System.Web.UI.WebControls.Button btnEmployeeUpdate;

      protected System.Web.UI.WebControls.DataGrid EmployeeGrid;

      public EmployeesUpdateable()
      {
        Page.Init += new System.EventHandler(Page_Init);
      }

      private void Page_Load(object sender, System.EventArgs e)
      {
        if (!IsPostBack)
        {
          //Executed on first request only
          try
          {
            //Create the Connection
            SqlConnection conn =
              new SqlConnection(@"Data Source=(local)\NetSDK;Initial
Catalog=Northwind;User ID=sa;pwd=;");

            //Create a SqlAdapter object
            adp = new SqlDataAdapter();

            //Create a select command for the adapter
            SqlCommand selectCmd = new SqlCommand("Select * FROM
Employees",
                conn);
            //Assign this command to the SelectCommand of the adapter
            adp.SelectCommand = selectCmd;

            //Create an update command for the adapter
            SqlCommand updateCmd =
              new SqlCommand("UPDATE Employees SET FirstName=@FirstName, "
+
                "LastName=@LastName WHERE EmployeeID=@EmployeeID", conn);
            //Add the FirstName, LastName, and EmployeeID
            //parameters to the command
            updateCmd.Parameters.Add("@FirstName", SqlDbType.NVarChar,
10);
            updateCmd.Parameters["@FirstName"].SourceColumn = "FirstName";
            updateCmd.Parameters.Add("@LastName", SqlDbType.NVarChar, 20);
            updateCmd.Parameters["@LastName"].SourceColumn = "LastName";
            updateCmd.Parameters.Add("@EmployeeID", SqlDbType.Int);
            updateCmd.Parameters["@EmployeeID"].SourceColumn =
"EmployeeID";
```

Listing 4.2   EmployeesUpdateable.aspx.cs (continued)

```
            //Assign this command to the UpdateCommand of the adapter
            adp.UpdateCommand = updateCmd;
            //Create a delete command for the adapter
            SqlCommand deleteCmd =
              new SqlCommand("DELETE FROM Employees WHERE " +
                "EmployeeID=@EmployeeID", conn);
            //Add the EmployeeID parameter to the command
            deleteCmd.Parameters.Add("@EmployeeID", SqlDbType.Int);
            deleteCmd.Parameters["@EmployeeID"].SourceColumn =
"EmployeeID";
            //Assign this command to the DeleteCommand of the adapter
            adp.DeleteCommand = deleteCmd;

            //Create an insert command for the adapter
            SqlCommand insertCmd =
              new SqlCommand("INSERT INTO Employees (FirstName, LastName)
" +
                "VALUES (@FirstName, @LastName)", conn);
            //Add the first name and last name parameters to the command
            insertCmd.Parameters.Add("@FirstName", SqlDbType.NVarChar,
10);
            insertCmd.Parameters["@FirstName"].SourceColumn = "FirstName";
            insertCmd.Parameters.Add("@LastName", SqlDbType.NVarChar, 20);
            insertCmd.Parameters["@LastName"].SourceColumn = "LastName";
            //Assign this command to the DeleteCommand of the adapter
            adp.InsertCommand = insertCmd;

            //Create a DataSet object
            ds = new DataSet();
            //Create an Employees table in the DataSet and fill it with
            //the data collected from SelectCommand of the SqlDataAdapter
            adp.Fill(ds, "Employees");

            //Bind the DataGrid
            EmployeeGrid.DataSource = ds.Tables["Employees"].DefaultView;
            EmployeeGrid.DataBind();

            //Add these objects to this client's session state
            Session.Add("adp", adp);
            Session.Add("ds", ds);
        }
        catch (SqlException sqlEx)
        {
            Response.Write("SqlException: " + sqlEx.ToString());
        }
        catch (Exception Ex)
        {
```

Listing 4.2   EmployeesUpdateable.aspx.cs (continued)

```
        Response.Write("Exception: " + Ex.ToString());
    }
  }
  else
  {
    //Executed on Post Back only
    //Retrieve the objects from the client's session state
    ds = (DataSet)Session["ds"];
    adp = (SqlDataAdapter)Session["adp"];
  }
}

private void Page_Init(object sender, EventArgs e)
{
  //
  // CODEGEN: This call is required by the ASP.NET Windows Form
  // Designer.
  //
  InitializeComponent();
}


#region Web Form Designer generated code
/// <summary>
/// Required method for Designer support - do not modify
/// the contents of this method with the code editor.
/// </summary>
private void InitializeComponent()
{
  this.btnEmployeeAdd.Click += new
    System.EventHandler(this.btnEmployeeAdd_Click);
  this.btnEmployeeUpdate.Click += new
    System.EventHandler(this.btnEmployeeUpdate_Click);
  this.EmployeeGrid.ItemCommand += new
    System.Web.UI.WebControls.DataGridCommandEventHandler(
      this.OnItemClicked);
  this.Load += new System.EventHandler(this.Page_Load);
}
#endregion

protected void OnItemClicked(object source, DataGridCommandEventArgs e)
{
  //Get the index of the item that was selected
  int itemindex = (int)e.Item.ItemIndex;

  if (e.CommandName == "Select")
  {
    //Save the index of the selected item in the view state
    ViewState["SelectedItemIndex"] = itemindex;
```

Listing 4.2 EmployeesUpdateable.aspx.cs (continued)

```
      //Fill the edit boxes with the selected employees name
      DataRow selectedRow = ds.Tables["Employees"].Rows[itemindex];
      txtFirstNameEdit.Text = selectedRow["FirstName"].ToString();
      txtLastNameEdit.Text = selectedRow["LastName"].ToString();
      //Enable the edit controls
      txtFirstNameEdit.Enabled = true;
      txtLastNameEdit.Enabled = true;
      btnEmployeeUpdate.Enabled = true;
    }
    else
    {
      try
      {

        //Delete the selected employee
        ds.Tables["Employees"].Rows[itemindex].Delete();


        //Update the database
        adp.Update(ds, "Employees");


        //Update the session DataSet
        Session["ds"] = ds;


        //Rebind the DatGrid
        EmployeeGrid.DataSource = ds.Tables["Employees"].DefaultView;
        EmployeeGrid.DataBind();
      }
      catch (SqlException sqlEx)
      {
        Response.Write("SqlException: " + sqlEx.ToString());
      }
      catch (Exception Ex)
      {
        Response.Write("Exception: " + Ex.ToString());
      }
    }
  }

private void btnEmployeeAdd_Click(object sender, System.EventArgs e)
  {
    try
    {
      //Get a new row
      DataRow newRow = ds.Tables["Employees"].NewRow();

      //Set the FirstName and LastName fields
      newRow["FirstName"] = txtFirstNameAdd.Text;
      newRow["LastName"] = txtLastNameAdd.Text;
```

Listing 4.2 EmployeesUpdateable.aspx.cs (continued)

```
        //Add the new row to the DataSet
        ds.Tables["Employees"].Rows.Add(newRow);

        //Update the database
        adp.Update(ds, "Employees");
        //Refill the DataSet, so that we can get the EmployeeID
        //of the newly added employee
        ds.Clear();
        adp.Fill(ds, "Employees");

        //Update the session DataSet
        Session["ds"] = ds;

        //Rebind the DatGrid
        EmployeeGrid.DataSource = ds.Tables["Employees"].DefaultView;
        EmployeeGrid.DataBind();

        //Clear the edit boxes
        txtFirstNameAdd.Text = "";
        txtLastNameAdd.Text = "";
      }
      catch (SqlException sqlEx)
      {
        Response.Write("SqlException: " + sqlEx.ToString());
      }
      catch (Exception Ex)
      {
        Response.Write("Exception: " + Ex.ToString());
      }
    }

    private void btnEmployeeUpdate_Click(object sender, System.EventArgs e)
    {
      try
      {
        //Change the FirstName and LastName field of the selected row
        //in the DataSet
        DataRow selectedRow = ds.Tables["Employees"].
          Rows[(int)(ViewState["SelectedItemIndex"])];

        selectedRow["FirstName"] = txtFirstNameEdit.Text;
        selectedRow["LastName"] = txtLastNameEdit.Text;

        //Update the database
        adp.Update(ds, "Employees");

        //Update the session DataSet
        Session["ds"] = ds;
```

Listing 4.2 EmployeesUpdateable.aspx.cs (continued)

```
            //Rebind the DataGrid
            EmployeeGrid.DataSource = ds.Tables["Employees"].DefaultView;
            EmployeeGrid.DataBind();
            //Clear the edit controls and disable them
            txtFirstNameEdit.Text = "";
            txtFirstNameEdit.Enabled = false;
            txtLastNameEdit.Text = "";
            txtLastNameEdit.Enabled = false;
            btnEmployeeUpdate.Enabled = false;
        }
        catch (SqlException sqlEx)
        {
            Response.Write("SqlException: " + sqlEx.ToString());
        }
        catch (Exception Ex)
        {
            Response.Write("Exception: " + Ex.ToString());
        }
    }
  }
}
```

Listing 4.2   EmployeesUpdateable.aspx.cs (continued)

Let's walk through the code-behind file starting with the Page_Load method. Notice that we've used the IsPostBack property of the Page to create a section of code that is executed only the first time the client requests the page. Similarly, there is a section that is executed only on a postback. We've created a SqlConnection, SqlAdapter, and Select-Command for the SqlAdapter just as in earlier examples. Then we create an Update-Command with this code.

```
SqlCommand updateCmd = new SqlCommand("UPDATE Employees SET " +
   FirstName=@FirstName, LastName=@LastName WHERE
EmployeeID=@EmployeeID",
   conn);
```

Because we're using the SQL Server managed provider, this is how we specify a parameterized SQL statement. Notice that we have used named parameters such as @FirstName. With the SQL Server managed provider, you cannot specify parameters using the "?", as you can do with the OLE DB managed provider. When using an OleDb-Command and specifying parameters using the "?", the order in which you add parameters to the Parameters collection of the OleDbCommand must be the same order as one in which the parameters appear in the SQL staterment. With the SqlCommand object, the order in which parameters are added does not matter as they are matched up by name. After we've created the updateCmd object, we need to add the three parameters: @FirstName, @LastName, and @EmployeeID. This is done with the following code:

```
updateCmd.Parameters.Add("@FirstName", SqlDbType.NVarChar, 10);
updateCmd.Parameters["@FirstName"].SourceColumn = "FirstName";
updateCmd.Parameters.Add("@LastName", SqlDbType.NVarChar, 20);
updateCmd.Parameters["@LastName"].SourceColumn = "LastName";
updateCmd.Parameters.Add("@EmployeeID", SqlDbType.Int);
updateCmd.Parameters["@EmployeeID"].SourceColumn = "EmployeeID";
```

The Add() method of the Parameters collection has several overloads. The one that we've used for the @FirstName and @LastName parameters takes the name of the parameter, the type of the parameter, and the size in bytes of the parameter. The overload that we've used for the @EmployeeID parameter just takes the name and type. This works well for types that are a fixed size like the Int because we shouldn't have to remember the size if it is fixed anyway. Also notice that for each parameter, we have set the *SourceColumn* property. This is used to specify which column in a DataSet table should correspond to a particular parameter. Whenever the UpdateCommand is called for a particular row in the Employees table, the values in the FirstName, LastName, and EmployeeID columns will be used for the values of the @FirstName, @LastName, and @EmployeeID parameters, respectively. There will be more on this a little later. The next thing we need to do is assign this SqlCommand to the UpdateCommand property of the SqlDataAdapater with this code.

```
adp.UpdateCommand = updateCmd;
```

The DeleteCommand and InsertCommand properties of the SqlDataAdapter have been set up similarly to the UpdateCommand. Then a DataSet is created, and the Employees table is filled just as before. The last thing that is done on the first request of the page is to store the newly created SqlDataAdapter and the DataSet in the client's session state. This is done so that we don't have to re-create them and refill the DataSet on each post back of the page, which would always require a call to the database. Session state is covered in more detail in Chapter 5. For now, just know that when an object is added to the client's session state, it is stored on the server side in memory on the Web server, on a remote server, or in a SQL Server database. On subsequent requests, any objects in the client's session state are restored and available for use. We've added the DataSet and SqlAdapter to the session state with this code:

```
Session.Add("adp", adp);
Session.Add("ds", ds);
```

In the section of the Page_Load handler that is executed only on postbacks, you can see that we've fetched the DataSet and SqlDataAdapter objects from the session state and placed them back in the appropriate member variables of the Page class.

```
ds = (DataSet)Session["ds"];
adp = (SqlDataAdapter)Session["adp"];
```

We'll cover the many factors that need to be taken into account when storing objects in a client's session state later in this chapter. Take caution when using session state. We could have avoided using session state altogether by executing the code in the if(!IsPostBack) section on every request of the page, regardless of whether it was a postback. Then we would be making unnecessary calls to the database, which isn't desirable either.

Let's move on to the OnItemClicked method, which is wired to the ItemCommand event of the EmployeeGrid DataGrid. The first thing that is done is getting the index of the item that was selected with this code.

```
int itemindex = (int)e.Item.ItemIndex;
```

The passed-in DataGridCommandEventArgs argument is used to retrieve the Item-Index of the item that was selected. Because this handler gets called when the user clicks on the Select or the Delete LinkButton, we need to determine which one was clicked by using the *CommandName* property of the DataGridCommandEventArgs argument as follows:

```
if (e.CommandName == "Select")
```

We set the name of the command that would correspond to each link button when we created the LinkButtons in the .aspx file by setting the CommandName attribute as follows:

```
<asp:ButtonColumn Text="Select" HeaderText="Select"
CommandName="Select">
</asp:ButtonColumn>
<asp:ButtonColumn Text="Delete" HeaderText="Delete"
CommandName="Delete">
</asp:ButtonColumn>
```

When the Select button is clicked, first the index of the selected item is saved in the Page View state. Recall from Chapter 2, "Anatomy of an ASP.NET Page," that ASP.NET stores Web Control and HTML Server Control property value information in the Page View state so that the state of controls is preserved between page requests. Similarly, we can store our own information in the View state of the page and retrieve that information on subsequent requests. The index of the selected item is saved in the View state with the following code.

```
ViewState["SelectedItemIndex"] = itemindex;
```

Next, get the DataRow object representing the selected row, and use it to fill the edit boxes used for editing an employee:

```
DataRow selectedRow = ds.Tables["Employees"].Rows[itemindex];
txtFirstNameEdit.Text = selectedRow["FirstName"].ToString();
txtLastNameEdit.Text = selectedRow["LastName"].ToString();
```

The edit boxes and the Update button are then enabled so that the client can modify the selected row if desired. When the Delete button is clicked, we call the *Delete()* method of the selected row in the Employees table of the DataSet. At this point, that row is now marked for deletion in the DataSet; however, it has not been deleted from the database. The SqlAdapter has an *Update()* method, which is used to reconcile changes made in the DataSet back to the database. The Update method has several overloads, but the one we're using here takes two parameters: a DataSet object and the table name within the DataSet that we wish to update. Here is the code:

```
//Delete the selected employee
ds.Tables["Employees"].Rows[itemindex].Delete();
//Update the database
adp.Update(ds, "Employees");
```

When the Update() method is called, the SqlDataAdapter will basically traverse through all of the changed rows in the Employees table and call the appropriate command for each one. If the row is marked for deletion, the DeleteCommand will be called for that row and the parameters of the DeleteCommand will be filled in from the columns of the row. If the row has been edited, the UpdateCommand will be called, and if it is a newly added row the InsertCommand will be called. Once again, any parameters of these commands will be filled in from the columns of the appropriate row.

After the Update() method has been called, we need to save the changed DataSet object back to the view state, otherwise, we will still have the original DataSet in the View state, which will not reflect the changes that we have made:

```
Session["ds"] = ds;
```

Last, the DataGrid is rebound to the DataSet so that the changes are reflected back to the client. If we skip this step, the deleted row will still appear on the page because the DataGrid will be repopulated from the previously stored View state.

When the Add button is clicked, the btnEmployeeAdd_Click handler is called. We need to add a new row to the Employees table and then set its FirstName and Last-Name column values to the text entered in the edit boxes. The DataTable object has a *NewRow()* method, which returns a new DataRow object with the appropriate schema for the table. We call the NewRow() method for the Employees table and save the returned DataRow object with this code.

```
DataRow newRow = ds.Tables["Employees"].NewRow();
```

We then set the FirstName and LastName column values and then add the new row to the Employees table. Note that the NewRow() method does not actually add a row to the table. It only creates a DataRow object for you with the appropriate schema for the table. To actually add the row to the table, we must call the add method of the Rows collection for the table.

```
//Set the FirstName and LastName fields
newRow["FirstName"] = txtFirstNameAdd.Text;
newRow["LastName"] = txtLastNameAdd.Text;

//Add the new row to the DataSet
ds.Tables["Employees"].Rows.Add(newRow);
```

Once again, we call the Update() method of the SqlDataAdapter to actually add the row to the database. Because the EmployeeID column of the Employees table is an Identity column, the EmployeeID for this new row won't be created until the row is actually added to the database. The value that is created for it will not be updated automatically in the DataSet object. There are several ways to get this value back from the database, but for this example we simply clear the DataSet out and refill it using the SqlDataAdapater. This will return all of the rows of the Employees table, including the row that was just added.

```
ds.Clear();
adp.Fill(ds, "Employees");
```

The Clear() method removes all tables and rows from the DataSet. If we had failed to call this method before calling Fill() we would have ended up with duplicate records in the DataSet. Alternatively, we could have called the Clear() method on the Rows collection of the Employees table.

Once again, we restore the new DataSet in the session state and rebind the DataGrid. Then the edit boxes are cleared out so that we have a clean slate for next time.

When the Update button is clicked, the btnEmployeeUpdate_Click handler is called. First, get a DataRow object that represents the selected row in the DataSet, by using the Rows collection of the Employees table and the index of the selected item that we saved in the View state like this:

```
DataRow selectedRow = ds.Tables["Employees"].
  Rows[(int)(ViewState["SelectedItemIndex"])];
```

Values are returned from the ViewState property as object types, so it is necessary to convert or cast them to their appropriate type, which explains the cast to an int type here. Next, use the selectedRow object to update the FirstName and LastName columns with the text entered in the edit boxes. As in the previous example, we call the Update() method of the SqlDataAdapter to send the changes to the database, restore the DataSet in the session state, rebind the DataGrid, and reset all of the edit controls for next time. This page can be seen in Figure 4.4.

As we've already mentioned, this wasn't the most appropriate way to implement this functionality. The DataSet wasn't very easy to use in this sort of scenario and if we hadn't saved it in the session state each time, we would have had to make an extra call to the database to repopulate it on each page request. That would be entirely inefficient and unnecessary. Storing the DataSet in the session state has its own caveats and pitfalls that need to be evaluated, so that isn't the best choice either. In addition, up to this point we haven't used stored procedures, which we highly recommend for performance as well as maintenance reasons. In the next section, we'll rework this example a few times using the SqlDataReader object and stored procedures, and finally we'll encapsulate all of the Employee table manipulation inside of a working Employees class.

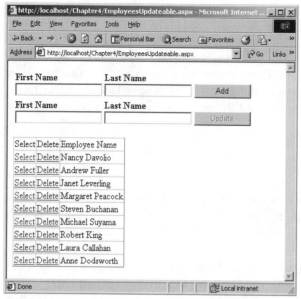

Figure 4.4 EmployeesUpdateable.aspx.

DataReader

The SqlDataReader and OleDbDataReader classes provide fast, forward-only access to the data source. The DataReader classes provide greater performance over using a DataSet and a DataAdapter to retrieve data. In our experience with .NET Web applications, we have found that using the SqlDataReader in combination with the SqlCommand class provides the best performance and ease of use. In most cases, using the DataSet class for a connectionless Web-based application is more trouble than it's worth and offers less performance. The DataReader classes do not provide the ability to house multiple tables, relationships, or schema, but these types of features are best used in long-running applications where a DataSet class can be created and maintained for an extended period of time.

The DataReader classes must be used in conjunction with the Command classes. You will use the *ExecuteReader()* method of a SqlCommand or OleDbCommand object, whose return value is either a SqlDataReader or OleDbDataReader object. Then you can simply call the *Read()* method of the DataReader object to traverse through the returned record set. The Command classes also have an *ExecuteNonQuery()* method, which should be used whenever your Command will be executing a SQL statement in which no record set will be returned. The return value of this method is the number of rows that were affected by the SQL statement. Although no record set is returned, you can still return output parameters. This can be useful in situations such as inserting new records into a table that has an identity field. You can return the newly created identity value via an output parameter.

Once you have used the ExecuteReader() method of the Command object to retrieve a DataReader, the Connection object associated with the Command remains in use. The Connection object will be unavailable for any other use until the *Close()* method of the DataReader has been called. It is important to always call the Close() method when you have finished with the DataReader.

There are a few public properties of the DataReader classes that will prove useful. There is a Boolean *IsClosed* property, which returns true if the DataReader is closed and false otherwise. The *FieldCount* property can be used to determine how many columns are in the current record of the DataReader. The *RecordsAffected* property can be used to determine how many records the last SQL statement affected. It will not tell you how many records were returned if the SQL statement was a SELECT statement, but instead it will tell you how many records were modified if it was an INSERT, UPDATE, or DELETE statement.

When reading through the records in a DataReader, the values in particular columns can be accessed using the DataReader's indexer. You can supply either a column ordinal or a column name like this:

```
string strFirstName = (string)myReader[2];
-or-
string strFirstName = (string)myReader["FirstName"];
```

The indexer returns a value of type object, so you will need to either cast or convert it to whatever data type the column contains, as we did above with the FirstName column string type. For string type columns, you could also call the ToString() method as follows:

```
string strFirstName = myReader["FirstName"].ToString();
```

Because the ToString() method returns a string representation of the object, this works fine for string type columns. The ToString() method can also be used on non-string type columns, and a string representation of the data type will be returned. There is another way to retrieve the specific data types that you want from particular columns. There are numerous *Get...()* methods, such as GetString(), GetBoolean(), GetByte, and GetInt32(). These methods do not provide any type conversion, so if you call GetInt32(), the value in that column needs to already be of type Int32.

NOTE You can determine the data type of a column at runtime by calling the *GetType()* method, which returns a System.Type object representing the data type of the column.

The only problem with using these methods is that you have to pass them the column ordinal as a parameter. We do not suggest hard-coding column ordinal numbers because if your table structure changes, you've just broken all of your code. There is also a *GetOrdinal()* method, which takes the column name as a parameter and returns the column ordinal. So you could do something like this:

```
string strFirstName =
   myReader.GetString(myReader.GetOrdinal("FirstName"));
```

Hard-coding the column ordinals in your code will provide a slight performance increase because no lookup will have to be performed to find the correct column from the column name. We don't feel that the performance increase outweighs the risk that you take of breaking your code by doing something as simple as inserting a new column into your table.

Another useful method of the DataReader is the *IsDBNull()* method. This method will tell you whether the value in a particular column is NULL. If you have columns in your tables that allow NULL values, it is a good idea to make sure that a particular field is not NULL before you try to retrieve a data type from it. An exception will be thrown if you try to convert a NULL value to a particular data type or if you try to use one of the Get...() methods on it. For instance, the following code will throw an exception if the value of the ReportsTo column is NULL.

```
int intReportsTo = myReader.GetInt32(myReader.GetOrdinal("ReportsTo"));
```

It is better to check for the NULL condition ahead of time and set intReportsTo to some value that signifies a NULL in your code, such as a -1, for example. You could check for the NULL condition like this:

```
if (myReader.IsDBNull(myReader.GetOrdinal("ReportsTo")))
{
  intReportsTo = -1;
}
else
{
  int intReportsTo =
myReader.GetInt32(myReader.GetOrdinal("ReportsTo"));
}
```

Let's rework the example from the preceding section using the SqlDataReader class and the SqlCommand class. We'll remove all of the DataSet and SqlDataAdapter code and rewrite the entire example. For this example, we'll still hard-code the SQL statements, just so you can see what is happening a little more clearly. The code for this example can be downloaded as part of the Chapter4 project from the companion Web site and is called EmployeesWithReader.aspx. In the next example, we'll start using some stored procedures to speed things up a notch. Once again, we're going to provide the full source for the code-behind class. The .aspx file will not change too much. You can remove this line from the top of the .aspx file.

```
<%@ Import namespace="System.Data" %>
```

Instead of having one column for the employee name, let's break the name out into First Name and Last Name columns. In addition, we'll be using the EmployeeID of the Employees table as the DataKeyField of the DataGrid. The declaration of the grid will change to the following code:

```
<asp:datagrid id=EmployeeGrid runat="server" AutoGenerateColumns="False"
  DataKeyField=EmployeeID>
  <Columns>
```

```
      <asp:ButtonColumn Text="Select" HeaderText="Select"
        CommandName="Select">
      </asp:ButtonColumn>
      <asp:ButtonColumn Text="Delete" HeaderText="Delete"
        CommandName="Delete">
      </asp:ButtonColumn>
      <asp:BoundColumn HeaderText="First Name" DataField="FirstName">
      </asp:BoundColumn>
      <asp:BoundColumn HeaderText="Last Name" DataField="LastName">
      </asp:BoundColumn>
    </Columns>
</asp:datagrid>
```

The source for the code-behind file can be found in Listing 4.3.

```
using System;
using System.Collections;
using System.ComponentModel;
using System.Data;
using System.Data.SqlClient;
using System.Drawing;
using System.Web;
using System.Web.SessionState;
using System.Web.UI;
using System.Web.UI.WebControls;
using System.Web.UI.HtmlControls;

namespace Chapter4
{
  /// <summary>
  /// Summary description for EmployeesWithReader.
  /// </summary>
  public class EmployeesWithReader : System.Web.UI.Page
  {
    private string m_strConnectionString = @"Data
Source=(local)\NetSDK;Initial Catalog=Northwind;User ID=sa;pwd=;";
    private SqlDataReader reader;
    private SqlConnection conn;

    protected System.Web.UI.WebControls.TextBox txtFirstNameAdd;
    protected System.Web.UI.WebControls.TextBox txtLastNameAdd;
    protected System.Web.UI.WebControls.Button btnEmployeeAdd;
    protected System.Web.UI.WebControls.TextBox txtFirstNameEdit;
    protected System.Web.UI.WebControls.TextBox txtLastNameEdit;
    protected System.Web.UI.WebControls.Button btnEmployeeUpdate;

    protected System.Web.UI.WebControls.DataGrid EmployeeGrid;
```

Listing 4.3 EmployeesWithReader.aspx.cs

```csharp
public EmployeesWithReader()
{
  Page.Init += new System.EventHandler(Page_Init);
}

private void Page_Load(object sender, System.EventArgs e)
{
  if (!IsPostBack)
  {
    //Executed on first request only
    try
    {
      //Create the Connection
      conn = new SqlConnection(m_strConnectionString);
      //Open the connection
      conn.Open();

      //Create a command to retrieve the data
      SqlCommand selectCmd = new SqlCommand(
        "Select * FROM Employees;SELECT * FROM Customers", conn);

      //Get a SqlDataReader
      reader = selectCmd.ExecuteReader();

      //Bind the DataGrid
      EmployeeGrid.DataSource = reader;
      EmployeeGrid.DataBind();
    }
    catch (SqlException sqlEx)
    {
      Response.Write("SqlException: " + sqlEx.ToString());
    }
    catch (Exception Ex)
    {
      Response.Write("Exception: " + Ex.ToString());
    }
    finally
    {
      if (reader != null)
        //Close the reader
        reader.Close();
      if (conn != null)
        //Close the connection
        conn.Close();
    }
  }
}
```

Listing 4.3 EmployeesWithReader.aspx.cs (continued)

```
    private void Page_Init(object sender, EventArgs e)
    {
      //
      // CODEGEN: This call is required by the ASP.NET Windows Form
      // Designer.
      //
      InitializeComponent();
    }


    #region Web Form Designer generated code
    /// <summary>
    /// Required method for Designer support - do not modify
    /// the contents of this method with the code editor.
    /// </summary>
    private void InitializeComponent()
    {
      this.btnEmployeeAdd.Click +=
        new System.EventHandler(this.btnEmployeeAdd_Click);
      this.btnEmployeeUpdate.Click +=
        new System.EventHandler(this.btnEmployeeUpdate_Click);
      this.EmployeeGrid.ItemCommand += new System.Web.UI.WebControls.
        DataGridCommandEventHandler(this.OnItemClicked);
      this.Load += new System.EventHandler(this.Page_Load);
    }
    #endregion

    protected void OnItemClicked(object source, DataGridCommandEventArgs e)
    {
      //Get the EmployeeID of the employee that was selected
      int intEmployeeID =
(int)EmployeeGrid.DataKeys[(int)e.Item.ItemIndex];

      if (e.CommandName == "Select")
      {
        //Save the selected EmployeeID to the view state
        ViewState["SelectedEmployeeID"] = intEmployeeID;

        //Fill the edit boxes with the selected employees name
        txtFirstNameEdit.Text = e.Item.Cells[2].Text;
        txtLastNameEdit.Text = e.Item.Cells[3].Text;


        //Enable the edit controls
        txtFirstNameEdit.Enabled = true;
        txtLastNameEdit.Enabled = true;
        btnEmployeeUpdate.Enabled = true;
      }
```

Listing 4.3   EmployeesWithReader.aspx.cs (continued)

```
    else
    {
      try
      {
        //Create the Connection
        conn = new SqlConnection(m_strConnectionString);
        //Open the connection
        conn.Open();

        //Create a delete command
        SqlCommand deleteCmd = new SqlCommand(
          "DELETE FROM Employees WHERE EmployeeID=@EmployeeID;" +
          "SELECT * FROM Employees", conn);
        //Add the EmployeeID parameter to the command
        deleteCmd.Parameters.Add("@EmployeeID", SqlDbType.Int);
        //Set the @EmployeeID parameter
        deleteCmd.Parameters["@EmployeeID"].Value = intEmployeeID;

        //Execute the command
        reader = deleteCmd.ExecuteReader();

        //Rebind the DatGrid
        EmployeeGrid.DataSource = reader;
        EmployeeGrid.DataBind();
      }
      catch (SqlException sqlEx)
      {
        Response.Write("SqlException: " + sqlEx.ToString());
      }
      catch (Exception Ex)
      {
        Response.Write("Exception: " + Ex.ToString());
      }
      finally
      {
        if (reader != null)
          //Close the reader
          reader.Close();
        if (conn != null)
          //Close the connection
          conn.Close();
      }
    }
  }

private void btnEmployeeAdd_Click(object sender, System.EventArgs e)
{
  try
  {
```

Listing 4.3   EmployeesWithReader.aspx.cs (continued)

```
      //Create the Connection
      conn = new SqlConnection(m_strConnectionString);
      //Open the connection
      conn.Open();

      //Create an insert command
      SqlCommand insertCmd = new SqlCommand(
        "INSERT INTO Employees (FirstName, LastName) VALUES " +
        "(@FirstName, @LastName);SELECT * FROM Employees", conn);
      //Add the first name and last name parameters to the command
      insertCmd.Parameters.Add("@FirstName", SqlDbType.NVarChar, 10);
      insertCmd.Parameters.Add("@LastName", SqlDbType.NVarChar, 20);
      //Set the parameters
      insertCmd.Parameters["@FirstName"].Value = txtFirstNameAdd.Text;
      insertCmd.Parameters["@LastName"].Value = txtLastNameAdd.Text;

      //Execute the command
      reader = insertCmd.ExecuteReader();

      //Rebind the DatGrid
      EmployeeGrid.DataSource = reader;
      EmployeeGrid.DataBind();

      //Clear the edit boxes
      txtFirstNameAdd.Text = "";
      txtLastNameAdd.Text = "";
    }
    catch (SqlException sqlEx)
    {
      Response.Write("SqlException: " + sqlEx.ToString());
    }
    catch (Exception Ex)
    {
      Response.Write("Exception: " + Ex.ToString());
    }
    finally
    {
        if (reader != null)
          //Close the reader
          reader.Close();
        if (conn != null)
          //Close the connection
          conn.Close();
    }
}

private void btnEmployeeUpdate_Click(object sender, System.EventArgs e)
{
```

Listing 4.3   EmployeesWithReader.aspx.cs (continued)

```
      try
      {
        //Create the Connection
        conn = new SqlConnection(m_strConnectionString);
        //Open the connection
        conn.Open();

        //Create an update command for the adapter
        SqlCommand updateCmd = new SqlCommand(
          "UPDATE Employees SET FirstName=@FirstName, LastName=@LastName
" +
            "WHERE EmployeeID=@EmployeeID;SELECT * FROM Employees",
conn);
        //Add the FirstName, LastName, and EmployeeID
        //parameters to the command
        updateCmd.Parameters.Add("@FirstName", SqlDbType.NVarChar, 10);
        updateCmd.Parameters.Add("@LastName", SqlDbType.NVarChar, 20);
        updateCmd.Parameters.Add("@EmployeeID", SqlDbType.Int);
        //Set the parameters
        updateCmd.Parameters["@FirstName"].Value =
txtFirstNameEdit.Text;
        updateCmd.Parameters["@LastName"].Value = txtLastNameEdit.Text;
        updateCmd.Parameters["@EmployeeID"].Value =
          (int)ViewState["SelectedEmployeeID"];

        //Execute the command
        reader = updateCmd.ExecuteReader();

        //Rebind the DatGrid
        EmployeeGrid.DataSource = reader;
        EmployeeGrid.DataBind();

        //Clear the edit controls and disable them
        txtFirstNameEdit.Text = "";
        txtFirstNameEdit.Enabled = false;
        txtLastNameEdit.Text = "";
        txtLastNameEdit.Enabled = false;
        btnEmployeeUpdate.Enabled = false;
      }
      catch (SqlException sqlEx)
      {
        Response.Write("SqlException: " + sqlEx.ToString());
      }
      catch (Exception Ex)
      {
        Response.Write("Exception: " + Ex.ToString());
      }
      finally
      {
```

Listing 4.3 EmployeesWithReader.aspx.cs (continued)

```
            if (reader != null)
              //Close the reader
              reader.Close();
          if (conn != null)
              //Close the connection
              conn.Close();
      }
    }
  }
}
```

Listing 4.3 EmployeesWithReader.aspx.cs (continued)

Let's review the listing and see how it works. First of all, there are three private class member variables. The m_strConnectionString variable holds the connection string so that we don't have to keep defining this throughout the code. In a real application, we would store this connection string in the registry, an XML file, or the Web.Config file; we would not hard-code it into the application as done here. We've also declared Sql-DataReader and SqlConnection member variables. In the Page_Load method, there is some code that should be executed only on the first request of the page by a particular client. We've created a new SqlConnection and then called the Open() method. The connection has to be opened before the ExecuteReader() method is called, or an exception will be thrown. The ExecuteReader() method is called and returns a Sql-DataReader object, which is saved in the SqlDataReader member variable.

```
//Create the Connection
conn = new SqlConnection(m_strConnectionString);
//Open the connection
conn.Open();

//Create a command to retrieve the data
SqlCommand selectCmd = new SqlCommand(
"Select * FROM Employees;SELECT * FROM Customers", conn);

//Get a SqlDataReader
reader = selectCmd.ExecuteReader();
```

Once we have the SqlDataReader, the DataGrid can bind directly to it by setting the DataSource of the grid equal to the SqlDataReader and then calling the Bind() method.

```
EmployeeGrid.DataSource = reader;
EmployeeGrid.DataBind();
```

All of this is wrapped up in a try block with two catch handlers for the SqlException and Exception type exceptions. Last, there is a finally block, where the SqlDataReader and SqlConnection objects are closed. This is a good place to put this because this code will be executed whether an exception occurs or not.

```
finally
{
  if (reader != null)
    //Close the reader
    reader.Close();
  if (conn != null)
    //Close the connection
    conn.Close();
}
```

In the OnItemClicked handler, we save the EmployeeID of the employee that was selected. We set the DataKeyField attribute of the DataGrid to the EmployeeID column of the employees table when we declared the grid in the .aspx file. Now we can access the key of the row that was selected by indexing into the DataKeys property of the EmployeeGrid.

```
int intEmployeeID = (int)EmployeeGrid.DataKeys[(int)e.Item.ItemIndex];
```

If the user clicked the Select button, the selected EmployeeID is saved into the view state, just as we saved the SelectedItemIndex in the previous example. The edit boxes are then filled with the selected employee's name by accessing the cell values of the selected item.

```
txtFirstNameEdit.Text = e.Item.Cells[2].Text;
txtLastNameEdit.Text = e.Item.Cells[3].Text;
```

As before, the edit controls are all enabled. If the user has clicked the Delete button, a connection to the database is opened. Then a SqlCommand object is created to execute the delete.

```
//Create a delete command
SqlCommand deleteCmd = new SqlCommand(
  "DELETE FROM Employees WHERE EmployeeID=@EmployeeID;" +
  "SELECT * FROM Employees", conn);
//Add the EmployeeID parameter to the command
deleteCmd.Parameters.Add("@EmployeeID", SqlDbType.Int);
//Set the @EmployeeID parameter
deleteCmd.Parameters["@EmployeeID"].Value = intEmployeeID;
```

At this point, we're still using parameterized queries, although we could have just as easily formatted a command string and put the EmployeeID directly in the string. We've stuck with the parameterized query because we are going to start using stored procedures in the next example. Stored procedures allow us to simply come back and change the SQL command text in the code to the name of the stored procedure, and all of my parameters for passing values to the stored procedure will already be set up. Because we aren't using the DataSet anymore, there is no need to set the SourceColumn of the parameters. Instead, the *Value* now needs to be set directly, done in the last line in the previous code. Notice that there are actually two SQL statements that are going to be executed when this command is executed. First, the selected record is deleted by the EmployeeID, and second, all of the records of the Employees table are selected again. We need to reselect the records of the Employees table so that we can rebind the DataGrid to reflect the changes that were just made. We're knocking out both statements with one call to the database. The SqlCommand is executed, and the DataGrid is bound to the reader just as in the Page_Load method.

The btnEmployeeAdd_Click and btnEmployeeUpdate_Click handlers are implemented much the same as the delete code. SqlConnection and SqlCommand objects are created. The parameters of the SqlCommand object are set, the command is executed, and the DataGrid is rebound to the returned SqlDataReader. There aren't any new concepts introduced in these handlers. This page should look and function exactly the same as the preceding example, with the exception that the employee name is divided into two columns now.

Wrapping It Up in a Class

Now that we know how to access data let's go ahead and redo the Employees example properly. In this section, we're going to create an Employee class. This class will have properties for several but not all of the columns in the Employees table. It will be able to populate itself, update, delete, and create new Employees. It will also have a static method that will return an ArrayList of Employee objects that can be used to bind to things such as a DataGrid. In addition, we'll use stored procedures rather than hard-coded SQL statements. We recommend using stored procedures for just about all of your SQL Server database access. If modifications need to be made to a SQL statement, the stored procedure can be updated on the fly. No source code modifications need to made and deployed. On top of that, stored procedures are already precompiled and will therefore provide a performance increase over hard-coded SQL statements. Much of the code in the Employee class is not new. You should recognize a lot of the code from the preceding Employees examples. We've included most of the source for the Employee class in Listing 4.4, but we have left out the sections that don't pertain to this discussion. The full source is available for download at the companion Web site.

```
using System;
using System.Data;
using System.Data.SqlClient;
using System.Collections;

namespace Chapter4
{
    /// <summary>
    /// Summary description for Employees.
    /// </summary>
    public class Employee
    {
        //private member variables
        private int m_intEmployeeID;
        private string m_strLastName = string.Empty;
```

Listing 4.4   Employee.cs

```csharp
      private string m_strFirstName = string.Empty;
      ...
      //Other member variables go here
      ...
      //public properties
      public int EmployeeID
      {
        get { return m_intEmployeeID; }
      }

      public string LastName
      {
        get { return m_strLastName; }
        set { m_strLastName = value; }
      }

      public string FirstName
      {
        get { return m_strFirstName; }
        set { m_strFirstName = value; }
      }
      ...
      //Other properties go here
      ...


      //Default constructor
      public Employee()
      {
      }

      public Employee(SqlDataReader reader)
      {
        LoadFromReader(reader);
      }

      public void LoadFromReader(SqlDataReader reader)
      {
        try
        {
          //These columns don't allow nulls
          m_intEmployeeID =
            reader.GetInt32(reader.GetOrdinal("EmployeeID"));
          m_strLastName = reader["LastName"].ToString();
          m_strFirstName = reader["FirstName"].ToString();
          //These columns do allows nulls so check for the NULL condition
          //for any value types other than string.
          m_strTitle = reader["Title"].ToString();
          m_strTitleOfCourtesy = reader["TitleOfCourtesy"].ToString();
```

Listing 4.4   Employee.cs (continued)

```
          if (reader.IsDBNull(reader.GetOrdinal("HireDate")))
          {
            m_dteHireDate = DateTime.MinValue;
          }
          else
          {
            m_dteHireDate =
              reader.GetDateTime(reader.GetOrdinal("HireDate"));
          }

        m_strAddress = reader["Address"].ToString();
        m_strCity = reader["City"].ToString();
        m_strPostalCode = reader["PostalCode"].ToString();
        m_strCountry = reader["Country"].ToString();
        m_strHomePhone = reader["HomePhone"].ToString();
        m_strExtension = reader["Extension"].ToString();
      }
      catch (SqlException sqlEx)
      {
        //Throw this exception
        throw new Exception
          ("Database exception occured in Employee.GetByID()", sqlEx);
      }
      catch (Exception Ex)
      {
        //Throw this exception
        throw new
          Exception("Exception occured in Employee.LoadFromReader()", Ex);
      }
    }


    //Use this method to get an ArrayList of all Employees
    public static ArrayList GetAll(SqlConnection conn)
    {
      SqlDataReader reader = null;
      //Create the Employee ArrayList
      ArrayList arrEmployees = new ArrayList();

      try
      {
        //Create a command to retrieve the data
        SqlCommand selectCmd = new
          SqlCommand("Northwind.dbo.sp_GetAllEmployees", conn);
        selectCmd.CommandType = CommandType.StoredProcedure;

        //Get a SqlDataReader
        reader = selectCmd.ExecuteReader();
```

Listing 4.4 Employee.cs (continued)

```
      //Create the Employee objects
      while (reader.Read())
      {
        arrEmployees.Add(new Employee(reader));
      }
    }
    catch (SqlException sqlEx)
    {
      //Throw this exception
      throw new Exception
        ("Database exception occured in Employee.GetByID()", sqlEx);
    }
    catch (Exception Ex)
    {
      //Throw this exception
      throw new Exception("Exception occured in Employee.GetAll()", Ex);
    }
    finally
    {
      if (reader != null)
      {
        //Close the reader
        reader.Close();
      }
    }

    //Return the ArrayList
    return arrEmployees;
  }


  //Use this method to get an employee from the database
  //given his EmployeeID
  public static Employee GetByID(SqlConnection conn, int
intEmployeeID)
  {
    SqlDataReader reader = null;
    Employee employee = null;

    try
    {
      //Create a select command
      SqlCommand selectCmd = new
        SqlCommand("Northwind.dbo.sp_GetEmployee", conn);
      selectCmd.CommandType = CommandType.StoredProcedure;
      //Add the parameters
      selectCmd.Parameters.Add("@EmployeeID", SqlDbType.Int);
```

Listing 4.4 Employee.cs (continued)

```
      //Set the parameter values
      selectCmd.Parameters["@EmployeeID"].Value = intEmployeeID;

      //Execute the command
      reader = selectCmd.ExecuteReader();

      if (reader.Read())
      {
        employee = new Employee(reader);
      }

      return employee;
    }
    catch (SqlException sqlEx)
    {
      //Throw this exception
      throw new Exception
        ("Database exception occured in Employee.GetByID()", sqlEx);
    }
    catch (Exception Ex)
    {
        //Throw this exception
        throw new Exception(
          "Exception occured in Employee.DeleteByID()", Ex);
    }
    finally
    {
      if (reader != null)
      {
        //Close the reader
        reader.Close();
      }
    }
  }


//Use this method to Add an employee to the database
public void Add(SqlConnection conn)
{
  try
  {
    //Create an insert command
    SqlCommand insertCmd = new
      SqlCommand("Northwind.dbo.sp_AddEmployee", conn);
    insertCmd.CommandType = CommandType.StoredProcedure;
    //Add the parameters
    insertCmd.Parameters.Add("@LastName", SqlDbType.NVarChar, 20);
    insertCmd.Parameters.Add("@FirstName", SqlDbType.NVarChar, 10);
```

Listing 4.4 Employee.cs (continued)

```
        insertCmd.Parameters.Add("@Title", SqlDbType.NVarChar, 30);
        insertCmd.Parameters.Add("@TitleOfCourtesy", SqlDbType.NVarChar,
          25);
        insertCmd.Parameters.Add("@HireDate", SqlDbType.DateTime);
        insertCmd.Parameters.Add("@Address", SqlDbType.NVarChar, 60);
        insertCmd.Parameters.Add("@City", SqlDbType.NVarChar, 15);
        insertCmd.Parameters.Add("@PostalCode", SqlDbType.NVarChar, 10);
        insertCmd.Parameters.Add("@Country", SqlDbType.NVarChar, 15);
        insertCmd.Parameters.Add("@HomePhone", SqlDbType.NVarChar, 24);
        insertCmd.Parameters.Add("@Extension", SqlDbType.NVarChar, 4);
        //Set the parameter values
        insertCmd.Parameters["@LastName"].Value = m_strLastName;
        insertCmd.Parameters["@FirstName"].Value = m_strFirstName;
        insertCmd.Parameters["@Title"].Value = m_strTitle;
        insertCmd.Parameters["@TitleOfCourtesy"].Value =
          m_strTitleOfCourtesy;
        insertCmd.Parameters["@HireDate"].Value = m_dteHireDate;
        insertCmd.Parameters["@Address"].Value = m_strAddress;
        insertCmd.Parameters["@City"].Value = m_strCity;
        insertCmd.Parameters["@PostalCode"].Value = m_strPostalCode;
        insertCmd.Parameters["@Country"].Value = m_strCountry;
        insertCmd.Parameters["@HomePhone"].Value = m_strHomePhone;
        insertCmd.Parameters["@Extension"].Value = m_strExtension;

        //Execute the command
        insertCmd.ExecuteNonQuery();
      }
      catch (SqlException sqlEx)
      {
        //Throw this exception
        throw new Exception
          ("Database exception occured in Employee.GetByID()", sqlEx);
      }
      catch (Exception Ex)
      {
        //Throw this exception
        throw new Exception("Exception occured in Employee.Add()", Ex);
      }
    }


  //Use this method to Update this employee to the database
  public void Update(SqlConnection conn)
  {
    ...
    //This method is exactly like the Add command except it calls
    //a different stored procedure.
  }
```

Listing 4.4   Employee.cs (continued)

```
//Use this method to delete this employee from the database
public void Delete(SqlConnection conn)
{
  DeleteByID(conn, m_intEmployeeID);
}


//Use this method to delete an employee from the database
//given his EmployeeID
public static void DeleteByID(SqlConnection conn, int intEmployeeID)
{
  try
  {
    //Create a delete command
    SqlCommand deleteCmd = new
      SqlCommand("Northwind.dbo.sp_DeleteEmployee", conn);
    deleteCmd.CommandType = CommandType.StoredProcedure;
    //Add the parameters
    deleteCmd.Parameters.Add("@EmployeeID", SqlDbType.Int);
    //Set the parameter values
    deleteCmd.Parameters["@EmployeeID"].Value = intEmployeeID;

    //Execute the command
    deleteCmd.ExecuteNonQuery();
  }
  catch (SqlException sqlEx)
  {
    //Throw this exception
    throw new Exception
      ("Database exception occured in Employee.GetByID()", sqlEx);
  }
  catch (Exception Ex)
  {
    //Throw this exception
    throw new Exception(
      "Exception occured in Employee.DeleteByID()", Ex);
  }
  }
}
}
```

Listing 4.4 Employee.cs (continued)

Keep in mind that this class is designed not only for use with ASP.NET applications, but also for use with any other type of application. In a lot of real-world scenarios, some of your applications may be Web based and some may be fat client applications. For example, in our car parts business, the public Web site is an ASP.NET application;

however, the applications that are used to maintain the parts database, handle pricing, invoices, and purchase orders are probably more suited to fat client applications. For this reason, we choose to implement our database access classes in a way that can be used effectively by both types of applications. Some of the methods used here could be changed to better suit a Web-only approach. All of the methods in the Employee class take at least one parameter, a SqlConnection, which is expected to be opened. We will still be opening a SqlConnection from within our code-behind classes. This allows the class user to reuse one connection for multiple things. If we had created, opened, and closed a connection within the Employee class, we would have taken this freedom away from any potential users of the class. Many of the member variables and property declarations were left out of the listing to save space. The full source code can be found in the Chapter4 project available for download from the Web site.

We provided a constructor that takes a SqlDataReader as a parameter. This makes it easy to traverse through the records of a SqlDataReader and create new Employee objects for each record. This constructor calls the LoadFromReader() method, passing the SqlDataReader along. The LoadFromReader() method simply fills in the member variables of the object by pulling column values out of the SqlDataReader, as we have already seen. There is one thing to note here. Notice that although many of the columns, such as Title and TitleofCourtesy, allow NULL values, we have not bothered to check for the NULL condition using IsDBNull(). Because these columns are string values, we can use the ToString() method to get their values. In effect, we're calling ToString() on the object type that is returned by the SqlDataReader indexer. The point is, if the value in the Title column is null, calling the ToString() method will not throw an exception. If the value of the HireDate column is NULL and we attempt to call the SqlDataReader.GetDateTime() function on that column it will throw an exception, so we need to check for the NULL condition there. By not checking for NULL on the strings, we save a little processing time.

The static GetAll() method returns an ArrayList of Employee objects, which we use to bind the DataGrid to the page. The method calls a stored procedure that returns all rows in the Employees table. The returned SqlDataReader object is then used to traverse through the records and fill the ArrayList with new Employee objects.

```
while (reader.Read())
{
  arrEmployees.Add(new Employee(reader));
}
```

This is done inside of a while loop. The Read() method will return true until the end of the record set is reached. Inside the while loop, passing the reader to the overloaded constructor creates a new Employee object, which is then added to the ArrayList. Once again, we make sure to close the SqlDataReader in the finally block. We do not close the SqlConnection; that is the client's responsibility.

The rest of the methods of this class do not contain anything that we haven't already seen other than the use of the ExecuteNonQuery() method of the SqlCommand class. This method is used to call any stored procedures that will not return a record set.

Now let's take a look at how to use this class from within an ASP.NET page. We'll rewrite the Employees example to use this class. Although we provided access to columns of the Employees table other than EmployeeID, FirstName, and LastName, we'll just stick to using those for the example. The source for the modified methods of the new code-behind class is provided in Listing 4.5. No changes were necessary to the .aspx file from the previous example.

```csharp
private void Page_Load(object sender, System.EventArgs e)
{
  if (!IsPostBack)
  {
    //Executed on first request only
    try
    {
      //Create the Connection
      conn = new SqlConnection(m_strConnectionString);
      //Open the connection
      conn.Open();

      //Bind the DataGrid
      EmployeeGrid.DataSource = Employee.GetAll(conn);
      EmployeeGrid.DataBind();
    }
    catch (SqlException sqlEx)
    {
      Response.Write("SqlException: " + sqlEx.ToString());
    }
    catch (Exception Ex)
    {
      Response.Write("Exception: " + Ex.ToString());
    }
    finally
    {
      //Close the connection
      conn.Close();
    }
  }
}


protected void OnItemClicked(object source, DataGridCommandEventArgs e)
{
  //Get the EmployeeID of the employee that was selected
  int intEmployeeID = (int)EmployeeGrid.DataKeys[(int)e.Item.ItemIndex];

  if (e.CommandName == "Select")
  {
    //Save the selected EmployeeID to the view state
    ViewState["SelectedEmployeeID"] = intEmployeeID;

    //Fill the edit boxes with the selected employees name
    txtFirstNameEdit.Text = e.Item.Cells[2].Text;
    txtLastNameEdit.Text = e.Item.Cells[3].Text;
```

Listing 4.5 EmployeesFinal.aspx.cs

```
      //Enable the edit controls
      txtFirstNameEdit.Enabled = true;
      txtLastNameEdit.Enabled = true;
      btnEmployeeUpdate.Enabled = true;
    }
    else
    {
      try
      {
        //Create the Connection
        conn = new SqlConnection(m_strConnectionString);
        //Open the connection
        conn.Open();

        //Delete the employee from the database
        Employee.DeleteByID(conn, intEmployeeID);

        //Rebind the DataGrid
        EmployeeGrid.DataSource = Employee.GetAll(conn);
        EmployeeGrid.DataBind();
      }
      catch (SqlException sqlEx)
      {
        Response.Write("SqlException: " + sqlEx.ToString());
      }
      catch (Exception Ex)
      {
        Response.Write("Exception: " + Ex.ToString());
      }
      finally
      {
        //Close the connection
        conn.Close();
      }
    }
}

private void btnEmployeeAdd_Click(object sender, System.EventArgs e)
{
    try
    {
      //Create the Connection
      conn = new SqlConnection(m_strConnectionString);
      //Open the connection
      conn.Open();

      //Create a new employee
      Employee emp = new Employee();
      //Set the employees First Name and Last Name
```

Listing 4.5   EmployeesFinal.aspx.cs (continued)

```
      emp.LastName = txtLastNameAdd.Text;
      emp.FirstName = txtFirstNameAdd.Text;
      //Add the employee to the database
      emp.Add(conn);

      //Rebind the DataGrid
      EmployeeGrid.DataSource = Employee.GetAll(conn);
      EmployeeGrid.DataBind();

      //Clear the edit boxes
      txtFirstNameAdd.Text = "";
      txtLastNameAdd.Text = "";
   }
   catch (SqlException sqlEx)
   {
     Response.Write("SqlException: " + sqlEx.ToString());
   }
   catch (Exception Ex)
   {
     Response.Write("Exception: " + Ex.ToString());
   }
   finally
   {
     //Close the connection
     conn.Close();
   }
}

private void btnEmployeeUpdate_Click(object sender, System.EventArgs e)
{
   try
   {
     //Create the Connection
     conn = new SqlConnection(m_strConnectionString);
     //Open the connection
     conn.Open();

     //Get the selected employee by EmployeeID
     Employee emp = Employee.GetByID(conn,
       (int)ViewState["SelectedEmployeeID"]);
     //Update the employees First Name and Last Name
     emp.LastName = txtLastNameEdit.Text;
     emp.FirstName = txtFirstNameEdit.Text;
     //Update the employee to the database
     emp.Update(conn);

     //Rebind the DataGrid
     EmployeeGrid.DataSource = Employee.GetAll(conn);
     EmployeeGrid.DataBind();
```

Listing 4.5   EmployeesFinal.aspx.cs (continued)

```
      //Clear the edit controls and disable them
      txtFirstNameEdit.Text = "";
      txtFirstNameEdit.Enabled = false;
      txtLastNameEdit.Text = "";
      txtLastNameEdit.Enabled = false;
      btnEmployeeUpdate.Enabled = false;
    }
    catch (SqlException sqlEx)
    {
      Response.Write("SqlException: " + sqlEx.ToString());
    }
    catch (Exception Ex)
    {
      Response.Write("Exception: " + Ex.ToString());
    }
    finally
    {
      //Close the connection
      conn.Close();
    }
  }
```

Listing 4.5   EmployeesFinal.aspx.cs (continued)

In the Page_Load method, we open a SqlConnection and pass it to the static Employee.GetAll() method. The returned ArrayList is used to bind to the DataGrid.

```
EmployeeGrid.DataSource = Employee.GetAll(conn);
EmployeeGrid.DataBind();
```

One thing to keep in mind when binding to custom-created classes is that all fields that you wish to access from the class must be exposed as properties. You cannot bind to public member variables, so make your member variables private and expose them with a public property that provides the read/write access that you desire.

In the OnItemClicked handler, we modify the section of code that provides the delete functionality to use the Employee class. The static DeleteByID() method was called passing the SqlConnection and the selected EmployeeID.

```
Employee.DeleteByID(conn, intEmployeeID);
```

Next, rebind the DataGrid by calling the GetAll() method again. This results in two calls to the database, a situation that isn't optimal. To get around this, we could write a new method on the Employee object that not only deletes an employee record, but also returns an ArrayList of the remaining employees. This method wouldn't be too useful in any type of application except a Web application, which is why we have chosen not to implement it that way. Not to mention that it doesn't make good logical sense from an object-oriented standpoint. It would, though, eliminate a database call.

The btnEmployeeAdd_Click handler also creates a new Employee object. It then sets the FirstName and LastName properties and calls the Add() method, which adds it to the database.

```
//Create a new employee
Employee emp = new Employee();
//Set the employees First Name and Last Name
emp.LastName = txtLastNameAdd.Text;
emp.FirstName = txtFirstNameAdd.Text;
//Add the employee to the database
emp.Add(conn);
```

The btnEmployeeUpdate_Click handler is implemented in a manner similar to the add handler, with the exception that first we retrieve the selected employee from the database by using the EmployeeID. This obtains all of the other fields that are used in the Employee class but are not being used in this example. If we just filled in the First-Name and LastName fields and called the Update() method of the Employee class, the values of all of the other fields would be wiped out in the database.

```
//Get the selected employee by EmployeeID
Employee emp = Employee.GetByID(conn,
  (int)ViewState["SelectedEmployeeID"]);
//Update the employees First Name and Last Name
emp.LastName = txtLastNameEdit.Text;
emp.FirstName = txtFirstNameEdit.Text;
//Update the employee to the database
emp.Update(conn);
```

Componentizing your code in this way cleans up your GUI client code and makes it really easy to make business logic changes in one place. If it becomes necessary, you can provide Web application-specific methods to your components that might make things a little more efficient or cut down on the number of calls that need to be made to the database.

Connection Pooling

The last topic of data access that we'd like to cover is connection pooling. Creating and establishing a connection to a database is a somewhat costly operation. Connection pooling is a mechanism of sharing connection objects between multiple users of an application so that connection creation is not always necessary. The idea is that when a connection is closed in a section of code, it is not really closed. Instead, it is returned to a pool of open connections ready to be reused. When a new section of code needs an open connection, an existing connection is pulled from the pool and reused, avoiding the costly connection process.

If you are using the OleDbConnection class, the provider handles connection pooling automatically. You get it for free and do not have to do anything to manage it yourself. If you are using a SQL Server database and therefore the SqlConnection class, connection pooling is handled for you through the use of Windows 2000 component services, but you are provided with the ability to manage certain options of the pooling process yourself. The rest of this section will explain the connection pooling mechanism for the SqlConnection class.

Connection pools are unique by connection string. If a SqlConnection object is created using a connection string for which there is currently no pool, a new pool will be created. At this time, the pool will create and add to the pool as many connection objects as specified by the minimum pool size. If a pool for that connection string already exists, then a connection object will be returned from the pool if one is available. If there are no available, unused connections in the pool, and the pool has not reached its maximum size (which is configurable), a new connection will be created, added to the pool, and returned to the requester. If the pool has already reached its maximum size, then the connection request will be queued. As soon as a connection is available it will be assigned to the first requester in the queue. A requester will wait for a connection from the pool only as long as specified in the ConnectionTimeout property of the SqlConnection class. When assigned a connection from the pool, the connection will be returned to the pool when the user calls the Close() method.

There are several pooling options that you can set via key/value pairs in the ConnectionString property of the SqlConnection class. The three most important keys are *Pooling, Max Pool Size,* and *Min Pool Size.* Pooling can be set to true, which is the default, or false, and it simply determines whether connection pooling is used. Max Pool Size sets the maximum number of connections that the pool can grow to accommodate; its default value is 100. Min Pool Size sets the number of connections that should be created and added to the pool when the pool is initially created. The default value is 0, which means that no additional connections will be created at pool creation time.

Using connection pooling is quite simple; if you are happy with the defaults mentioned previously, you don't have to do anything at all. If you want to adjust the pool, you simply add or change the appropriate keys in the connection string. Here is what our connection string would look like for creating a pool with a Max Pool Size of 150 and a Min Pool Size of 25.

```
@"Data Source=(local)\NetSDK;Initial Catalog=Northwind;
    User ID=sa;pwd=;Max Pool Size=150;Min Pool Size=25"
```

Wrapping Up the Chapter

In this chapter, we scratched the surface of the power that ADO.NET provides. We'll be building further on the techniques introduced in this chapter when we start building a real-world application in Chapter 6. We hope that you have enough information on ADO.NET to do nearly everything that you need for a Web-based application at this point.

In the next chapter, we will cover the rest of the ASP.NET essentials that we need to start developing a real-world application. In addition, we'll cover some more advanced data binding techniques that will enable you to add some real power to your pages.

Creating More Advanced ASP.NET Pages

In the previous chapters we have covered the basics of ASP.NET. We have seen how to use Web Server Controls and the event-driven programming model that is now available in ASP.NET. We've covered database access and how we can bind our server-side controls to various data sources. We've also covered the very useful code-behind programming methodology that allows us to separate the code that makes our page work and the code that makes up our user interface.

In this chapter, we'll introduce some more advanced concepts to build on what we already know. We'll cover the HttpRequest, HttpResponse objects, and Cookies and see how we can provide greater customization of client sessions and remember users between visits to our site. We'll also see how we can store our own information in the client's ViewState and store objects in memory on the server-side with Session and Application variables. After covering this information we will have seen the majority of ASP.NET fundamentals, We'll finish off the chapter by showing how you can write your own custom page class on which to base all of your pages. This ability allows you to easily reuse common code throughout your pages. We'll then introduce user controls, another concept that allows you to reuse common user interface objects across your pages. The last section of the chapter will cover some more advanced Data Binding techniques with the DataGrid and introduce the DataList and Repeater controls for the first time.

After covering the topics in this chapter, you will have all of the information you need to build very robust Web applications.

Communicating with the Browser

As Web programmers our primary responsibility is to communicate with our clients through an Internet browser. We can send information to the client through Http-Response object. All of the Web Server Controls that we covered in Chapter 3, "Server Controls," use this object behind the scenes to render their output to the stream of data that will be sent to the client. The client's data is sent back to the server and is accessible through the use of the HttpRequest object. Through the HttpRequest object, data such as query string parameters and form values can be retrieved. ASP.NET uses the HttpRequest object to populate our server-side controls with any data that the client may have provided. In this section, we'll see how we can use the HttpResponse and HttpRequest objects directly to perform some advanced operations.

HTTP cookies are not new. Cookies allow us to store information in memory or on disk on the client's machine. This is one way of enabling us to remember who a client is between page requests. We'll cover how ASP.NET exposes cookies to us in this section as well.

The Response Object

As we mentioned earlier, the HttpResponse object is used to send data to the client. All of the Web Server Controls use this object behind the scenes. It is still possible to use the HttpResponse object directly in our code to render output to the client. Although ASP.NET provides such a powerful framework for writing Web applications through the use of the built-in objects and controls, sometimes it is desirable for very simple pages and for debugging purposes to use the HttpResponse object directly.

The Response object is also used for buffering output on the server. By default, an ASP.NET page will not be transmitted to the client's browser until it has been completely processed on the server. In the case of a long-running page that delivers a lot of content to the client or performs lengthy operations, it might be a good idea to send the output of the page periodically before the entire page has been processed. This could provide a better user experience, as the user won't have to wait for a long period of time before viewing the content of the page.

One fundamental operation that we need to perform quite commonly is redirecting the client to another resource on the Web. This action is also handled by the Http-Response object and will be covered in this section.

The HttpResponse object is also responsible for caching content on the Web server to improve performance. We won't cover this concept in this section, but it will be covered in Chapter 10, "Debugging and Optimization."

Generating Content Programmatically

To understand the response object, you must know how the Web server communicates with the browser. When the browser requests a page from the server, it is actually making a temporary connection via a TCP/IP socket. Sockets provide for two-way conversations, so when the server is ready to send the page back to the browser, it does so over the socket channel. When programs use sockets, they write data to the socket using the functions provided in the socket library. The TCP/IP protocol then moves the bytes of data from one machine to the other; it may even break the data apart into packets and add special headers to route the data back and forth between the two machines. The connection stream can be written via the HttpResponse object, which is exposed as the Response property of the Page object, from which all ASP.NET pages are derived.

Normally in a classic ASP page, the content that is sent to the browser comes from HTML with code strategically placed throughout it within special tags. In the case of ASP.NET, this same technique can be used, but typically the aspx file for the page will consist of server-side controls. The code in the script or code-behind class will interact with these controls and the HTML around them, to create the content that is sent to the browser.

There are times when you will want to write content directly to the browser. For example, if a page is merely required for testing some action on the server, then it may be easier just to send the output directly without fancy formatting or the need for controls. Or, you can use this method when type or layout of the data is not known until runtime. For example, if there is a need to traverse through a collection of objects and each object's properties as well, it may be useful to have freedom from a defined layout and to write data directly as it is discovered. Again, this is a technique probably put to best use in debugging and development only. This could be useful when looking for an elusive cookie value during development. The usefulness of writing directly to the browser is limited to large, production-quality ASP.NET apps. In these cases, the programmer will most often know exactly what the format of the data will be and can get more benefit from using a predetermined layout.

The following is an example of how to send output to the browser using Http-Response. Remember that the output you send with HttpResponse will ultimately be displayed by the browser, so formatting can be done simply by sending HTML. To run the following example, create a new WebForm and replace its Page_Load function with the following:

```
protected void Page_Load(object sender, System.EventArgs e)
{
Response.Write(string.Format("The date is: {0}<br>",
DateTime.Now.ToShortDateString()));

    Response.Write(string.Format("<i>The time is: <b>{0}</b></i><br>",
DateTime.Now.ToShortTimeString()));
}
```

The results of this in the browser are shown in Figure 5.1, which displays the current date and time on the Web server.

In addition to sending purely code-generated text, HttpResponse allows you to send the contents of an entire file to the browser. For example, you may want to dynamically load and display a file in the browser but don't want to write code to open and read the file and then write it out manually. One example might be to dynamically load HTML from a file to display in part of your page based on some business logic. It could also be useful for displaying other HTML files within an ASP.NET page, for example, to display a copyright header across the top of all pages in a Web app without using user controls.

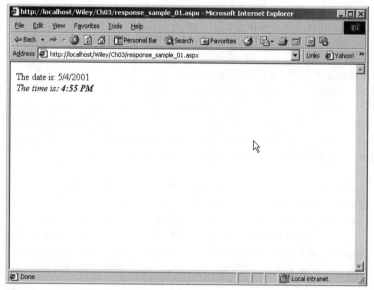

Figure 5.1 Response output.

The following example sends files to the browser in three different ways. First, we send a header line using one line of code that will be included in all pages in an application. Notice that the HTML file we send here has no HTML, HEAD, or BODY tags in it because these are included in the aspx page already. Later in this chapter, when we learn about User Controls, we will see that they act similarly, and shouldn't have these tags either. Then, we send a file that is formatted as standard text and one formatted as HTML.

```
//Send a file containing a header line
Response.WriteFile("top_border.htm");

//Send plain text
Response.Write("<B>Begin unformatted file contents</B><BR>\r");
Response.WriteFile("wiley.txt");
Response.Write("<B>End unformatted file contents</B><BR><BR>\r");

//Send text formatted for browser
Response.Write("<B>Begin formatted file contents</B><BR>\r");
Response.WriteFile("wiley_formatted.txt");
Response.Write("<B>End formatted file contents</B><BR><BR>\r");
```

This example opens and reads a file manually, adds HTML line breaks to it, and sends the data via HttpResponse. This third example is more work, but it can be used to show any text file in the browser with its intended line breaks intact. Notice also that the WriteFile method looks for the file in the Web directory, and the OpenRead method requires a full path to find the file. The File object is for working with files in any type of application, while HttpResponse.WriteFile is for Web apps, where the files needed often reside in the same folder or virtual directory as the ASP.NET pages.

```
//Read plain text, format it for browser, send it
Response.Write("<B>Begin programmatically formatted file
  contents</B><BR>\r");

//Open and read the file
  string path = "f:\\meyneh\\fileshare\\wiley\\ch03\\wiley.txt";

System.IO.StreamReader sr =
  new System.IO.StreamReader(System.IO.File.OpenRead(path));

System.Text.StringBuilder sb =
  new System.Text.StringBuilder(sr.ReadToEnd());

//Replace linefeeds with browser linefeed
sb.Replace("\r", "<BR>\r");
sr.Close();

//Send to browser
Response.Write(sb.ToString());
Response.Write("<B>End programmatically formatted file
  contents</B><BR>\r");
```

To run these samples, create a new WebForm, and place any of the preceding code lines into its Page_Load function. If you run this example, you'll see the contents of the file as well as the header bar across the top of the page, as shown in Figure 5.2.

NOTE When creating a header this way, it will not benefit from some of the advanced caching features available to the built-in Server Controls discussed later in the book.

Redirection

Another common use of HttpResponse is for redirection. When a page is requested, your logic may dictate that the browser should request a different page instead. For example, if you want the user to be rerouted to a login page because they are not yet logged in, you would use redirection. When you call HttpResponse.Redirect, the server sends an HTTP header to the browser that tells it to request another page instead and includes which page to request. Redirection cannot occur after nonheader content has been sent to the browser; doing so will cause an exception.

```
protected void Page_Load(object sender, System.EventArgs e)
{
    Response.Redirect("http://www.wiley.com");
}
```

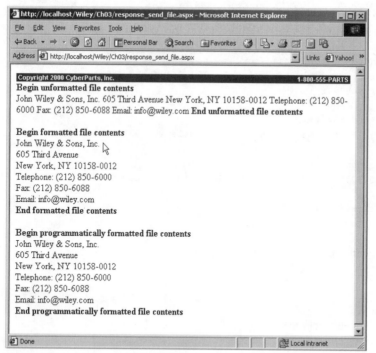

Figure 5.2   More response output.

When you request this page that calls the redirect method, you are immediately sent to another page. You can redirect at any time in your code, but it is important to remember that an HttpException will be thrown if output has already been sent to the browser. The following code throws this exception. You will see the ASP.NET red and yellow unhandled exception page when the exception occurs, and all processing of the page will stop. Any unhandled exception in an ASP.NET page automatically generates a page that displays detailed exception information, including the source code location and stack trace. Exception handling was covered in detail in Chapter 4, "Database Access."

NOTE In Windows 2000 you are less likely to encounter output sent before calling HttpResponse.Redirect because output is buffered by default, and it is unlikely that any content will have been sent to the browser when you call Redirect.

```
protected void Page_Load(object sender, System.EventArgs e)
{
    Response.Write("You will never see this text");
    Response.Flush();
    Response.Redirect("http://www.wiley.com");
}
```

If you were able to view the source of the HTML generated by a redirect, it would look something like this:

```
<meta http-equiv="Refresh" content="0; url=http://www.wiley.com">.
```

If you were to create an HTML page that just redirects the browser to another page, the code shown here is all that would be needed.

There is one more thing to be aware of when using Response.Redirect(). When ASP.NET performs a Redirect it automatically throws a ThreadAbortException. This exception can be caught just as any other exception. However, this is a special exception that will be automatically re-thrown after any catch blocks have been executed. This means that we have to be careful when using a Response.Redirect() inside of a try block. It might be necessary to provide an empty catch block specifically for the ThreadAbortException in some cases, just to prevent any general catch blocks from being executed due to a Response.Redirect().

Cookies

Cookies have been one of the most important aspects of programming interactive Web applications since the beginning. ASP.NET does not disappoint in this area and provides an object-oriented way to set and retrieve cookies on the browser. Although you probably already understand the use of cookies, let's briefly review them here because they are used as one of the fundamental building blocks of the WileyParts online shopping application that we'll create in Chapter 6, "Applying What We've Learned So Far."

Because HTTP is a connectionless protocol, it is difficult to treat a browser as an always-connected client application. Most Web-based applications rely on resources residing on the server that are particular to one user on one browser. In a traditional, rich-client application, the state of the session is stored on the client in its programming logic.

One way to simulate a rich-client application on the Web is to employ cookies that store data on the client. Even though cookies are not robust enough to store complex session-related objects like database connections or business objects, they can be used effectively by storing just enough data to allow the code on the server to re-create the real data objects whenever the user visits the site. Let's learn how to use the Response object read and write cookies in the browser.

ASP.NET provides four related classes for working with cookies:

- HttpCookie
- HttpCookieCollection
- HttpResponse
- HttpRequest

The Response object has a property called Cookies, which is an HttpCookieCollection of HttpCookie objects. When a browser makes a request to the server, it sends all of the cookies for the server (by its address or domain name) in the HTTP header of the request. ASP.NET loads these cookies into the collection for you. To access the cookies, simply index them in the collection. When information is sent to the browser in a cookie, you can determine whether you want it to exist on the client only while the browser is open or whether you want it to remain on the client machine after the browser is closed. The difference in how long the cookie will live in the browser determines whether you have a Persistent Cookie or a Session Cookie. Session Cookies are those that live only as long as the browser is open, whereas a Persistent Cookie is one that exists until its expire date, or indefinitely.

Both types of cookies are useful. For example, if a user logs into a Web application, you may want to store his or her userid in the browser as the user navigates among the pages in the application. You may want to require the user to reenter his or her login credentials if the browser is closed and opened again. This is crucial in environments where more than one person may be using a machine to access Web applications. For example, imagine if you were using a browser in a public library or college to access your bank account online. If the banking application keeps your login credentials in a cookie while you are using the application, that information definitely should be gone before the next user sits down at that same machine. If not, the next user could browse to your banking application and be authenticated as you—not the desired functionality. This is a case where you would want to implement Session Cookies that will cease to exist as soon as the browser is closed.

There may be situations in which you want information to be stored on the client for a much longer period of time. A persistent cookie is perfect for storing information such as user preferences, user visit counts, and other simple information that is distinct to each user. An example of this is an online shopping Web site or a member-based forum Web site. In these cases, a Persistent Cookie will keep the user's information over long periods of time, so that the items in the user's cart or his or her forum login information will be intact the next time the user visits. In general, it is safe to use Persistent Cookies in applications that will be accessed from personal machines in people's homes or offices, rather than from public or shared computers.

As far as your code is concerned, the main difference between setting a Session Cookie and a Persistent Cookie is the expiration time. Session Cookies have no expiration time set; thus, they are stored only in memory while the browser is open. Persistent cookies, on the other hand, do have expiration dates associated with them, but the dates can be set as far into the future as you want. There is no limit on the amount of days, week, or years a Persistent Cookie can be set to last.

Let's create and send a session a cookie to the browser that we will read back from the browser in the next section. Create a new WebForm, and replace its Page_Load function with the following:

```
protected void Page_Load(object sender, System.EventArgs e)
{
    //set a temporary cookie
    HttpCookie tempcookie = new HttpCookie("WileyTempCookie");
    tempcookie.Values.Add("userid", "1250");
    Response.Cookies.Add(tempcookie);
}
```

Run the example, and look in the cookies location on your client machine. In Windows 2000, this should be C:\Documents and Settings\<your user name>\Cookies\. You will not find this cookie anywhere on the hard drive because it is in memory only—it is not stored anywhere. Now try the following code, which will set a Persistent Cookie:

```
protected void Page_Load(object sender, System.EventArgs e)
{
    //set a persistent cookie
```

```
        HttpCookie perscookie = new HttpCookie("WileyPersistentCookie");
        perscookie.Expires = Convert.ToDateTime("12/01/03 16:00");
        perscookie.Values.Add("userid", "1250");
        Response.Cookies.Add(perscookie);
    }
```

This cookie, as opposed to the one in the previous example, can be found on the hard drive, in the cookie storage location. The Persistent Cookie was, in fact, stored and will exist there after the browser closes.

Now let's read the cookie from the browser request and display its value. For the following example, run the previous Session Cookie example to set the cookie. Then run this example. Don't close the browser first, or else the cookie will be gone! After you have run it once while the Session Cookie still exists, close the browser. Then run the example in a new browser.

```
protected void Page_Load(object sender, System.EventArgs e)
{
    //read cookie from browser via the cookie collection
    HttpCookie cookie = Request.Cookies["WileySessionCookie"];

    if (cookie == null)
    {
        //cookie not found
        Response.Write("Session cookie not found<BR>");
    }
    else
    {
        //cookie found
        string s = cookie.Values["userid"].ToString();

        //cookie empty or not
        if (s.Trim().Length == 0)
        {
            Response.Write("Cookie was found, but is empty<BR>");
        }

        else
        {
            Response.Write(string.Format("Cookie value: {0}<br>", s));
        }
    }
}
```

You will see that the cookie cannot be found. Session Cookies are maintained as long as at least one browser is open, and not necessarily the one in which you accessed the page that set the cookie. This is important for situations in which a Web application opens additional browser windows that would still need to access the cookie.

To read the Persistent Cookie, use the code from the previous example but change the cookie name to reflect that of the Persistent Cookie. This code should open the cookie and read its value even if all browser windows have been closed and reopened.

Modify the first line of the Page_Load function in the previous example code as follows, to see this in action:

```
HttpCookie cookie = Request.Cookies["WileyPersistentCookie"];
```

Now, let's try an example that will read all of the set cookies. To do this, we will have to loop through the Request.HttpCookies collection and get each HttpCookie from it. In order to read the actual data stored in each cookie, we have to perform another loop because a single cookie can have multiple values. Fortunately, we can do this easily in C# with the foreach construct. This is very similar to that which has been a part of VB for a long time.

How do we know that these objects can take part in foreach loops? In .NET, if an object implements the IEnumerable interface, it supports the foreach construct being applied to it. There are other ways to ensure that an object supports the foreach construct, but they are outside the scope of this book and have to do with meeting certain requirements imposed by the .NET common language runtime. Objects that are derived from IEnumerable most likely have an internal structure that consists of a collection of some other type of object. In the documentation, we see that the Http-CookieCollection implements this interface; it does so because it contains one or many instances of the HttpCookie object, hence the term Collection.

When the example is run, note the ASP.NET_SessionId cookie that may show up. This is the cookie that ASP.NET uses to keep track of a client across connections. When using the session management that is provided by ASP.NET, the key stored in this cookie is used to look up session data stored in memory on the server. This is turned on in the configuration of the entire Web application and will be discussed later in the book. It is interesting to note, though, that ASP.NET employs the same techniques we are using here. If you decide to use the ASP.NET session state management functionality, you will be using cookies behind the scenes. Again, we'll go into heavy detail on this in later chapters. Here is the sample to read all currently set cookies:

```
protected void Page_Load(object sender, System.EventArgs e)
{
    //Get the names of all cookies
    foreach(string cookiename in Request.Cookies)
    {
        //Get the cookie with this name
        HttpCookie cookie = Request.Cookies[cookiename];

        //Get all of this cookie's values names
        foreach(string valuename in cookie.Values)
        {
            Response.Write(string.Format(
                "cookiename: {0} valuename: {1} value: {2}<br>",
                cookiename,
                valuename,
                cookie[valuename]));
        }
    }
}
```

Figure 5.3   Read all cookies.

The output is shown in Figure 5.3. You can see that for each cookie, all of its names and values are displayed. This is one simple example of when using Reponse.Write might be an easy solution to displaying output.

QueryString and Forms Collections

In most Web applications, the user navigates through multiple pages. This is similar to a standard thick-client application whose interface consists of multiple windows and dialogs. But because HTTP is a connectionless protocol, there must be a mechanism by which parameters can be passed between the pages. One way would be by storing values in cookies and then reading those values when the next page is loaded. This, however, would be a poor solution to this problem. Although doing so would work, cookies are meant to store data for longer periods of time, and parameters need to exist only long enough to allow the browser to request the next page. For this reason, it is often simpler to use a QueryString to pass values along.

There are two ways to send parameters from one Web page to another: in a query string or in a form. Let's first talk about the query string. In the query string, parameters are concatenated onto the URL in a name-value type scheme. When the server receives a request for a page, it then parses the URL and makes these parameters and their values available to the code for the page, in this case the code-behind class. (If you're not using code-behind, the in-line script can use the parameters, too. In this book we use code-behind classes.) In the case of ASP and ASP.NET, these are available in a collection called QueryString, which is a member of the HttpRequest class, which in turn is a member of the HttpPage class. The HttpPage class is the class from which your code-behind class is derived. The code for your page can get these values and use them however needed to perform your program logic.

Using query string parameters is a very common and simple way to pass data from one page to another, but it is also somewhat limited and comes with some important caveats.

There are several ways to put the parameters into the query string. First, because parameters are just text added to the end of the URL of the page to which you are passing them, you can write the code to do this yourself. This is common and easy, but there are rules you should follow. If the parameters' values can have spaces or other special characters, they need to be converted into characters that are allowed in an URL. If you ever look at an URL with parameters at the end, you will notice things like %20. For example, we ran a search on Microsoft's Web site and found that the following parameters were passed when the search page was called: http://searchmicrosoft. com/us/SearchMS25.asp?qu=Hello%20World&so=RECCNT.

It was actually much longer, but we copied only a small portion. Because URLs require special treatment, such as replacing spaces with "%20," the ASCII char for a space, you'll need to do this when building a query string URL in your code. In ASP, or even many other Web programming tools, the framework does this for us. In ASP.NET, you simply encode your parameters by calling HttpServerUtility's UrlEncode method, which is exposed to all ASP.NET pages as a variable named Server.

Let's create a very simple query string and pass it. To try this, create a WebForm, drag a Button onto it, and handle the click event for it. Just double-click the button in the WebForm designer to cause the IDE to link up the handler for you. (Refer to Chapter 2, "Anatomy of an ASP.NET Page," if you've forgotten how to do this.) Then paste in the relevant code:

```
protected void Button1_Click(object sender, System.EventArgs e)
{
    string parms =
    Server.UrlEncode("searchstring=ford f-150&category=fullsized
trucks");
    Response.Redirect("anotherpage.aspx?" + parms);
}
```

In the code we call a page that does not exist, so you should get the 404 error in the browser. However, the important thing is that you see the parameters we passed in the URL, properly encoded into valid HTTP resource request. It looks like this: http://localhost/Wiley/Ch05/anotherpage.aspx?searchstring%3dford+f50%26category%3 full+sized+trucks.

The second most common way to pass parameters from one page to another is to use an HTML Form. We won't go into detail about forms processing in HTML, so pick up an HTML or CGI resource for more information. A definitive resource on the subject is www.w3.org. ASP.NET pages have only one form, as opposed to classic ASP where often there are multiple forms on a page. Trying to have more than one form in a WebForm can cause undesired behavior.

When a form is used in an HTML or ASP page, the names and values of all of the input controls within the form are sent to the called page when the form is posted. They are not sent on the end of the URL, but rather placed in the body of the HTTP request made by the browser. As a result, they are retrieved by the Forms collection, rather than by accessing the QueryString collection. There are much more important differences than just this, though.

First, there are no limits to the amount of data that can be passed when using a form. There can be any number of controls in a form, and thus any number of name-value pairs sent. Query strings are limited in length to around 2000 bytes because there are limits to the size of URLs in the HTTP protocol. This is also a benefit when you don't want your users to see what's being passed because the parameters will not be seen in the browser's address bar. It prevents a dubious user from molesting the parameters by hand in an attempt to foul up the works or access pages he or she may not otherwise be able to access.

Second, it is less programming on your part if you don't have to create a query string in your code. When using forms, all of the variables are sent in the request automatically for you.

You also won't find the need to access the forms collection nearly as much as you might have in classic ASP, if ever at all. The forms collection was the main way to view what users entered into input controls in classic ASP. In ASP.NET, however, you don't need to read a collection of names and values because the controls are available to your server-side code as control objects and present in your code-behind class as member variables. These objects expose their values in their properties. Using the controls directly is much easier than looking up a value in the forms collection. In fact, in the large enterprise-level applications on which we have used ASP.NET, we have yet to need the forms collection at all. One example in which this difference is helpful is if you had many dynamically created input controls on your page and you wanted to loop through them to look for certain text or make a property the same on all of them. Looping through all of the controls on the page is not quite as easy, and it requires you to treat each one of them based on its type of control. The forms collection, on the other hand, exposed all of the values as simple name-value pairs.

Note that an ASP.NET form's action property is set so that the form is submitted to the same page. Yes, the form is submitted back to "itself." This is uncommon in classic ASP, although it is equally common for classic ASP forms to submit to another page that is set up to read the parameters and act on them. In ASP.NET, the same code that generated the page originally is called when the form is submitted. Translation: The events that occur from button clicks, item selections, and so on are all handled in the same code class that is the page itself. For example, if you had an edit and save button in an classic ASP Form, you typically would have the Save button submit its containing form to a page that is specifically set up to receive the form and implement the save logic. Then, another page would be called on the edit button's submission to perform the edit logic. This requires three pages: the one with the buttons, each in its own form, and one to handle each of the form submissions. Because pages submit back to themselves in ASP.NET, you now only need one page and one form. The server-side code knows which handler to call at the appropriate time from the JavaScript that is generated by ASP.NET.

Because forms are such a tightly integrated part of WebForms in ASP.NET and we will rarely if ever need to programmatically retrieve them, we are not going to do any examples on the subject here. Just keep what we have discussed in mind when writing your applications, as it gives some insight to how WebForms are intended to be used.

Web.Config

The Web.Config file is an XML configuration file that should be located in the root virtual directory of your ASP.NET applications. There are many things that can be configured through the use of this file, including debug settings, session state, and tracing. ASP.NET application configuration settings are inherited hierarchically. At the top of the hierarchy is the machine.config file, which is installed with the .NET framework and located in the %windir%\Microsoft.NET\Framework\Version\CONFIG directory. All ASP.NET applications inherit from the configuration settings made in this file. These settings can be overridden by any changes that you make in Web.Config files throughout the virtual directories of your application.

This hierarchical inheritance allows us to adjust application settings throughout various virtual directories in our application, but still maintain a base configuration file in the root directory of our application. All of the configuration information in the Web.Config file resides between the <configuration> and </configuration> tags. Inside these tags settings are defined with configuration sections. There are many preconfigured sections provided with ASP.NET, such as <appsettings>, <authentication>, and <compilation>. We won't reproduce a full list of all of the available sections here, but you can easily find the list in the MSDN library.

The <appsettings> section is used for adding application-specific settings such as a database connection string. We can add name-value pairs to this section of the configuration file and access these within our code at runtime. Let's look at an example of adding a database connection string to the <appsettings> section:

```
<appSettings>
  <add key="dsn" value="Data Source=(local)\NetSDK;
    Initial Catalog=Northwind;User ID=sa;pwd=;" />
</appSettings>
```

To access this setting from within our code, we use the System.Configuration.ConfigurationSettings class. This class has a property called *AppSettings*, which is a collection of the name-value pairs that we specified in our Web.Config file. We could retrieve the dsn value that we specified previously with this code:

```
String dsn =
System.Configuration.ConfigurationSettings.AppSettings["dsn"]
```

As an example of the hierarchical nature of the Web.Config files let's assume that we have included the dsn value in the <appsettings> section of the Web.Config file located in the root virtual directory of our application. The default security setting specified in the machine.config file allows all users to have access to an application. Let's assume that in our virtual root directory Web.Config file, we have not specified any other security settings, which means that we will inherit the value from the machine.config file and allow all users access to our application.

We now add a virtual directory called Secure under our root virtual directory, so our directory structure looks like this:

```
Application Root
    -> Secure
```

We then install a Web.Config file in the Secure directory and specify security settings that disallow all users other than administrators. The result is that any resources located in the root directory are accessible by all users and as programmers we can access the dsn setting that we specified in the root Web.Config file. Any resources in the Secure virtual directory are accessible only by administrators; however, we can still access the dsn setting specified in the root Web.Config file. This is a good thing. We have to specify only our dsn in the root Web.Config file, and we can still access it from any virtual directory located under the root directory. We still have the freedom to specify different application settings in our subordinate virtual directories, such as different security rights.

We didn't cover exactly how to specify security settings here, but we will cover that in detail in Chapter 8, "Security and Membership." We will also be covering several other sections of the Web.Config file throughout the remainder of the book.

The Global.asax file

The global.asax file is an important part of all ASP.NET applications. Similar to and compatible with the Global.asa file in classic ASP, the Global.asax is an optional file that allows you to write code pertaining to the HttpApplication object, which represents the entire ASP.NET application with which you are working.

To use the Global.asax file, it must be resident in the root directory of the IIS application of your project. Visual Studio .NET creates a stub file for you with all of the major application event handlers. It is compiled and turned into an object derived from the HttpApplication class that represents an ASP.NET application.

One important fact about this file is that if it changes, .NET recompiles it automatically, and it will rerun the next time a client hits the server. This ensures that your application is in sync with any changes made to the file, which is important especially if this file has application configuration code in it. This works only if you are not using a code-behind file. If you do use code-behind classes in the Visual Studio .NET projects, changes to the Global.asax.cs file are not tracked by the server and must be recompiled manually.

Here is the class declaration inside Global.asax:

```
public class Global : System.Web.HttpApplication
{
  protected void Application_Start(Object sender, EventArgs e)
  {
  }
```

```
    protected void Session_Start(Object sender, EventArgs e)
    {
    }
    protected void Application_BeginRequest(Object sender, EventArgs e)
    {
    }
    protected void Application_EndRequest(Object sender, EventArgs e)
    {
    }
    protected void Session_End(Object sender, EventArgs e)
    {
    }
    protected void Application_End(Object sender, EventArgs e)
    {
    }
}
```

Let's go through each of these functions in more detail. We'll start with the application events.

Application_Start

The Application_Start event is fired the first time any client requests a page from the server application. This is, of course, only the application you are working on, which consists of all pages existing in the virtual directory on the server. Remember that this has nothing to do with any other applications or pages served from different locations on the Web server.

You could use this event to load global variable (application variables) so that all code throughout the application has fast access to certain data. For example, if you need some values read from the registry and used in your Web code somewhere, it might be a good idea to read them at the start of the application and cache them in memory instead of reading the registry every time the code needs the information. This would be even more applicable if you have a requirement to read from hard storage, which can be much slower than reading from the registry and would not scale well if the code had to do it often or for many users. This event works only with data that is static throughout the typical life of the application. If the data needs to be refreshed daily, you could put IIS on a periodical reset schedule, which would force this event to occur at the first user request after the restart. (There are better methods of refreshing data on a daily basis, and they are discussed in Chapter 10.) When using this technique, remember to force a restart of the application after you make a change to data that is cached in this event, as in a registry change, by running a net stop followed by a net start at a command prompt, or simply running iisreset. Also notice that each time you compile your project in Visual Studio .NET, the application is restarted, so the first request for a page after a compile will fire this event.

NOTE It is important to remember that running iisreset will stop and start the Web service. This will stop and start all running Web applications as well. If your Web server is running applications that make use of inproc session state, restarting the server will terminate all of the current sessions.

Let's create an example in which we use some of the .NET file access objects to write the output to disk so we can see some of these events in action. Why don't we write to a browser? Because a browser is more related to the session rather than to the application. For this example, we want to look at an application event. In fact, there isn't even a request or response object available in this context to write to, so we'll just write the output to a file as HTML so the output file can be opened in a browser. We can then refresh the page to see the changes, instead of having to keep reopening a text file. We didn't write to the event log that we used in our previous code because the Windows Event Viewer applet doesn't support showing all of the event messages in one window; you must open another dialog and view each event one at a time. Listing 5.1 shows us the example code.

```
namespace Ch03
{
    using System;
    using System.Collections;
    using System.ComponentModel;
    using System.Web;
    using System.Web.SessionState;
    using System.IO;

    /// <summary>
    ///             Summary description for Global.
    /// </summary>
    public class Global : System.Web.HttpApplication
    {
        public void WriteEventToFile(string message)
        {
            //Simply open and write a file as a stream writer object.
            string filename = "c:\\appevents.htm";
            StreamWriter sw = new StreamWriter(filename, true);
            sw.WriteLine(string.Format("{0} at {1:hh:mm:ss:ms}<br>",
                message,
                DateTime.Now));
            sw.Close();
        }

        protected void Application_Start(Object sender, EventArgs e)
        {
            WriteEventToFile("Application_Start event fired");
        }

        protected void Session_Start(Object sender, EventArgs e)
        {
        }

        protected void Application_BeginRequest(Object sender, EventArgs
e)
```

Listing 5.1   Application events in Global.asax

```
        {
        }

        protected void Application_EndRequest(Object sender, EventArgs e)
        {
        }

        protected void Session_End(Object sender, EventArgs e)
        {
        }

        protected void Application_End(Object sender, EventArgs e)
        {
        }
    }
}
```

Listing 5.1   Application events in Global.asax (continued)

The stub event handlers are automatically inserted by Visual Studio .NET. Now when you compile the application, you will get the start event when you first request a page. You can request any page; we requested one from a previous example in the Ch03 application. Figure 5.4 shows the file we wrote displayed in the browser as soon as the page was received.

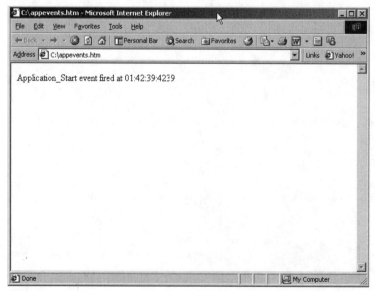

Figure 5.4   Application_Start event.

There are some things you cannot do in the Application_Start event, like access some Web-related objects. For example, there is no session object at this point, so if you try to access it, you will fire an exception that tells you that the object is not available in this context. There are other events that should happen soon after, in which you can use the session object. Most other objects in the framework outside of those in the System.Web namespace are available, however.

Application_BeginRequest

The Application_BeginRequest event fires every time a client requests a page. This is a great feature to expose in ASP.NET because it allows you to write code based on each and every page request. There was no way to do this in classic ASP; similar functionality might have been implemented in an ISAPI extension, for example.

One use for this event would be a page request counter. For example, you could set up a database stored procedure that atomically increments a counter for the number of times pages are requested. In the Application_BeginRequest event, you could call this procedure for every request. Another example would be to store the hit count for each page in the application, then display the most requested pages by querying each page's request count. Another example would be to reroute each request to a certain page by calling RequestRewritePath, which would force the request to go to a programmatically defined path.

Application_EndRequest

The Application_EndRequest event fires at the end of each request. This event is always listed immediately after Application_BeginRequest. In fact, on our Pentium PII 500 MHz machine, if there is no processing in these events, it is usually less than a millisecond between them.

Application_End

Whenever an application is shut down completely, the Application_End event is fired. This could occur when all the sessions have timed out, the Web project is recompiled in Visual Studio .NET, or the Global.asax file is modified when it is script based (not code-behind based). Remember, stopping the Web site doesn't stop the application and call this event. Doing so merely stops the Web server from *responding* to requests. Even removing the application from the Internet Service Manager snap-in will not kill the application. To truly cause this event to fire, reset the server via running an iisreset at a command prompt.

We will go more into depth on some of the advanced aspects of the HttpApplication object later in this chapter, such as session management and user information.

Session Management and Variable Scope

In Web applications, the server sees each request as a single, connectionless client request. Unlike a client/server-based application, the server does not distinguish multiple pages requested by a single client as related to one another in any way. Of course, we already know this because we have been dealing with the connectionless HTTP protocol for years and finding ways to make believe that the server knows each client distinctly and knows that multiple requests from the same client are actually one user session. There are several techniques for doing this in ASP. NET applications, including Session events, Session variables, and State variables. You could implement a way to relate multiple requests as one session yourself, by using cookies, for example. But ASP.NET uses cookies to support Sessions already, so why not use this built-in feature?

Session Events

There are two Session-related events that occur during the lifetime of a session: Session_Start and Session_End. These are both part of the HttpApplication class, and thus they are implemented in the Global.asax file of your Web application.

The Session_Start event can be used for any initialization pertaining to each user. For example, if your code depends on a unique number for each user other than the session ID, you could create it here and store it in a session variable for future use. Or, you could use this time to take a time stamp of the time the user first logged on. One of the most common things to do here is to set up a hit counter to keep track of every user session ever created.

The other event related to sessions is the Session_End event, which fires when the session times out. This event doesn't fire when a user leaves the site or closes the browser, but after the timeout period set in the Web.Config file has elapsed. Don't rely on it too much; it has long been rumored that this event is unreliable. Until this is acknowledged to be either true or false by Microsoft, we recommend using this event sparingly and not for important tasks.

Because sessions are stored in memory on the server by default, if you are running a Web app behind a load-balanced or clustered server farm, a user must always hit the same server for every request, to make sure the session is available in the pages. To do this, most load-balancing redirectors on the market support sticky sessions, where all requests from a specific user are always routed to the same server, thus solving this potential dilemma.

Session Variables

Session variables are a means to store data across multiple page requests. This is similar to using a global variable across all of the windows in a traditional client/server-based application. For example, let's say that a user makes the first page request in an application and is required to enter his or her name into a Web Form. The next page the user visits may need to know his or her name also, but the server doesn't relate the two requests in any way. So, the user's name could be stored in the Session variable to be accessed on any page in the application. When ASP. NET creates a session for a user, on the first page request, a unique number called the Session ID is generated via a complex algorithm and stored in a special cookie on the user's browser. The next time the user requests a page in the same application, ASP.NET looks for that cookie, gets the Session ID, and uses it to look up the session object for that user. In this session object can be stored variables, declarable and settable entirely at runtime. The server has an in-memory data structure that holds all of the session variables your code sets for an individual user, and this gives the notion of a connected session to the otherwise connectionless HTTP protocol.

How do you set the variable in the session? First, sessions have to be enabled by having the sessionState section set up properly in the applications Web.Config file. Here is a snippet of the file, showing the sessionState section:

```
<sessionState
  mode="InProc"
  stateConnectionString="tcpip=127.0.0.1:42424"
  sqlConnectionString="data source=127.0.0.1;user id=sa;password="
  cookieless="false"
  timeout="20"
/>
```

The code shown is the default code for ASP.NET applications created in Visual Studio .NET. The mode=InProc line make the session storage live inside the memory of the Web server. If you have the standard versions of ASP.NET, this is the option you will likely use. The premium versions of ASP.NET support storing session variables in a separate application or in SQL Server. Those options are more of a configuration issue rather than a programming issue, and they are outside the scope of the book. The cookieless=false option means that the session management uses HTTP cookies to store a key with which to locate a user's session variables. This is the default, and when used, requires that all of your visitors have browsers that allow cookies. The timeout variable states that sessions will cease to exist after the user has not requested a page in the allotted time. By default, this is set to 20 minutes.

All that is needed to store a variable in the session state, once the previous configuration entries are in place, is code along these lines:

```
Session["username"] = "jsmiley";
```

or

```
Session.Add("username", "jsmiley");
```

It's that simple; the variable is stored on the server and related to the Session ID stored on the user's browser. The difference between the two lines of code is purely programmer preference, as they both do the same thing. Now throughout every page in the application, the username can be retrieved with code like this:

```
String uname = (string)S.ession["username"];
```

It is important to note that session variables are stored in memory on the server, and not on disk. This means, of course, that if the server dies for any reason, this state information is lost completely. Likewise, if the user lets the session expire by waiting past the timeout time before requesting a page, the session will be deleted. This behavior is by design because if a user is using a public Internet PC, say in a library, for example, and he or she forgets to log off, we don't want the next user to be able to access his or her banking data because the session is still "connected." It is also interesting to note that as long as the server remains running, even if a session is ended because a user timed out or left the application, the same Session ID will be used if the user starts a new session by requesting a page again. This saves the server the extra work of creating a new Session ID and setting a cookie when one already exists for a user.

In the next example, we have two pages, one that asks the user for his or her name and another that displays it back. The name entered is stored in a Session variable across the two page requests.

```
<%@ Page language="c#" Codebehind="SessionVariableSet.aspx.cs"
AutoEventWireup="false" Inherits="Chapter5.SessionVariables" %>

<HTML>
  <HEAD>
    <meta name="GENERATOR" Content="Microsoft Visual Studio 7.0">
    <meta name="CODE_LANGUAGE" Content="C#">
  </HEAD>
  <body>
    <form method="post" runat="server">
      <P>
        Enter your name in the field, then click Go.
      </P>
      <P>
        <asp:TextBox id=TextBox1 runat="server">
        </asp:TextBox>
        <asp:Button id=Button1 runat="server" Text="Go">
        </asp:Button>
      </P>
    </form>
  </body>
</HTML>
protected void Button1_Click(object sender, System.EventArgs e)
{
   //Set the session var and go to next page.
   Session["name"] = TextBox1.Text;

   //Create an object and store in session state.
   MyPerson person = new MyPerson(TextBox1.Text, "", "", "");
   Session["person"] = person;

   Response.Redirect("SessionVariableRead.aspx");
}
```

For the code-behind class, we showed only the Button1 click handler. In the code, we set two Session variables, one to store merely the name as a string and one to hold a MyPerson object reference created with the name entered. The reason for this is to show you that Session variables can be of any type. For the page that retrieves the Session variables, we show you only the Page_Load method from the code-behind file. No UI elements are used because the content is generated by Response.Write calls.

```
protected void Page_Load(object sender, System.EventArgs e)
{
  //Read the session var and display it.
  string name = (string)Session["name"];
  Response.Write("You entered: " + name + "<br>");

  //Read the object from session and display the name.
  MyPerson person = (MyPerson)Session["person"];
  Response.Write("From person object: " + person.FirstName);
}
```

Using Session state can go a long way toward making robust Web applications, but be aware of its limitations. Take care not to store things in Session state that are overly large or use valuable resources like database connections. If you have a large object that needs to be accessed across multiple pages, consider storing just enough information in Session state to allow you create an instance of this type of object at will. This will allow you to let the object go out of scope on one page and then be re-created on the next page from information stored in Session state. Although your application incurs the cost of cleaning up and re-creating an object multiple times, in some cases this may be better than holding many large objects in memory on the server. This is a design technique that's well documented and can be put to good use in Web applications, if deemed best for overall performance and stability. See Figures 5.5 and 5.6 to see these samples in action.

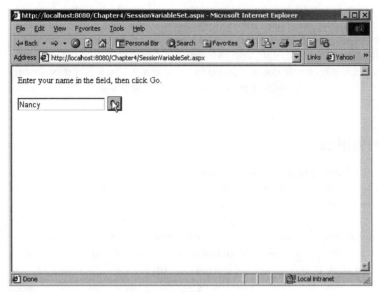

Figure 5.5 Setting a Session variable.

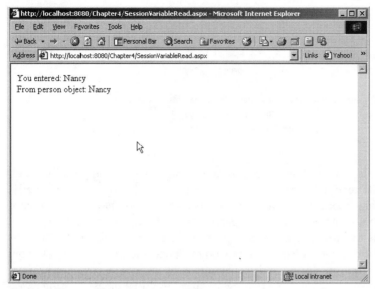

Figure 5.6 Reading a Session variable.

Although we didn't show it in our code for simplicity's sake, the retrieval of a variable from Session state should be wrapped in a try...catch block to make sure the variable exists. To remove a variable from Session state, simply call Session.Remove, Session.RemoveAt, or Session.RemoveAll. These methods are self-explanatory and will remove a single variable by its name or index or will remove all variables. Session.Clear removes all variables as well. In addition, you can completely abandon your session by calling Session.Abandon, which will cause the server to clear any Session state variable and end the session. This may take some time because the server doesn't attempt to do this until it is idle.

ViewState Variables

There is another type of variable that you can store across page requests called View State variables. These are stored in the browser, but not as cookies. The data you store in these variables is not kept on the server and has nothing to do with sessions. Instead, it uses the built-in ViewState mechanism of ASP.NET to store string type data in the hidden View state variable on the browser. The server sends this special variable to the browser with each and every page (unless is turned off). It stores information and variables about the current state of objects on the browser, so they can be preserved across the page requests and properly re-created on the next visit to the server, with no user code needed. You can set your own variables to be stored in this composite variable, to be accessed in another page's code. This is very much like the technique popular in classic ASP where a variable was stored in programmer-defined hidden input controls when sent to the server. To set a variable in this fashion in the ViewState object, use something along these lines:

```
ViewState["uname"] = "Rebecca";
```

And to retrieve it, use something like this:

```
String suname = (string)ViewState["uname"];
```

This is very similar in syntax to using session variables. There is one major difference, however. Unlike Session variables that can hold virtually any type of data including object references, the ViewState can hold only string data. This means that, of course, you can store things like strings and numbers, but to store an object, it must inherit from the ISerializable interface and thus must support its own serialization. In fact, when you try to store an object in the ViewState, if it cannot be serialized (which ASP.NET attempts automatically) an exception is thrown. When you have a case of needing a nonserializable object across multiple pages, you can employ the tactics described in the Session variables section and store only enough simple data to allow re-creation of the desired object. Note that it is very common to store strings and numbers in ViewState, both of which are serializable. Again, because this functionality is quite simple, it needs no example code and is best left up to your own experimentation.

Application Variables

Application variables are those that are stored on the server and available to all code in an entire ASP.NET application. This is analogous to a global variable, but used across multiple clients, instead of multiple code modules or windows. For example, an application may need a piece of data stored in the registry. It may make sense to read the registry only at the start of the application and have it available to all code without having to access the registry each time. This variable can hold any type of data, just like a Session variable, and it is subject to the same caveats. Don't store too many large objects or resource-intensive ones in these variables because they exist on the server for the life of the application. Notice, though, that these rules are not always as important for Application variables as Session variables because there are many more sessions than applications usually. To set an application variable use code like this:

```
Application["dsn"] = ReadDsnFromReg();
```

And to retrieve, use code like this:

```
sting dsn = (string)Application["dsn"];
```

Page Subclassing

All ASP.NET, applications are object oriented due to the fact that they are .NET Framework applications that run within the CLR.

In this section, we will not attempt to describe all of the virtues of deriving one object from another; that is left up to the readers and their object-oriented design books. I will, however, describe the hugely useful design method of deriving an

ASP.NET page from a base class page that supports a set of functionality that could be used by most or all of the pages in an application.

The example page class we will use in this section is only the beginning of the page class that will be extended and used throughout the Wiley Web Parts application that we build in this book. Although it includes some real-world features, it is only a sample of how to implement page subclassing in ASP.NET.

Normally, when you create an ASP.NET page with Visual Studio .NET, the page class will be created for you based on the filename you give the page. This page class is derived from the System.Web.UI.Page class by default. This is much like using VC++ to create windows in MFC applications; the MFC AppWizard will create a stub class based on the class name chosen and derived from a base window class that is part of the Microsoft Foundation Class. In this stub class, you would implement the custom behavior, which gives your window its functionality. The same applies in ASP.NET. While this is a common and effective way to start your page, most Web applications consist of multiple pages, and it is good design practice to share commonly used code by means of a common base class.

You can derive your own page class using Visual Studio .NET in two steps. First, make the base class, which needs to be derived at some level from the System.Web.UI.Page class. Then, simply change the class declaration of your page to be derived from your new base class, instead of the default System.Web.UI.Page that Visual Studio .NET supplied. One thing to note is that with other object frameworks, many base classes require you to pass in parameters or are derived from multiple classes. In .NET, using custom base classes is easier because the framework designers have minimized the use of constructors on classes that are likely to be subclassed a lot. This makes it easier to write our own subclasses because we won't have to implement any extra constructors.

As you create ASP.NET applications, you may find that many of them have common functionality. This could be because of your company's unique business model or because there is a consistency requirement for all applications across the entire organization. For example, an application we recently completed needed to track everything the user typed into the search fields on an e-commerce site in order to determine which topics were searched for most frequently and the most common spellings. We used a base page class to add functionality to every page that allowed user inputs to be logged to the database.

Let's take a look at an example. First, we will add functionality that will read and write cookie values on the client browser, which is commonly used in Web apps. In addition, we will add some base class functionality that will write entries to the Event Log. Note that at this point in the samples, we are not using robust error handling for simplicity's sake.

Using the same cookie functionality we described earlier in this chapter, we made one change: We overloaded the WriteCookie function to handle Session and Persistent Cookies. Other than that, it is the same code.

As for the event logging, we create an event source for the current page and write the log message. We used this.ToString() for the source name. This has the added benefit of allowing us to see which page the event came from in the Windows event viewer application. You could also use this in an object model so that you could see at a glance what object was causing the events. Using ToString() shows the full type name of the class with its namespace, which is ASP.PageSubclass_aspx, instead of the actual page name of PageSubclass.aspx, but it still tells us where in the application the event came from. When an Event Source is created, access to the Windows registry is required. By default, an ASP.NET application does not have access to the registry.

ASP.NET applications are set to run under a Windows user account called ASPNET, which is only a member of the Users security group. To allow an ASP.NET application to have access to the registry, make the ASPNET user a member of the Administrators group. The code for the base class is shown in Listing 5.2.

```
using System;
using System.Web;
using System.Diagnostics;

/// <summary>
///          Summary description for PageBase.
/// </summary>
public class PageBase: System.Web.UI.Page
{
    public PageBase ()
    {
    }

    protected void WriteEventLogEntry(string sMessage,
        EventLogEntryType type)
    {
        // Create the source if it does not already exist.
        if (!EventLog.SourceExists(this.ToString()))
        {
            EventLog.CreateEventSource(this.ToString(), "Wiley");
        }

        //Create an EventLog and set the source.
        EventLog log = new EventLog();
        log.Source = this.ToString();

        //Write the message to the event log.
        log.WriteEntry(sMessage);
    }

    protected void WriteCookie(string cookiename,
        string key, string val)
    {
        //Create or open the cookie and set its value.
        HttpCookie cookie = new HttpCookie(cookiename);
          cookie.Values.Add(key, val);
        Response.Cookies.Add(cookie);
    }

    protected void WriteCookie(string cookiename,
        string key, string val, DateTime expires)
    {
        //Create or open the cookie and set its value.
        HttpCookie cookie = new HttpCookie(cookiename);
        cookie.Expires = expires;
```

Listing 5.2   A base class for ASP.NET pages

```
            cookie.Values.Add(key, val);
            Response.Cookies.Add(cookie);
        }

        protected string ReadCookie(string cookiename, string key)
        {
            //Try to open the cookie we want.
            HttpCookie cookie = Request.Cookies[cookiename];
            if (cookie == null)
            {
                //The cookie was not found, so return blank.
                return "";
            }
            else
            {
                //The cookie was found, so read the key desired.
                return cookie.Values[key].ToString();
            }
        }
    }
}
```

Listing 5.2   A base class for ASP.NET pages (continued)

Notice the line using System.Diagnostics at the top of the code. This is the namespace in which the EventLog object lives. Because the Windows event viewer applet doesn't provide a way to delete the event log, the log will remain on the computer after the application is gone. Calling EventLog.Delete will delete the log. Remember to call EventLog.DeleteEventSource first, so subsequent calls to check for existence of this source will fail and force the source and log to be created again (at least in the code we are using here).

The code for a sample class that derives from this base class is shown in Listing 5.3.

```
namespace Ch05
{
    using System;
    using System.Collections;
    using System.ComponentModel;
    using System.Data;
    using System.Drawing;
    using System.Web;
    using System.Web.SessionState;
    using System.Web.UI;
    using System.Web.UI.WebControls;
    using System.Web.UI.HtmlControls;

    /// <summary>
```

Listing 5.3   A page deriving from a custom base class

```
///                    Summary description for example10.
/// </summary>
public class PageSubclass : PageBase
{
    public PageSubclass()
    {
        Page.Init += new System.EventHandler(Page_Init);
    }

    protected void Page_Load(object sender, System.EventArgs e)
    {
        //Use event logging functionality from the base class.
        WriteEventLogEntry("Page_Load in example10.aspx",
            System.Diagnostics.EventLogEntryType.Information);
    }

    protected void Page_Init(object sender, EventArgs e)
    {
        InitializeComponent();
    }

    private void InitializeComponent()
    {
        this.Load += new System.EventHandler(this.Page_Load);
    }
}
}
```

Listing 5.3   A page deriving from a custom base class (continued)

Notice that the main page class is derived from the base class and that we are able to call the protected function from it with no special code other than a simple call. This is standard object-oriented fare, and it is an intrinsic part of C#. We will build on this example throughout the book to add more features to the base class.

User Controls

User controls provide the ability to reuse user interface code across multiple pages. They provide a simple way to combine multiple Web or HTML server controls into a reusable Web Form element that can be placed on multiple pages. Navigational or menu bars that are used consistently throughout a Web application are prime candidates to be converted to a user control. Prior to ASP.NET this sort of code reuse would have been done through the use of server-side includes, which simply allowed you to include the code from another file at the point that you declare the include directive. User controls provide more functionality than this, however. Once a user control has been added to a Web Form, its properties and methods can be accessed and programmed against just like HTML or Web Server Controls.

User controls are created very similarly to Web Forms. They can be created with or without the code-behind method. Of course, code-behind is still the recommended way to go; however, the code-behind class for a user control inherits from System.Web.UI.UserContol rather than System.Web.UI.Page as for Web Forms. User-Control indirectly inherits from System.Web.UI.Control just as the Page class and therefore has the same base properties and events as the Page class. A user control can support all of the same UI elements as a Web Form, including the HTML and Web Server Controls. The major difference between a Web Form and a user control is that user controls cannot be requested directly. They can be used only inside the context of a Web Form. In addition, user controls should not contain <html>, <body>, or <form> elements as these will already exist on the page in which the user control is added. Most importantly, your user control should not declare <form> elements. One other important difference between a user control and Web Form is that of naming convention. As opposed to having a .aspx file extension like a Web Form, user controls should have a .ascx file extension.

Let's work up a fairly simply example of a user control. In Visual Studio .NET, create a new Web user control item called NavBar.ascx. By default, Visual Studio .NET will create an .ascx file and an accompanying code-behind C# file for you. If you examine the .ascx file that was created, you will see a Control directive like this:

```
<%@ Control Language="c#" AutoEventWireup="false"
    Codebehind="NavBar.ascx.cs" Inherits="Chapter5.NavBar"%>
```

This is in place of a Page directive, which you use for a Web Form. The valid attributes for the Control directive are a subset of the attributes available for the Page directive. Now let's add the following to the page:

```
<asp:Label id=lblMessage runat="server" />
<p></p>
<asp:Button id=btnPageOne runat="server" Text="Page One" />
  
<asp:Button id=btnPageTwo runat="server" Text="Page Two" />
```

We've added one Label control, which will display a message that states which page the user is currently viewing. The two Button controls will link between two pages called PageOne.aspx and PageTwo.aspx, which we'll be creating shortly. In the code-behind file, be sure to declare member variables for all three controls like this:

```
protected System.Web.UI.WebControls.Label lblMessage;
public System.Web.UI.WebControls.Button btnPageOne;
public System.Web.UI.WebControls.Button btnPageTwo;
```

Note the use of the *public* access modifier on the two Button controls. We will be accessing these two controls from the pages on which we include the navbar user control, so the public access is necessary. Add the following line of code to the Page_Load method.

```
lblMessage.Text = "Current Page is <b>" + Request.Path + "</b>";
```

This will simply set the text of the lblMessage Label control to tell us which page we are currently viewing. This isn't all that useful, but at this point we just want to demonstrate that the events inherited from the Control class are still available to us in a user control.

Last, we need to handle the Click event for each of the two Button controls like the following:

```
private void btnPageOne_Click(object sender, System.EventArgs e)
{
  Response.Redirect("PageOne.aspx");
}
private void btnPageTwo_Click(object sender, System.EventArgs e)
{
  Response.Redirect("PageTwo.aspx");
}
```

That's all the functionality we're going to add to the NavBar at this point. Now we need to create a couple of pages on which we can use the NavBar control. Create two new Web Forms called PageOne.aspx and PageTwo.aspx. To enable us to declare our NavBar in an .aspx file we first add an @Register directive to the .aspx file. Add the following directive to the top of PageOne.aspx and PageTwo.aspx.

```
<%@ Register TagPrefix="Chapter5" TagName="NavBar" Src="./NavBar.ascx"
%>
```

The *TagPrefix* attribute is used to declare an alias for the namespace in which the control is located. Here it is set to Chapter5, which happens to be the namespace name. This would become much more useful if we had a really long namespace name. The *TagName* property is set to NavBar and is the value that will be used to refer to this control when we declare it for use in the page. The *Src* attribute must be set to either the absolute or relative location of the user control .ascx file. Now we can declare an instance of the NavBar control inside the <form> tags of both PageOne.aspx and PageTwo.aspx like this:

```
<Chapter5:NavBar id=NavBar1 runat="server" />
```

Notice that Chapter5:NavBar reflects the choices that we made for the TagPrefix and TagName attributes of the Register directive. We've assigned an ID to the control of NavBar1 and set the runat attribute, just as we would for an HTML or Web Server Control. Now to demonstrate how easy it is for us to access properties or elements of the user control from a Web Form, we'll add a bit of code that will disable the button that provides the link to the current page. In the code-behind files for PageOne and PageTwo, add the following member declaration.

```
protected NavBar NavBar1;
```

Now we can access our NavBar control, NavBar1, and manipulate or call any accessible properties or methods. In the Page_Load method of the PageOne Web Form, add the following code.

```
NavBar1.btnPageOne.Enabled = false;
```

And in the Page_Load method of the PageTwo Web Form, add this code.

```
NavBar1.btnPageTwo.Enabled = false;
```

Compile the project and navigate to the page. Experiment by clicking on the buttons. You should see that the message at the top of the screen should always state which page we are currently viewing, which is done by the NavBar control itself in the Page_Load method. In addition, if you are viewing PageOne.aspx the Page One button is disabled, and when you are viewing PageTwo.aspx the Page Two button is disabled. The buttons are part of the NavBar control, but we were able to successfully manipulate the state of the buttons from the Web Form page in which the control was added. A screen shot of what this should look like can be seen in Figure 5.7.

User control properties can be set declaratively at design time as well as at runtime. This is done by setting the desired user control properties within the declarative tag via the use of name-value attribute pairs. For an example of this, let's add a property to our NavBar user control that will set the text of the message. In the code-behind file for the NavBar, add the following code.

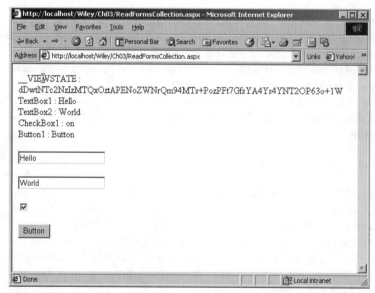

Figure 5.7   The NavBar control.

```
public string Message
{
  get { return lblMessage.Text; }
  set { lblMessage.Text = value; }
}
```

In addition, remove any code that is in the Page_Load method for the NavBar. Now that we have a public property on the NavBar control, we can set it at design time from PageOne.aspx and PageTwo.aspx. Change the declaration of the NavBar control in the PageOne.aspx file as follows:

```
<Chapter5:NavBar id=NavBar1 runat="server" Message="This is Page One"/>
```

Likewise, change the declaration in the PageTwo.aspx file to this:

```
<Chapter5:NavBar id=NavBar1 runat="server" Message="This is Page Two"/>
```

If you view the page in your browser now, you'll see that the text of the message was set successfully.

More Advanced Data Binding

In Chapters 3 and 4, we discussed Data Binding, which is ASP.NETs built-in way to display data in the controls on our pages. There are a few controls that need more explanation when on the subject of Data Binding because they are much more robust than some of the simpler controls we learned about. These controls are the DataGrid, the DataList, and the Repeater.

DataGrid

We looked at the DataGrid in Chapter 3 to some extent. We didn't go into all of its features, though, because to do so properly requires more robust data than we created in that section of the book. Now that we've learned how to pull data from a real database, let's revisit the DataGrid and look into some of its more powerful features.

Paging

Because the DataGrid is rendered as an HTML table, there is no client-side support for scrolling through rows or otherwise seeing only a portion of the rows at one time. While it is true that you could put a DataGrid inside a span whose overflow style is set to scroll, this is good only for fixing the vertical size of a grid holding a small number of rows. Besides, we want to do things on the server whenever possible, to maintain better support for a wide variety of browsers. So what do we do when we want to see only a portion of the rows in a set of data? We can either custom code our pages to load only the data currently needed, or we can use the DataGrid's robust paging features.

Paging in the DataGrid means just what you would expect, that no matter how many rows of data are in the data source, we are going to show only a fixed number of rows per page, with navigation facilities to move through the data when needed. To do this, the DataGrid supports both automatic paging and custom paging.

Automatic Paging

To set up your DataGrid to automatically page through the data source, we simply set the AllowPaging property to true and the PageSize to the number of rows we want to see on each page. When the table is rendered, it will have a new row added to the bottom (or top) called the pager. The pager row is created just like any other row, and it has the type defined in the ListItemType enum as Pager. This will be useful later when we handle events each time a new row is created when the DataGrid is being generated. But for now, what we really care about is that the pager is a row that displays LinkButton links that allow the user to traverse forward and backward, as well as to each page in the data. These are created for you automatically by ASP.NET, but they can be customized, which we will look at later.

When an auto-paging DataGrid is bound, it determines which rows to display based on which link the user clicked or the first page when the page is first loaded. All you have to do to make this work is handle the PageIndexChanged event of the DataGrid, set the CurrentPageIndex property, and rebind to the data. The CurrentPageIndex property can be set from the event arguments, which exposed the NewpageIndex property. As you have probably figured out by now, the full data is bound to the grid, but only some rows are shown when it is rendered. Although only the visible data is actually sent to the browser, it's clearly not the most desirable behavior to have the grid read all of the data in the first place. When the binding first occurs, the DataGrid calculates how many pages there are by the total amount of items in the data source divided by the PageSize properties value. When the current page needs to be shown, the DataGrid indexes into the data source for the correct items. For this reason, the object used as the data source must inherit from the ICollection interface, which supports indexing its items. Note that attempting to use automatic paging when binding to a non-ICollection-derived object results in an error. For those times, as well as when we don't want to read a whole data set when showing just one page, we must resort to custom paging. Here is an example snippet of paging from an ArrayList data source. The DataGrid is simple, as is the code. In many cases, the code would be bound to a set of data from a database.

```
protected void Page_Load(object sender, System.EventArgs e)
{
  if (!IsPostBack)
  {
    LoadData();
    DataGrid1.DataBind();
  }
}

protected void LoadData()
{
  ArrayList arr = new ArrayList();
```

```
    arr.Add(new MyPerson("Hank", "Meyne", "594-66-8745", "124598"));
    arr.Add(new MyPerson("James", "Jones", "595-36-4887", "136598"));
    arr.Add(new MyPerson("Tim", "Smith", "569-87-1584", "915184"));
    arr.Add(new MyPerson("St. John", "Smythe", "595-84-8745", "435689"));
    arr.Add(new MyPerson("Robin", "Fisher", "594-48-7485", "030518"));
    arr.Add(new MyPerson("Linda", "Blake", "595-63-5412", "865375"));
    arr.Add(new MyPerson("Robert", "Thomas", "569-81-2259", "738642"));
    arr.Add(new MyPerson("Alex", "Smythe", "595-14-5441", "916284"));
    arr.Add(new MyPerson("Ray", "Stewart", "593-68-7714", "976431"));
    DataGrid1.DataSource = arr;
}

protected void DataGrid1_PageIndexChanged(object source,
    System.Web.UI.WebControls.DataGridPageChangedEventArgs e)
{
    DataGrid1.CurrentPageIndex = e.NewPageIndex;
    LoadData();
    DataGrid1.DataBind();
}
```

And the aspx code for the DataGrid is:

```
<asp:DataGrid
    id="DataGrid1"
    runat="server"
    PageSize="3"
    AllowPaging="True">
</asp:DataGrid>
```

Figure 5.8 shows this code running, and in Figure 5.9 we see the same DataGrid except with numbered pages.

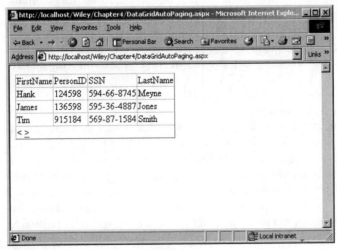

Figure 5.8   Automatic paging.

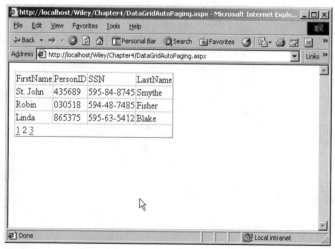

Figure 5.9 Automatic paging with page numbers.

Notice that we rebind the grid each time we handle a PageIndexChanged event. In this case, we could have simply bound to the data on every page load, regardless of the IsPostBack state. But, we want to keep postbacks in mind in case we are loading the page for a reason other than a PageIndexChanged on the grid. For example, if there were a button on the page that has a server-side click handler, we may not need to waste time rebinding the grid if its page index isn't changing.

Custom Paging

Deploying a data-paging page, as in the previous example, is great for simple displays of data where the total amount of rows is relatively small. This would not, however, be a good solution in cases where the superset of the data is large because with automatic paging, all of the data is retrieved each time the grid is bound; the grid just displays the data for the current page. What if there were a half million rows of data? Obviously, the automatic paging mechanism would perform dismally in this case. To solve this kind of problem, we can use custom paging to get only the data we need for the current page.

When using custom paging, what we are really doing is using the DataGrid to display data from a data source, but also to provide feedback events to tell us which page the user wants to see. The DataGrid itself is not performing any logic to filter the data in any way; we must handle this with our code. The event that is important to us in this case is again the PageIndexChanged event. In this event, we are informed of which page in the data the user wishes to see by the NewPageIndex property of the events argument. If, for example, the property is 4, which tells us that we need to get the fourth page of data from the real data source and bind the grid to this subset. This would usually mean calling a stored procedure or SQL statement specially written to return just those rows. To enable custom paging, we set the DataGrid's AllowCustom-Paging and AllowPaging properties to true. Also, we must set the VirtualItemCount property to the maximum number of rows in the entire data set. This is needed by the DataGrid so that it will know how many pages there are, and thus how many times the user can click next or previous. Setting this property should be done at the beginning of the user's experience on this Web page so the grid will always show the correct amount of page links, or next and previous links. As well, this might be a good place to show the user how many rows are available in total.

For the following example, we use a class-scoped array of strings to represent the total set. This would be analogous to an entire table in a database in a real application. When the user asks for a certain page of the data, we are notified by an event, and we can build our data set to which to bind. In this case, we are just loading a small portion of the total data by adding two strings at a time into an ArrayList from the string array.

```
//Sample data
private string[] m_data = new string[10]
  {"Hank", "Stacy", "Millie", "Sam", "Molly",
 "Toby", "Martin", "Alex", "Jill", "Larry"};


protected void Page_Load(object sender, System.EventArgs e)
{
  if (!IsPostBack)
  {
    DataGrid1.VirtualItemCount = m_data.Length;
    LoadData(0);
  }
}


protected void LoadData(int intStart)
{
  //Create the data source just for one page
  ArrayList arr = new ArrayList(DataGrid1.PageSize);
  for (int i = intStart; i < intStart + DataGrid1.PageSize; i++)
  {
    arr.Add(m_data[i]);
  }
  DataGrid1.DataSource = arr;
  DataGrid1.DataBind();
}


private void DataGrid1_PageIndexChanged(object source,
  System.Web.UI.WebControls.DataGridPageChangedEventArgs e)
{
  //Go to the next page in the data
  DataGrid1.CurrentPageIndex = e.NewPageIndex;
  LoadData(e.NewPageIndex * DataGrid1.PageSize);
}
```

And the aspx code is a simple DataGrid with the appropriate properties set:

```
<asp:DataGrid
  id="DataGrid1"
  runat="server"
  PageSize="1"
  AllowPaging="True"
  AllowCustomPaging="True"
  ShowHeader="False">
</asp:DataGrid>
```

Figure 5.10 shows this page in action.

Sorting

Sorting a DataGrid can happen on several levels. You can populate it by binding to a sorted list of items. You can program buttons or links on your page to define the sort criteria or order, and you can program accordingly. Or, you can use the built-in sorting features. The DataGrid supports sorting by rendering the header text of the columns as LinkButtons, which can be clicked to invoke sorting on that particular column. To set this up in your DataGrid, you must set the AllowSorting property to true as in Listing 5.4 and optionally set the sorting options on each column. If the AutoGenerate-Columns property is set to true and you don't define your own BoundColumns, then every column will be sortable. If you do define BoundColumns, then you must set sorting options on each of them. Once the options are set up, you simply handle the sort event of the grid and reload the data accordingly. As we would expect, it is possible to find out which column was clicked, so that the sorting can be done on a per-column basis.

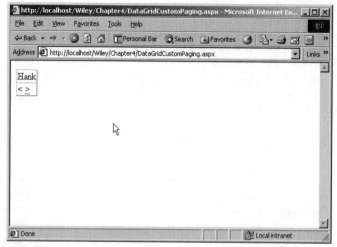

Figure 5.10   Custom paging.

For the first example, we'll look at a simple sorting method, which allows sorting on every column of the DataGrid. Of course, all columns from the data source are shown because AutoGenerateColumns is not explicitly set to false.

```
<%@ Page language="c#" Codebehind="DataGridSort.aspx.cs"
AutoEventWireup="false" Inherits="Chapter5.DataGridSort" %>

<HTML>
  <HEAD>
    <meta name="GENERATOR" Content="Microsoft Visual Studio 7.0">
    <meta name="CODE_LANGUAGE" Content="C#">
  </HEAD>
  <body>
    <form method="post" runat="server">
      <asp:DataGrid id=DataGrid1 runat="server" AllowSorting="True">
      </asp:DataGrid>
    </form>
  </body>
</HTML>
```

Listing 5.4 DataGridSort.aspx

```
namespace Chapter5
{
  using System;
  using System.Collections;
  using System.ComponentModel;
  using System.Data;
  using System.Drawing;
  using System.Web;
  using System.Web.SessionState;
  using System.Web.UI;
  using System.Web.UI.WebControls;
  using System.Web.UI.HtmlControls;
  using System.Data.SqlClient;

  public class DataGridSort : System.Web.UI.Page
  {
    protected System.Web.UI.WebControls.DataGrid DataGrid1;

    public DataGridSort()
    {
      Page.Init += new System.EventHandler(Page_Init);
    }
```

Listing 5.5 DataGridSort.aspx.cs

```csharp
protected void Page_Load(object sender, System.EventArgs e)
{
  //Read data In the default order.
  if (!IsPostBack) ReadData("employeeid");
}

protected void ReadData(string sortcolumn)
{
  //Create the sql statement with the sort syntax.
  string sql = "select employeeid, lastname, firstname, title from
    employees order by " + sortcolumn;

  //Open database, and read data.
  SqlConnection cn = new
    SqlConnection(@"DataSource=(local)\NetSDK;InitialCatalog=
    Northwind;UserID=sa;pwd=;");
  cn.Open();
  SqlCommand cmd = new SqlCommand(sql, cn);
  SqlDataReader reader = cmd.ExecuteReader();

  //Bind grid.
  DataGrid1.DataSource = reader;
  DataGrid1.DataBind();

  //Clean up.
  reader.Close();
  cn.Close();
}

protected void Page_Init(object sender, EventArgs e)
{
  InitializeComponent();
}

private void InitializeComponent()
{
  this.DataGrid1.SortCommand += new
    System.Web.UI.WebControls.DataGridSortCommandEventHandler(
    this.DataGrid1_SortCommand);

  this.Load += new System.EventHandler(this.Page_Load);
}

protected void DataGrid1_SortCommand(object source,
  System.Web.UI.WebControls.DataGridSortCommandEventArgs e)
{
 //Reload the data from the database
  ReadData(e.SortExpression);
}
}
}
```

Listing 5.5   DataGridSort.aspx.cs (continued)

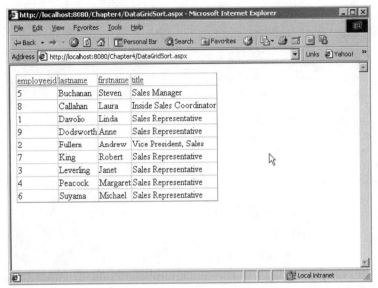

Figure 5.11   DataGrid default sorting.

You can see the sorting grid in Figure 5.11; now let's examine the code. The Page_Load in Listing 5.5 reads the data for the first time in the default order, but only on the first request of the page. This is because a click on one of the column headers will cause a trip to the server, at which time we will alter the data reading sequence; we don't want to read the data twice per trip just because the Page_Load always runs. So, we simply handle the SortCommand, which happens whenever a header LinkButton is clicked and includes the header text in the event argument. Because the header text is the column name, we can simply pass that into the Sql statements order by clause and reload the data in the new order. Now let's look at supporting sorting on only certain columns. In this sample, we need to modify only the aspx file. The code-behind class is unchanged.

```
<%@ Page language="c#" Codebehind="DataGridSortColumns.aspx.cs"
AutoEventWireup="false" Inherits="Chapter5.DataGridSortColumns" %>

<HTML>
  <HEAD>
    <meta name="GENERATOR" Content="Microsoft Visual Studio 7.0">
    <meta name="CODE_LANGUAGE" Content="C#">
  </HEAD>
  <body>
    <form method="post" runat="server">
      <asp:DataGrid id=DataGrid1 runat="server" AllowSorting="True"
        autogeneratecolumns="False">
```

Listing 5.6   DataGridSortColumns.aspx

```
        <Columns>
          <asp:BoundColumn DataField="EmployeeID"
            SortExpression="EmployeeID" HeaderText="Employee ID">
          </asp:BoundColumn>
          <asp:BoundColumn DataField="FirstName"
            SortExpression="FirstName" HeaderText="First Name">
          </asp:BoundColumn>
          <asp:BoundColumn DataField="LastName"
            SortExpression="LastName" HeaderText="Last Name">
          </asp:BoundColumn>
          <asp:BoundColumn DataField="Title" HeaderText="Title">
          </asp:BoundColumn>
        </Columns>
      </asp:DataGrid>
    </form>
  </body>
</HTML>
```

Listing 5.6 DataGridSortColumns.aspx (continued)

Refer to Figure 5.12 to see the grid in action. In the aspx DataGrid code in Listing 5.6, we turned off AutoGenerateColumns and set up a few bound columns to show only the data we want to see instead of every column in the data source. Because we set the SortExpressions explicitly to the name of the columns in the database, we are able to use the same code to alter the Sql statement, as in the previous example. We also left the last column nonsortable, simply by not setting up a SortExpression in its bound column code. Notice, however, that the AllowSorting property must still be set to true for the entire DataGrid.

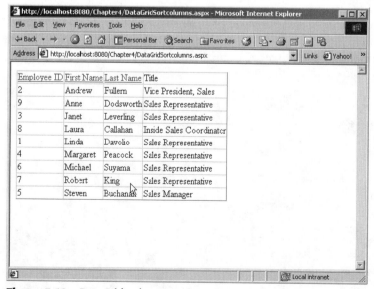

Figure 5.12 DataGrid column sorting.

Data Binding Events

When binding to data in a DataGrid, there are several techniques for customizing the data that is displayed on each row. One way is to use the DataFormatString attribute of the columns, which allows you to set the format using the same format specifiers used in the static String.Format method. Or you could add a template column and set up your own custom view of the data being bound. This could be mixed with a function defined in the aspx file (so it will be in the same class that gets created for the page at runtime), and you could call it to format your data. This would include using the Container object and accessing the DataItem property to have access to the native data object being bound. But, in some cases, it may be suitable to handle the ItemData-Bound event, which is fired every time a row is created in a DataGrid. Handling this event is a great way to perform any processing you need to do on each row. In the following example, we will load the same data as we did last time, but this time let's highlight any employee title that contains the word "President" in its title. Also, similar to the example in the MSDN Library, we'll add a line number to the items in the grid.

```
<%@ Page language="c#" Codebehind="DataGridItemDataBound.aspx.cs"
AutoEventWireup="false" Inherits="Chapter5.DataGridItemDataBound" %>

<HTML>
  <HEAD>
    <meta content="Microsoft Visual Studio 7.0" name=GENERATOR>
    <meta content=C# name=CODE_LANGUAGE>
  </HEAD>
  <body>
    <form method=post runat="server">
      <asp:datagrid id=DataGrid1 runat="server">
        <Columns>
          <asp:BoundColumn HeaderText="Line number">
          </asp:BoundColumn>
        </Columns>
      </asp:datagrid>
    </form>
  </body>
</HTML>
```

Listing 5.7 DataGridItemDataBound.aspx

```
namespace Chapter5
{
  using System;
  using System.Collections;
  using System.ComponentModel;
  using System.Data;
  using System.Drawing;
```

Listing 5.8 DataGridItemDataBound.aspx.cs

```
using System.Web;
using System.Web.SessionState;
using System.Web.UI;
using System.Web.UI.WebControls;
using System.Web.UI.HtmlControls;
using System.Data.SqlClient;

public class DataGridItemDataBound : System.Web.UI.Page
{
  protected System.Web.UI.WebControls.DataGrid DataGrid1;

  public DataGridItemDataBound ()
  {
    Page.Init += new System.EventHandler(Page_Init);
  }

  protected void Page_Load(object sender, System.EventArgs e)
  {
    if (!IsPostBack) ReadData();
  }

  protected void ReadData()
  {
    string sql = "select employeeid, lastname, firstname, title from
      employees";

    SqlConnection cn = new
      SqlConnection(@"DataSource=(local)\NetSDK;InitialCatalog=
      Northwind;UserID=sa;pwd=;");
    cn.Open();
    SqlCommand cmd = new SqlCommand(sql, cn);
    SqlDataReader reader = cmd.ExecuteReader();

    DataGrid1.DataSource = reader;
    DataGrid1.DataBind();

    reader.Close();
    cn.Close();
  }

  protected void Page_Init(object sender, EventArgs e)
  {
    InitializeComponent();
  }

  private void InitializeComponent()
  {
    this.DataGrid1.ItemDataBound += new
      System.Web.UI.WebControls.DataGridItemEventHandler(
      this.DataGrid1_ItemDataBound);
```

Listing 5.8 DataGridItemDataBound.aspx.cs (continued)

```
        this.Load += new System.EventHandler(this.Page_Load);
    }

    protected void DataGrid1_ItemDataBound(object sender,
      System.Web.UI.WebControls.DataGridItemEventArgs e)
    {
      //Check to make sure it is a normal row.
      if ((e.Item.ItemType == ListItemType.Item) ||
        (e.Item.ItemType == ListItemType.AlternatingItem))
      {

        //Add the line number.
        e.Item.Cells[0].Text = e.Item.ItemIndex.ToString();

        //Cast the DataItem to a database row object.
        string title =

((System.Data.Common.DbDataRecord)e.Item.DataItem)["Title"].ToString();

        //Color cell on specified title.
        if (title.IndexOf("President") > 0)
        {
          e.Item.Cells[4].BackColor = Color.Yellow;
        }
      }
    }
  }
}
```

Listing 5.8   DataGridItemDataBound.aspx.cs (continued)

In this example, we used both AutoGenerateColumns and a BoundColumn. Refer to Figure 5.13 to see the grid in action. Notice that in Listing 5.8 we did not use a DataField attribute on the BoundColumn. If left alone, this column would just have remained blank because we didn't tell the grid which data to put there. Instead, we used this column in code to add the line numbers for each row. When we discovered that a row had "President" in the title, we colored that cell yellow. Remember, as we have mentioned before, we must cast the DataItem out to whatever type of object is contained in the data source. In this case, because we used an SqlDataReader to bind to, we had to cast to the DbDataRecord object, which is what makes up each record in a DataReader.

Now you have learned some of the more powerful features of the DataGrid. We didn't look into everything the DataGrid supports, like in-place editing of rows, but we will cover something along those lines soon enough. Next, let's move on to two more controls that allow you to create an advanced customized view of your data: the DataList and the Repeater.

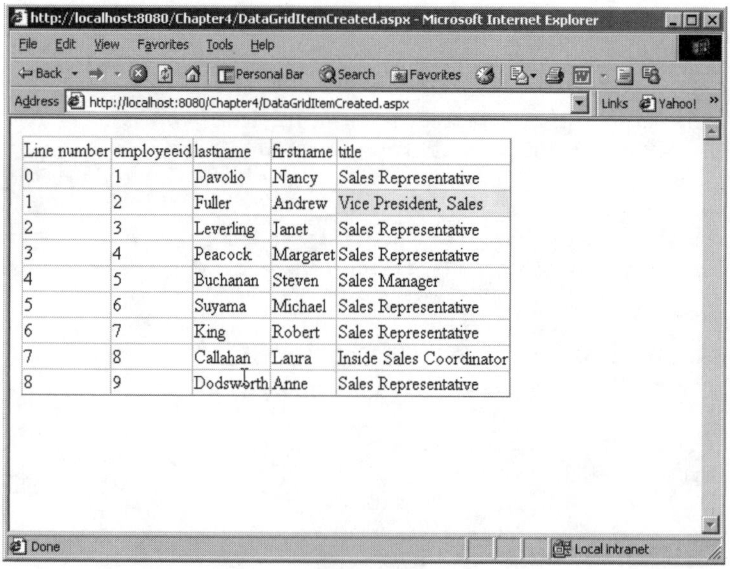

Line number	employeeid	lastname	firstname	title
0	1	Davolio	Nancy	Sales Representative
1	2	Fuller	Andrew	Vice President, Sales
2	3	Leverling	Janet	Sales Representative
3	4	Peacock	Margaret	Sales Representative
4	5	Buchanan	Steven	Sales Manager
5	6	Suyama	Michael	Sales Representative
6	7	King	Robert	Sales Representative
7	8	Callahan	Laura	Inside Sales Coordinator
8	9	Dodsworth	Anne	Sales Representative

Figure 5.13 DataGrid ItemDataBound event.

DataList

The DataList is similar to a DataGrid, but it has automatic layout functionality. The DataList requires you to define each of the items or "rows" yourself, using standard HTML or ASP.NET Server Controls. In effect, this makes a DataList much like a DataGrid with only TemplateColumns defined. This allows you to create virtually any look you want on the items in the data source. In this example, we will use HTML tables and ASP.NET HyperLink controls to create employee information blocks with a distinct separation between them. As for the HyperLinks that we included, they link to pages that don't exist, but they are provided to add a more complete look to the example.

```
<%@ Page language="c#" Codebehind="DataListSimple.aspx.cs"
AutoEventWireup="false" Inherits="Chapter5.DataListSimple" %>

<HTML>
  <HEAD>
    <meta name="GENERATOR" Content="Microsoft Visual Studio 7.0">
    <meta name="CODE_LANGUAGE" Content="C#">
  </HEAD>
  <body>
    <form method="post" runat="server">
```

Listing 5.9 DataListSimple.aspx

```
    <asp:DataList id=DataList1 runat="server" RepeatColumns=3>
      <ItemTemplate>
        <table BackColor=LemonChiffon Border=0 Width=180px
          CellPadding=0
          CellSpacing=0>
          <tr>
            <td bgcolor=Gold>
              <font face=Arial size=2><b>Employee
                Information</b></font>
            </td>
          <tr>
            <td bgcolor=LemonChiffon>
              <table cellpadding=0 cellspacing=0>
                <tr>
                  <td width=100px>
                    <font face=Arial size=2><b>Last Name</b></font>
                  </td>
                  <td>
<%# ((System.Data.Common.DbDataRecord)Container.DataItem)["LastName"] %>
                  </td>
                </tr>
                <tr>
                  <td>
                    <font face=Arial size=2><b>First Name</b></font>
                  </td>
                  <td>
<%# ((System.Data.Common.DbDataRecord)Container.DataItem)["FirstName"] %>
                  </td>
                </tr>
              </table>
            </td>
          </tr>
          <tr>
            <td bgcolor=LemonChiffon>
              <br>
              <asp:HyperLink CssClass=LinkClass ID=link1
                ImageUrl="images/viewicon.gif" Runat=server
                NavigateUrl='<%# string.Format("view.aspx?id={0}",
((System.Data.Common.DbDataRecord)Container.DataItem)["EmployeeID"]) %>' />

              <asp:HyperLink CssClass=LinkClass ID="Hyperlink1"
                ImageUrl="images/matchicon.gif" Runat=server
                NavigateUrl='<%# string.Format("match.aspx?id={0}",
((System.Data.Common.DbDataRecord)Container.DataItem)["EmployeeID"]) %>' />
            </td>
          </tr>
        </table>
        <br>
```

Listing 5.9   DataListSimple.aspx (continued)

```
        </ItemTemplate>
      </asp:DataList>
    </form>
  </body>
</HTML>
```

Listing 5.9   DataListSimple.aspx (continued)

```
namespace Chapter5
{
  using System;
  using System.Collections;
  using System.ComponentModel;
  using System.Data;
  using System.Drawing;
  using System.Web;
  using System.Web.SessionState;
  using System.Web.UI;
  using System.Web.UI.WebControls;
  using System.Web.UI.HtmlControls;
  using System.Data.SqlClient;

  public class DataListSimple : System.Web.UI.Page
  {
    protected System.Web.UI.WebControls.DataList DataList1;

    public DataListSimple()
    {
      Page.Init += new System.EventHandler(Page_Init);
    }

    protected void ReadData()
    {
      string sql = "select employeeid, lastname, firstname, title from
        employees";
      SqlConnection cn = new
      SqlConnection(@"DataSource=(local)\NetSDK;InitialCatalog=Northwind;
        UserID=sa;pwd=;");
      cn.Open();
      SqlCommand cmd = new SqlCommand(sql, cn);
      SqlDataReader reader = cmd.ExecuteReader();

      DataList1.DataSource = reader;
      DataList1.DataBind();

      reader.Close();
      cn.Close();
```

Listing 5.10   DataListSimple.aspx.cs

```
    }

    protected void Page_Init(object sender, EventArgs e)
    {
      InitializeComponent();
    }

    private void InitializeComponent()
    {
      this.Load += new System.EventHandler(this.Page_Load);
    }

    private void Page_Load(object sender, System.EventArgs e)
    {
      ReadData();
    }
  }
}
```

Listing 5.10   DataListSimple.aspx.cs (continued)

Notice that on the declaration of the DataList in Listing 5.9, we set the Repeat-Columns to 3. This makes the list render with three columns of whatever your template looks like, by however many rows needed. Another interesting setting we could have applied is RepeatLayout. Setting this to table causes the DataList to render as a table; setting it to flow causes it to render in-line, like normal HTML text. It is up to you to determine how you want to do it; in many cases, the end result will look similar for either setting. By default, the DataList renders items vertically in rows. If you have RepeatColumns set to more than 1, there would be fewer rows vertically. But it is also possible to set the RepeatDirection to horizontal. This causes all of your items to be displayed in a horizontal line. Unfortunately, this can quickly cause your items to run off the right side of the screen, causing a large amount of horizontal scrolling. For the preceding code, the results are shown in Figure 5.14.

Now let's look at editing data in a DataList. The DataList supports this much the way the DataGrid does, in that it allows you to define buttons (or LinkButtons or ImageButtons) with the special CommandNames: edit, cancel, and selected. In this example, we use the edit and cancel commands. If there is any type of button control (or any control that has the CommandName property) in an item template that has the CommandName set to edit, then the DataLists EditCommand event will be fired automatically on its click. Likewise for cancel and select, which cause the CancelCommand and SelectCommand events to be fired, respectively. If you need to have your own user-defined command you want to handle in the item, set the CommandName to whatever you want, then test for it in the ItemCommand event, which is fired for every button-type control in the DataList. Note that in addition to their respective events, the ItemCommand is fired even when you click an edit, select, or cancel control. You'll see in Listing 5.11 where we take care of exactly this behavior. Note that you don't handle controls' events directly when they are in a DataList template because their events are bubbled up to the container, which is the DataList itself. This is why we handle these events thrown by the DataList itself.

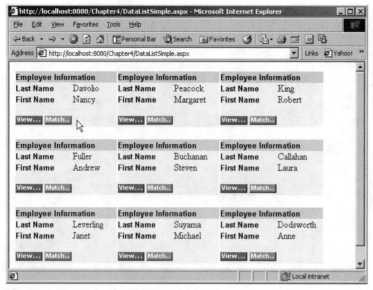

Figure 5.14 A simple DataList.

What does all of this mean to us in practice? Take the EditCommand event, for example. When the EditCommand event is fired because the user clicked a button-type control whose CommandName is edit, we set the EditItemIndex of the DataList to the currently clicked item. This causes the DataList to be re-created using the EditItem-Template UI in place of the current item clicked. We set up the EditItemTemplate to have textboxes and other editable controls in it so that we can modify the data and later save it. If we follow the same logic for a SelectCommand, the SelectedItemTemplate UI will be drawn for the currently selected item. When we want to handle something other than these natively supported commands, we set the CommandName to our own text. For example, if we set it to save, then the ItemCommand event will be fired, where we can test for the CommandName of "save" in the event arguments and do as we please. Let's look at an example that does just this. We will read from and update the data source with simple select statements to make the example easy to understand. Incorporating these techniques with the more advanced data objects discussed earlier in the chapter will be left as an exercise for the reader.

```
<%@ Page language="c#" Codebehind=" DataListEdit.aspx.cs"
AutoEventWireup="false" Inherits="Chapter5.DataListEdit" %>

<HTML>
  <HEAD>
    <meta name="GENERATOR" Content="Microsoft Visual Studio 7.0">
    <meta name="CODE_LANGUAGE" Content="C#">
  </HEAD>
```

Listing 5.11 DataListEdit.aspx

```
<body>
<form method="post" runat="server">
  <asp:DataList id=DataList1 runat="server" DataKeyField="EmployeeID">
    <ItemTemplate>
      <table BackColor=LemonChiffon Border=0 Width=200px CellPadding=0
        CellSpacing=0>
        <tr>
          <td bgcolor=Gold>
            <font face=Arial size=2><b>Employee Information</b></font>
          </td>
        </tr>
        <tr>
          <td bgcolor=LemonChiffon>
            <table cellpadding=0 cellspacing=0>
              <tr>
              <td width=100px>
                <font face=Arial size=2><b>Employee ID</b></font>
              </td>
              <td>
<%# ((System.Data.Common.DbDataRecord)Container.DataItem)["EmployeeID"] %>
              </td>
            </tr>
            <tr>
              <td width=100px>
                <font face=Arial size=2><b>Last Name</b></font>
              </td>
              <td>
<%# ((System.Data.Common.DbDataRecord)Container.DataItem)["LastName"] %>
              </td>
            </tr>
            <tr>
              <td>
                <font face=Arial size=2><b>First Name</b></font>
              </td>
              <td>
<%# ((System.Data.Common.DbDataRecord)Container.DataItem)["FirstName"] %>
              </td>
            </tr>
          </table>
        </td>
      </tr>
      <tr>
        <td bgcolor=LemonChiffon>
          <br>
          <asp:ImageButton ID="ImageButton1"
            ImageUrl="images/editicon.gif"
            Runat=server CommandName="edit" />
        </td>
```

Listing 5.11   DataListEdit.aspx (continued)

```
          </tr>
        </table>
        <br>
    </ItemTemplate>
    <EditItemTemplate>
      <table BackColor=LemonChiffon Border=0 Width=200px CellPadding=0
        CellSpacing=0>
        <tr>
          <td bgcolor=Gold>
            <font face=Arial size=2><b>Employee Information</b></font>
          </td>
        </tr>
          <tr>
            <td bgcolor=LemonChiffon>
              <table cellpadding=0 cellspacing=0>
                <tr>
                  <td width=100px>
                    <font face=Arial size=2><b>Employee ID</b></font>
                  </td>
                  <td>
<%# ((System.Data.Common.DbDataRecord)Container.DataItem)["EmployeeID"]%>
                  </td>
                </tr>
                <tr>
                  <td width=100px>
                    <font face=Arial size=2><b>Last Name</b></font>
                  </td>
                  <td>
                    <asp:textbox
                      id=TextBox1 Width=100px runat=server text='
<%#((System.Data.Common.DbDataRecord)Container.DataItem)["LastName"]%>' />
                  </td>
                </tr>
                <tr>
                  <td>
                    <font face=Arial size=2><b>First Name</b></font>
                  </td>
                  <td>
                    <asp:textbox id=TextBox2 Width=100px runat=server
                      text='
<%# ((System.Data.Common.DbDataRecord)Container.DataItem)["FirstName"]
%>'/>
                  </td>
                </tr>
              </table>
            </td>
          </tr>
          <tr>
            <td bgcolor=LemonChiffon>
```

Listing 5.11   DataListEdit.aspx (continued)

```
                           <br>
                           <asp:ImageButton ID="ImageButton2"
                              ImageUrl="images/saveicon.gif" Runat=server
                              CommandName="save" />

                           <asp:ImageButton ID="ImageButton3"
                              ImageUrl="images/cancelicon.gif" Runat=server
                              CommandName="cancel" />
                      </td>
                   </tr>
               </table>
           <br>
        </EditItemTemplate>
     </asp:DataList>
   </form>
 </body>
</HTML>
```

Listing 5.11 DataListEdit.aspx (continued)

```
namespace Chapter5
{
  using System;
  using System.Collections;
  using System.ComponentModel;
  using System.Data;
  using System.Drawing;
  using System.Web;
  using System.Web.SessionState;
  using System.Web.UI;
  using System.Web.UI.WebControls;
  using System.Web.UI.HtmlControls;
  using System.Data.SqlClient;

  public class DataListEdit : System.Web.UI.Page
  {
    protected System.Web.UI.WebControls.DataList DataList1;
    protected System.Web.UI.WebControls.TextBox TextBox1;
    protected System.Web.UI.WebControls.TextBox TextBox2;

    public DataListEdit()
    {
      Page.Init += new System.EventHandler(Page_Init);
    }
    protected void ReadData()
    {
      string sql = "select employeeid, lastname, firstname, title from
```

Listing 5.12 DataListEdit.aspx.cs

```
    employees";
  SqlConnection cn = new
  SqlConnection(@"DataSource=(local)\NetSDK;InitialCatalog=Northwind;
  UserID=sa;pwd=;");
  cn.Open();
  SqlCommand cmd = new SqlCommand(sql, cn);
  SqlDataReader reader = cmd.ExecuteReader();

  DataList1.DataSource = reader;
  DataList1.DataBind();

  reader.Close();
  cn.Close();
}

protected void Page_Init(object sender, EventArgs e)
{
  InitializeComponent();
}

private void InitializeComponent()
{
  this.DataList1.ItemCommand += new
    System.Web.UI.WebControls.DataListCommandEventHandler(
    this.DataList1_ItemCommand);

  this.DataList1.CancelCommand += new
    System.Web.UI.WebControls.DataListCommandEventHandler(
    this.DataList1_CancelCommand);

  this.DataList1.EditCommand += new
    System.Web.UI.WebControls.DataListCommandEventHandler(
    this.DataList1_EditCommand);

  this.Load += new System.EventHandler(this.Page_Load);
}

private void Page_Load(object sender, System.EventArgs e)
{
  if (!IsPostBack) ReadData();
}

protected void DataList1_EditCommand(object source,
  System.Web.UI.WebControls.DataListCommandEventArgs e)
{
  DataList1.EditItemIndex = e.Item.ItemIndex;
  ReadData();
}

protected void DataList1_CancelCommand(object source,
```

Listing 5.12   DataListEdit.aspx.cs (continued)

```
        System.Web.UI.WebControls.DataListCommandEventArgs e)
    {
        DataList1.EditItemIndex = -1;
        ReadData();
    }

    protected void DataList1_ItemCommand(object source,
        System.Web.UI.WebControls.DataListCommandEventArgs e)
    {
        //Handle the save command.
        if (e.CommandName == "save")
        {
            //Get the data key for item, which is EmployeeID.
            int empid =

Convert.ToInt32(DataList1.DataKeys[e.Item.ItemIndex].ToString());

            //Find the updated controls in the template item.
            TextBox txtLastName = (TextBox)e.Item.FindControl("TextBox1");
            TextBox txtFirstName = (TextBox)e.Item.FindControl("TextBox2");

            //If found, update datasource.
            if ((txtLastName != null) && (txtFirstName != null))
            {
                SaveData(empid, txtFirstName.Text, txtLastName.Text);
            }

            //Take out edit mode and reload data to show changes.
            DataList1.EditItemIndex = -1;
            ReadData();
        }
    }

    private void SaveData(int empid, string fname, string lname)
    {
        //Create an update query.
        string sql = string.Format("update employees set lastname = '{0}',
            firstname = '{1}' where EmployeeID = {2}", lname, fname, empid);
        SqlConnection cn = new
        SqlConnection(@"DataSource=(local)\NetSDK;InitialCatalog=Northwind;
            UserID=sa;pwd=;");
        cn.Open();
        SqlCommand cmd = new SqlCommand(sql, cn);

        //Run the update query to save the data.
        cmd.ExecuteNonQuery();
        cn.Close();
    }
  }
}
```

Listing 5.12 DataListEdit.aspx.cs (continued)

Let's look at what we did. Listing 5.11 seems like a lot of code, but most of it is UI layout and Visual Studio .NET-generated code. As we discussed earlier, we have ImageButtons in both the ItemTemplate and the EditItemTemplate. The one in the ItemTemplate with the edit icon has the CommandName "edit" so that when it is clicked we handle the EditCommand handler. In this handler we set the item to be edited and reload the data. This time, the browser gets different contents for this item, specifically that which is defined in the EditItemTemplate, which uses TextBoxes, bound to the first and last name of the employee. Because the data is loaded into textboxes, it can be edited. When the user clicks the save ImageButton, the ItemCommand event handler is invoked, which tests for the CommandName of "save," which was set in the save ImageButton. In this handler things get a little tricky. First, we must test for the correct CommandName of "save." Even though we have only one user-defined CommandName in the page, don't just handle it without first testing. If you do, you will run this code when the "edit" and "cancel" command events are fired as well. Clearly this would fail because we are looking for UI controls that may not exist during those events. Then we call the FindControl method of the item to get the TextBox values the user modified. We can't access these controls directly via a class-level variable like normal because they are created only when the EditItemTemplate is used and must be accessed dynamically through FindControl. When we find the controls, we can get their text and save the record to the database. Notice also that we used the DataKeyField to store the unique record with each row, which we discussed earlier in the book. In Figure 5.15, you can see the layout before the edit action; Figure 5.16 shows the layout during the edit; and Figure 5.17 shows the edited and saved contents.

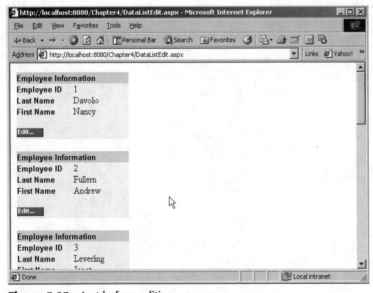

Figure 5.15 Just before editing.

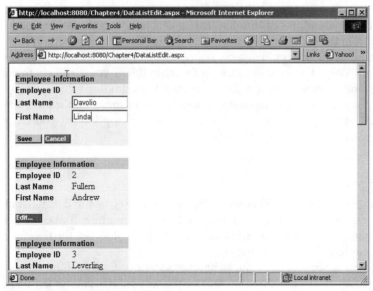

Figure 5.16   During the edit phase.

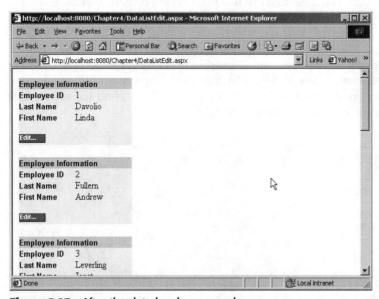

Figure 5.17   After the data has been saved.

We will skip some other features of the DataList, such as selecting an item, using styles to simplify the look and feel of different items, and handling the item creation events just as we did in the DataGrid. We don't want to go into too much depth with these controls because doing so would just be regurgitating much of what is available in the MSDN Library. We just wanted to touch on the main things you are likely to do with these controls and show you some more interesting Data Binding techniques. As we use these and other controls throughout the book's main sample application, we will go more into detail whenever needed. For now, you can apply what you have learned here to your own DataList experiments.

Repeater

The Repeater is similar to the other list controls, but it could be considered somewhat lightweight. It has no support for paging, sorting, selecting, or editing. It also has no default layout format. Where the DataGrid has a default layout of a grid, the Repeater relies entirely on your templates for its display.

In this example, we use some of the same techniques as before, for Data Binding and setting up the ItemTemplate. But, in this case, we need to set up the SeparatorTemplate as well, so that the items will be on "rows." To do this we simply supply a <br> as the HTML content to be inserted between each item. If we left this out, the elements would just be flowed onto the page, and they would be much less readable. Remember, the DataGrid and DataList don't require this because they already support a row-like layout by default. We tried to add a few different techniques for this sample. Instead of using a table to format each item, we used ASP.NET Label Server Controls. This illustrates that Server Controls can be used just like plain HTML content in your templates. We bind in the same fashion as before, but this time we included more data. There is one field called "notes" in the database, which was too large to display for every item. So, in Listing 5.13 we added two LinkButtons to control its visibility. To handle their clicks, we set them up according to the discussion in the DataList section and gave them CommandNames of ShowNotes and HideNotes, respectively. When handling the ItemCommand event, we check for which one was clicked, find the appropriate controls, and either show or hide them accordingly.

```
<%@ Page language="c#" Codebehind="RepeaterSimple.aspx.cs"
AutoEventWireup="false" Inherits="Chapter5.RepeaterSimple" %>

<HTML>
  <HEAD>
    <meta name="GENERATOR" Content="Microsoft Visual Studio 7.0">
    <meta name="CODE_LANGUAGE" Content="C#">
  </HEAD>
  <body>
  <form method="post" runat="server">
  <asp:Repeater id=Repeater1 runat="server">
    <ItemTemplate>
      <table BorderStyle=Solid BorderWidth=2 BorderColor=navy
CellPadding=0
```

Listing 5.13 RepeaterSimple.aspx

```
      CellSpacing=0>
        <tr>
         <td>
           <asp:label BackColor=LightBlue Font-Name=arial Font-Size=9pt
           Font-Bold=true ID=Label1 Runat=server Width=100px
           Height=100%>
           Name
           </asp:label>

           <asp:label BackColor=Lightsalmon Font-Name=arial Font-
           Size=9pt
           Font-Bold=false ID=Label2 Runat=server Width=200px>
            
<%# ((System.Data.Common.DbDataRecord)Container.DataItem)["FirstName"] %>
<%# ((System.Data.Common.DbDataRecord)Container.DataItem)["LastName"] %>
           </asp:label><br>

           <asp:label BackColor=LightBlue Font-Name=arial Font-Size=9pt
           Font-Bold=true ID="Label3" Runat=server Width=100px>
           Title
           </asp:label>

           <asp:label BackColor=Lightsalmon Font-Name=arial Font-
           Size=9pt
           Font-Bold=false ID="Label4" Runat=server Width=200px>
            
<%# ((System.Data.Common.DbDataRecord)Container.DataItem)["Title"] %>
           </asp:label><br>

           <asp:label BackColor=LightBlue Font-Name=arial Font-Size=9pt
           Font-Bold=true ID="Label5" Runat=server Width=100px>
           Address
           </asp:label>

           <asp:label BackColor=Lightsalmon Font-Name=arial Font-
           Size=9pt
           Font-Bold=false ID="Label6" Runat=server Width=200px>
            
<%# ((System.Data.Common.DbDataRecord)Container.DataItem)["FirstName"] %>
<%# ((System.Data.Common.DbDataRecord)Container.DataItem)["City"] %>,
<%# ((System.Data.Common.DbDataRecord)Container.DataItem)["Region"] %>
<%# ((System.Data.Common.DbDataRecord)Container.DataItem)["PostalCode"] %>
           </asp:label><br>

           <asp:label BackColor=LightBlue Font-Name=arial Font-Size=9pt
           Font-Bold=true ID="Label7" Runat=server Width=100px>
           Birthday
           </asp:label>

           <asp:label BackColor=Lightsalmon Font-Name=arial Font-
           Size=9pt
```

Listing 5.13 RepeaterSimple.aspx (continued)

```
                    Font-Bold=false ID="Label8" Runat=server Width=200px>
                     
                    <%# string.Format("{0:MM/dd/yyyy}",
((System.Data.Common.DbDataRecord)Container.DataItem)["BirthDate"]) %>
                    </asp:label><br>

                    <asp:label BackColor=LightBlue Font-Name=arial Font-Size=9pt
                    Font-Bold=true ID="Label9" Runat=server Width=100px>
                    Notes
                    </asp:label>

                    <asp:LinkButton CommandName="ShowNotes"
                    BackColor=Lightsalmon
                    Font-Name=arial Font-Size=9pt Font-Bold=false
                    ID="LinkButton1"
                    Runat=server Width=200px>
                     Show notes...
                    </asp:LinkButton><br>

                    </td>
                </tr>

                <tr>
                  <td>
                    <asp:label visible=false BackColor=Lightsalmon Font-
                    Name=arial
                    Font-Size=9pt Font-Bold=false ID="lblNotes" Runat=server
                    Width=300px>
<%# ((System.Data.Common.DbDataRecord)Container.DataItem)["Notes"] %>

                        <asp:LinkButton visible=false CommandName="HideNotes"
                        BackColor=Lightsalmon Font-Name=arial Font-Size=9pt
                        Font-Bold=false ID="lnkHideNotes" Runat=server>
                        Hide notes
                        </asp:LinkButton><br>
                    </asp:label>
                  </td>
                </tr>
           </table>
      </ItemTemplate>

      <SeparatorTemplate>
        <br>
      </SeparatorTemplate>
   </asp:Repeater>
   </form>
  </body>
</HTML>
namespace Chapter5
{
```

Listing 5.13 RepeaterSimple.aspx (continued)

```
using System;
using System.Collections;
using System.ComponentModel;
using System.Data;
using System.Drawing;
using System.Web;
using System.Web.SessionState;
using System.Web.UI;
using System.Web.UI.WebControls;
using System.Web.UI.HtmlControls;
using System.Data.SqlClient;

public class RepeaterSimple : System.Web.UI.Page
{
  protected System.Web.UI.WebControls.Repeater Repeater1;

  public RepeaterSimple()
  {
    Page.Init += new System.EventHandler(Page_Init);
  }

  protected void Page_Init(object sender, EventArgs e)
  {
    InitializeComponent();
  }

  private void InitializeComponent()
  {
    this.Repeater1.ItemCommand += new
      System.Web.UI.WebControls.RepeaterCommandEventHandler(
      this.Repeater1_ItemCommand);
    this.Load += new System.EventHandler(this.Page_Load);
  }

  private void Page_Load(object sender, System.EventArgs e)
  {
    ReadData();
  }

  protected void ReadData()
  {
    string sql = "select * from employees";
    SqlConnection cn = new
    SqlConnection(@"DataSource=(local)\NetSDK;InitialCatalog=Northwind;
      UserID=sa;pwd=;");
    cn.Open();
    SqlCommand cmd = new SqlCommand(sql, cn);
    SqlDataReader reader = cmd.ExecuteReader();

    Repeater1.DataSource = reader;
```

Listing 5.14   RepeaterSimple.aspx.cs

```
    Repeater1.DataBind();

    reader.Close();
    cn.Close();
}

protected void Repeater1_ItemCommand(object source,
    System.Web.UI.WebControls.RepeaterCommandEventArgs e)
{
    if (e.CommandName == "ShowNotes")
    {
        Label lblNotesDisplay = (Label) e.Item.FindControl("lblNotes");
        lblNotesDisplay.Visible = true;
        LinkButton lnkHideNotesDisplay = (LinkButton)
            e.Item.FindControl("lnkHideNotes");
        lnkHideNotesDisplay.Visible = true;
    }

    if (e.CommandName == "HideNotes")
    {
        Label lblNotesDisplay = (Label) e.Item.FindControl("lblNotes");
        lblNotesDisplay.Visible = false;
        LinkButton lnkHideNotesDisplay = (LinkButton)
            e.Item.FindControl("lnkHideNotes");
        lnkHideNotesDisplay.Visible = false;
    }
}
}
}
```

Listing 5.14 RepeaterSimple.aspx.cs (continued)

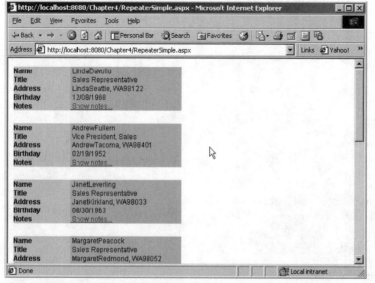

Figure 5.18 Repeater with hidden notes.

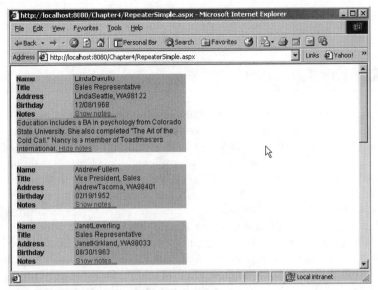

Figure 5.19   Repeater with visible notes.

Figure 5.18 shows the list before clicking the notes button, and Figure 5.19 shows it once the notes appear. Here's a trick to make a Repeater insert a separator after every *other* item. Handle the ItemCreated event for the repeater and use a toggling variable. The <br> literal control is added at the correct time, when the item being created is, in fact, a SeparatorTemplate item, and two rows have been created. This is helpful because the Repeater doesn't allow you to code for this directly in the templates. Note that if you want to break on more than every other line, or if you are using headers and footers, this code could be modified slightly to handle that as well.

```
private bool m_bNewRow;
...
protected void Repeater1_ItemCreated(object source,
    System.Web.UI.WebControls.RepeaterItemEventArgs e)
{
  if (e.Item.ItemType == ListItemType.Separator)
  {
    if (m_bNewRow)
    {
      e.Item.Controls.Add(new LiteralControl("<br>"));
    }
    m_bNewRow = !m_bNewRow;
  }
}
```

As you can see, the Repeater can work well in read-only situations, especially where complex data items need to be displayed. For simpler items that can easily fit into a single row in a strictly grid-like layout, the DataGrid may be easier to code. But for super customization, the DataList and Repeater make for a power pair of controls at your disposal.

Wrapping Up the Chapter

In this chapter we covered the remainder of the ASP.NET fundamentals that we will need to develop real-world applications. We covered the Request and Response objects, as well as cookies, query strings, and forms. We introduced the concept of Session state and global variables and showed you a few application-level events that you can handle. We then introduced the concept of Page Subclassing and demonstrated how useful it can be for reusing common functionality throughout a Web application. Finally, we looked at some advanced Data Binding techniques and some nice features of the advanced binding controls. We didn't cover all of the things that can be done with these objects and controls. This book is not intended to be a reference for all of the things in the ASP.NET portions of the framework, but rather a resource on how to put a lot of features to use in a full-sized application. Having said that, now we can move into the next phase of the book, which jumps right into some real-world code examples, and we can start putting together a set of real-world Web applications using ASP.NET and C#.

Applying What We've Learned So Far

So far we have looked at the ASP.NET technology and seen how you can accomplish a lot of typical Web programming tasks with it. We've taken a look at most of the new server-side controls, and we have done some comparing and contrasting between this technology and the previous-generation technology. Keep in mind that by no means did we perform an exhaustive account of the objects and controls in the framework. To cover every single detail about them would simply be rewriting what is already covered so well in the MDSN Library. In this book, we want to give you some good foundational, real-world instruction by example on using the framework.

This chapter introduces the sample Web application that you'll be using throughout the rest of this book.

An Online Car Parts Retailer

There are so many different types of example programs to choose from, such as contact management, call center workflow, portal sites, or customer relationship management (CRM). Because many programmers intend to use ASP.NET to build consumer-based online services, we chose to take the somewhat standard route of developing an online store. While a more interesting type of application would be fun, an online store sample will best reflect the use of ASP.NET in the real world.

Our online car parts retailer sells parts and accessories for selected Chevrolet models. It is designed to scale well to include all makes and models of all cars, should any of our readers ever need to put together a real online car parts house! But the real lesson here is to use ASP.NET for the entire program, rather than browser script on the very front end, ASP on the "server" front end, COM in the middle, and who knows what kind of data access pulling up the rear. As you've seen throughout this book, we no longer need a hodge-podge of tools and technologies to complete a full-blown Web app—it can all be done in one place, with one tool, at one time.

We'll create the online store in phases, adding more functionality and new topics throughout the rest of the book. To begin with, we'll build a simple system where shoppers visit, select products, and check out. Then, we will add a business-to-business (B2B) feature to the application, namely exposing the store's inventory to other businesses via SOAP Web Services. After that, we will study some of the external services we can tap, such as a shipping pricing service.

This application demonstrates building an application in modular components from beginning to end. First, we'll create a simple database model in which all of our data will reside. Then, we'll develop an object model, which we will call the middle tier. This is the same way we have been doing multitiered architectures for years (using the Windows DNA paradigm), but this time it will all be in a common language and programming model. This middle tier will prevent the presentation layer from having to interact directly with the data; thus, you can substitute any data source as long as the interface to the middle tier remains the same (or similar, at least). Then, to make up the presentation layer, we will use as many of the great new features of ASP.NET as we can. We will refrain from resorting to any of the previous-generation methods of Web programming as much as possible, so we won't use any browser script, such as JavaScript, Jscript, or ECMAScript (except the script generated by ASP.NET). As for COM objects, we certainly won't be programming those ourselves; it will all be done as .NET objects.

NOTE Because the code is very extensive, we've included only code snippets throughout, with thorough explanation. All of the code for the sample project can be downloaded from the companion Web site, located at www.wiley.com/compbooks/meyne. In fact, the sample project could be a good starting point for your online retail store, if you are so inclined!

The Database Model

The first step for this project is to develop a database on which this Web site will run. We've chosen to use MSDE for the data provider, and we will use the SQL Server managed provider of ADO.NET for data access. A diagram of the database model can be seen in Figure 6.1. This database model has been simplified somewhat, but it will provide us with everything we need for a basic, yet operational e-commerce site.

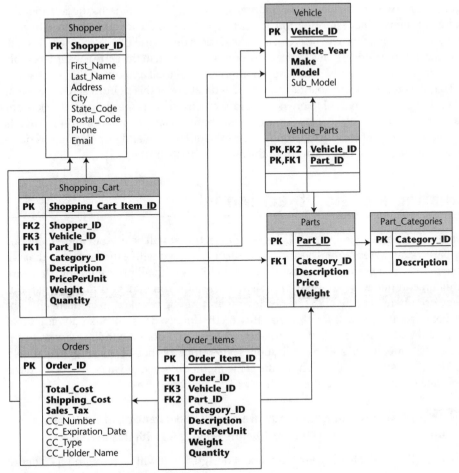

Figure 6.1 WileyParts database model.

Here is a quick run-down of the data flow through this database. At some point during a shopper's visit to our Web site, we will create an entry for the shopper in the Shopper table. The Shopper_ID field of this table is an identity column, so when we create an entry we will be given a unique ID for the shopper that will be the key to tracking what the shopper has in his or her cart and any orders that he or she has placed. When a shopper searches for a part, he or she will choose one of the vehicles in the Vehicle table. The shopper will then choose one of the part categories in the Part_Categories table. Once we have the Vehicle_ID and the Part_Category_ID we can search the Parts table in conjunction with the Vehicle_Parts table for any parts that match the shopper's search criteria. If the shopper chooses to add a part to his or her cart, a record will be created in the Shopping_Cart table that contains the Shopper_ID and all of the pertinent information about the part. Once the shopper decides to purchase the part, an entry will be created in the Orders table, and one or more entries will be created in the Order_Items table representing each item in the cart. The Orders table will contain the user's credit card information and the total amount of the purchase.

That is as far as we are going to go with the database at this point. There are several other things that we would likely need to implement, such as the ability to track order status and shipping. We'll get to some of these things in later chapters, but some of it is beyond the scope of this book. Complete scripts for creating and populating this database are available for download from the companion Web site.

Creating a Basic Object Model

Let's begin by building several C# classes or objects that will be used to implement our car parts retailer Web store. These objects will be designed with a methodology that we have found to be useful and workable in the field. As with all programming, there are a million and one ways to solve a problem with code. You may find that the methodology used here doesn't suit your needs or that it can be tweaked to be more efficient for your specific project. Realize that this methodology does not take advantage of some of the more powerful object-oriented features, nor does it handle every code situation that can arise in a Web application. We use it in this book because it is relatively clean-cut and simple to read. This is the same methodology that was introduced in the *Wrapping It Up in a Class* section in Chapter 4, "Database Access."

NOTE Make sure you review and have a good understanding of the *Wrapping It Up in a Class* section in Chapter 4 before moving on with this example.

This section won't teach you object model design, but it will focus on the specifics of implementing an object model with C# and then using it in a Web application. Although these objects are geared to be more efficient for Web application use, they could still easily be used by a Win Forms application. If you do decide to implement a model like this one in a non-Web application, it would probably need to be expanded on to provide maximum efficiency for that usage scenario. For instance, we won't be using the DataSet object in any of these classes, and it might make more sense to do so with a Win Form application.

We created an object for each one of the tables that will provide the required functionality to work with the data in that table. The exception is the Vehicle_Parts table. Because this is just a utility table used to provide a many-to-many relationship between the Vehicle table and the Parts table, there is no object for access to this table. In addition, we implement only methods that will be used by the Web site. We won't implement any methods that might be used by a back-end administration application for maintaining the site. So, let's start examining the implementation of this object model.

WileyObject

The WileyObject class is a base class from which the rest of the objects will inherit. For the most part, it provides error tracking and logging functionality. The class has a protected method called LogError, which is used for logging any errors that occur in the code of an inherited class. When an error occurs in an inherited class, we will catch the exception, log it, and then throw it up to the next caller. Also in this class is another logging method called WriteToLog, which is static in case there are any static methods in the application that need this functionality. The code for the logging methods is as follows:

```
protected void LogError(string s)
{
  try
  {
    //Open the log, create it if it does not exist
    if (!EventLog.Exists("Wiley"))
    {
      //Create the log
      EventLog.CreateEventSource(ToString(), "Wiley");
    }
    else
    {
      //Make sure that this source exists.  If it doesn't, create it.
      if (!EventLog.SourceExists(ToString()))
      {
        //Create the source
        EventLog.CreateEventSource(ToString(), "Wiley");
      }
    }

    EventLog evtLog = new EventLog(String.Empty, ".", ToString());

    //Write the message to the log
    evtLog.WriteEntry(s, EventLogEntryType.Error);
  }
  catch (Exception e)
  {
    //Throw this exception
    throw e;
  }
}
```

The method will add the error message to the WileyParts Windows Event Log and will use the fully qualified name of the inherited class as the event source. Note that this code is very similar to that provided in the base page class introduced in Chapter 5, "Creating More Advanced ASP.NET Pages."

This class isn't too complex. The nicest thing about it is the ability to log errors to the Event Log easily. With a Web application, sometimes you can end up with errors in your code that may not be entirely detrimental to the application. They may go completely unnoticed to your users, but they could cause data or performance problems. If you carefully catch exceptions and log them to the Event Log, you can examine the error messages on a daily basis until you've cleaned up all of the problems. This is particularly useful during the testing, debugging, and installation phases of an application. In addition to logging errors to the Windows Event Log, you could include your own custom logging, such as to an HTML file, for example.

WileyConnection

The WileyConnection object is nothing but a wrapper object for a SqlConnection. The SqlConnection class is sealed, so you can't inherit from it; however, you can write a class that has a SqlConnection as a private member variable that is exposed via a public property. What are the advantages of doing this? For this particular application there aren't really any advantages. The advantage lies in the ability to use the WileyConnection object in all of your code and not care which managed provider connection object is being encapsulated inside the WileyConnection class. You also wouldn't care if the WileyConnection object changed to encapsulate a connection object from a different managed provider; the managed provider connection objects implement the same interfaces, so your code will still work.

Let's look at a scenario where this is useful. Assume that you are writing a Web application that needs to access an Oracle database initially. You know that down the road, management wants to migrate to SQL Server 2000. Because there isn't an Oracle managed provider yet, you will have to use the OLE DB managed provider. If you encapsulate the OleDbConnection object inside of a custom class such as the WileyConnection object, then later on when you need to migrate to SQL Server, you can simply change the WileyConnection class, and the rest of your code should still work. If you have spread references to the OleDbConnection class throughout your code, then you could have quite a bit of rewriting to do. The following code wraps up the SqlConnection object inside of the WileyConnection object as a demonstration. If you really wanted to go ahead with this concept, you would also need to write classes to encapsulate other classes in the SqlClient namespace such as the SqlDataReader and SqlCommand. Here is the code for the WileyConnection object:

```
public class WileyConnection : WileyObject
{
  //Member variables
  private SqlConnection m_conn;

  //Properties
  public SqlConnection Connection
  {
    get {return m_conn;}
  }
```

```csharp
//The constructor takes a connection string and automatically opens
//the connection
public WileyConnection(string strConnectionString)
{
  Open(strConnectionString);
}


public bool Open(string strConnectionString)
{
  try
  {
    //Make sure this connection isn't already open
    if (m_conn != null)
    {
      if (IsOpen())
        return true;
    }

    m_conn = new SqlConnection(strConnectionString);
    m_conn.Open();
  }
  catch(Exception ex)
  {
    WileyObject.WriteToLog(ex.ToString(), "WileyDatabase");
    throw new Exception("Failed to open database", ex);
  }

  return true;
}

//Is this connection already open?
public bool IsOpen()
{
  try
  {
    //If the connection is already open, just return true
    if (m_conn.State == ConnectionState.Open)
      return true;
    else
      return false;
  }
  catch(Exception ex)
  {
    WileyObject.WriteToLog(ex.ToString(), "WileyDatabase");
    throw new Exception("Failed to determine if database is open",
ex);
  }
}

  //Close the connection
```

```
public bool Close()
{
  try
  {
    if (m_conn == null)
      return true;

    m_conn.Close();
  }
  catch(Exception ex)
  {
    WileyObject.WriteToLog(ex.ToString(), "WileyDatabase");
    throw new Exception("Failed to close database", ex);
  }
  return true;
}
}
```

An alternate approach would be to code to the interface IDbConnection in all of our client code because the managed provider connection classes, SqlConnection and OleDbConnection, implement this interface. We could create a custom connection factory class that creates and returns SqlConnection objects. In our client code, we could call this connection factory class to retrieve a connection object and then call the methods of the connection object via the IDbConnection interface. If we need to change to use the OleDbConnection object in the future, we just change our custom connection factory class, and everything will still work fine in our client code. As mentioned previously, to reap full benefit from this approach you would need to do the same sort of thing for the Command (IDbCommand interface) and DataReader (IdataReader interface) objects. The downside to this is that these common interfaces do not provide access to all of the functionality of the managed provider classes. If you need to access some method or property that is not a part of the common interface, you would still have to cast the interface to the provider-specific class in your client code, which would negate all of the benefit of coding to the common interface. Having said all of that, in our experience it is rare that companies will change database vendors very often. It isn't cost effective for a company to implement SQL Server today and replace it with Oracle or some other database within a few years. The approach that you take in your applications should be on a case-by-case basis.

Vehicle

The Vehicle object encapsulates the Vehicle table. It is implemented in the same manner as the Employee class from Chapter 4. The first thing that shoppers at our Web site are going to need to do is identify for which vehicle they need to find parts. They will do so by selecting a vehicle year from a drop-down box, which will then provide them with a list of Chevrolet models that were available during that year. There are two static methods that we use directly from our Web application to get this information. The first is *GetVehicleYears()*. This method returns an ArrayList of integers that are the distinct vehicle years that exist in the Vehicle table. It creates the ArrayList by using a Sql-Command object to call a stored procedure and then iterating through the rows returned in the SqlDataReader and adding each vehicle year to the ArrayList. The second method is *GetVehiclesByYear()*, which will again return an ArrayList, but this time the ArrayList is filled with Vehicle objects representing all of the vehicles that exist for the year.

PartCategory

The PartCategory is an extremely small object used for encapsulating an extremely small table. After the shopper has selected his or her vehicle, he or she will then need to select a part category such as Engine, Electrical, or Transmission. This will allow us to narrow the part search down to a small subset of parts for the chosen vehicle. All we really need to do is get a list of all of the categories in the Part_Categories table so that we can give the shopper a list from which to choose. The static *GetAllCategories()* method will return an ArrayList of PartCategory objects, to which we can bind an ASP.NET control.

Part

After the shopper has selected his or her vehicle and part category, we will call the *Get-PartsByVehicleAndCategory()* static method of the Part object. Following suit with the other objects, this method calls a stored procedure that gets the matching parts from the Parts table. It then uses the returned SqlDataReader to create an ArrayList of Part objects that will be returned and bound to an ASP.NET control.

Shopper

The Shopper object encapsulates the Shopper table and provides access to the shopper's cart and any orders that have been placed. When the shopper wants to add something to his or her cart, we will create an entry in the Shopper table if one does not already exist. To do this, we'll use the *Add()* method, which calls a stored procedure that takes parameters for all of the fields of the Shopper table and inserts a new record. The stored procedure is called with a SqlCommand object, and the values that are used for the parameters passed to the stored procedure will be the values in the corresponding member variables of the Shopper object. The add method calls a stored procedure named sp_AddShopper, shown here:

```
INSERT INTO WileyParts.dbo.Shopper
(First_Name, Last_Name, Address, City, State_Code, Postal_Code, Phone,
  Email)
VALUES
(@FirstName, @LastName, @Address, @City, @StateCode, @PostalCode,
@Phone,
  @Email)

-- Get the shopper's ID
```

```
SET @ShopperID = @@IDENTITY

RETURN 0
```

Here is the code for the Add() method:

```
public void Add(WileyConnection conn)
{
try
  {
    //Call a stored procedure to add this shopper to the database
    SqlCommand cmd = new SqlCommand("WileyParts.dbo.sp_AddShopper",
      conn.Connection);
    cmd.CommandType = CommandType.StoredProcedure;

    //Create the output parameter for the ShopperID
    cmd.Parameters.Add("@ShopperID", SqlDbType.Int);
    cmd.Parameters["@ShopperID"].Direction = ParameterDirection.Output;

    cmd.Parameters.Add("@FirstName", SqlDbType.VarChar, 20);
    cmd.Parameters["@FirstName"].Value = m_strFirstName;
    cmd.Parameters.Add("@LastName", SqlDbType.VarChar, 50);
    cmd.Parameters["@LastName"].Value = m_strLastName;
    cmd.Parameters.Add("@Address", SqlDbType.VarChar, 60);
    cmd.Parameters["@Address"].Value = m_strAddress;
    cmd.Parameters.Add("@City", SqlDbType.VarChar, 15);
    cmd.Parameters["@City"].Value = m_strCity;
    cmd.Parameters.Add("@StateCode", SqlDbType.VarChar, 2);
    cmd.Parameters["@StateCode"].Value = m_strStateCode;
    cmd.Parameters.Add("@PostalCode", SqlDbType.VarChar, 10);
    cmd.Parameters["@PostalCode"].Value = m_strPostalCode;
    cmd.Parameters.Add("@Phone", SqlDbType.VarChar, 24);
    cmd.Parameters["@Phone"].Value = m_strPhone;
    cmd.Parameters.Add("@Email", SqlDbType.VarChar, 40);
    cmd.Parameters["@Email"].Value = m_strEmail;

    //Execute the command
    cmd.ExecuteNonQuery();

    //Get the shopper's ID
    m_intShopperID = (int)cmd.Parameters["@ShopperID"].Value;
  }
  catch(Exception ex)
  {
    WileyObject.WriteToLog(ex.ToString(), "Shopper");
    throw new Exception("Failed to load shopper from reader", ex);
  }
}
```

The Add() method sets up a SqlCommand object with the appropriate parameters, including an output parameter to return the Shopper_ID of the newly inserted row. The stored procedure inserts a row into the Shopper table using the passed-in parameters. If this insert statement fails in any way, a SQLException will be thrown. This is why it is important to wrap up your database code inside of try/catch blocks, as is done with the Add() method. If an exception occurs, the error message of the exception is added to the errors collection of the Shopper object and the Add() method will return false. This will allow the client code to detect if an error has occurred and then display an appropriate error message. If the insert statement is successful, the stored procedure sets the @ShopperID output parameter equal to @@IDENTITY, which will be the Shopper_ID of the last inserted record. The add method then sets the m_intShopperID member variable to the value passed back in the @ShopperID parameter with this code.

```
m_intShopperID = (int)cmd.Parameters["@ShopperID"].Value;
```

Very similar to the Add() method, there is an *Update()* method that can be called to change or add any information about the shopper, such as name, address, and phone number. Remember, once an entry has been made for the shopper in the Shopper table, he or she will be assigned a Shopper_ID. This ID can then be used to retrieve the shopper's information using the static *GetShopperByID()* method, which will return a Shopper object populated with the shopper's data.

In addition to the properties for all of the fields of the Shopper table, a *ShoppingCart* property is provided for accessing an ArrayList of *ShoppingCartItem* objects. There is also an *Orders* property for accessing an ArrayList of *Order* objects. To populate the ArrayList of ShoppingCartItems, the *GetShoppingCart()* method will need to be called. This is not done automatically; so if you don't need to retrieve the items in the shopper's cart for a particular page, the extra database call won't be performed. After we've retrieved the items in the shopper's cart, several helper methods will give us the Sub Total, Shipping Cost, Sales Tax, and the Total Cost of all of the items in the cart. These methods are ingeniously named *GetCartSubTotal()*, *GetCartShippingCost()*, *GetCartSalesTax()*, and *GetCartTotalCost()*. We can also empty the shopper's cart by calling the *EmptyCart()* method and get the number of items in the shopper's cart (without actually getting the items in the cart) with the *GetShoppingCartItemCount()* method.

Last, there is a *CheckOut()* method. Before we go through the code for this method, let's first look at the remaining objects, which will all be used inside of the CheckOut() method.

ShoppingCartItem

The ShoppingCartItem object is used to maintain the shopper's shopping cart. It is responsible for adding, deleting, and updating records in the Shopping_Cart table. There is an *Add()* method for adding new records, much like that of the Shopper object. There is also a *Delete()* method, which will delete a record from the table, thereby removing an item from a shopper's cart. A static *Delete()* method is also provided, which is more commonly used by a Web application because it doesn't require an instance of the ShoppingCartItem object. Once a shopper has added an item to his or her cart, he or she will be allowed to update the quantity of a particular item. To do this, we'll use the static *UpdateQuantityByID()* method.

Order and OrderItem

The OrderItem object simply provides access to the Order_Items table and at present allows us only to add items to the table using its Add() method. When a shopper checks out, one order item will need to be created for each item in the shopper's cart. In addition, one and only one record will need to be created in the Orders table. This is done with the Order object. The Order object also has an Add() method that adds an entry to the Orders table and retrieves the Order_ID of the newly added record, just as the Shopper.Add() method retrieved the Shopper_ID. The client code should never have a need to call the OrderItem.Add() method directly. Instead, it should call the Order.AddOrderItem() method, shown here:

```
public void AddOrderItem(WileyConnection conn, SqlTransaction trans,
   int intVehicleID, int intPartID, int intCategoryID,
   string strDescription, decimal decPricePerUnit, int intQuantity,
   float fltWeight)
{
   //Create a new OrderItem
   OrderItem item = new OrderItem();
   //Fill in the members
   item.OrderID = m_intOrderID;
   item.VehicleID = intVehicleID;
   item.PartID = intPartID;
   item.CategoryID = intCategoryID;
   item.Description = strDescription;
   item.PricePerUnit = decPricePerUnit;
   item.Weight = fltWeight;
   item.Quantity = intQuantity;

   //Add the item to the database
   item.Add(conn, trans)

   //Add the item to the OrderItem collection
   m_arrOrderItems.Add(item);
}
```

This method takes parameters for all of the fields necessary to create an OrderItem object in addition to the WileyConnection and a SqlTransaction object. (We'll discuss the SqlTransaction in the "Checking Out" section that follows.) It creates the OrderItem object, sets the appropriate properties, and then calls it's Add() method. If all goes well, the new OrderItem object is added to the collection of the Order object.

Checking Out

Now we can go back and look at the CheckOut() method of the Shopper object.

```
public void CheckOut(WileyConnection conn, string strCCNumber,
   string strCCExpirationDate,
```

```
      string strCCType, string strCCHolderName, out int NewOrderId)
{
  NewOrderId = 0;

  //Get the shopping cart
  GetShoppingCart(conn);

  //Create a new Order object
  Order ord = new Order();
  ord.ShopperID = m_intShopperID;
  ord.TotalCost = GetCartTotalCost();
  ord.ShippingCost = GetCartShippingCost();
  ord.SalesTax = GetCartSalesTax();
  ord.CCNumber = strCCNumber;
  ord.CCExpirationDate = strCCExpirationDate;
  ord.CCType = strCCType;
  ord.CCHolderName = strCCHolderName;

  //Start a transaction
  SqlTransaction trans = conn.Connection.BeginTransaction();

  //Add the order to the database
  try
  {
    ord.Add(conn, trans);
  }
  catch(Exception ex)
  {
    //Roll back the transaction
    trans.Rollback();

    WileyObject.WriteToLog(ex.ToString(), "Shopper");
    throw new Exception("Failed to add order - rolled back trans", ex);
  }

  //Iterate through the shopping cart items and create order items
  foreach (ShoppingCartItem item in m_arrShoppingCart)
  {
    //Add an item to the order
    try
    {
      ord.AddOrderItem(conn, trans, item.VehicleID, item.PartID,
        item.CategoryID, item.Description,
        item.PricePerUnit, item.Quantity, item.Weight);
    }
    catch(Exception ex)
    {
      //Roll back the transaction
      trans.Rollback();
```

```
            WileyObject.WriteToLog(ex.ToString(), "Shopper");
            throw new Exception("Failed to checkout - rolled back trans", ex);
        }
    }


    //Commit the transaction
    trans.Commit();

    //Add the order to the collection
    m_arrOrders.Add(ord);

    //Empty the shopper's cart
    EmptyCart(conn);

    //Make OrderId available to caller
    NewOrderId = ord.OrderID;
}
```

This method will be called when the shopper has entered his or her credit card information and confirmed his or her desire to check out. We won't be providing code for calling a credit card validation service in this book. Normally, you would need to validate the given credit card information with one of the numerous credit card validation services on the Internet before calling the CheckOut method. The GetShoppingCart() method is called to retrieve all of the items in the shopper's cart. Then a new Order object is created, and its properties are filled in with the information that is retrieved from the shopping cart, along with the passed-in credit card information.

What we need to do here is first create an entry in the Orders table and then create one or more entries in the Order_Items table. If there is any failure during this process, we will want to clean up any changes that we have made to the database. We won't want an entry in the Orders table that doesn't have corresponding entries in the Order_Items table and vice versa. One solution to this is to use a *SqlTransaction*. This object is provided by the SQL Server managed provider and is used to represent a Transact-SQL transaction. Here is how it works: To start a transaction and acquire a SqlTransaction object, call the SqlConnection.BeginTransaction() method. This method executes the BEGIN TRANSACTION statement on the connection.

```
SqlTransaction trans = conn.Connection.BeginTransaction();
```

We use the Connection property of the WileyConnection object to access the encapsulated SqlConnection object directly and call the BeginTransaction method. We could easily add a BeginTransaction() method to the WileyConnection class to do this for us. The BeginTransaction() method has several overloads that allow you to specify transaction names and isolation levels, but we don't need that functionality here. The SqlTransaction object that is returned is saved in a variable for future use. Once we have a SqlTransaction object, it is the key to controlling the transaction. The Rollback() and

Commit() methods are available to roll back or commit the transaction. Any SqlCommand that should participate in the transaction needs to be given a reference to the SqlTransaction object. Notice that the connection as well as the SqlTransaction are passed into the Order.Add() method as follows:

```
//Add the order to the database
try
{
  ord.Add(conn, trans);
}
catch(Exception ex)
{
  //Rollback the transaction
  trans.Rollback();

  WileyObject.WriteToLog(ex.ToString(), "Shopper");
  throw new Exception("Failed to add order - rolled back trans", ex);
}
```

Inside the Order.Add() method, the SqlTransaction is assigned to the SqlCommand object by setting the Transaction property.

```
//Set the transaction that the command will execute under
cmd.Transaction = trans;
```

If the Order.Add() method fails, an Exception will be thrown. In the CheckOut() method this is caught, and if Order.Add() fails, the exception is logged and thrown up to the calling code, and the Rollback() method of the SqlTransaction object is called and the method returns false. If Order.Add() is successful, an Order_ID will be available for us to assign to the order items that we need to create. This will be the ID that will be given to the shopper so that he or she can track the order. We haven't provided any order tracking facilities yet, so the shopper would just have to call Wiley Parts on the phone. After we have an Order_ID, we need to iterate through the items in the shopping cart and use the information available in each ShoppingCartItem to call the Order.AddOrderItem() method. Once again, pass in the SqlTransaction object, which gets passed down further to the OrderItem.Add() method and is assigned to the SqlCommand object used there. Again, if there is any failure the SqlTransaction.Rollback() method is called.

If the order and order items were created successfully the transaction is committed by calling SqlTransaction.Commit(). The Order object is then added to the Orders collection of the Shopper object. The EmptyCart() method is then called to clear the shopper's cart because those items have already been checked out. Last, the method output parameter, NewOrderId, is set to the OrderID of the newly added order. This ID can be used by the client application to provide the OrderID to the shopper for his or her reference.

WileyPageBaseClass

All of the ASP.NET pages that we write for this application will inherit from the Wiley-PageBaseClass object. This is the same class that was created in Chapter 3, "Server Controls," with a few additions that we will cover here. Recall that this class inherits from System.Web.UI.Page. The methods that were added to the base class in Chapter 3 will remain. Those methods provided an easy way to write to the event log and read and write cookies. The functionality that we added to this class provides an easy way to handle connections to the database.

The first functionality added is a protected WileyConnection member variable. This variable has been declared (m_conn), along with a protected property for accessing it. The property declaration looks like this:

```
protected WileyConnection DBConnection
{
  get
  {
    if (m_conn != null)
    {
      //Make sure the connection is open
      if (m_conn.IsOpen())
      {
        //return the connection
        return m_conn;
      }
    }

    //The connection isn't opened yet, so let's open it
    OpenDBConnection();

    return m_conn;
  }
}
```

Whenever we need to call a method on one of the objects that requires a WileyConnection parameter, we use the *DBConnection* property. The get accessor of the property always makes sure that the returned WileyConnection object is valid and opened for use. If the connection is not already open, the *OpenDBConnection()* method is called, which looks like this:

```
protected bool OpenDBConnection()
{
  //Check to see if this connection is already open
  if (m_conn != null)
  {
    if (!m_conn.Open(ConfigurationSettings.AppSettings["dsn"]))
    {
```

```
        //Navigate to the error page
        Response.Redirect(this.ErrorPage);
        return false;
    }

    return true;
  }

  m_conn = new
    WileyConnection(ConfigurationSettings.AppSettings["dsn"]);

  return true;
}
```

First, this method checks to see if there is already a valid WileyConnection object. If so, it calls the Open() method and, if there are no errors, it returns true. Notice that the connection string that is passed to the open method is retrieved from an AppSetting key named dsn. We will need to add the dsn key to the <appsettings> section of our Web.Config file, as we discussed in the Web.Config section of Chapter 5. If there is no valid WileyConnection object, then a new one is created. The connection is opened in the constructor of the WileyConnection object, so this is all taken care of in one clean step.

Next there is a *CloseDBConnection()* method.

```
protected void CloseDBConnection()
{
  if (m_conn != null)
    m_conn.Close();
}
```

This method ensures that the connection to the database is closed and once again redirects the user to the error page if an error occurs. The last thing of note in this class is that we have wired up a handler for the Page.Unload event in the constructor with this line of code.

```
Page.Unload += new System.EventHandler(Page_Unload);
```

The Unload event occurs when the page is unloaded from memory. This is a great place to clean up resources such as database connections. Here is the simple implementation.

```
private void Page_Unload(object sender, EventArgs e)
{
  //Close the database connection
  CloseDBConnection();
}
```

All that we need to do is call the CloseDBConnection() method, and the database connection will be closed. One thing: The CloseDBConnection() method can be called at any time, and although it will be called when the page is unloaded from memory, there may be times when you would want to call it manually. For example, if you've opened a database connection and are done with it, but your page has a lengthy operation that must be performed afterward, you could call CloseDBConnection manually rather than wait for it to be called automatically when the page unloads.

That's all that has been added to this class. We think that you will find the database connection features very handy and easy to use in your client code.

WileyControlBaseClass

This class is identical to WileyPageBaseClass with the exception that it inherits from System.Web.UI.UserControl rather than System.Web.UI.Page. We will use this class as the base class for any user controls that we create.

Creating the User Interface

Now that we have a usable data model and set of objects to support the functionality of the business, we will create the user interface to the actual Web application. One of the design goals of this application is to achieve as much abstraction as possible between the user interface and the business logic and database system. To meet this requirement, we won't have any data access in the application whatsoever. Nowhere will we access any of the data without doing so through the object model. We will employ many of the framework controls and objects that we have studied so far in the book, and we will use ASP.NET Sessions and ViewState for keeping application information across trips to the server. We've limited our code in the book to the lines under discussion; complete code for all of the pages in the application is available on the companion Web site. Let's jump right into the app starting with the application startup code in Global.asax.

The WileyError Page

The WileyError page is used to show that an error has occurred. If an exception is thrown on any of the pages in the application, we go directly to this page. In the

QueryString used to request this page, we pass the error message so that it can be displayed to the user. We could have set up a default error message in IIS to be displayed whenever there is a scripting error, but handling this manually lends more power to us; we could not have passed the error message if we had let IIS handle the error automatically. Figure 6.2 is an example of the error page in action.

Here is a code snippet for displaying the error page:

```
try
{
    //Application code here
}
catch(Exception ex)
{
    ShowErrorPage(ex);
}
```

Of course, the ShowErrorPage method is in the base class, and it can easily be called from anywhere in the application to provide a consistent feedback to problems encountered. Plus, making this call in every exception is a simple way to ensure the user never sees the standard unhandled exception screen generated by the system.

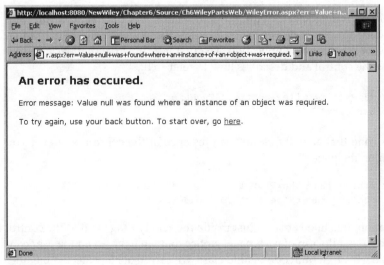

Figure 6.2   The error page.

The HeaderBar User Control

The HeaderBar is a user control, which we discussed in Chapter 5. This control displays the logo and a simple navigation menu on top of all the pages of the application. This is not just a couple of links, as many menus are. The HeaderBar user control is a smart menu; it will display a link to go to the cart page only if it determines that there are, in fact, items in the cart. It also dynamically displays a greeting to the user, which helps the user see that the application knows who he or she is. Although it is not a problem to go to the cart page when there are no cart items, it would be a problem to go there if the shopper had not been assigned a valid shopper ID yet. Alternately, we could handle checking for items in the cart page or even in the user control, but this example demonstrates that you can perform useful operations in a user control.

NOTE Remember not to include a <form> tag in a user control, which can cause problems in ASP.NET. Also, there is no need to include <html>, <title>, or <head> tags in a user control because the control will be a part of the page in which it is used, which will have already provided the tag. If you are relying on styles or a link to a style sheet in your user control, the styles that are included in the main page will not be applied to the user control when viewing it inside the Visual Studio .NET IDE; the styles will take effect in the browser at runtime, however.

Although there is nothing special required in the ascx file of the user control, there are at least two extra lines of code needed in the page that hosts the user control that will appear in every page in this application. The first is a directive that declares that the page may use the control and describes how to refer to it:

```
<%@ Register TagPrefix="wiley_control" TagName="HeaderBar"
  src="Headerbar.ascx" %>
```

The second is code that actually declares an instance of the control wherever you want it to appear on the page:

```
<wiley_control:headerBar ShowProfileLink="true" ShowCartLink="true"
ShowShopLink="false" runat="server" ID="HeaderBar1" />
```

In this application, this line is placed just inside the <body> tag, so that the control will be displayed first at the top of each page. Notice that we have given the user control an ID of HeaderBar1. In our code-behind class, we can create a protected member variable of type headerBar, and then access it in code, like this:

```
protected headerBar HeaderBar1;
...
HeaderBar1.Visbile = true;
HeaderBar1.ShowProfileLink = true;
```

In the next code snippet we will see what our code-behind in the user control does. First, it checks in Session state to see if there is a valid shopper object. There will be a shopper object only during the visit of the shopper, so if the shopper is making his or her first request to the application, this object will not yet exist. If the shopper object exists, we show or hide user interface objects, links in this case, accordingly. If the shopper object does not exist, we must look in the cookies collection to determine if he or she has been here before. If so, we read the shopper ID from the cookie, load the shopper object into Session state, and continue. If the shopper has no cookie for our site, then we must create the shopper object for the first time. Once it is created by the call to Shopper.Add(), again we store the new shopper object in Session state and continue. The only difference for a new shopper is that we don't yet know his or her name, so we simply refer to him or her as "New Shopper."

Also here is the code that limits access to the cart page if there are no cart items. It renders the cart link invisible when appropriate. The aspc page is very simple and has only an image for the logo and a few HyperLink controls for navigation. Also in the code-behind file are the public properties for each of the programmable features of the user control. In this code snippet, we show you a public property called ShowProfileLink, which is set in the declaration of the control in an aspx file, as seen in the previous snippet. Because we included the user control in the aspx code pages at design time, we can set these properties there. When the control is loaded, it can create its user interface based on the properties. If we didn't expose these properties, then the containing page would have no way to customize the user control. There are a few other properties, but for this example, we are looking at just this one.

```csharp
private bool m_blnShowProfileLink = false;
public bool ShowProfileLink
{
  get { return m_blnShowProfileLink; }
  set { m_blnShowProfileLink = value; }
}

...

private void Page_Load(object sender, System.EventArgs e)
{
  try
  {
    Shopper shopper = (Shopper)Session["ShopperObject"];

    if (shopper == null)
    {
      //There is no shopper in the session state, so look for it in the
      //cookies.
      string strShopperID = ReadCookie("WileyParts", "ShopperId");

      if (strShopperID.Length > 0)
      {
```

```csharp
        /* If the lenth of the string returned by ReadCookie is greater
         * than 0, then the client has a ShopperId in his cookie
         * collection. Create a shopper object, and store it in session
         * state. */

        shopper = Shopper.GetShopperByID(DBConnection,
          Convert.ToInt32(strShopperID));

        Session["ShopperObject"] = shopper;
      }
      else
      {
        //The client does not have a ShopperID yet, so create one for him.
        shopper = new Shopper();
        shopper.Add(DBConnection);

        //Save the new shopper in session state.
        Session["ShopperObject"] = shopper;

        //Write the ShopperId to an indefinite persistant cookie cookie.
        WriteCookie("WileyParts", "ShopperId",
          shopper.ShopperID.ToString(), DateTime.MaxValue);
      }

      //No shopper object yet, so show links accordingly.
      lnkProfile.Visible = false;
      lnkViewCart.Visible = false;
      lblShopper.Text = "";
    }

    //Show links accordingly.
    int count;
    shopper.GetShoppingCartItemCount(DBConnection, out count);
    if (count > 0)
      lnkViewCart.Visible = m_blnShowCartLink;

    lnkShop.Visible = m_blnShowShopLink;
    lnkProfile.Visible = m_blnShowProfileLink;

    //Now show shopper name if they have entered one yet.
    if (shopper.FirstName.Trim().Length > 0)
      lblShopper.Text = string.Format("Welcome: {0}",
        shopper.FirstName);
    else
        lblShopper.Text = "Welcome: New Shopper";
  }
  catch(Exception ex)
  {
    ShowErrorPage(ex);
  }
}
```

The VehicleSelect Page

The VehicleSelect page is the first page of the application; this is the entry point for public users. The user will be presented with a drop-down list of years for vehicles. When the user selects a year, he or she will be presented with all of the vehicles in our database for that year. When the user selects a vehicle, he or she will move to the next page. This page, like all of the pages in this application, has been kept simple, so you can see just what is important, without a lot of complexity. Now let's look at the aspx code that lays out the grid. Notice how we chose to set the AutoGenerateColumns property to false because we want to see only a specific portion of the Vehicle objects in our display. Our DataGrid is quite simple and consists of the Make, Model, a custom HeaderStyle, and a ButtonColumn so that the user can actually choose a vehicle from the list.

```
<asp:DataGrid font-size=9pt AutoGenerateColumns=false Width=100%
  id=grdVehicles datakeyfield="VehicleID" runat="server">

  <Columns>
    <asp:ButtonColumn Text="Buy Parts" ItemStyle-Width=80px
      CommandName="Select">

    </asp:ButtonColumn>

    <asp:BoundColumn HeaderText="Make" DataField="Make">
    </asp:BoundColumn>

    <asp:BoundColumn HeaderText="Model" DataField="FullModel">
    </asp:BoundColumn>
  </Columns>

  <HeaderStyle Font-Bold="True" ForeColor="White" BackColor="Maroon">
  </HeaderStyle>
</asp:DataGrid>
```

As in the section on the DataGrid, the HeaderStyle template item describes the look of the header row. In this simple grid, we don't have to include a FooterStyle because the grid has no footer. The built-in ButtonColumn is used with the CommandName of "Select" and some simple bound columns. Remember that we needed to set the Auto-GenerateColumns property to false; otherwise, the columns would be accompanied by all of the columns (properties) of each data source item. Because the ButtonColumn is a Select button, the SelectedIndexChanged event is fired when clicked. We chose to use the default hyperlink style ButtonColumn because it looks best with the thin rows in the grid. Now, let's look at the page-loading code in the code-behind file:

```
protected void Page_Load()
{
  if (!IsPostBack)
  {
    try
    {
```

```
            //Bind for available model years
            cboYear.DataSource = Vehicle.GetVehicleYears(DBConnection);
            cboYear.DataBind();
            cboYear.Items.Insert(0, "Select");
        }
        catch(Exception ex)
        {
            ShowErrorPage(ex);
        }
    }
    else
    {
        //Don't need this item after first selection is made.
        cboYear.Items.Remove("Select");
    }
}
```

Let's examine this code in more detail. First, everything is wrapped in a try...catch, and the error page is called if any exception is thrown. This is done throughout the entire application. Next, the drop-down list control is filled with the available years. To do this, we bind to the ArrayList of year strings that is returned by the Vehicle object. Because this page is derived from WileyPageBaseClass, the DBConnection variable is passed to the method. We didn't need to use the DataTextField or DataValueField because the data source contains only strings. If each year were enveloped in an object, then we would have had to provide the name of the property that we will want to use as the value and text of the list items. Because these properties are not set, the list calls ToString() on each object, in hopes that it will return a useful piece of data to be displayed in the list. Because the years are strings, they do support ToString(), which returns the actual year. When not in a PostBack situation, the string "Select" is inserted into the list. This serves two purposes: It shows the user a clue as to what to do first, and second, it forces the user to select a year. This causes the SelectedIndexChanged event to be fired for the control, which is where the code to get the vehicles resides. On the PostBack, we remove the "Select" from the list, so it won't cause problems in the handler code. Let's look at the code for when a user selects a year from the list.

```
protected void cboYear_SelectedIndexChanged(object sender,
    System.EventArgs e)
{
    try
    {
        //Make sure a year is selected
        if (cboYear.SelectedItem.Text == "Select") return;

        //Load vehicles for the selected year
        ArrayList data = Vehicle.GetVehiclesByYear(DBConnection,
            Convert.ToInt32(cboYear.SelectedItem.Text));

        lblFound.Text = string.Format("{0} vehicle(s) found", data.Count);

        if (data.Count > 0)
```

```
      {
        //Bind for available model years
        grdVehicles.DataSource = data;
        grdVehicles.DataBind();
        lblFound.Visible = true;
      }
    }
    catch(Exception ex)
    {
      ShowErrorPage(ex);
    }
  }
```

First, while inside the try...catch the GetVehiclesByYear method is called on the Vehicle object and the returned ArrayList used for binding in the DataGrid. Next, we get the count of the items found to display in a label and finally bind the DataGrid to the ArrayList of vehicles.

NOTE When binding a control such as a DataGrid to a collection such as an ArrayList, it is sometimes nice to show the count of the rows before or after the grid. In an ArrayList, this can be found by simply accessing the Count property. In an array, we can use the Length property. A SqlDataReader is different in that it is forward-only and does not know its contents until it has read them all. For this reason, there is no count or length property on it. In that case, we can simply have our control bind to the SqlDataReader, then get the count of items in the control. Most controls support this; the DataGrid exposes it through the Items.Count property.

When the user selects a vehicle from the list, theDataGrids SelectedIndex event will be fired, because there is a ButtonColumn with a CommandName of 'Select' in the grid. An item in this ButtonColumn is what the user will click. Now for the code that handles a selection of a vehicle:

```
protected void grdVehicles_SelectedIndexChanged(object sender,
  System.EventArgs e)
{
  try
  {
    //Store the user's vehicle choice for later use.
    Session["CurrentVehId"] =
      grdVehicles.DataKeys[grdVehicles.SelectedIndex].ToString();

  }
  catch(Exception ex)
  {
    ShowErrorPage(ex);
  }
    Response.Redirect("categories.aspx");
}
```

The currently selected vehicle ID is stored in a Session state variable for later use. This works well in this particular application; passing the vehicle ID via a QueryString would be less than ideal because the next page called doesn't use it, but the one after it does. Using the QueryString would have required us to pass it along twice. Next, we call Redirect to move to the next page. Redirect is the standard method used to move between pages in server-side code. Figure 6.3 shows the resulting page in action after the user has selected a year.

That's all there is to the vehicle selection page. Try to imagine what the code would look like in classic ASP for this page. This code, in ASP.NET, is far more elegant, clean, and maintainable. Now let's move on to the second page, the categories page.

The Categories Page

The Categories page allows the user to select a category in which to search for parts. This time, we used a DataList. We could easily have used a DataGrid as on the VehicleSelect page, but we wanted to get some practice with the more advanced DataList. Using the DataList allows us to customize fully what is in each cell of the grid, as opposed to forcing us to use just the ButtonColumns and BoundColumns of the DataGrid. By using the DataList, we are able to help keep more of the categories on the same screen, without scrolling as much, due to the fact that the DataList supports multiple columns with the RepeatColumns property. When the user selects a category, he

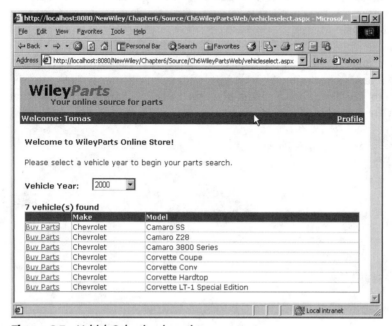

Figure 6.3 VehicleSelection in action.

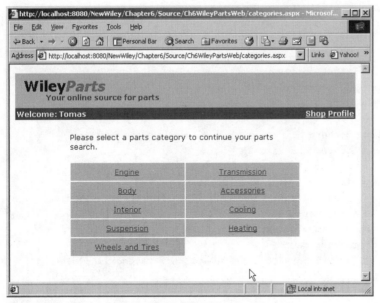

Figure 6.4   The Categories page in action.

or she will be sent to the next page, which will show parts for only the selected category. When the page loads, the DataList binds to the collection of categories returned from the call to the GetAllCategories method. Figure 6.4 shows the page in action.

First, we'll look at the aspx code, in which we create a DataList to display the categories. Each category is displayed as a HyperLink control, inside a small table to add a box shape around each item. You can see the table in the item template, along with its contents, which is a LinkButton bound to the Description property of the bound category object. For each record (or object in this case) that is in the data source, an HTML table will be created from the ItemTemplate. Notice how we also bound to the CatagoryID for the CommandArgument on each HyperLink so that we can easily check which category the user wants in the server-side code.

> **NOTE** We used the CommandName to store the key of the category so that we can determine which category was selected in the code-behind class. We could have used the DataKeyField just as we did on the DataGrid in the VehicleSelect page, but we wanted to use this technique here as an alternative. Also remember that in order to bind in the aspx code, we had to include the Import statement to bring the correct namespace into scope.

```
<%@ Import Namespace="WileyParts.Objects" %>
.
.
.
<asp:DataList id=lstCategories repeatcolumns=2 runat="server">
  <ItemTemplate>
    <table width=200px bgcolor=tan cellpadding=5>
      <tr>
        <td align=center>
          <font face=verdana size=2>

            <asp:linkbutton width=100% text='
              <%# ((PartCategory)Container.DataItem).Description %>'
              Runat=server
              CommandName='select'
              CommandArgument='
            <%#((PartCategory)Container.DataItem).CategoryID.ToString()
%>'>

            </asp:linkbutton>
          </font>
        </td>
      </tr>
    </table>
  </ItemTemplate>
</asp:DataList>
```

Now, let's look at the page load code, which simply binds the DataList to the categories data source.

```
protected void Page_Load(object sender, System.EventArgs e)
{
  if (!IsPostBack)
  {
    try
    {
      //Bind for available model years
      lstCategories.DataSource =
        PartCategory.GetAllCategories(DBConnection);

      lstCategories.DataBind();
    }
    catch(Exception ex)
```

```
    {
      ShowErrorPage(ex);
    }
  }
}
```

When the user selects a category from the DataList, we will get the ItemCommand event in the code-behind because each DataList item has a LinkButton with its CommandName enabled. Remember that even though the user is clicking on a LinkButton control, the DataList raises the event because a DataList is able to bubble events up from its contained controls. In this handler, we redirect to the next page, passing the selected category ID along in the QueryString. This is where the CommandArgument comes in handy. We have access to the CommandName property through the DataListCommandEventArgs argument of the event handler. This is given to us by the framework, and with it we can determine the category ID because it was stored in this property to begin with.

```
protected void lstCategories_ItemCommand(object source,
   System.Web.UI.WebControls.DataListCommandEventArgs e)
{
   Response.Redirect(string.Format("partselect.aspx?catid={0}",
      e.CommandArgument));
}
```

The PartSelect Page

On the PartSelect page, the parts that are available for the specific year and vehicle that the user selected are loaded into a DataList. This is basically the products page of the shopping cart site. The user selects the items he or she wants to buy, and they are inserted into the cart. In the code for the page, we get the category ID from the QueryString and store it in the ViewState object. This means that it will be stored invisibly on the client's browser in a hidden field, so that it can be known on this page's next trip to the server. We could have stored this in another Session state variable, but we wanted to use a different technique this time. Next, retrieve the current vehicle ID from the Session variable, and set the DataSource for the DataList to the parts returned by calling GetPartsByVehicleAndCategory on the Part object. The vehicle is displayed in the caption on the screen so the user can check that he or she is looking at parts for the correct automobile. In this case, the vehicle information is displayed in a Label control. Figure 6.5 shows the page in action.

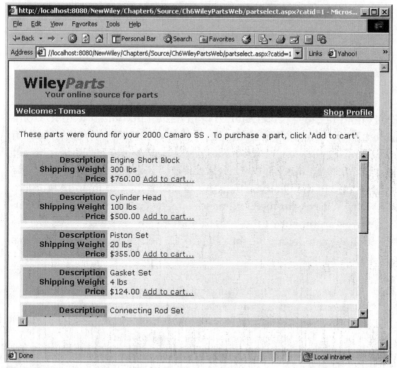

Figure 6.5 The parts selection page in action.

The following is the aspx code for the page. Remember, although we don't include it in the code that follows, we must use the Import directive to access the objects in the namespace, as we did in the previous example. We use a standard DataList again. As you can see, the DataList can quickly become a valued member of your programmer's toolbox when writing Web applications with ASP.NET.

```
<div style="height:300px;overflow:scroll;">
  <asp:DataList id=lstParts runat="server">
    <ItemTemplate>
      <table width=600px cellpadding=5>
        <tr bgcolor=lemonchiffon>
          <td>
            <font face=verdana size=2>
              <asp:label width=150px style="text-align:right"
                backcolor=tan font-bold=true runat=server>
                Description 
              </asp:label>

              <asp:label id=lblDesc runat=server Text='<%#
                ((Part)Container.DataItem).Description %>'>
              </asp:label>
              <br>

              <asp:label width=150px style="text-align:right"
```

```
                        backcolor=tan font-bold=true runat=server>
                        Price 
                      </asp:label>

                      <asp:label id=lblWeight runat=server Text='<%#
                        ((Part)Container.DataItem).Weight + " lbs" %>'>
                      </asp:label>
                      <br>

                      <asp:label width=150px style="text-align:right"
                        backcolor=tan font-bold=true runat=server>
                        Shipping Weight 
                      </asp:label>

                      <asp:label id=lblPrice runat=server Text='
                        <%# string.Format("{0:c}",
  ((Part)Container.DataItem).Price)
                        %>'>
                      </asp:label>

                      <asp:LinkButton Text="Add to cart..."
                        Runat=server
                        CommandName='add'
                        CommandArgument='
                          <%# ((Part)Container.DataItem).PartID.ToString() %>'>
                      </asp:LinkButton>
                    </font>
                  </td>
                </tr>
              </table>
          </ItemTemplate>
        </asp:DataList>
  </div>
```

Each part item is created from Label controls and a LinkButton. The LinkButton has a CommandName of "add" even though we don't use it in the server-side code. This gives us the option to add more buttons to each part item at a later date, such as a View Detail button that would display the specifications for the selected part. If we were to add another button, we would need to check the CommandName in the event handler to see which button was clicked. Here, because there is only one button, the CommandName of "add" is really optional. We have used more controls in the ItemTemplate this time, so you can see that the items in a DataList can be as complex as you need them to be. The controls are bound to the part objects from the data source in the usual fashion, except for the Price property, which makes use of the string.Format method to display it in a currency format. Also, notice how a standard HTML <div> tag adds scroll bars to the parts list. Next, we move on to the page-loading section of the code-behind.

```
protected void Page_Load(object sender, System.EventArgs e)
{
  try
```

```
{
    int catid =
Convert.ToInt32(Request.QueryString["catid"].ToString());
    ViewState["CatId"] = catid.ToString();
    int vehid = Convert.ToInt32(Session["CurrentVehId"].ToString());
    lstParts.DataSource =
Part.GetPartsByVehicleAndCategory(DBConnection,
        vehid, catid);

    lstParts.DataBind();

    //Load vehicle desc
    Vehicle vehicle = Vehicle.GetVehicleByID(DBConnection,
        Convert.ToInt32(Session["CurrentVehId"]));

    lblVehicleDesc.Text = string.Format("{0} {1}", vehicle.VehicleYear,
        vehicle.FullModel);
    }
    catch(Exception ex)
    {
        ShowErrorPage(ex);
    }
}
```

When the user selects a part to buy, the ItemCommand event is fired for the DataList. In this function, the part selected is added to the cart. When the user selects a part, a new ShoppingCartItem object is created, and its data is populated. This object is filled by interrogating the DataList for the respective controls in each item, via calling FindControl.

NOTE We could have saved the part IDs in the DataKeyField of the DataList and then loaded the real Part object when an item was selected. Then, we could have built the ShoppingCartItem from the Part item instead of having to interrogate the DataList controls for their values. That would have required another query from the database to get the part, when most of the properties of the part already exist in the list item. Plus, this shows you an alternative to always going to the database for the needed data.

In this handler, we also need to determine whether the shopper has given us his or her personal information yet. We do this by checking the Boolean IsComplete property of the Shopper object. This property checks all of the required fields of the Shopper object. If data exists for all of the required fields the property will return true; otherwise, it will return false. Here is what the handler looks like:

```
protected void lstParts_ItemCommand(object source,
    System.Web.UI.WebControls.DataListCommandEventArgs e)
{
    bool blnFirstItem = false;
    try
    {
```

```
//Get the shopper object out of the session state
Shopper shopper = (Shopper)Session["ShopperObject"];

if (shopper.IsComplete)
{
  //Set the FirstItem flag to true so that we know to redirect the
  //user to the profile page to acquire or confirm his personal
  //information.
  blnFirstItem = true;
}

//Add part to cart
ShoppingCartItem item = new ShoppingCartItem();
item.CategoryID = Convert.ToInt32(ViewState["CatId"].ToString());
item.Description = ((Label)e.Item.FindControl("lblDesc")).Text;
item.PartID = Convert.ToInt32(e.CommandArgument);
item.PricePerUnit =
  Convert.ToDecimal(((Label)e.Item.FindControl(
  "lblPrice")).Text.Replace("$", ""));

item.Quantity = 1;
item.ShopperID = shopper.ShopperID;
item.VehicleID = Convert.ToInt32(Session["CurrentVehId"]);
item.Weight = Convert.ToInt32(((Label)e.Item.FindControl(
  "lblWeight")).Text.Replace(" lbs", ""));

item.Add(DBConnection)

catch(Exception ex)
{
  ShowErrorPage(ex);
}
  if (blnFirstItem)
    //Go to profile page
    Response.Redirect("profile.aspx");
  else
    //Go to cart page
    Response.Redirect("cart.aspx");  }
}
```

The Profile Page

The profile page is the place where the user enters his or her demographic information. This is stored across visits and is reloaded via a cookie the next time the shopper visits the site. The page is a simple data-entry page, consisting of TextBoxes, a DropDown-List, and an ImageButton with which to save the input. You can see what the page looks like in Figure 6.6; then we move straight into the aspx code, of which we will look at only a small snippet.

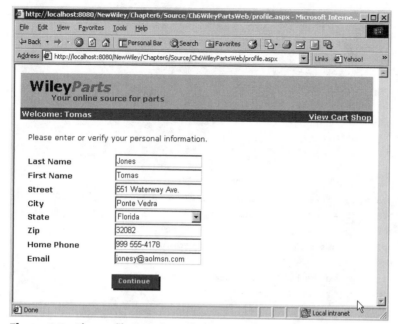

Figure 6.6   The profile page in action.

```
<asp:label width="150px" font-bold="true" runat="server" id="Label7">
  Home Phone</asp:label>

<asp:textbox itemstyle-width="200px" runat="server"
  id="txtHomePhone"></asp:textbox>

<asp:RequiredFieldValidator id="RequiredFieldValidator6" runat="server"
  ErrorMessage="Required Field" ControlToValidate="txtHomePhone">
  </asp:RequiredFieldValidator>

<br>

<asp:label width="150px" font-bold="true" runat="server" id="Label8">
  Email</asp:label>

<asp:textbox itemstyle-width="200px" runat="server"
id="txtEmail"></asp:textbox>

<asp:RequiredFieldValidator id="RequiredFieldValidator7" runat="server"
  ErrorMessage="Required Field" ControlToValidate="txtEmail">
  </asp:RequiredFieldValidator>

<br>
```

```
<br>

<asp:label width="150px" font-bold="true" runat="server"
  id="Label9"></asp:label>

<asp:Imagebutton alttext="Continue" ImageUrl="images/continue.gif"
  runat="server" id="btnContinue"></asp:Imagebutton>
```

The aspx code is made up of simple entry fields with validation controls attached. The only thing worth mentioning is the blank Label control before the ImageButton. This ensures that the button lines up directly underneath the controls above it. The code-behind code is straightforward as well. When the page is loaded, the shopper's information in displayed in the fields, and when the user clicks the Save button, the shopper's information is updated via a call to Shopper.Save. We included only a few states in the list for the example, but the list might be better suited to Data Binding to states stored in a database.

```
protected void Page_Load(object sender, System.EventArgs e)
{
  try
  {
    if (!IsPostBack)
    {
      //Load states into list
      cboState.Items.Add(new ListItem("", ""));
      cboState.Items.Add(new ListItem("Alabama", "AL"));
      cboState.Items.Add(new ListItem("Florida", "FL"));
      cboState.Items.Add(new ListItem("Georgia", "GA"));
      cboState.Items.Add(new ListItem("North Carolina", "NC"));
      cboState.Items.Add(new ListItem("South Carolina", "SC"));

      //Load any existing shopper contact info
      Shopper shopper = (Shopper)Session["ShopperObject"];
      txtCity.Text = shopper.City.Trim();
      txtEmail.Text = shopper.Email.Trim();
      txtFirstName.Text = shopper.FirstName.Trim();
      txtHomePhone.Text = shopper.Phone.Trim();
      txtLastName.Text = shopper.LastName.Trim();
      txtStreet.Text = shopper.Address.Trim();
      txtZip.Text = shopper.PostalCode.Trim();

      //Load correct state
      for(int i = 0; i < cboState.Items.Count; i++)
      {
        if (cboState.Items[i].Value == shopper.StateCode)
        {
          cboState.SelectedIndex = i;
          break;
        }
      }
    }
```

```
      }
    }
    catch(Exception ex)
    {
      ShowErrorPage(ex);
    }
  }


  protected void btnContinue_Click(object sender,
    System.Web.UI.ImageClickEventArgs e)
  {
    try
    {
      //Save shopper's info
      Shopper shopper = (Shopper)Session["ShopperObject"];
      shopper.City = txtCity.Text.Trim();
      shopper.Email = txtEmail.Text.Trim();
      shopper.FirstName = txtFirstName.Text.Trim();
      shopper.Phone = txtHomePhone.Text.Trim();
      shopper.LastName = txtLastName.Text.Trim();
      shopper.Address = txtStreet.Text.Trim();
      shopper.PostalCode = txtZip.Text.Trim();
      shopper.StateCode = cboState.SelectedItem.Value;
      shopper.Update(DBConnection);

    }
  catch(Exception ex)
  {
    ShowErrorPage(ex);
  }
    //Redirect to cart page
    Response.Redirect("cart.aspx");
  }
```

The Cart Page

The cart page is one of the most complex pages in the whole application. On this page, the user will be able to see what he or she has placed in the cart so far, as well as delete items and edit their quantities. First, we load the cart by loading the shopper and calling the GetShoppingCart method to which the cart's DataList is bound. When we load the DataList, we handle things a little differently than in other pages so far. For the footer of the cart, we want to show the cart totals, so we will need to know when during the Data Binding stage the DataList is ready to create the last row of the cart—the footer. For the footer, we have controls that are embedded in the Footer Template of the DataList, as we do for the different controls used while editing the cart item. First, let's look at the page in action in Figure 6.7; then we will look into the aspx code.

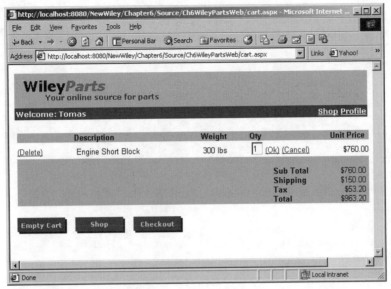

Figure 6.7 The shopping cart page in action.

```
<asp:DataList id=lstCart datakeyfield="ShoppingCartItemID"
runat="server">
  <HeaderTemplate>
    <div style="background-color:tan">
      <font face=arial size=2>
        <asp:label width=100px font-bold=true runat=server>
        </asp:label>

        <asp:label width=220px font-bold=true runat=server>
          Description
        </asp:label>

        <asp:label width=80px font-bold=true runat=server>
          Weight
        </asp:label>

        <asp:label width=120px font-bold=true runat=server>
          Qty
        </asp:label>
```

```
              <asp:label width=80px font-bold=true runat=server
                style="text-align:right">
                Unit Price
              </asp:label>
          </font>
        </div>
    </HeaderTemplate>


    <ItemTemplate>
      <div>
        <font face=arial size=2>
          <asp:LinkButton width=100px Text="(Delete)" CommandName="delete"
            runat=server>
          </asp:LinkButton>

          <asp:label width=220px runat=server><%#
            ((ShoppingCartItem)Container.DataItem).Description %>
          </asp:label>

          <asp:label width=80px runat=server><%#
            ((ShoppingCartItem)Container.DataItem).Weight + " lbs" %>
          </asp:label>

          <asp:label width=20px runat=server><%#
            ((ShoppingCartItem)Container.DataItem).Quantity %>
          </asp:label>

          <asp:LinkButton Text="(Change)" width=100px CommandName="edit"
            runat=server>
          </asp:LinkButton>

          <asp:label width=80px runat=server style="text-align:right"><%#
            string.Format("{0:c}",
              ((ShoppingCartItem)Container.DataItem).PricePerUnit)%>
          </asp:label>
        </font>
      </div>
    </ItemTemplate>


    <EditItemTemplate>
      <div>
        <font face=arial size=2>
          <asp:LinkButton width=100px Text="(Delete)" CommandName="delete"
            runat=server>
          </asp:LinkButton>

          <asp:label width=220px runat=server><%#
            ((ShoppingCartItem)Container.DataItem).Description %>
          </asp:label>

          <asp:label width=80px runat=server><%#
            ((ShoppingCartItem)Container.DataItem).Weight + " lbs" %>
          </asp:label>
```

```
      <asp:TextBox width=20px runat=server   id=txtQty text='<%#
        ((ShoppingCartItem)Container.DataItem).Quantity %>'>
      </asp:TextBox>

      <asp:LinkButton Text="(Ok)" CommandName="update"
        runat=server>
      </asp:LinkButton>

      <asp:LinkButton Text="(Cancel)" CommandName="cancel"
        runat=server>
      </asp:LinkButton>

      <asp:label width=80px runat=server
        style="text-align:right"><%#
        string.Format("{0:c}",((ShoppingCartItem)Container.DataItem).
        PricePerUnit)%>
      </asp:label>
    </font>
  </div>
</EditItemTemplate>

<FooterTemplate>
  <div style="background-color:tan">
    <font face=arial size=2>
      <br>
        <asp:label width=450px font-bold=true runat=server>
        </asp:label>

        <asp:label width=80px font-bold=true runat=server>
          Sub Total
        </asp:label>

        <asp:label width=80px runat=server id=lblSubTotal
          style="text-align:right">
        </asp:label>
        <br>

        <asp:label width=450px font-bold=true runat=server>
        </asp:label>

        <asp:label width=80px font-bold=true runat=server>
          Shipping
        </asp:label>

        <asp:label width=80px runat=server id=lblShipping
          style="text-align:right">
        </asp:label>
        <br>

        <asp:label width=450px font-bold=true
          runat=server></asp:label>
```

```
      <asp:label width=80px font-bold=true
         runat=server>Tax</asp:label>

      <asp:label width=80px runat=server id=lblTax style="text-
         align:right">
      </asp:label>
      <br>

      <asp:label width=450px font-bold=true
         runat=server></asp:label>

      <asp:label width=80px font-bold=true runat=server>
         Total
      </asp:label>

      <asp:label width=80px runat=server id=lblTotal
         style="text-align:right">
      </asp:label>
    </font>
  </div>
 </FooterTemplate>
</asp:DataList>
</P>
<asp:Hyperlink id=lnkCheckOut  ImageUrl="images/checkout.gif"
  NavigateURL="checkout.aspx" runat=server
  altText="Checkout">
</asp:HyperLink> 

<asp:ImageButton id=btnEmptyCart ImageUrl="images/emptycart.gif"
  runat=server altText="Empty Cart">
</asp:ImageButton>
```

In the aspx page, we have created a DataList, just as we have on other pages thus far. But, this time, we are using a dedicated template for the different parts of the grid. For the cart items, we are displaying the item information nicely formatted in Label controls in the ItemTemplate, which are bound to the ShoppingCartItem objects in the data source. For the HeaderTemplate, we are defining static Label controls simply to display the text that makes up the column headers. For the FooterTemplate, as mentioned before, we are using Label controls again, but this time to display the cart summary information. What is probably the most complex part of the DataList is the Edit-ItemTemplate. In this template, we use Labels to show some of the cart item data, but we also use a TextBox and a few link buttons, with which the user can change the quantity of any item in the cart. We will study this more in detail, but first let's look at how the page is loaded and how the items are created during the data binding stage. We will need to reuse the code that loads the page in several places, so we have placed it in a method called LoadPage(), which will be called by the Page_Load method.

```
protected Shopper m_shopper = null;

protected void Page_Load(object sender, System.EventArgs e)
{
```

```
    if (!IsPostBack)
    {
      LoadPage();
    }
}

private void LoadPage()
{
  try
  {
    m_shopper = (Shopper)Session["ShopperObject"];
    m_shopper.GetShoppingCart(DBConnection);

    if (m_shopper.ShoppingCart.Count == 0)
    {
      btnEmptyCart.Visible = false;
      lnkCheckOut.Visible = false;
      lblCartEmpty.Visible = true;
      lstCart.Visible = false;
    }
    else
    {
      btnEmptyCart.Visible = true;
      lnkCheckOut.Visible = true;
      lblCartEmpty.Visible = false;
      lstCart.DataSource = m_shopper.ShoppingCart;
      lstCart.DataBind();
    }
  }
  catch(Exception ex)
  {
    ShowErrorPage(ex);
  }
}

protected void lstCart_ItemDataBound(object source,
  System.Web.UI.WebControls.DataListItemEventArgs e)
{
  try
  {
    //Create totals row
    if (e.Item.ItemType == ListItemType.Footer)
    {
      ((Label)e.Item.FindControl("lblSubTotal")).Text =
        string.Format("{0:c}", m_shopper.GetCartSubTotal());

      ((Label)e.Item.FindControl("lblShipping")).Text =
        string.Format("{0:c}", m_shopper.GetCartShippingCost());

      ((Label)e.Item.FindControl("lblTax")).Text =
string.Format("{0:c}",
        m_shopper.GetCartSalesTax());
```

```
    ((Label)e.Item.FindControl("lblTotal")).Text =
string.Format("{0:c}",
        m_shopper.GetCartTotalCost());
    }
  }
  catch(Exception ex)
  {
    ShowErrorPage(ex);
  }
}
```

In the LoadPage() function, we get the shopper from the Session variable and store it at the class level. Then, we get the cart item from the object model, and if there are items, we bind the DataList to them. If there are no items in the cart, we inform the shopper of this fact and refrain from displaying an empty DataList. The calls to perform the data binding are typical; however, we handle the ItemDataBound event for the DataList so that we can perform special action when the DataList is in the process of creating its footer section. The controls in the FooterTemplate are available at this point because the DataList has created them while creating the DataLists contents. This is where we insert our own values for the cart summary information, which is exposed as properties of the shopper object. This technique is not unique to the FooterTemplate creation, but it is available on every item created by the DataList. We could have checked for the ListItemType.Item, or ListItemType.Header if we wanted to, and we would then have access directly to the controls in those respective templates. Notice that we have to use FindControl to get the control at runtime, then cast it out to the type we know is in the template. We don't have design-time access to these controls because they are not really created until the DataList is generated at runtime.

Now let's look at what happens when the user clicks on one of the links in a cart item. To allow editing of the quantity of an item in the cart, we set the CommandName of the Change Qty LinkButton to "edit"; when the user clicks the button, the EditCommand event is fired. The EditItemIndex of the DataList in this handler is set to the clicked items index, and the page is reloaded with the EditItemTemplate drawn in place of the current item. The DataList handles this redrawing of the grid with the correct template on the correct item automatically. The TextBox that appears allows the user to update the quantity of the item in the cart. Also, the Ok and Cancel buttons are displayed, with the CommandNames of "update" and "cancel," respectively. In our code-behind, just as when the DataList fires the EditCommand event when the Change Qty link is clicked, the UpdateCommand, DeleteCommand, and CancelCommand events are fired when their respective controls are clicked. We can see in the code snippet that in the UpdateCommand handler, we get the value of the TextBox in the template and change the cart item's quantity via the object model. We then reload the page to show the current changes. Last, we have the Empty Cart button, which simply calls on the object model to empty the items in the cart, then reloads the page so the cart will be shown as empty.

```
protected void lstCart_EditCommand(object source,
  System.Web.UI.WebControls.DataListCommandEventArgs e)
{
  lstCart.EditItemIndex = e.Item.ItemIndex;
  LoadPage();
}


protected void lstCart_UpdateCommand(object source,
  System.Web.UI.WebControls.DataListCommandEventArgs e)
{
  try
  {
    //Save changes to cart item.
    int itemid = Convert.ToInt32(lstCart.DataKeys[e.Item.ItemIndex]);
    int qty =

Convert.ToInt32(((TextBox)e.Item.FindControl("txtQty")).Text.Trim());

    ShoppingCartItem.UpdateQuantityByID(DBConnection, itemid, qty);

    //Clear edit row
    lstCart.EditItemIndex = -1;

    //Reload page
    LoadPage();
  }
  catch(Exception ex)
  {
    ShowErrorPage(ex);
  }
}

protected void lstCart_CancelCommand(object source,
  System.Web.UI.WebControls.DataListCommandEventArgs e)
{
  lstCart.EditItemIndex = -1;

    //Reload page
  LoadPage();
}

protected void btnEmptyCart_Click(object source,
  System.Web.UI.ImageClickEventArgs e)
{
  try
  {
    m_shopper = new Shopper();
    m_shopper.GetShopperByID(DBConnection, (int) Session["ShopperId"]);
    m_shopper.EmptyCart(DBConnection);
```

```
    //Reload page
    LoadPage();
  }
  catch(Exception ex)
  {
    ShowErrorPage(ex);
  }
}

protected void lstCart_DeleteCommand(object source,
  System.Web.UI.WebControls.DataListCommandEventArgs e)
{
  try
  {
    //Delete item
    int itemid = Convert.ToInt32(lstCart.DataKeys[e.Item.ItemIndex]);
    ShoppingCartItem.DeleteByID(DBConnection, itemid);

    //Reload page
    LoadPage();
  }
  catch(Exception ex)
  {
    ShowErrorPage(ex);
  }
}
```

The DataKeyField is used to hold the ShoppingCartItemID. This allows the various command handlers of the DataList to know which row in the database is being affected. The DataList in this case really shows how powerful it can be when an application needs to edit data that exists in a tabular format. In the case of the shopping cart, it works perfectly.

The Checkout Page

The checkout page is fairly simple. It allows the user to enter his or her payment information. Our sample online store takes credit cards, so we will create a generic credit card entry area and finalize the order for the shopper. Of course, we don't include any code to perform a real credit card transaction; we will leave that up to you. We simply approve the transaction and complete the purchase. The profile page is shown in the next section.

The first thing the page does is check to see if the shopper is valid. It does this by looking at the Shopper.IsComplete property to see if the shopper's data is complete enough to check out. If not, the user is redirected to the profile page, where the needed information can be input. We'll look at the Page_Load code here, but because the aspx code is nothing more than a few TextBoxes, an ImageButton, and a DropDownList, we won't show it here. A screenshot of the page can be seen in Figure 6.8.

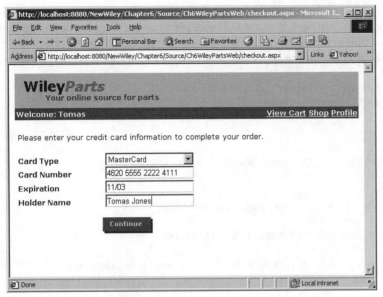

Figure 6.8 The checkout page.

```
protected void Page_Load(object sender, System.EventArgs e)
{
  if (!IsPostBack)
  {
    Shoppershopper=null;
    try
    {
      shopper = (Shopper)Session["ShopperObject"];

    }
    catch(Exception ex)
    {
      ShowErrorPage(ex);
    }
    //Make sure the shopper profile is complete
    if (!shopper.IsComplete)
      Response.Redirect("profile.aspx");
  }
}
```

When the user clicks the Continue ImageButton, the following code runs. When we call the Shopper.CheckOut method, we need to pass in an out variable to get the new order ID. The reason for passing in a variable to get the new order ID instead of collecting a return value is merely in case the programmer ever decides that it should return various success codes about the transaction against the credit card. Although this application doesn't do that, it is a good example of using the common language runtime's out parameter modifier. Once we have completed the CheckOut, we pass the new order to the final page of the app. Other than that, this handler is self-explanatory.

```
protected void btnContinue_Click(object sender,
  System.Web.UI.ImageClickEventArgs e)
{
  try
  {
    Shopper shopper = (Shopper)Session["ShopperObject"];

    int id;
    shopper.CheckOut(DBConnection, txtCardNumber.Text,
txtExpiration.Text,
        cboCardType.SelectedItem.Value, txtHolderName.Text, out id);

    //Store the order id on the server so it won't be in the url.
    Session.Add("OrderID", id);

  }
  catch(Exception ex)
  {
    ShowErrorPage(ex);
  }
    //Go to ordercomplete page
    Response.Redirect("ordercomplete.aspx");
}
```

The OrderConfirmation Page

This is perhaps the simplest page in that all it does is thank the user for shopping, displays the new order ID, and presents an invoice of the items that were purchased. To create the invoice, we use a simple DataGrid to display the items in the order. In addition, we display the cart totals, as the shopper's information.

We won't study this page in detail because it doesn't introduce anything new; it just uses the same controls we have seen in the other pages. Do note, however, that the page is not called with the order ID in the QueryString because that would be a security breech. If the order ID were in the URL, the user could modify it in the browser's address bar and view other people's orders and credit card information. In your applications, you may want to perform some text translation on the credit card numbers whenever they are displayed to the user. Many companies use X in place of all but the last four digits. This prevents anyone from stealing the credit card number, but it helps the shopper determine which card was used for the purchase. You can see the page in Figure 6.9.

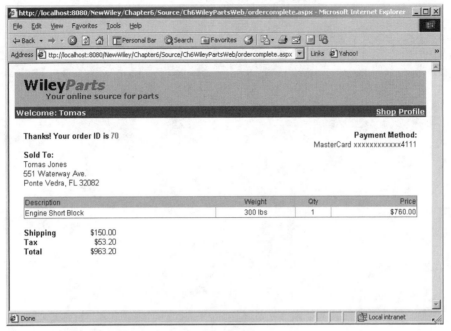

Figure 6.9   The OrderConfirmation page in action.

Wrapping Up the Chapter

Now we have seen all of our objects and controls in action. We have created a simple, yet usable and modifiable Web shopping cart application. We have put many different techniques to use in this chapter, and we hope that you can expand on them in your own applications. In fact, we intended for this sample shopping cart to be usable as a starting foundation for any reader who wishes to implement a real online store. Now, we will move on to add extra functionality and peripheral applications to this one.

Web Services

Business applications often need to share information and programming tasks among themselves. With the onset of the Internet, there is an unlimited number of resources that might be helpful to your application, by providing specialized data or functionality. In the past, businesses have been able to communicate together, often by means of dedicated point-to-point channels and sometimes by proprietary protocols or objects. This has met the needs of applications so far, but a new technology is emerging that will facilitate this kind of collaboration between businesses and programs in a much better way. This way is called XML Web services.

What Are XML Web Services?

XML Web services are a way for applications to share data and business logic, over the Web, using nonproprietary standard protocols, such as XML and HTTP, which are supported in a wide variety of environments. The formal name for them is XML Web services, though some might refer to them as ASP.NET Web services. Actually, ASP.NET just provides a means for you to produce or consume XML Web services. Microsoft does not have a lock on this technology; most other vendors, including IBM, HP, and Sun, have their own implementations as well. Because XML Web services are based on XML on HTTP, which is public technology, applications running in any type of environment could theoretically share data and business logic through Web services, no matter on what platform they were built. Web services are a new twist on a not-so-new idea. The idea has been around for a while, but not in such a robust and universal, environment-independent way.

In the past, XML Web services were much less robust, portable, and easy to use. For example, if you were writing a retail commerce application, you might need to calculate the shipping price for a particular product based on the customer's shipping location, the weight of the package, the shipping service level or priority, and the seller's location. To provide the shipping service and calculations, you may have relied on, say, Turbo Shipping Company, Inc. Turbo, knowing that so many people need to calculate the price of shipping, must provide a way for its clients to do so. Before Web services, Turbo had several options, but each had its own set of caveats.

One option for Turbo was to distribute its shipping price data so that clients could import the data into their local data stores and access it through whatever code means they want to use. The problem with this is that when Turbo changes its shipping data, all clients are going to have to get the updated data and import it into their systems again, clearly not the best solution. This is particularly bad when clients' data is out of sync with Turbo's, and they charge their customers the wrong amount.

The next option Turbo had was to open its data up across a proprietary network and allow clients to access it through a set of APIs or objects. Of course, this is not the best solution because clients have to maintain their connection and configuration to this network and support whatever means of programming is required to use the objects or APIs required for accessing the data, another less-than-perfect solution. What if Turbo had implemented its objects to pull shipping prices in Microsoft's DCOM? That wouldn't be much use to a client who used Unix. Turbo would have to provide and maintain libraries of this functionality for many different operating systems.

For another option, Turbo could create a Web page that takes parameters and responds with a string that contains the shipping price information embedded in it. This is good in that most operating systems support requesting Web pages over HTTP, and the data would always be real-time and up to date. The problems with this solution are that the calling program might have to make complex programming calls to request content from a Web server and that there is no good way to get the results back from the call in an object-oriented manner. The results are embedded in a string, which is not object based and must be parsed by the client application.

Enter XML Web services. A Web service is very much like Turbo's third option—the Web page that returns the shipping prices for programs to parse. But instead of returning string data, a Web service can return the results as an object when combined with the SOAP protocol and be called in an object-oriented way. The calling program doesn't have to make low-level socket connections and send HTTP GET requests and then read off the returned stream. Nor do we have to parse anything in the response to make sense of the data. With a Web service, we call the shipping pricing functionality, over the Web, with object-oriented syntax, and we have the answer given back to us as an object, with little in the way to limit how robust the object can be.

NOTE SOAP is the Simple Object Access Protocol, which allows us to invoke methods over the network using HTTP. It also handles the details that allow us to manipulate objects returned from Web services in an object-oriented way. Web services actually return their results in XML; SOAP converts the XML into objects for our applications to use.

For example, take a look at the psuedocode for a client or calling-application that follows. In the past, if we wanted to request data from a Web server to use in our application, we might use something along these lines:

```
SendRequestToServer()
{
  SocketConnetion conn = new
    SocketConnection("http://www.turboshipping.com/", 80)

  conn.SendString("POST /ShippingService.asp HTTP/1.1")
  conn.SendString("Host: ")
  conn.SendString("Content-Type: application/x-www-form-urlencoded")
  conn.SendString("Content-Length: length")
  conn.SendString("weight=5.5")
  conn.SendString("zipfrom=32082")
  conn.SendString("zipto=10101")
}


HandleResponseFromServer()
{
  String shipinfo = ServerResponse.Readbuffer(20);
  //Parse the results, example results: 5.75, 6.80, 7.95, 10.50, 26.00
  String StandardPrice = shipinfo.Tokenize(",")
  String 3DayPrice = shipinfo.Tokenize(null)
  String 2DayPrice = shipinfo.Tokenize(null)
  String OverNightPrice = shipinfo.Tokenize(null)
  String OverNightSaturdayPrice = shipinfo.Tokenize(null)
}
```

This abstract code snippet opens up a call to the server and requests the resource by the standard HTTP protocol means. Then, when the results are returned, they are parsed for the data parts, to be used in the business logic. Now, with .NET Web services, the code to accomplish the same task is simple:

```
GetShippingPrice()
{
  TurboShippingService turbo = new TurboShippingService()
  TurboShippingInfo info = turbo.GetShippingInfo(5.5, "32082", "10101");
}
```

In the second psuedocode snippet, you can see how easy and object oriented it is to get the shipping information. You create an object that represents the Web service, call the function you need, and get the results back as an object. The results don't have to be objects; they can be simple data types as well. You can send objects to the function, and you can even do so by reference, meaning that you can send a reference to an object and have it modified by the code on the server. Arrays are supported as well. And in the case that there is an application somewhere that needs to access Turbo's shipping prices, but there is no SOAP support on that system, all is not lost. Non-SOAP environments (which there will be very few of in the future, we hope) can always make the Web service call and simply access the results in their XML format. This doesn't leverage all of the ease-of-use benefits of SOAP, but it still allows the caller to get at the data in a robust and industry-standard way.

Quite a bit easier, wouldn't you say? With the old way, we are essentially making a manual call to the URI on the Web and then dealing with the data to make it usable. Sure, there are better ways to call a Web page from code than by directly writing to a socket, like using the MFC classes like the CInernetSession or the API calls to open a file over the Internet, but even these methods require a fair amount of programming. And there still is the problem of what to do with the results.

How Do Web Services Work?

How does all of this work? SOAP, as mentioned previously, is the protocol that makes it all possible. SOAP is a nonproprietary way for invoking programming logic across standard Web protocols. It also provides a mechanism for converting XML that is sent over the Web, either to or from a Web service, into objects. SOAP provides a definition for messages to be sent to make calls over the Web. ASP.NET Web services also use SOAP for enveloping the XML into objects for us.

When you make a call to a Web service that will return an object like the Turbo-ShippingInfo class, the actual contents of the object, and not a binary object, are sent over the wire. Because we are calling the Web service over the HTTP protocol, it returns its results as a stream of text, formatted in XML. Then, once the stream of XML has been received by the calling program, it is deserialized into objects by the framework. At that point, the objects are ready for use.

Of course, there is much more to calling a Web service than what we saw in the preceding simple psuedocode. Most of the gory details are handled for you both by the .NET common language runtime and by special tools that generate some of the low-level code for you. When you need to use a Web service in a Visual Studio.NET application, you can simply use the Web Reference tool, or Wsdl.exe, which is part of the .NET SDK. These tools will create the code you need to treat the Web services as objects and the shell classes that the Web service uses so that your application will have an understanding of their layout. Because of this, calling a Web service is easy and can be integrated into virtually any kind of application with little effort. And because XML and HTTP are heavily supported by most modern operating systems, SOAP support can easily be added at the application level via APIs and tool kits. Web services can be created and consumed by applications regardless of where they are, what they run on, and how they were written.

Uses for Web Services

Let's talk about some more examples of where Web services could be used in the enterprise. Imagine a large bank's corporate headquarters, where there are several thousand employees using 20 different enterprise applications to do their various jobs. Now imagine that 10 of those 20 applications are running as rich client applications on various Windows platforms written in MFC, ATL, VB, and Access; 5 are running on Unix and Solaris machines written in Java and C++; and the other 5 are Web based, served from various Webs servers from IIS with ASP to Unix with Perl/CGI programs. This scenario is not completely out of the question for some companies that have their IT fragmented across the organization and the country. Now comes the tough part. Every single application needs to be able, for one reason or another, to pull up the contact information for the 100,000 customers in the company's master database. How does the typical company solve this programming problem? Unfortunately, the typical company often has many redundant, disparate chunks of code that all access the same data, each in its own way. Some systems make calls through COM or DCOM objects to get the contact info, some via Java RMI or CORBA methods; still others might call the database directly from SQL libraries on Unix. Obviously, this leads to many problems, not the least of which is the amount of code and support needed to accomplish all of this. On top of that is the administration of all of these database connections and credentials, not to mention what happens when the table layout changes slightly. Half of the apps in the organization might be in need of repair and recompile at that point.

A Web service that has a simple object-based interface that allows listing, searching, adding, deleting, and updating of the customer contact database could be this fictional company's savior. If these programs all accessed the contact information using this Web service, several problems would be solved. First, a consistent programming model could be used by all applications that need the information, no matter what type of language or OS they were developed on. SOAP is destined to be available to all development environments in the future, and most already have the means to make HTTP calls over the Internet. Second, the interface to the data can be abstracted to the underlying data structure. What if the customer tables change or even get ported to a completely different brand of database server? Using the Web service as the single point of access to this data, it is the only code that needs to be modified. As long as the objects and Web service interface remain the same, all consuming programs will continue to work without interruption. Imagine how much money could be saved in just one instance of having to modify the customer database slightly if only one app—the Web services app—has to be changed. Another major benefit is that because Web services are called over the Internet, the only thing the consuming app really needs in production is a valid Internet connection allowing it to be used outside of the corporate network.

While the preceding scenario might be a typical problem inside of the private computing environment of a company, Web services can also help in the public domain, where a company may wish to share its data with anonymous users over the Web. The Food and Drug Administration's master list of approved drugs for both prescription and over-the-counter use comes to mind. Currently the lists are available for download from the FDA Web site as fixed row length data files. Once downloaded, they must be put into the user's database for use in a program or read directly from the files. It might be a great benefit to all programs that rely on up-to-date drug information if they could access Web services for the data.

As one more example, imagine a Web-based communication system where one company maintains a Web chat server with chatting functionality exposed as Web services. With that system in place, it would be very easy to embed chat capabilities into any consumer- or business-based rich client application. Taking it even a step further, a PC-based consumer application could implement its user interface in the client machine but get all of its business logic and functionality via Web service calls. This would keep every user on the same version and eliminate piracy. It could also usher in the new notion of application rental over the Web.

For all of these reasons, SOAP and ASP.NET Web services will be major new players in the future of both consumer- and business-based applications. Now let's jump right in and start creating Web services.

Web Services in Visual Studio .NET

We saw in Chapter 2, "Anatomy of an ASP.NET Page," that Visual Studio .NET makes developing Web Forms a lot easier than using Notepad. This holds true with Web services as well, so all of the Web services that we develop in this chapter will be done with Visual Studio .NET. Let's dive right in and create a new Web service project.

Start by choosing File, New, Project from the menu bar. In the Project Types list, select Visual C# Projects, and then select ASP.NET Web Service in the Templates list on the right. Name the project WileyPartsServices, and if you are using a default setup, leave the location as http://localhost. A screenshot of what this dialog looks like can be seen in Figure 7.1.

A Web service project is no different from a Web application project. The only difference in the default project templates that are created is that the Web application project adds one extra reference to the System.Drawing class. In addition, when the projects are initially created, a Web application project creates a single Web Form called Web-Form1.aspx, while a Web Service project creates a single Web service called Service1. asmx. The rest of the files in the projects are identical. In fact, you can easily add a Web Form to a Web Service project and, just as easily, add a Web service to a Web application project. As we saw in Chapter 2 when we created our first Web application project, Visual Studio .NET will create a new virtual directory in IIS with the same name as the project.

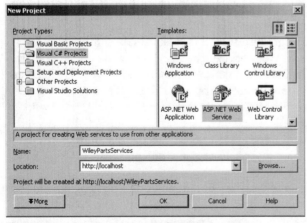

Figure 7.1 Creating a new Web service project.

The only files that might be new to you in this project are Service1.asmx and Service1.asmx.cs. These are the files added by the template that make up the default Web service. By default, this Web service is set up to use code-behind. Because Web services don't have user interfaces, there is only one line in the Service1.asmx file:

```
<%@ WebService Language="c#" Codebehind="Service1.asmx.cs"
  Class=" WileyPartsServices.Service1" %>
```

This line is a WebService directive, which is similar to a Page directive used for Web Forms. The only values of this directive used by the runtime are the *Language* and *Class* values. The Codebehind value is used by Visual Studio .NET to keep track of the code-behind class that belongs to this Web service. The class that is specified in the Class value can be implemented in the .asmx file, or it can be implemented in a .NET assembly that must be made available in the bin directory of the Web application where the service will reside.

Let's take a look at the code behind file, Service1.asmx.cs. The first thing to note is the declaration of the Service 1 class:

```
public class Service1 : System.Web.Services.WebService
```

It is derived from System.Web.Services.WebService. Although inheriting this class is done by default when using Visual Studio.NET, it is not necessary. Inheriting from the WebService class will provide you with access to ASP.NET objects, just as the Page class does. The WebService class exposes the *Application*, *Session*, *User*, and *Server* objects as properties. In addition, there is a *Context* property, which is of type Http-Context and exposes the Request and Response objects. If you don't need to access any of these things, then you don't need to derive your class from WebService.

WebMethod Attribute

We can make any public method of our code-behind class callable from the Web by applying the WebMethod attribute to it. The template class provides a HelloWorld Web service example, which is commented out:

```
[WebMethod]
public string HelloWorld()
{
  return "Hello World";
}
```

You can have as many methods as you wish within your code-behind class, but only those that have the WebMethod attribute applied to them will be callable from the Web.

The WebMethod attribute has a few optional properties that we can specify to control and describe the behavior of the Web service. To specify properties of a C# attribute, you specify the properties inside of parentheses immediately following the attribute name as follows:

```
[WebMethod(property=value)]
```

The *BufferResponse* property can be set to true or false. This property controls whether the response from a Web service is buffered entirely before it is sent back to the caller. True is the default setting and requires the entire response to be buffered before it is sent back to the caller. When BufferResponse is set to false, the response will be buffered and returned to the client in 16-kilobyte sections. In most cases, you will stick with the default setting of true, unless your Web method returns a rather large amount of data.

The *CacheDuration* property controls the time in seconds that ASP.NET should cache the results of the Web method call for a unique parameter set. This is set to 0 by default, so no caching occurs.

The *Description* property is the one that you will use most often. It simply allows you to specify a text string that will be displayed to potential consumers of your Web service when description documents are generated. We'll see where this description text shows up for us in Visual Studio .NET when we write a few applications that consume our Web services later in the chapter.

If you need to provide session support with your Web method, use the *EnableSession* property. If EnableSession is set to true, you can store values in the session state and when the same client makes another Web method call, you can retrieve the value from the session state, just as with an ASP.NET page.

All of the methods exposed by a particular Web service (.asmx file) must have unique names. If you are exposing a method of a class that has several overloads and you want to expose all of the overloads, which all have the same name, you have a problem. You can use the *MessageName* property to solve this problem. The Message-Name property allows you to specify an alias name for a particular method without having to change the name of the method in the class definition. For example, if we had a method called Echo that had two overloads, we could use the *MessageName* property as follows:

```
[WebMethod(MessageName="EchoString"]
public string Echo(string s)
{
  return s;
}
[WebMethod(MessageName="EchoInteger")]
public string Echo(int i)
{
  return i.ToString();
}
```

WebService Attribute

The WebService attribute can be applied to a class that contains exposed Web methods. Its primary purpose is to declare the XML namespace to which the Web method should belong. The Visual Studio .NET Web service template does not implement this attribute, and if a namespace is not specified the namespace will default to http://tempuri.org. Your Web methods need to belong to a somewhat unique namespace to allow Web method consumers to distinguish them from other services on the Web.

Typically, the namespace is set to the URL of the company Web site. The namespace, though, does not have to point to a real live Web site. You declare the namespace by setting the *Namespace* property of the WebService attribute.

You can also provide some descriptive text for the Web methods that are provided by setting the *Description* property of the WebService attribute. When we create our Wiley Parts Web services in the next section we will apply a WebService attribute to our class like this.

```
[WebService(Namespace="http://www.wileyparts.com/",
  Description="Methods to aid in retrieving automobile parts from
WileyParts")]
```

Now that we have seen how Visual Studio.NET handles Web Service projects, let's take a look at some examples of Web services and what they can do.

Creating Web Services

Unlike other examples in the book, each of these examples is created in its own ASP.NET Web Services project. We will create simple WinForms applications to call the services. The companion Web site has two solutions for each example: a project for the Web service and a project for the WinForms calling application.

> **NOTE** We can certainly call services from our ASP.NET Web applications, but we wanted to show a real separation between the service and its client. A rich-client caller emphasizes this perfectly. As for the source code of the examples, we will show only the relevant code from any WinForms we use because this book doesn't really intend to explain WinForms.

The nice thing about .NET is that all applications use the same syntax, object-oriented features, and framework, so the examples in WinForms can port easily into ASP.NET Web projects. In fact, disregarding any of the UI programming in these samples, the code to call the Web services could be cut and pasted directly into an ASP.NET Web page. The full source code for the WinForms examples is available for download from the companion Web site, if you are interested. The first Web service will create a nicely formatted proper name from name parts commonly found in business data. This type of functionality would normally be in written client-side code, and we wouldn't expect it of a Web service. Neither would we get much use out of the HelloWorld method that VSN generates for us by default. It is a good example, however, of passing some simple types and getting some results.

Returning a String with a Web Service

This is one of the simplest forms of a Web service—one with simple parameters that returns a simple string. For this first code example we list the entire contents of the file for the Web service. In future examples, we'll list only the code that is relevant to the example itself. To build this example, create a new ASP.NET Web service project called Example1Svc, and add a new Web service to it called Example1Service. Then, add the bold code in Listing 7.1 into the class, and build.

```
using System;
using System.Collections;
using System.ComponentModel;
using System.Data;
using System.Diagnostics;
using System.Web;
using System.Web.Services;

namespace Example1Svc
{
  public class Example1Service : System.Web.Services.WebService
  {
    public Example1Service()
    {
      InitializeComponent();
    }

    private void InitializeComponent()
    {
    }

    /// <summary>
    /// Clean up any resources being used.
    /// </summary>
    protected override void Dispose( bool disposing )
    {
    }

    [WebMethod(Description="Formats parts of a name into a proper
name.")]
    public string FormatProperName(string strSalutation, string
      strLastName, string strFirstName, string strSuffix)
    {
      if (!strSalutation.EndsWith(".")) strSalutation += ".";
      return string.Format("{0} {1} {2} {3}", strSalutation,
strFirstName,
        strLastName, strSuffix);
    }
  }
}
```

Listing 7.1   A Web service with simple data types

The file looks very similar to that of a regular aspx WebForm page. This makes sense because a Web service is just another form of a Web page. Because Web services are derived by default from System.Web.Services.WebService, they have access to many of the same features used in WebForms, such as Session state and the response object via the Context object. Because this derivation is optional, you may chose not to subclass System.Web.Services.WebService. In that case, you would have to use other measures to access some commonly used features. It's fine in most cases to leave the base class declaration there, however, especially because Visual Studio.NET includes it automatically.

The WebMethod attribute above the FormatProperName method tells the compiler that this is a Web service method. As with any other class you write, if you need to have private methods inside this class, feel free to do so and leave off the WebMethod attribute. Set the Description inside the attribute so that it would be displayed when the user views the service in a Web browser.

Because we can actually think of Web services as Web pages that output their results in XML, we know that we could call them directly with a browser. When we browse to the Web service location with our browser, however, we see a nicely formatted screen created for us by the ASP.NET Framework. A line in the machine.config file on the server maps .asmx requests to a specific class in the framework that displays this page to us. This page displays the names and descriptions of the available methods. If we drill into these methods by clicking on their links, an interface allows us to provide parameters and call the method from within our browser. This is a boon when programming Web services because it is a great tool for debugging your Web method outputs. To test the code in Listing 7.1 using the framework-generated test mechanism, simply point your Web browser to the Example1Service.asmx file. Figures 7.2, 7.3, and 7.4 are what we see when we do this in Internet Explorer.

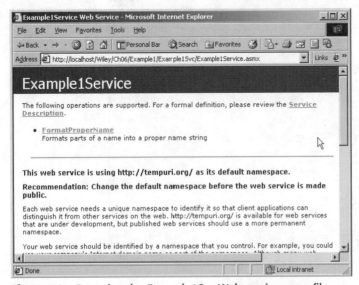

Figure 7.2   Browsing the Example1Svc Web service asmx file.

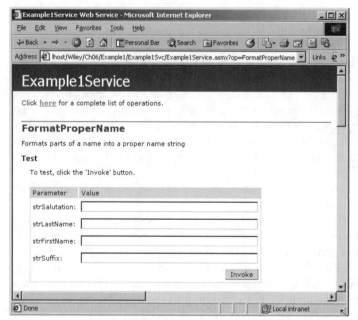

Figure 7.3   Browsing the Example1Svc–FormatProperName method.

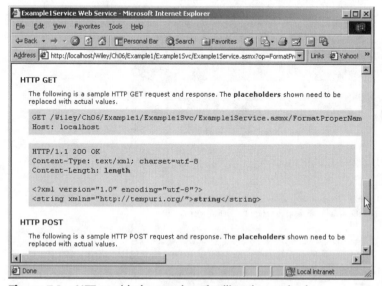

Figure 7.4   .NET provided examples of calling the method.

When looking at the browser as shown in Figure 7.4, scroll down to see the examples that are displayed to understand how you could call this Web service method. In particular, look at the HTTP Get method used for calling it; we could use the following in the browser to manually call the method:

```
http://localhost/wiley/Ch07/Example1/Example1Svc/Example1Service.asmx/
FormatProperName?strSalutation=string&strLastName=String&strFirstName=
String&strSuffix=string
```

Later, we will rely on Visual Studio .NET and the .NET Framework to help us call these Web methods from code without having to worry about these details. But when we point the browser to this address, we see the same thing we saw when we clicked the Invoke button on the ASP.NET-generated test page. In the Figure 7.5 example, we replaced the variable values in the query string to some real name parts.

We can also see in the test harness the SOAP call example, as in Figure 7.4. The SOAP call looks different than the HTTP Get call above.

```
POST /Wiley/Ch07/Example1/Example1Svc/Example1Service.asmx HTTP/1.1
Host: localhost
Content-Type: text/xml; charset=utf-8
Content-Length: length
SOAPAction: "http://tempuri.org/FormatProperName"

<?xml version="1.0" encoding="utf-8"?>
<soap:Envelope xmlns:xsi="http://www.w3.org/2001/XMLSchema-instance"
xmlns:xsd="http://www.w3.org/2001/XMLSchema"
xmlns:soap="http://schemas.xmlsoap.org/soap/envelope/">
  <soap:Body>
    <FormatProperName xmlns="http://tempuri.org/">
      <strSalutation>string</strSalutation>
      <strLastName>string</strLastName>
      <strFirstName>string</strFirstName>
      <strSuffix>string</strSuffix>
    </FormatProperName>
  </soap:Body>
</soap:Envelope>
```

This SOAP call uses an HTTP Post to make the call to the Web method. In the header there is a SOAPAction parameter, which tells the Web service the full name of the method being called. In the body of the request, you can see the XML that makes up the SOAP method call and the parameters sent. In the example generated by .NET, there are placeholders shown for the parameters, but if you had the proper tools, mainly an application with which you could submit HTTP requests manually, you could send this SOAP header with real data in the parameters to invoke the Web method. We won't go that far in this book; making manual SOAP calls is never necessary with .NET clients.

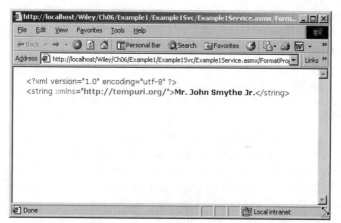

Figure 7.5 Calling the FormatProperName method manually via a HTTP Get command.

Now that we've seen some of how a Web service is created and viewed with some of the tools provided by ASP.NET, how do we actually use it from within our applications? When we want to use a Web service in any type of .NET application in Visual Studio .NET, we use the Add Web Reference tool. This is similar to adding a .NET or even a COM reference in Visual Studio .NET, as well as adding a reference in VB6. In this case, however, we are instructing Visual Studio .NET to browse out to the actual Web service, discover the Web service's interface, and write a wrapper class for us to use when calling it. Visual Studio .NET's Add Web Reference feature is actually calling a command-line application in the Framework SDK called Wsdl.exe. Wsdl.exe is the actual program that creates the wrapper classes for us. Like many features of Visual Studio past and present, the IDE calls out to the external programs to do their jobs. Remember, the compiler and linker themselves are separate programs called by Visual Studio every time you click Build. That sounds like a lot, but it is only a few clicks on your end when you are working inside of Visual Studio .NET.

When we go through these steps, we are actually browsing the server on which the Web service lives. In this case, we browse all the way down to the folder where the Web service is. Clicking on the link to the vsdisco file returns XML. This XML is called the *discovery information*, and it tells the calling application, in this case the Visual Studio .NET IDE, which methods are in this service and the URL to call to learn more about the methods. This URL is a link to what is known as the *Web Service Definition Language* (WSDL). It is the contract for using the Web service; it defines the types and interface that the Web service supports so that your client will know how to make calls to it. Viewing the WSDL for any Web service is easy: Just browse to the link shown. For our example, the link is http://localhost/Wiley/Ch07/Example1/Example1Svc/Example1Service.asmx?wsdl.

This link calls the asmx page, the Web service, with a query string parameter of wsdl. This is handled by all Web services, and it returns the actual WSDL XML, shown in Figure 7.6.

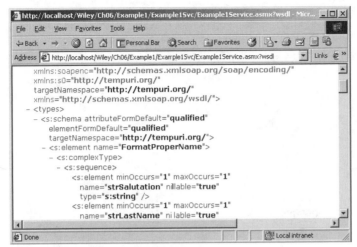

Figure 7.6   WSDL for Example1Svc.

The contract shows the interface of the FormatProperName method, the only method in the service at this point, so that the caller can adhere to it and generate code and classes to represent it on the client side. The URIs in the xmlns tags above the interface information are used as distinct namespaces for the XML document. For a better understanding of XML and its namespaces, please refer to an XML reference; a good online resource is www.w3c.org.

When you make a Web reference, Visual Studio .NET writes a wrapper class for you that makes the calls to the Web service from within your code. The wrapper class can be viewed by looking in the Project Explorer of Visual Studio .NET and drilling down into the Web Reference node. If your explorer is set to view all files, you will see the C# file that wraps the Web reference calls up into objects for our use. The Add Web Reference tool creates our Web reference code in a namespace named after the server. In this case, the namespace is localhost, which we can see in the Project Explorer in Figure 7.7.

NOTE You probably want to know what UDDI is because it appears as an option for searching for Web services in the Add Web Reference tool or Visual Studio .NET. UDDI is the Universal Description, Discovery, and Integration standard. This is a directory of Web services on the Internet. Just as you would search for any other type of Web resource using a search engine on the Web, the UDDI is a searchable repository for services available from business everywhere. As Web services become more popular, programmers will be able to search for functionality in UDDI repositories. The standards define a way that services can expose their features both programmatically, and through discovery documents and service descriptions.

Figure 7.7   Project Explorer showing the Web reference.

The classes that are created for us by using the Add Web Reference are important only to our code; as programmers using the Web services, we really won't care too much about their contents. Just so that we'll be clear on what's happening in there, feel free to look at the generated code. In it you will notice that the methods that are available in the Web service are mimicked in this class. This class's sole purpose is to wrap and represent the Web service and its methods to our calling code. The wrapper class methods take the same parameters and have the same return types as the Web methods; basically the wrapper class has the same interface as the real Web service. By doing this, we can write code that will access the Web service using its published interface. Although the calls we will make in our code look like we are calling the Web methods directly, we are actually calling this wrapper class, which is in turn calling the Web method over the Web using the SOAP framework. The wrapper includes both synchronous and asynchronous calls for each method, which gives us some flexibility in how we design our client applications. The synchronous calls are the most commonly used, and they will behave just like any other synchronous call, whether over the Web or not. The asynchronous calls could be useful for longer-running calls to Web methods, but they would also require that the programmer implement code that supports asynchronous calling of functions. The most common way to do this is by using timers, or multiple threads, which requires advanced programming techniques, such as locking and thread safety. To call Web services asynchronously would not be within the scope of this book because it wouldn't really explain anything new to us regarding how SOAP, XML Web services, or their objects work for typical programmers.

Now let's create a sample application that makes use of this Web service. For this example, we will use a WinForms application. Although the book is about ASP.NET, we feel that many readers will likely implement Web services to be used by client applications other than those written as ASP.NET applications. As you will see, the code to actually make Web service calls is application-type agnostic and can be used as-is in any other application, including an ASP.NET application. The steps involved are creating a WinForms project and creating a Web reference to the Example1Svc Web

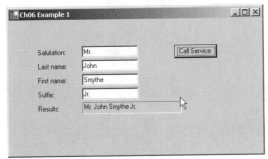

Figure 7.8 A simple WinForms form calling a simple Web service.

service. Then, employ a simple button handler on a WinForms form. We access the service by instantiating an object whose type name is the name of the Web service. In this example, because we are calling Example1Service, we instantiate an object of type Example1Service. The constructor to the service takes no parameters, and as soon as it is instantiated, we can call any Web method we want on it. The same goes for properties; in addition to the Web methods in the service, if there are properties, we can use them now as well. Keep in mind that the first call to a newly compiled Web service will respond slowly, just as does any other ASP.NET application first being loaded. When we make the call to the FormatProperName method, we receive the string return value and use it at will. The calling code looks like this:

```
private void button1_Click(object sender, System.EventArgs e)
{
  Cursor = Cursors.WaitCursor;
  Example1Service svc = new Example1Service();
  label6.Text = svc.FormatProperName(textBox1.Text.Trim(),
    textBox3.Text.Trim(),
    textBox2.Text.Trim(),
    textBox4.Text.Trim());
  Cursor = Cursors.Default;
}
```

Returning an Array of Strings with Web Services

For the next example, let's create a simple method that will create and return a string array and return it as a return value to the caller. This would be a good way to return a simple list from a database, such as cities or states to be displayed in a selection control. The following snippet creates and returns an array of strings, loaded with names. The names, of course, would have come from somewhere important, like a database, for example. To create this example, create a new ASP.NET Web Service project called Example2Svc, and add a new Web service called Example2Service. Then, add the following Web method to the Web service class.

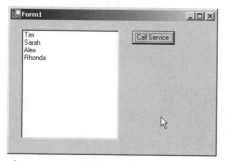

Figure 7.9   Calling a Web service that returns an array.

```
[WebMethod]
public string[] GetNames()
{
  string[] s = new string[4];
  s[0] = "Tim";
  s[1] = "Sarah";
  s[2] = "Alex";
  s[3] = "Rhonda";
  return s;
}
```

Figure 7.9 shows the calling code, which is implemented as a WinForms application. Just as in the Example1Service client, this code is completely portable to any other type of application.

```
private void button1_Click(object sender, System.EventArgs e)
{
  Cursor = Cursors.WaitCursor;
  Example2Service svc = new Example2Service();
  string[] names = svc.GetNames();
  foreach(string name in names)
  {
    listBox1.Items.Add(name);
  }
  Cursor = Cursors.Default;
}
```

Returning an Object and an Array of Objects with Web Services

In the preceding example, the server allocated the string array and returned it to the client, but we aren't accessing memory from the client that has been allocated on the server. What has actually happened is that ASP.NET has serialized the array into a SOAP-compliant format and the Web Reference Proxy object unserializes it into an array on the client. This is how we can be returned a loaded array from across the Web. This also allows us to send a "pointer," or an empty object reference, to the server to be filled in.

In this next example, we will call a Web method to return to us a real business object. This is the type of Web service functionality that will be the most common for most programmers. This example, like the last, shows us the power of SOAP to return an object that was allocated on the server to our application. To create this example, create a new Web service project called Example3Svc, and add a new Web service called Example3Service. Into this service add the following method and class:

```
[WebMethod]
public ComputerProduct GetComputerProduct()
{
  return new ComputerProduct("1542", "Turbo Laser Printer XL2",
    Convert.ToDecimal(439.95));
}


//In a separate class...
public class ComputerProduct
{
  private string m_strSku;
  private string m_strDescription;
  private decimal m_decPrice;

  public ComputerProduct() {}

  public ComputerProduct(string strSku, string strDesc, decimal
decPrice)
  {
    m_strSku = strSku;
    m_strDescription = strDesc;
    m_decPrice = decPrice;
  }

  public string Sku
  {
    set { m_strSku = value; }
    get { return m_strSku; }
  }

  public string Description
  {
    set { m_strDescription = value; }
    get { return m_strDescription; }
  }

  public decimal Price
  {
    set { m_decPrice = value; }
    get { return m_decPrice; }
  }
}
```

The calling code for this simply retrieves a ComputerProduct object and displays some of its properties to the user:

```
private void button1_Click(object sender, System.EventArgs e)
{
   Cursor = Cursors.WaitCursor;
   Example3Service svc = new Example3Service();
   ComputerProduct pr = svc.GetComputerProduct();
   textBox1.Text = pr.Sku;
   textBox2.Text = pr.Description;
   textBox3.Text = pr.Price.ToString();
   Cursor = Cursors.Default;
}
```

We defined a class on the server called ComputerProduct. This class is public in the Web service and therefore can be used by callers of the service. Callers can use the class just as if it were defined in their local code, as well as receive it as a return value, or pass it as a parameter to methods on the Web service. Notice how we are able to use the ComputerProduct class in the client code even though it is defined in the Web service code. The WSDL allowed Visual Studio .NET to learn the layout of the Computer-Products class so that it could create code to represent it in the Web Reference wrapper code. In fact, if you browse to the C# file of the wrapper code, you will see this class definition at the bottom of the file. It is important to realize that only public properties are defined in the client's version of the ComputerProducts class. Any code, such as a method, could not be sent to the client because these SOAP objects are not based on binary objects, but on XML text. Because XML is not a binary protocol, it is able to handle only the data types in the objects defined on the server. This will have a little impact on how you write objects that are destined to live inside Web services. For example, if the ComputerProducts class had a method on it called SaveComputerProduct, defined in the version in the Web service, it would not appear in the client-side Computer-Products class at all. In order to save the client-side version of a ComputerProduct object, you would have to implement another Web service method that provides that functionality. For example, you may have a Web method that has this form:

```
SaveClientComputerProduct(ComputerProduct pr) {...}.
```

Don't think of this as a limiting factor; you can still do all of the things you need to do, just lay them out differently. Here is another example that allocates memory on the server, fills it with new ComputerProducts objects, and returns the new, full array of objects in a ref parameter to the caller: Using the same Web service project Example3Svc, add the following Web method. The ComputerProduct class remains unchanged.

```
[WebMethod]
public int GetComputerProducts(ref ComputerProduct[] ComputerProducts)
{
  ArrayList arr = new ArrayList();

  arr.Add(new ComputerProduct("1542", "Turbo Laser Printer XL2",
    Convert.ToDecimal(439.95)));
  arr.Add(new ComputerProduct("1984", "Turbo Dot Printer DT5S",
    Convert.ToDecimal(269.95)));
  arr.Add(new ComputerProduct("0687", "Turbo Jet Printer PC300",
    Convert.ToDecimal(189.90)));

  ComputerProducts =
(ComputerProduct[])arr.ToArray(typeof(ComputerProduct));
  return 3;
}
```

And here is the caller code, which retrieved the array of objects from the server, iterates them with a foreach loop, and displays their properties:

```
private void button2_Click(object sender, System.EventArgs e)
{
  Cursor = Cursors.WaitCursor;
  ComputerProduct[] ComputerProducts = null;
  Example3Service svc = new Example3Service();
  svc.GetComputerProducts(ref ComputerProducts);
  foreach(ComputerProduct ComputerProduct in ComputerProducts)
  {
    string[] subs = new string[3];
    subs[0] = ComputerProduct.Sku;
    subs[1] = ComputerProduct.Description;
    subs[2] = ComputerProduct.Price.ToString();
    listView1.Items.Add(new ListViewItem(subs));
  }
  Cursor = Cursors.Default;
}
```

Both of these examples are displayed in one client window, shown in Figure 7.10. This last example gives us another great example of allocating resources on the server and having SOAP take care of matching those allocations on the client. In this case, we sent a reference to an empty array to the Web method, and when the method returned, the array was populated.

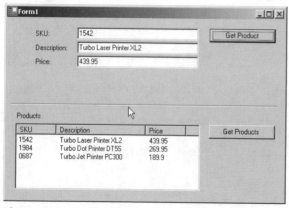

Figure 7.10   Calling more advanced Web services.

Using XmlInclude in a Web Service

In this next example, we return an object whose type is not known statically.

To do this, we set up the ComputerProduct class as in the previous example, but this time we derive it from the Products class, which has one property of its own. In the Web method that returns one of these objects, it returns a Product rather than a ComputerProduct. Now, because a ComputerProduct is a Product, we can safely run this code, but unfortunately, SOAP will not know by looking at the method interface what types of objects it uses, and thus what types of objects will be generated on the client. All of this is due to the simple fact that the classes that are generated for us to use in our client code are learned about not at runtime, but statically by the WSDL in the discovery phase when we add the Web reference. Returning a ComputerProduct object cast as a Product object is a runtime behavior; therefore, the client won't know about this until runtime.

But when using a method where type other than the return type is actually passed back when the call is made the client needs to be able to determine the type at runtime. To handle these cases, we must delve into the System.Xml.Serilization namespace and use the XmlInclude attribute on the Web method that returns derived types. Because SOAP serializes the parameters and return values into XML when you call a Web method, we use this attribute of the serialization library to help us out. By using something like this:

```
[XmlInclude(typeof(ComputerProduct))]
```

at the declaration of the Web method, we instruct the call to WSDL to return the interface for the ComputerProduct class in addition to those of the classes that are directly in the method parameters or return type. In fact, when we do this, you will see that this class is also defined in the wrapper code for the Web service. After all, if our client is going to be dealing with ComputerProducts, it needs to know the layout of both Product and ComputerProduct.

Keep in mind that you don't have to use XmlInclude on any class type that is exposed directly in the parameters or return values of a Web method. Nor must you use it for class types that are not included in the method interface, but are members of the objects that are included. For example, if you have a Web method that returns a Person, and the Person class has a property of type Phone (another class defined in the Web service code), you don't need to use XmlInclude on the Phone class. It will be learned about automatically because it can be determined statically. Even at design time, the Person class will expose the Phone class to the Wsdl program, which creates the callable wrapper. The same thing is true for a base class. If we were returning a ComputerProduct, which is derived from a Product, the system would know about the Product class outside of runtime. When returning a Product, and not its derived ComptuterProduct, it is impossible to tell which classes are derived from Product without the XmlInclude. Think about the code for the Product, it has no reference whatsoever to the ComputerProduct class. In fact, it is quite normal that the programmer of the Product class designed his or her class never even to know or care what gets derived from it, if anything. The next example uses this technique. Create a new Web service project called Example4Svc, and add a new Web service called Example4-Service. To it, add the following code:

```
[WebMethod]
[XmlInclude(typeof(ComputerProduct))]
public Product GetComputerProduct()
{
  return new ComputerProduct("1542", "Turbo Laser Printer XL2",
    Convert.ToDecimal(439.95));
}

public class Product
{
  private string m_strTypeName;

  public Product() {}

  public string TypeName
  {
    set { m_strTypeName = value; }
    get { return m_strTypeName; }
  }
}

public class ComputerProduct : Product
{
  private string m_strSku;
  private string m_strDescription;
  private decimal m_decPrice;

  public ComputerProduct() {}

  public ComputerProduct(string strSku, string strDesc, decimal
decPrice)
  {
```

```
      m_strSku = strSku;
      m_strDescription = strDesc;
      m_decPrice = decPrice;
      base.TypeName = "Computer Hardware and Software";
    }

    public string Sku
    {
      set { m_strSku = value; }
      get { return m_strSku; }
    }

    public string Description
    {
      set { m_strDescription = value; }
      get { return m_strDescription; }
    }

    public decimal Price
    {
      set { m_decPrice = value; }
      get { return m_decPrice; }
    }
  }
}
```

And the client code looks like this, which displays the resulting object cast out to the desired type, as can be seen in action in Figure 7.11:

```
private void button1_Click(object sender, System.EventArgs e)
{
  Cursor = Cursors.WaitCursor;
  Example4Service svc = new Example4Service();
  Product pr = svc.GetComputerProduct();
  textBox1.Text = ((ComputerProduct)pr).Sku;
  textBox2.Text = ((ComputerProduct)pr).Description;
  textBox3.Text = ((ComputerProduct)pr).Price.ToString();
  textBox4.Text = pr.TypeName;
  Cursor = Cursors.Default;
}
```

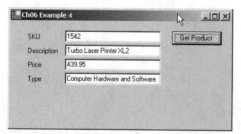

Figure 7.11 Calling a Web service that uses XmlInclude.

Allow Upload of a File to the Web Server with Web Services

This example creates a Web Service that allows us to easily send files to the Web server. This could be useful for something as simple as uploading an image or document to be saved on a server with an employee record, for example. On the other hand, it could be used to upload code in a Web service-based source control system, which supports Internet upload and download of all kinds of files.

To send a file to the server, we will create a Web service application called Example-5Svc and add a Web service called Example5Service. Include the following Web method:

```
[WebMethod()]
public void SendFile(Byte[] bytes, string filename)
{
  FileStream fs = new FileStream(filename, FileMode.OpenOrCreate);
  fs.Write(bytes, 0, bytes.Length);
  fs.Close();
}
```

The Web method is quite simple. It merely takes a byte array of data, the filename to create on the server as a string. Of course, the filename would probably be given to the client by the server before or during this call so we could check if it exists. We probably don't want to allow someone to arbitrarily create (or overwrite) files on our server! In fact, we could employ some simple method whereby the server assigns a filename for us, maybe using a GUID or hash scheme, and returns the name to our calling code. Or, the calling code could request the filename in another call altogether, then pass that into the call that sends the file. Once the array of bytes is on the server, it is saved to a file using standard methods.

The code that calls this service would look something like this:

```
private void SendFileToServer()
{
  FileStream fs = new FileStream("C:\\filetosend.txt", FileMode.Open);
  Byte[] bytes = new Byte[fs.Length];
  fs.Read(bytes, 0, (int) fs.Length);
  fs.Close();

  FileWebService svc = new FileWebService();
  svc.SendFile(bytes,"C:\\filestosend.txt");
}
```

This code is simple as well. It reads the file from the local machine into a byte array and sends this to the Web service as a parameter. This could be a nice alternative to using an FTP-based file transfer mechanism in your applications. This code could be used to transfer an image as well, but to transfer content other than plain text, you would need to encode it into Base64 XML first, so that no special characters in the stream would be misinterpreted as a control value. When you plan to send massive amounts of data from a very large file using this service, consider compressing the file, sending, and then decompressing it on the server.

Expanding WileyParts with Web Services

Now that you have a basic understanding of Web services, let's expand our Wiley Parts business by adding some. The Web services we'll add will use the same object model that we created in Chapter 6, "Applying What We've Learned So Far." The Web services that we'll make available will allow someone to search the Wiley Parts inventory and see the parts that we have to offer.

Wiley Parts Services

Let's put together the Web methods that will be provided by Wiley Parts. First, add a new Web service to the WileyPartsServices project called PartSearch. We need to be able to access the classes in the WileyParts.Database and WileyParts.Objects namespaces, so we have to add a reference to the WileyPartsObjects.dll. Be sure to include the following using statements at the top of the PartSearch.asmx.cs file:

```
using WileyParts.Database;
using WileyParts.Objects;
```

Apply the WebService attribute to the PartSearch class, as you learned in the previous section. All we have left to do is define the Web methods that we need. For now, we are going to expose the ability to get a list of the vehicle years for which we sell parts, our part categories, a list of vehicles given a specific year, and a list of parts given a VehicleID and CategoryID. Here are the Web methods that need to be added to Part-Search.asmx.cs.

```
[WebMethod(Description="Returns a list of available vehicle years as an
array of integers.")]
public int[] GetVehicleYears()
{
  //Open a connection
  WileyConnection conn = new
    WileyConnection(ConfigurationSettings.AppSettings["dsn"]);

  //Get the vehicle years
  ArrayList arrYears = Vehicle.GetVehicleYears(conn);

  //Close the connection
  conn.Close();

  //return an int[] from the ArrayList
  return (int[])arrYears.ToArray(typeof(int));
}

[WebMethod(Description="Returns a list of available vehicles for the
specified year.")]
public Vehicle[] GetVehiclesByYear(int intYear)
```

```
{
  //Open a connection
  WileyConnection conn = new
    WileyConnection(ConfigurationSettings.AppSettings["dsn"]);

  //Get the vehicles
  ArrayList arrVehicles = Vehicle.GetVehiclesByYear(conn, intYear);

  //Close the connection
  conn.Close();

  //return a Vehicle[] from the ArrayList
  return (Vehicle[])arrVehicles.ToArray(typeof(Vehicle));
}

[WebMethod(Description="Returns a list of the available part
categories.")]
public PartCategory[] GetAllCategories()
{
  //Open a connection
  WileyConnection conn = new
    WileyConnection(ConfigurationSettings.AppSettings["dsn"]);

  //Get the categories
  ArrayList arrCategories = PartCategory.GetAllCategories(conn);

  //Close the connection
  conn.Close();

  //return a PartCategory[] from the ArrayList
  return (PartCategory[])arrCategories.ToArray(typeof(PartCategory));
}

[WebMethod(Description="Returns a list of the parts when given a
VehicleID and CategoryID.")]
public Part[] GetParts(int intVehicleID, int intCategoryID)
{
  //Open a connection
  WileyConnection conn = new
    WileyConnection(ConfigurationSettings.AppSettings["dsn"]);

  //Get the parts
  ArrayList arrParts = Part.GetPartsByVehicleAndCategory(conn,
    intVehicleID, intCategoryID);

  //Close the connection
  conn.Close();

  //return a Part[] from the ArrayList
  return (Part[])arrParts.ToArray(typeof(Part));
}
```

As you can see, we've included the WebMethod attribute for each one of these methods and also defined the Description property. All four of these methods work pretty much the same way. A connection to the database is opened with the following lines of code:

```
WileyConnection conn = new
    WileyConnection(ConfigurationSettings.AppSettings["dsn"]);
```

Notice that we are retrieving the connection string from the AppSettings, just as we did in the Web application that was developed in Chapter 6. Next, the appropriate method is called to retrieve an ArrayList of a particular type. The database connection is then closed:

```
//Close the connection
conn.Close();
```

Last, an array of a particular type is returned from the method. Notice that the return type of all of the methods is an array of some type rather than an ArrayList. Any object that we wish to transmit via SOAP must be serializable. The ArrayList is not a serializable class, so we can't transmit it directly. The ArrayList does have a ToArray() method that can be used to retrieve an array of all of the items in the ArrayList. We can also specify the type of array to create by passing in a System.Type object. In the GetVehiclesByYear method, this is done with this line of code.

```
return (Vehicle[])arrVehicles.ToArray(typeof(Vehicle));
```

That's all there is to developing these Web services. Most of the work has already been done in the object model that we developed in Chapter 6. Now, let's test out a couple of them before we move on to writing applications that can access these Web services.

If you navigate to the PartSearch.asmx file in your browser, you should see a page similar to that shown in Figure 7.12. All four of the methods are listed there, along with the text to which we set the Description property of the WebMethod attribute. You can also see the text that we provided for the Description property of the WebService attribute at the very top. You can click on any of the Web method names, and a page will be displayed that will allow you to invoke the Web method through your browser. Figure 7.13 shows the page that is displayed when we clicked on GetVehiclesByYear. Further down the page (not shown) are samples of what the SOAP, HTTP-GET, and HTTP-POST request and response message should look like for accessing the Web method. To invoke this method, simply enter in a year, such as 2001, and click the Invoke button. A new browser window will be opened and will display the response of the HTTP-GET call of the Web method, as shown in Figure 7.14. The reponse contains a list of <Vehicle> tags, which shows that our Web service is working properly.

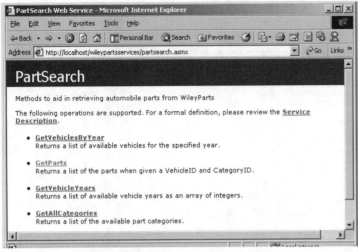

Figure 7.12   WileyPartsServices.

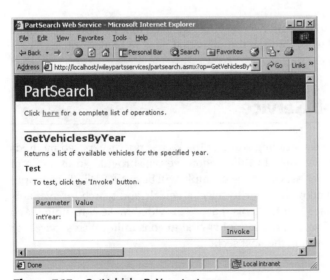

Figure 7.13   GetVehiclesByYear test page.

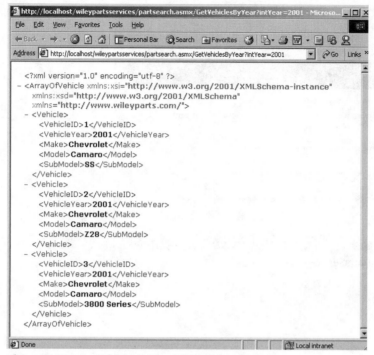

Figure 7.14   GetVehiclesByYear HTTP-GET response.

Now that we've seen how to create Web services, we need to learn how to use them in other applications. We'll walk through the steps that need to be performed to consume a Web service in the next section.

Consuming a Web Service

Consuming a Web service means calling some of the Web service's exposed methods from an application across the Web. In this section we will provide an example of consuming the Wiley Parts Web services. The example will be a .NET Win Form application written in C#. It will allow the user to select a vehicle and search for available parts for that vehicle. We'll see that the tools that are provided make consuming Web services a fairly easy task. The WSDL.exe tool is vital in consuming Web services, so we'll take a look at it right away in the next section.

WSDL.exe

The first thing that we need to do is generate a proxy class that can be included in a .NET application. This proxy class will allow us to call the Wiley Parts Web services. The WSDL.exe command-line utility provided as part of the .NET framework is used specifically for this purpose. Before we explain this utility further, there's one thing to note: If you are using Visual Studio .NET to create a .NET application, it will create proxy classes for you when you add a Web Reference to your application. We'll see how to do that in the next section. In spite of this built-in ability in Visual Studio .NET, the WSDL utility still has its uses, particularly if you are not using Visual Studio .NET for your development. The utility is installed by default in the Program Files\ Microsoft.NET\FrameworkSDK\bin directory. If you haven't included this directory in your environment path, do so now before proceeding with this section.

To execute the utility in its simplest form, you need to provide a URL or path to a WSDL contract. If you want to accept the default values for all of the switches of the utility, then specifying the WSDL contract is all you need to do. Figure 7.15 shows an example of creating a C# proxy class for the PartSearch Web service. We retrieved the WSDL contract for the Web service by appending the URL with ?wsdl. The last line in the screen shot shows that a file called PartSearch.cs was created. This tells us two things. First, by default the name of the file that is created takes the same name as the service, which is PartSearch in this case. Second, the fact that the extension is .cs tells us that the utility creates C# proxy classes by default. The WSDL.exe utility has many switches that we can use to control it. A few of the more common ones are the following:

/language:<language> Used to specify the language in which the proxy class should be generated. The valid values are CS, VB, or JS for C#, Visual Basic.NET, and JavaScript respectively. The default is CS.

/out:<filename> Used to specify a path and/or filename for the output. The default is the current path and the name of the service along with the appropriate extension, depending on the value of the /language switch.

/namespace:<namespace> Used to specify a namespace in which the proxy class should be wrapped. By default, the class will not be wrapped in a namespace at all.

/protocol:<protocol> Valid values are SOAP, HttpGet, and HttpPost. The default is SOAP.

We won't go through all of the details of the proxy class that was generated for our PartSearch service, but we would like to point out a few important details. The class that was generated inherits from System.Web.Services.Protocols.SoapHttpClientProtocol. Inside the class, three public methods were generated for every Web method that was exposed by the Web service. One of these methods will take the exact same name as the Web method and is used for calling the Web method synchonously. The other two methods take the same name as the Web method preceded by Begin and End. These two methods are used for calling the Web method asynchronously. Here are the three methods that were generated for the GetVehicleYears Web method.

Figure 7.15   Running the WSDL.exe Utility.

```
[System.Diagnostics.DebuggerStepThroughAttribute()]
[System.Web.Services.Protocols.SoapDocumentMethodAttribute("http://www.
wileyparts.com/GetVehicleYears",
  RequestNamespace="http://www.wileyparts.com/",
  ResponseNamespace="http://www.wileyparts.com/",
  Use=System.Web.Services.Description.SoapBindingUse.Literal,

ParameterStyle=System.Web.Services.Protocols.SoapParameterStyle.Wrapped)
]
[return: System.Xml.Serialization.XmlArrayItemAttribute("int",
  IsNullable=false)]
public int[] GetVehicleYears()
{
  object[] results = this.Invoke("GetVehicleYears", new object[0]);
  return ((int[])(results[0]));
}


[System.Diagnostics.DebuggerStepThroughAttribute()]
public System.IAsyncResult BeginGetVehicleYears(
  System.AsyncCallback callback, object asyncState)
{
  return this.BeginInvoke("GetVehicleYears", new object[0], callback,
  asyncState);
}


[System.Diagnostics.DebuggerStepThroughAttribute()]
public int[] EndGetVehicleYears(System.IAsyncResult asyncResult)
{
  object[] results = this.EndInvoke(asyncResult);
  return ((int[])(results[0]));
}
```

At the bottom of the generated class you will see something like this.

```
public class Vehicle : WileyObject {
}


[System.Xml.Serialization.XmlIncludeAttribute(typeof(Part))]
[System.Xml.Serialization.XmlIncludeAttribute(typeof(PartCategory))]
[System.Xml.Serialization.XmlIncludeAttribute(typeof(Vehicle))]
public class WileyObject {
}


public class Part : WileyObject {
}


public class PartCategory : WileyObject {
}
```

We don't know about you, but something doesn't look right with this to us. All of the custom classes that we used in our Web methods are defined here, which is great, but they are all empty. Class members are created only for public member variables and properties that provide both a get and set accessor. None of the classes that we used has public member variables, and all of the properties that we provided had only get accessors. We can fix this problem by going back to our WileyPartsObjects project and defining set accessors for all of the properties. After you've done that, you can rereference the WileyPartsObjects.dll, recompile the WileyPartsServices project, and then run the WSDL.exe utility again. This is what the classes defined in the generated proxy class will look like after doing so.

```
public class Vehicle : WileyObject {
   public int VehicleID;
   public int VehicleYear;
   public string Make;
   public string Model;
   public string SubModel;
}


[System.Xml.Serialization.XmlIncludeAttribute(typeof(Part))]
[System.Xml.Serialization.XmlIncludeAttribute(typeof(PartCategory))]
[System.Xml.Serialization.XmlIncludeAttribute(typeof(Vehicle))]
public class WileyObject {
}

public class Part : WileyObject {
   public int PartID;
   public int CategoryID;
   public string Description;
   public System.Decimal Price;
   public System.Single Weight;
}

public class PartCategory : WileyObject {
   public int CategoryID;
   public string Description;
}
```

This looks better, but something is still a little funny. Member variables have been created for all of the properties that we provided in the classes rather than properties. The member variables have taken on the same name as the properties that we provided. This is rather inconvenient. If we need to bind some kind of control to these classes, we will have to define properties manually, as binding will not work with public member variables. If we create new Web methods and need to run the utility again, the modifications that have been made to the generated classes will be lost. In a real-world project it is probably a good idea to extract these generated classes and place them in a separate source file, which will allow you to make custom modifications and not worry about losing them if the proxy class needs to be regenerated. If you do have to regenerate the proxy class, you can just delete any classes from the proxy class that you have modified to eliminate duplicate class definitions.

As you'll see in the next section, the WSDL.exe tool provides you with a little more control than adding a Web Reference to a project.

An Alternative .NET Client for Wiley Parts

Let's create a C# Win Form application that will utilize the Wiley Parts services. We won't explain how to write a WinForms application because this is a Web application book, but we will show you how to add a Web Reference to a project and use the proxy classes that are generated. If you are not familiar with developing WinForm applications, the full source code for this example can be downloaded from the companion Web site.

We created a C# Win Form project called WinFormWebServiceClient. To add a Web Reference to a project, you can right-click on the project in Solution Explorer and choose Add Web Reference. You should be presented with a dialog that looks similar to Figure 7.16. In the left-hand pane there is a link to the live Microsoft UDDI directory, where you can find any Web services that have been registered by various companies. There is also a link to the Test Microsoft UDDI directory and, last, a link to any Web references on the local Web server. If you click on the link for local Web services, the dynamic discovery file that should be located in the root directory of your default Web server will be found, which will enable the discovery of any Web services in that directory or any directory below it. A list of links to other discovery files that are found will be shown in the right-hand pane, as you can see in Figure 7.17. There are several to choose from on our machine. The WileyPartsServices discovery file is listed last. If we click on that link, the left-hand pane will display the same Web page that we saw in Figure 7.2, and the Add Reference button at the bottom of the dialog will become enabled. To add the Web reference to the project, click the button.

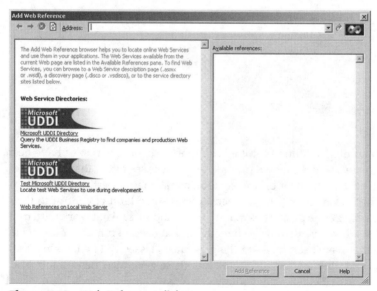

Figure 7.16 Web Reference dialog.

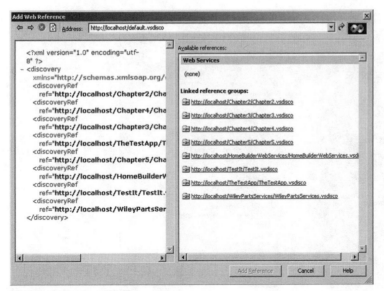

Figure 7.17   Local Web services.

After the Web reference is added, the Solution Explorer window should look like Figure 7.18. A Web References folder has been added, and a localhost folder is located inside of it. If we had referenced a Web service on some other Web site, the name of that Web site would have been used instead. In the localhost directory, four files have been created. The PartSearch.wsdl file is just the WSDL contract file that was retrieved from the Web service and used to create the PartSearch.cs file, which is the C# proxy class for calling the Wiley Parts Web methods. This is the exact same proxy file that we generated earlier with the WSDL.exe tool. By default, the proxy class is included inside of a namespace that takes the form of <Project Name>.<Web Site Name>. Our proxy class has been created inside of the WinFormWebServiceClient.localhost namespace. The Reference.map file keeps a list of the discovery documents and WSDL contract files that were found when the Web reference was made. The WileyPartsServices.disco file is a static discovery file for the Web service that we have referenced.

We added a few controls to a Win Form and wrote some simple code to populate those controls with the results of the Web method calls. When the form is first opened, the following code will be executed.

```
PartSearch search = new PartSearch();
cmbVehicleYears.DataSource = search.GetVehicleYears();

cmbCategories.DataSource = search.GetAllCategories();
```

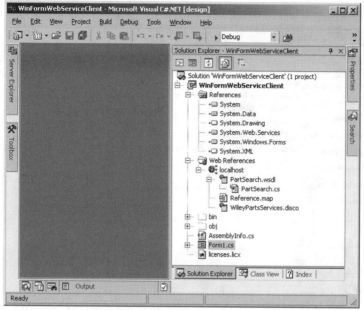

Figure 7.18 Solution Explorer with a Web Reference.

To call the Web methods, an instance of the PartSearch proxy class must be created. Our form has two combo boxes for displaying the available vehicle years and the part categories. As you can see, we have set the DataSource property of the cmbVehicle-Years control to the result of a call to the GetVehicleYears() Web method. Similarly, we have set the DataSource property of the cmbCategories control to the result of a call to the GetAllCategories() method. The last two lines of code need a little explaining. When combo boxes are bound to an array of objects, the text that is displayed for each object is the text returned by a call to the ToString() method on that object, unless the DisplayMember property of the combo box has been set to the name of a specific property on the object. The GetVehicleYears() Web method returns an integer array, and the int.ToString() method returns a string representation of the integer, which is what we want. The GetAllCategories() method returns an array of PartCategory objects. If you remember from the earlier discussion in this chapter, the PartCategory class is created for us in the PartSearch.cs proxy file and looks like this:

```
public class PartCategory : WileyObject
{
  public int CategoryID;
  public string Description;
}
```

The class that has been generated does not have a ToString() method. Even if our original PartCategory class had defined a ToString() method, that method implementation would not be reproduced in the proxy class. If we do not set the DisplayMember property of the cmbCategories combo box the ToString() method of the class will be called to get the display text. Because the PartCategory and WileyObject classes do not provide an override of the ToString() method, the Object.ToString() method, which returns the name of the class, will be called. We need to display the description of the category in the combo box, so we have set the DisplayMember to "Description". Additionally, we have set the ValueMember of the combo box to CategoryID because we will need that to make a call to the GetParts() Web method later on. There is still a problem, though. The DisplayMember and ValueMember properties must be set to the names of public properties that will be available on the object. The PartCategory class that was generated does not have any properties, but rather has two public member variables by the names of CategoryID and Description. When the cmbCategories combo box tries to bind at runtime, an exception will be generated and the program will fail. We need to expose these two member variables as properties like this.

```
public class PartCategory : WileyObject
{
  private int m_intCategoryID;
  private string m_strDescription;

  public int CategoryID
  {
    get { return m_intCategoryID; }
    set { m_intCategoryID = value; }
  }

  public string Description
  {
    get { return m_strDescription; }
    set { m_strDescription = value; }
  }
}
```

An important thing to note here is that, whatever is done to this class, there must be either public member variables or properties named CategoryID and Description. These exact names have been defined in the WSDL contract, and they need to be there for proper serialization and deserialization of the class. The PartCategory type is defined in the WSDL contract like this.

```
<s:complexType name="PartCategory">
  <s:complexContent mixed="false">
    <s:extension base="s0:WileyObject">
      <s:sequence>
        <s:element minOccurs="1" maxOccurs="1" name="CategoryID"
          type="s:int" />
        <s:element minOccurs="1" maxOccurs="1" name="Description"
          nillable="true" type="s:string" />
      </s:sequence>
    </s:extension>
  </s:complexContent>
</s:complexType>
```

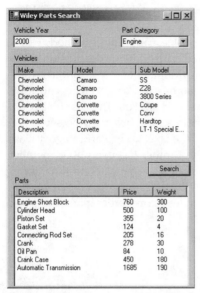

Figure 7.19   WinFormWebServiceClient.

Note the specific element names of CategoryID and Description. The point here is that often you will need to modify custom classes that are generated by a Web reference or the WSDL.exe tool. You need to be very cautious to maintain the original publicly accessible member variables and properties, or your Web method calls will cease to function properly. If you do manage to break something in a generated class, you can always refer to the WSDL contract and make sure that you have not removed or changed any required property names.

Calls to the GetVehiclesByYear() and PartSearch() Web methods are made very similarly to what we have already seen, so we will not show them here. You can check out the full source for this Win Form application by downloading the source code from the companion Web site. A screen shot of what it looks like is shown in Figure 7.19.

Wrapping Up the Chapter

In this chapter, we learned how to use XML Web services as a means to pass objects across the Web, as well as to call on business logic that exists on a Web server. Web services are a meaningful way to solve a host of business challenges, and with ASP.NET they are easy to implement and consume. While Web services can be used from any type of application, we have tried to show you how to use them from something other than a Web application. We do feel that many of you will consume Web services heavily in your ASP.NET Web applications, and the techniques you have learned in this chapter apply there equally well. Now we will move on to security and authentication in ASP.NET and discuss the means by which we can control access to our Web pages.

CHAPTER 8

Security and Membership

Web application security and authentication should be considered from the very beginning of your Web project, starting with the design phase. You must ensure that the design of the application allows the proper security measures to be implemented. For example, if you are designing an e-commerce application, any pages that collect personal information, such as credit card numbers, should be placed in separate directories where SSL can be implemented. If you are designing an intranet Web application that will contain information that should be accessible only by managers, those pages should also be separate. The larger the Web application, the more important security and authentication become, particularly if you have hyperlinks sprinkled throughout your pages.

In this chapter we cover how ASP.NET security works with the security features that are provided by IIS to further enhance security and authentication. We take a look at several different methods for implementing authentication. Finally, we will add an Orders Report to our Wiley Parts application and implement a security mechanism for accessing the report.

IIS Security

Internet Information Services has built-in security features that work independently of ASP.NET. These security features can be used along with Windows user account information to secure a Web application without requiring any code changes. You can configure IIS security for any Web site or virtual directory from Internet Services Manager. From the property page for a particular directory, select the Directory Security tab and click the Edit button under the Anonymous Access and Authentication Control section. You should see a dialog similar to the one in Figure 8.1. We'll cover these options in detail in the sections that follow.

Anonymous Access

When IIS receives a request from a client, it needs to process the request under a valid Windows account. This allows the operating system to grant or deny access to resources based on the user's security credentials. When the Anonymous Access checkbox is selected, IIS will not authenticate the client; instead, it will impersonate a specified user account on behalf of the client. When IIS is installed, a user account called IUSR_*ComputerName* is created and assigned to the Guests user group. This account is used by default whenever a directory is set to allow anonymous access. This user account can be changed manually by clicking the Edit button in the Anonymous Access section, which will display a dialog similar to Figure 8.2. From this dialog you can specify any user account that you wish. If the Allow IIS to Control Password checkbox is checked, IIS will automatically keep in synch with the password for the specified account, even if the password is changed.

Figure 8.1   IIS Authentication dialog.

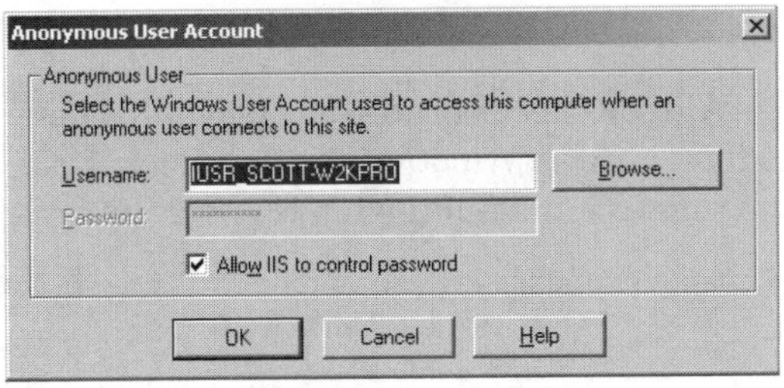

Figure 8.2   Anonymous access user account.

It is important to note that ASP.NET applications are set to run under the Windows ASPNET user account by default. This means that whenever access is requested for a resource that will be served by the ASP.NET ISAPI DLL (.aspx, .ascx, etc.), the ASPNET user account must have access to the resource as well, or access will be denied.

Anonymous access should be used for any areas of a Web application that do not need to be secured. This will be typical for Web sites that are open to the public, such as the sample Wiley Parts Web site, or general information areas of an intranet Web site. Keep in mind that IIS will be impersonating the IUSR_*ComputerName* account or an account that you have specified when anonymous access is enabled. If NTFS security changes are made that deny this account access to particular resources, anonymous users will be unable to access those resources. If anonymous access is the only authentication option chosen, attempting to request a resource that the anonymous account does not have access to will result in a page similar to Figure 8.3 being served up by IIS.

Figure 8.3   Access Denied Form.

Windows Authentication

Windows authentication allows us to use Windows security accounts to grant or deny access to areas of our Web site. There are three types of Windows authentication: Basic, Digest, and Integrated Windows authentication. Each has its own set of pros and cons.

Basic

Basic authentication is the most widely supported form of Windows authentication because it is part of the HTTP 1.0 specification and is supported by most browsers. In addition, it will work through proxy servers and firewalls. It is the least secure option, however, because user names and passwords are not encrypted before they are sent across the network.

When a client makes a request for a resource and has not yet been authenticated and authorized to access that resource, he or she will be prompted for username and password. The prompt displayed for acquiring the username and password depends on the browser used. Figure 8.4 shows the prompt displayed by an IE browser, and Figure 8.5 shows the prompt displayed by a version of the Opera browser. If the user supplies credentials that are denied access, the resulting action will vary from browser to browser. For example, with an IE browser, the user will be prompted for the username and password three times. After the third failed attempt, the page shown in Figure 8.3 will be displayed. With Version 3.62 of the Opera browser, the user will continually and endlessly be prompted for username and password.

Figure 8.4   Internet Explorer Basic authentication dialog.

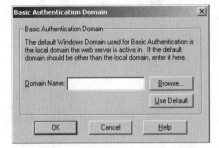

Figure 8.5 Opera Basic authentication dialog.

Remember that the username and password that the user is being asked to supply are a Windows username and password. It could be for an account on the Web server machine or for an account in a Windows domain. Neither of these prompts allows the user to specify a domain name. Domain credentials can be specified be entering the username in the form DOMAIN\username. With Basic authentication, we can specify the default domain to be used if none is specified on the server. When the Basic authentication check box on the dialog in Figure 8.1 is checked, the Edit button that is grayed out on the right side of the dialog becomes active. Clicking on this Edit button will display the dialog shown in Figure 8.6. As you can see from the text in the dialog, the default domain that is used is the one in which the Web server is active. You can change this to some other domain if you wish.

Figure 8.6 Basic authentication domain dialog.

Basic authentication is highly accessible and will be the most widely supported form of Windows authentication, but due to its vulnerability to the dreaded hacker it should be used sparingly and mainly in secure network situations.

Digest

Digest authentication works much the same as Basic authentication, but it is more secure. Passwords are sent as a hash value that is created from the original password, as opposed to sending the username and password across the wire without any type of encryption, as with Basic authentication. Just as with Basic authentication, Digest authentication will work properly through proxy servers and firewalls. Not all browsers support Digest authentication, though, because it was introduced in the HTTP 1.1 specification. In addition, it is supported only in domains with a Windows 2000 domain controller.

Integrated

Integrated Windows authentication is the most secure option. Usernames and passwords are not sent across the network at all. The client's browser will authenticate the user through a cryptographic exchange with the Web server. It is supported only by Internet Explorer 2.0 or later and does not work through HTTP proxy connections. If you are developing an intranet Web application, this will be the option that you will use most often.

When a client requests a resource under a Web site using Integrated Windows authentication, the credentials with which that the user logged on to the machine will be used to attempt to authenticate the user on the Web server first. If those credentials fail or are denied access to the requested resource, the user will be prompted for his or her credentials by a dialog similar to that shown in Figure 8.7.

If a client requests a resource under a Web site that is using Integrated Windows authentication with a browser other than Internet Explorer 2.0, he or she will likely see an error message that indicates that the authentication method is not supported. The error message displayed by Opera 3.62 can be seen in Figure 8.8.

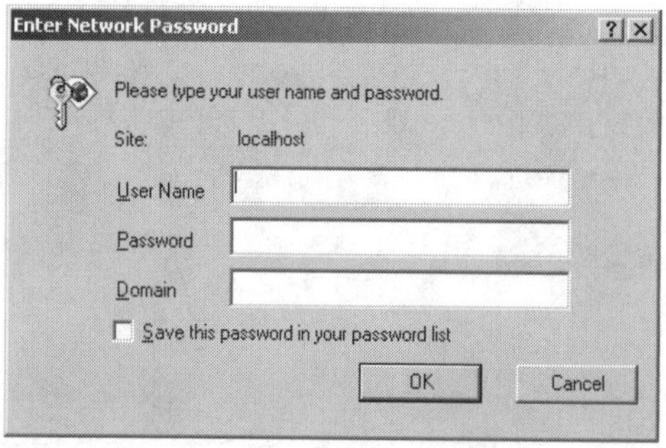

Figure 8.7   Integrated Windows authentication prompt.

Figure 8.8 Opera authentication error.

Integrated Windows authentication is very easy to use and extremely flexible. Its pitfalls are that it is supported only by Internet Explorer 2.0 or greater and that all users must have valid Windows accounts. If you are developing a large intranet Web site to be used on a predominantly Windows client network, you will definitely want to use this authentication option. It is not usually suitable, though, to public Internet Web site applications because all users must have a valid Windows account.

Mixing and Matching

It is important to know that these different authentication methods, including anonymous access, can all be used together. If anonymous access is selected, IIS will always attempt to authorize client requests using the anonymous user account first. If the anonymous account is denied access and Integrated Windows authentication is enabled, IIS will attempt to log the user on with his or her current credentials. If access is once again denied, the user will be prompted for a username and password. In the case that the user is not using a browser that supports Integrated Windows authentication and the Web site has Digest or Basic authentication enabled, those authentication methods will be attempted in their respective order.

For an example, let's assume that we have a directory structure such as the following:

```
Application (Accessible by anonymous)
    -> Secure (Not accessible by anonymous)
```

We have configured a Web site in IIS whose root directory is the Application directory, and we have enabled Anonymous Access, Basic, and Integrated Windows authentication through Internet Services Manager. The NTFS security settings for the Application directory allow everyone access, but the Secure directory allows access only to a user named Dave West. Let's assume then that Dave West is at work and is logged on to the network as himself. He then navigates to a page called default.htm in the Application directory with the latest version of Internet Explorer. IIS will first try to access the default.htm resource by using the anonymous user account. In this case, access is granted and the page is displayed. He then navigates to a page called TopSecret.htm, which is located in the Secure directory. Once again, IIS will attempt to access the resource using the anonymous user account, but this time access is denied. IIS will now attempt to access the resource using the other available forms of authentication. Integrated Windows authentication takes precedence over Basic authentication, so IIS will attempt to authenticate using this method next and will first try the user credentials with which Dave is logged on to his machine. In this case, he is logged on as Dave West, which does have access to the TopSecret.htm resource, and the page will be displayed without prompting Dave for his credentials.

Now Dave starts up his laptop, which is attached to the network, and logs on to the network once again. His laptop does not have any version of Internet Explorer, but instead has an Opera browser. Dave attempts to navigate to the TopSecret.htm resource using the Opera browser, but this time he is prompted for his username and password. Because Opera does not support Integrated Windows authentication, IIS attempts to authenticate Dave using Basic authentication. Basic authentication will not try to log Dave on using the credentials with which he logged on to his machine, so he is forced to enter his credentials once again. If he does, the TopSecret.htm page will be displayed. As long as he doesn't close his browser, he can continue to request other resources that he has access to without reentering his username and password.

As you can see, we can implement robust security through IIS without having to write any code whatsoever. In the sections that follow we will see how ASP.NET can be configured to work with IIS and implement security of its own.

ASP.NET Authentication

ASP.NET has the ability to authenticate users and enforce security restraints on its own as well as in concert with IIS. When IIS has granted access to a request for an ASP.NET page, or any other resource registered to be handled by aspnet_isapi.dll, the authentication information is passed on to the ASP.NET application for further authentication. Keep in mind that if IIS has authenticated a user, it will always be under a Windows account, whether it is the anonymous IUSR_*ComputerName* account or some other Windows account. It is this information that will be passed on to the ASP.NET application.

ASP.NET security is configured through the use of the Web.Config file, which should be located in the root virtual directory of the application. In this section, we concentrate specifically on the sections that pertain to security.

The sections of the Web.Config file that pertain to security are <authentication>, <identity>, and <authorization>. The <authentication> section is used to specify the type of authentication to be used for the virtual directory.

```
<authentication mode="Windows|Forms|Passport|None" />
```

As you can see in this line of code, as of now there are four choices for authentication: Windows, Forms, Passport, and None.

The <identity> section allows you to specify whether to use client impersonation. In a nutshell, this would allow you to make operating system calls on behalf of the original client. We could also specify a particular user account with which to impersonate. The <identity> section takes on the following form.

```
<identity impersonate="true|false"
   userName="username" password="password" />
```

To impersonate using the credentials supplied by IIS, simply set the impersonate option to true and leave out the username and password attributes. If you specify a username and password, that account will be impersonated instead. Impersonation must be used in conjunction with Windows authentication. To set up a scenario where ASP.NET impersonates each client request, the following would need to be present in the Web.Config file.

```
<authentication mode="Windows" />
<identity impersonate="true" />
```

NOTE We're not going to go into any more detail on impersonation in this book, but you should be aware that the capability exists and know how to enable it.

The <authorization> section is used to allow or deny access to specific users, roles, or verbs (HTTP transmission methods, GET, HEAD, POST, and DEBUG). It takes the following form in the Web.Config file.

```
<authorization>
  <allow users="comma-separated list of users"
    roles="comma-separated list of roles"
    verbs="comma-separated list of verbs" />
  <deny users="comma-separated list of users"
    roles="comma-separated list of roles"
    verbs="comma-separated list of verbs" />
</authorization>
```

Securing directories in this manner is referred to as URL authorization. For example, if we wanted to allow access to the Administrator account on our Web server and deny all other users access to a particular directory, we could use the following in the Web.Config file in that directory.

```
<authorization>
  <allow users="Scott-w2kpro\Administrator" />
  <deny users="*" />
</authorization>
```

Assuming that the authentication mode is set to Windows, if we attempt to access this page with Internet Explorer and are not logged on as the Administrator, Integrated Windows authentication will kick in and we will be prompted for a username, password, and domain. Just as before, if we fail to enter appropriate credentials three times, we will see an Access Denied page, shown in Figure 8.9. This time the error page is served up from ASP.NET and not IIS. You can see the difference if you compare Figure 8.9 and Figure 8.3.

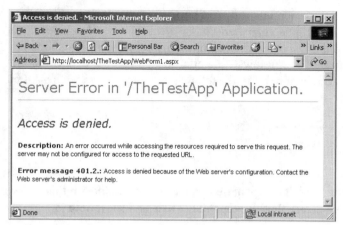

Figure 8.9   ASP.NET Access Denied page.

Two special identities can be used. The * can be used to specify all users, as we did in the previous example. The ? can be used to specify the anonymous user. The default setting in the machine.config file is to allow all users as follows.

```
<authorization>
  <allow users="*" />
</authorization>
```

ASP.NET will look through the list of <allow> and <deny> tags in the <authorization> section of the Web.config file until it finds the first match for the current user. If it is an <allow>, the request will be processed. If it is a <deny>, access to the resource will be denied. So, if we change the <authorization> section in the previous example and place the <deny> tag before the <allow> tag, no users will be granted access to resources, not even the Administrator account.

If you intend to use the <authorization> section to allow or deny access to Windows users, then the authentication mode must be set to Windows. If the authentication mode is set to something other than Windows, no Windows user accounts will be allowed access. In the previous example where only the Administrator account was allowed access, if the authentication mode was set to "None" the Administrator account would have been denied access.

For our Orders Report in the sample application, we'll need to implement different security strategies. The following sections demonstrate how to use Windows, Forms, and Passport authentication in the ASP.NET Web application.

Windows

Windows authentication is the simplest to implement via ASP.NET. To enable ASP.NET Windows authentication, you simply need to modify the <authentication> section of the Web.Config file as follows:

```
<authentication mode="Windows">
```

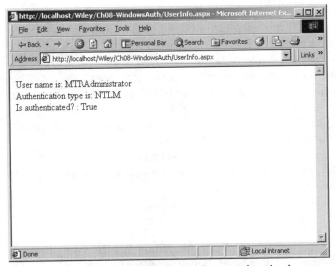

Figure 8.10   A User object with Windows authentication.

You should use ASP.NET Windows authentication in conjunction with any of the three forms of IIS Windows authentication. This type of authentication requires no code changes. Look at the User object when a user has been authenticated by Windows authentication. Here is some code that gives us access to the user object of the logged-on user. For this sample, create a new ASP.NET Web application called Chapter8WindowsAuth, and in it create a new WebForm called UserInfo. Inside the UserInfo Page_Load handler, insert the following code. We created a completely separate application for this example because we don't want to have to change the config file for the other samples in the chapter.

```
Response.Write(string.Format("User name is: {0}<br>",
User.Identity.Name));
Response.Write(string.Format("Authentication type is: {0}<br>",
  User.Identity.AuthenticationType));

Response.Write(string.Format("Is authenticated? : {0}<br>",
  User.Identity.IsAuthenticated));
```

When this code is run from a Page_Load event, we would see something similar to the page shown in Figure 8.10.

Forms

Forms authentication is a robust way to allow flexibility in how you authenticate your users. It is robust because the Forms mode allows you to perform whatever kind of action you desire when an unauthenticated user requests a page. Implementing Forms authentication requires programming in addition to configuration. Forms authentication also allows you to store your users' credentials in any format you like, including files and databases. In this example, we are going to make a copy of the WileyParts application from Chapter 6. This time, however, we are going to modify it to have a secure orders page, which will be in its own subproject called Chapter8Forms-Auth. Make a copy of the entire Ch6WileyPartsWeb project folder called Ch8Wiley-PartsWeb. In this new folder, create a folder called Secure, and in it, create a new ASP.NET Web application called Chapter8FormsAuth. In this application we will create a page that will display all of the orders made to the shopping site, but that will be protected by Forms authentication.

Like the other modes, the first step in implementing Forms-based authentication is done in the Web.Config file. In the Web.Config file of the new Chapter8FormsAuth project, modify the authentication section as follows.

```
<authentication mode="Forms">
```

Next, you must tell the server which page will be implementing the user validation and which users should be forced to log in by inserting the following code in the Config. Web file.

```
<forms loginUrl="login.aspx" name="WileyFormsSecurity" />
</authentication>
<authorization>
  <deny users="?" />
</authorization>
```

In the second line, we tell the server which file to redirect the users to when they are not authenticated; in this case, it's login.aspx. The name attribute tells the server what to name the cookie that is stored and passed back in the authentication form of each subsequent page. In the second line of the authorization section, we tell the server to deny access to any unauthorized user. The ? in the user's attribute stands for anonymous user; thus, any user logging on who is anonymous (not authenticated) will be redirected to the login.aspx page. The fact that these entries were made in the Web.Config file of the subfolder means that they apply only to the application at that level, in this case the Chapter8FormsAuth application in the Secure folder. This emphasizes the hierarchical nature of config files in .NET. The settings in any folder override the settings in the parent folder. This works nicely when we want to secure only a portion of the pages and leave some totally public.

Notice that even if we tried to allow a Windows user to access the resource by putting a <allow users="blueline1\tomj" /> entry in the authorization section, Tom would still be rerouted to the login page. The authentication mode is set to Forms, so the server doesn't care if a Windows user tried to access the page. This is not Windows authentication, so no luck for the user with a valid Windows account on the server—he must still log in using the Forms authentication page. Also note that if we include a <allow users="*" /> entry before the deny entry, we would be allowing any user to bypass the Forms authentication and directly access the protected resource. This is probably not the desired behavior in most cases. Now let's take a look at the login page code, which has the important line dealing with the actual authentication, in bold.

What does all of this mean to the application? When a page is requested in an application using Forms authentication, the first thing that ASP.NET does is to look for a cookie in the request header containing an authentication key that can tell the browser who the user is. If this cookie is not present, ASP.NET assumes that the user has not been authenticated for the current session. ASP.NET will automatically send the user to the page specified in the Web.Config file in the <loginUrl="login.aspx"> line. The ? in the line <deny users="?">, tells ASP.NET to reject any user who is not authenticated.

For the actual login page, create a new WebForm called login.aspx, in the Chapter8FormsAuth project. On the login.aspx page, you (the programmer) are responsible for authenticating the user however you wish. In most cases, you would want to display typical username and password entry fields and a button to invoke the authentication. For this example, we are building a simple page to go along with the Wiley Parts examples used so far. Here, we will create an orders page that an order-filler at Wiley Parts can access to view current orders that are waiting to be shipped. While our sample is simple and doesn't actually ship the orders, it is a perfect example of when you may want to disallow all but properly authenticated users to access the pages.

On this login page, we use a simple pair of ASP.NET TextBoxes, one for a username and one for a password. When the user enters credentials into these two fields and presses a server-side button, the code looks in the database for the user and password. If they are found, then the user is authenticated. If they are not found, a login failure message is displayed. The code to look in the database to authenticate the user will be added to the WileyPartsObjects DLL, also copied over from Chapter 6. The code for this modification is shown in Listing 8.1.

To tell the system that the user has been authenticated successfully, we rely on some helper functionality in the .NET framework System.Web.Security namespace. We call FormsAuthentication.RedirectFromLogin, which will send the user back to the original, secured page he or she requested. This time, however, a cookie is inserted into the request by the ASP.NET FormsAuthentication Provider. This is used by the system to verify that the user has been authenticated in each subsequent request the user makes in the session. This is how ASP.NET knows not to send the user back to the login page after he or she has already successfully authenticated.

The Name property of the User.Identity object on the Page class will be set to the now-authenticated user. This allows us to get the user's name and some other information, such as whether the authentication took place, the type (Forms in this case,) and the actual authentication ticket. when using Forms authentication. To see what the client is sending to the server when the user is authenticated, we wrote a small HTTP Server in C# to call with the login.aspx page. The server displays the requests that are sent to it. Here is the output from an authenticated call:

```
POST /tcp.aspx HTTP/1.1
Accept: image/gif, image/x-xbitmap, image/jpeg, image/pjpeg,
application/vnd.ms-
powerpoint, application/vnd.ms-excel, application/msword, */*
Referer: http://localhost/Wiley/Ch08-FormsAuth/login.aspx
Accept-Language: en-us
Content-Type: application/x-www-form-urlencoded
Accept-Encoding: gzip, deflate
```

```
User-Agent: Mozilla/4.0 (compatible; MSIE 6.0b; Windows NT 5.0; .NET CLR
1.0.291 4)
Host: localhost:8080
Content-Length: 48
Connection: Keep-Alive
Cache-Control: no-cache
Cookie: ASP.NET_SessionId=pvxxpxrnmzh32pb4ryz5q2b3;
WileyPartsSecurity=C145D82B0EDA61558060CE873CF4BA50208344ACD0E6A30B8980C
2F361FCE42C2740A06E3E777B214AC24BC1BC7140CEB696E5BC65AF66E6065F591FBCF8D
F8C


txtPwd=123&txtUid=hankm&btnLogin=Login
```

Notice the WileyPartsSecurity form item that was inserted by the system. The form is named by the name entry in the Web.Config file.

NOTE To do this trick, we simply had to change the form in the login.aspx page and make its action=http://localhost:8080/tcp.aspx, which is the simple HTTP server, with a bogus URI, just for good measure. Also, we had to remove the runat=server attribute from the form to keep ASP.NET from linking to it and setting it to post back to the page. Of course, doing this is a hack and renders the page useless, so be sure to change it back if you attempt these kinds of experiments.

Note that the User-Agent (which is how the browser identifies its type to the server) denotes that it supports the .NET common language runtime and the version thereof. Internet Explorer is a host for .NET common language runtime applications, just as is ASP.NET, and is a .NET exe file created by a .NET compiler.

Now back to the login page example. When the user enters his or her credentials into the form, if we don't find the credentials record when searching in the database for the user, we can assume the user is not allowed to be served the secured page. In that case, we simply display a message telling the user that the username and password combination was incorrect. In some cases, you may want to use this opportunity to send the user to a page where he or she can enter a new username and password, thus entering new "membership" information into the system on the fly. This would work well in public Web applications that need to support a large number of authenticated users. It may be best in a public site to allow the users to enter their own user account information to gain access to the system rather than having to administer users manually on the Web server side. In effect, we would be letting the user base do the user administration for us.

Because the authentication of the users is actually the burden of your code, you can perform this any way you like. How you decide to store the users' credentials information is entirely up to you. You could store the user credentials in an XML file on the server, or you could call in to some preexisting user database or a mainframe or offsite computer. Or, you may need an extra measure of security and require your users to enter two different passwords to log in. It's up to you; you may not even require passwords at all. Some form of a username is required, however, whether it takes the shape of an ID string, social security number, or email address. The user's name is used in the call to set the authorization, whether you call FormsAuthentication.SetAuthCookie or FormsAuthentication.RedirectFromLoginPage.

The .NET Framework supplies a robust set of objects that allow you maximum flexibility when using Forms authentication. The one most commonly used is the FormsAuthentication object mentioned previously. This object of the System.Web.Security namespace supports a set of static members for helping you with the chores of programming with the Forms.

If you decide to compile and run this example from the companion Web site, remember to include this alternate version of the WileyPartsObjects, not the one we created previously in Chapter 6, "Applying What We've Learned So Far." Note that we also added two other classes, the OrderList and OrderListItem classes. These are just to display the orders using database access techniques we learned in Chapter 4, "Database Access"; therefore, we won't study them here. Create a new class in the WileyPartsObjects project called UserAuth, as shown in Listing 8.1.

```
using System;
using System.Data;
using System.Data.SqlClient;
using System.Collections;
using WileyParts.Database;

namespace WileyParts.Objects
{
  /// <summary>
  /// Summary description for UserAuth.
  /// </summary>
  public class UserAuth : WileyObject
  {
    public UserAuth()
    {
      //
      // TODO: Add constructor logic here
      //
    }

    public static bool IsUserValid(string strUid, string strPwd,
      ref bool IsValid, WileyConnection conn)
    {
      try
      {
        //Call a stored procedure to get the parts for the given vehicle
        //and category
```

Listing 8.1 The UserAuth class in WileyPartsObjects

```
            SqlCommand cmd = new
SqlCommand("WileyParts.dbo.sp_IsUserAuthorized",
            conn.Connection);

        cmd.CommandType = CommandType.StoredProcedure;

        //Add the parameters
        cmd.Parameters.Add("@Uid", SqlDbType.VarChar, 20).Value =
strUid;
        cmd.Parameters.Add("@Pwd", SqlDbType.VarChar, 20).Value =
strPwd;
        cmd.Parameters.Add("@IsValid", SqlDbType.Bit).Direction =
          ParameterDirection.Output;

        //Execute the command
        cmd.ExecuteNonQuery();

        IsValid = Convert.ToBoolean(cmd.Parameters["@IsValid"].Value);
        return true;
    }
    catch(Exception ex)
    {
        WileyObject.WriteToLog(ex.ToString(), "UserAuth");
        throw new Exception("Failure while trying to authorize user",
ex);
    }
  }
 }
}
```

Listing 8.1   The UserAuth class in WileyPartsObjects (continued)

And here is the code that occurs on the login page, when the user enters his or her credentials:

```
private void btnLogin_Click(object sender, System.EventArgs e)
{
  //See if user is authorized.
  bool b = false;

  UserAuth ua = new UserAuth();
  if (!ua.IsUserValid(txtUid.Text.Trim(), txtPwd.Text.Trim(), ref b,
    DBConnection))
  {
    lblLogin.Text = ua.GetErrorsFormatted();
    lblLogin.Visible = true;
    return;
```

```
   }

   if (b)
   {
      //Valid, so continue on to application.
      FormsAuthentication.RedirectFromLoginPage(txtUid.Text.Trim(),
false);
   }
   else
   {
      //Invalid, so inform user.
      lblLogin.Text = "Invalid user name or password";
      lblLogin.Visible = true;
   }
}
```

Note that this is only the code-behind. We are not showing the user interface aspx code because it is a simple form with TextBoxes and a Button, which have been discussed at length already. The user will have entered his or her credentials into the appropriate fields and clicked the Login button. In the click event handler for the button, we check the database to see if he or she is a valid user. We use a simple technique of looking for the username and password in a user's table, and if one is found that exactly matches the entered text, the user is considered authorized. If not, we simply display a message to the user stating the obvious. In your applications, you might want to develop a more sophisticated way to store user credentials than we have here. Also note that we could have called the methods directly to let the system know the user is valid by replacing the FormsAuthentication.RedirectFromLoginPage with the following:

```
string redurl =
   FormsAuthentication.GetRedirectUrl(txtUid.Text.Trim(), false);

FormsAuthentication.SetAuthCookie(txtUid.Text.Trim(), false);
Response.Redirect(redurl);
```

In Figure 8.11, you can see what might be a typical form for authentication. If the user is authorized, we simply call FormsAuthentication.RedirectFromLoginPage(txtUid.Text.Trim(), false); in which we pass the user's authenticated login name and a value indicating whether we want the authentication to last beyond this user's session. In most cases, you will want to pass the value false and require the user to reauthenticate should he or she close all of the browsers and attempt to revisit the protected page. This would make sense in environments in which people may access the site from public computers such as in libraries or colleges, where we don't want a user to be able to log in to the site with the previous user's authenticated credentials. In this type of environment, you might want to display a message on your pages that reminds the user to shut down all browser windows when he or she is done accessing the site. Calling this static method will tell ASP.NET to redirect the user back to the original, protected page he or she first requested, this time as a fully authorized user. We don't have to tell the system where to redirect back to because the Forms authentication system takes care of this for us by providing the return URL in the QueryString to the login page.

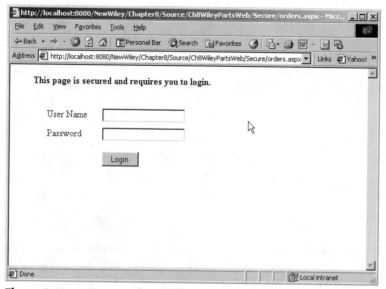

Figure 8.11   A Forms authentication login.aspx page.

Here is the code-behind class of the protected page that the user first tried to access. The call to FormsAuthentication.SignOut() will cancel the authorization and require the user to log back in the next time he or she requests a previously requested page in this application, regardless of whether the user has closed the browser. In fact, as soon as you call SignOut, which runs on the server, the user will be sent directly to the login page again because the form in the orders.aspx page is set to post back to itself (its action is orders.aspx). As soon as the user is no longer authenticated, the browser is told by the response to go to the login page all over again. Note that the only code in this snippet that is related to authentication is in bold; the rest of the code is just a review of earlier chapters.

```
private string m_strLast = "";

private void Page_Load(object sender, System.EventArgs e)
{
  try
  {
    if (!IsPostBack)
    {
      //Load table with orders.
      ArrayList arrOrderItems = OrderList.GetOrderList(DBConnection);

      DataGrid1.DataSource = arrOrderItems;
      DataGrid1.DataBind();
    }
  }
  catch(Exception ex)
```

```
  {
    Response.Write(ex);
  }
}


private void DataGrid1_ItemDataBound(object sender,
  System.Web.UI.WebControls.DataGridItemEventArgs e)
{
  //Don't display the same shopper text on more than one row.
  if (e.Item.Cells[0].Text == m_strLast)
  {
    e.Item.Cells[0].Text = "";
  }
  else
  {
    m_strLast = e.Item.Cells[0].Text;
  }
}


private void btnShip_Click(object sender, System.EventArgs e)
{
  //Look at the checkboxes and perform shipping code here.
  foreach(DataGridItem item in DataGrid1.Items)
  {
    if (((CheckBox)item.FindControl("chkShipped")).Checked)
    {
      Response.Write(string.Format("Shipped item {0}<br>",
item.ItemIndex));
    }
  }
}

private void btnLogout_Click(object sender, System.EventArgs e)
{
  //Sign the user out - unautheticate him
  FormsAuthentication.SignOut();
}
```

This page just displays a grid of parts (OrderItems) sold by Wiley Parts that are ready to be shipped. Although the code to access the orders works the same way as does much of the code in the previous chapter, we included a few tricks you can use in your apps, just because this page is a good place for them. Remember, only the btn-Logout_Click handler in bold is part of the authentication functionality.

As for the other parts of the code, first, we handled the ItemDataBound event of the DataGrid and held on to the text in the first column after every read of the data. With a simple comparison, we can prevent the same shopper name from showing up on every order item line in his or her order. This change merely cleans up the data from a viewing standpoint. We also allow the user to click a CheckBox on each row of the grid, providing the user with an interface to select order items to ship at this time. Of course, our code stops there, but you can see how we can read through the DataGrid back on the server and see which rows were marked as "shipped." In a real application, you may want to use code similar to this to read checked items, and their database IDs from the DataKeys collection, and call other code to do something with them. Here is the DataGrid code we set up to support the CheckBoxes on each row. It is the Template-Column that makes this possible. Review the code snippet, and then refer to Figure 8.12 to see it in action.

```
<asp:DataGrid id="DataGrid1" AutoGenerateColumns="false" runat="server">
  <Columns>
    <asp:BoundColumn HeaderText="Shopper"
      DataField="ShopperName"></asp:BoundColumn>

    <asp:BoundColumn HeaderText="Vehicle"
      DataField="VehicleDesc"></asp:BoundColumn>

    <asp:BoundColumn HeaderText="Description"
      DataField="Description"></asp:BoundColumn>

    <asp:BoundColumn HeaderText="Weight"
      DataField="Weight"></asp:BoundColumn>

    <asp:BoundColumn HeaderText="Qty"
      DataField="Quantity"></asp:BoundColumn>

    <asp:BoundColumn HeaderText="Unit $"
      DataField="PricePerUnit"></asp:BoundColumn>

  <asp:TemplateColumn>
    <ItemTemplate>
      <asp:CheckBox Runat="server" id="chkShipped" value="" />
    </ItemTemplate>
  </asp:TemplateColumn>
  </Columns>
</asp:DataGrid>
```

Here are some notes about designing Form-based authenticated apps. You can have your whole application protected via the Web.Config file, and you can cause redirection to any other page, including those not part of the protected app. You can even redirect to pages that are not of the aspx type. Of course, in that case you would have to program the return to the original page yourself because you probably would not have native access to the .NET FormsAuthentication object in a non ASP.NET page.

Remember that when crossing application boundaries, you won't be able to access Session variables in the login page. If you are authenticating a user who has already gone through some unprotected pages that set variables in the Session management objects in the application that sent them to a Forms authentication login page in a different application, you will not have access to the Session variables in the first application. You can set up authentication and authorization in a Web.Config file in a folder that is not an IIS application. Just leave out the tags that are related only to the application level, or ASP.NET will give you an error.

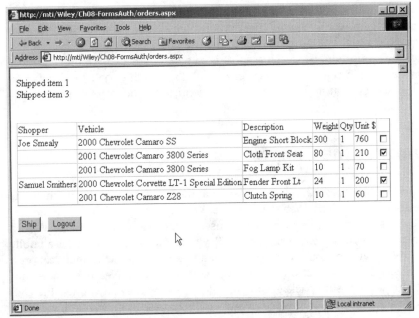

Figure 8.12   The secured orders.aspx page in action.

Note that if a user browses directly to the login page without being redirected there automatically by ASP.NET, unexpected behavior can result. In particular, the login page will not have a return URL sent to it and will attempt to redirect the user to the default.aspx page. If this page is not there, of course, the user will be given a 404 error. Keep this in mind if you have an application without a default page setup.

Passport

Microsoft's Passport Authentication Service is a type of Forms authentication, but the user login authentication process and credentials checking are performed not by you, but by the Passport service. A Passport login account is not just meant for your application, but can be used on other Passport-enabled sites as well. Under Passport Authentication, when a user requests a secured resource on your site for the first time in a session, he or she is redirected to the Passport site provided by Microsoft. Special parameters are encrypted and passed along in the QueryString to Passport including a unique ID representing the relationship your site has with Passport, as well as the URL of the original page the user requested. Passport will authenticate the user or allow him or her to set up a Passport account (credentials) at that time. When the user is authenticated by Passport, the user is redirected back to the requested page on your site and is granted access. When passport sends the redirection back to your site, it also sends an encrypted version of the key that the user will use in subsequent requests on your site. From this key, the Passport provider objects in ASP.NET will generate the Form to be used for your user's credentials.

Passport is an important authentication type, and it will assist the Web in general by allowing users to gain access to many Passport-enabled sites with one login. Microsoft does charge a fee to use Passport, but not to the user, only to the site wishing to use Passport for authentication. Because Passport is so new, and because more and more documents are emerging daily about its use, we will skip it in this book. Just know that the service exists and that it is an option for authenticating the users of your public Web site.

Wrapping Up the Chapter

In this chapter, we have seen the many different authentication and security methods that can be used for ASP.NET Web applications. We implemented Forms authentication on an Orders Report page, which requires users to log in to view that page. We did not implement any security schemes for our Wiley Parts Web site because it is a public Internet Web site that allows anonymous access and requires no user authentication.

In the next chapter, we will cover a few e-commerce essentials. Nearly every e-commerce Web site needs to ship packages to its customers. We'll see how to use the UPS online services to calculate shipping costs and verify addresses. In addition, we'll see how easy it is to send email with the .NET Framework.

Adding E-Commerce Essentials

Most e-commerce Web sites sell a physical product of some sort and ship the products to customers. Shipping the product to the customer is usually left to the experienced hands of one of the many shipping companies available. Those shipping companies usually offer varying levels of service and price. As a typical e-commerce site, the Wiley Parts site needs to be able to determine shipping service options and prices dynamically and allow the customer to choose the service that best suits him or her. In most cases, after the order is processed, we will want to email a copy of the invoice to the customer. In this chapter, we will develop some objects that can be used to retrieve shipping options and prices from the UPS Online services and then see how to send email under .NET.

Before we get into developing these handy objects, there are a few things that we need to cover. As is becoming the industry standard, we need to communicate with the UPS servers using XML. We're not going to cover XML itself in detail, as there are many very good resources on the subject already. We are going to cover a few of the tools provided in the framework for working with XML.

XML Tools

As commerce on the Internet continues to move forward, XML becomes increasingly important. Companies that wish to make Internet callable services available to others will more than likely do so through the use of XML in one form or another. We've already seen the power of XML Web services in Chapter 7, "Web Services," and how they simplify the whole process for us. XML Web services use SOAP, an XML standard for representing data and commands. When you are working with XML Web services, you won't need to come in direct contact with the underlying XML very often. There are many services available now on the Internet that use XML for communications, but they have not adopted the SOAP standard and are not Web services compatible. That means that to use those services, you won't be able to simply add a Web Reference to your project and start using them. To use these services, you will probably have to write some code that knows how to generate and read XML directly. Fortunately, the classes provided in the System.Xml namespace of the .NET Framework make working with XML data fairly easy. We're not going to cover the entire System.Xml namespace here, as it is quite broad. In fact, we are going to cover only the basics of three classes: XmlTextWriter, XmlTextReader, and XmlDocument.

XmlTextWriter

The System.Xml.XmlTextWriter should be used when you need to write some XML as fast as possible in a forward-only manner to some type of stream. It generates XML that conforms to the W3C 1.0 specifications. In general, you will create an XmlTextWriter, write the needed XML using the many Write... methods, and then close the XmlText-Writer. Perhaps the best way to demonstrate the XmlTextWriter is through a simple example.

Suppose that Wiley Parts needs to supply its parts inventory to a distributor in XML format. Let's work up an example of how we could go about creating an XML file of Wiley parts. We've created a Chapter9 project and a Web Form called XmlTools.aspx, which you can download from the companion Web site. For now, the page consists of one list box and one button. The list box will be filled with Wiley part categories. When the button is clicked, an XML file will be created for all of the parts in the selected category. It will be created in the root of the C drive and titled WileyParts.xml. Let's look at the code contained in the handler for the button click. Then we'll go through and explain it.

```
//Write the XML for list of parts
XmlTextWriter writer = new XmlTextWriter("C:\\WileyParts.xml",
   System.Text.Encoding.UTF8);
writer.WriteStartDocument();
//<WileyParts>
writer.WriteStartElement("WileyParts");

foreach (Part p in arrParts)
{
  //<Part>
  writer.WriteStartElement("Part");
  //<PartID>xxx</PartID>
  writer.WriteElementString("PartID", XmlConvert.ToString(p.PartID));
  //<Description>xxxxx</Description>
  writer.WriteElementString("Description", p.Description);
  //<Price>xxxxx</Price>
```

```
    writer.WriteElementString("Price", XmlConvert.ToString(p.Price));
    //<Weight>xxx</Weight>
    writer.WriteElementString("Weight", XmlConvert.ToString(p.Weight));
    //<Category>
    writer.WriteStartElement("Category");
    //<CategoryID>xxx</CategoryID>
    writer.WriteElementString("CategoryID", strCategoryID);
    //<Description>xxx</Description>
    writer.WriteElementString("Description", strCategoryDesc);
    //</Category>
    writer.WriteEndElement();
    //</Part>
    writer.WriteEndElement();
}

//</WileyParts>
writer.WriteEndDocument();
//Close the writer
writer.Close();
```

For the sake of saving space, we left out the code at the very beginning of this handler that actually retrieves an ArrayList of Part objects (arrParts) for the selected category. The complete code, however, is on the companion Web site. The first thing that is done in relation to generating the XML file is the creation of an XmlTextWriter.

```
XmlTextWriter writer = new XmlTextWriter("C:\\WileyParts.xml",
    System.Text.Encoding.UTF8);
```

We used the constructor to pass in the name of the file that we want to write to, and we have specified the encoding format. You can use any of the encoding types in the System.Text.Encoding enumeration. The XmlTextWriter constructor has three overloads.

```
public XmlTextWriter(TextWriter);
public XmlTextWriter(Stream, Encoding);
public XmlTextWriter(string, Encoding);
```

As you can see, the XmlTextWriter can write to a TextWriter, which would have its own encoding specified. It can also write to a stream and to a file. We'll be writing to a stream later when we write some classes to call the UPS Online services. To start the XML document out, call *WriteStartDocument()*.

```
writer.WriteStartDocument();
```

This will write the opening XML declaration. Right now, the version will always be 1.0, and the encoding attribute will be set appropriately depending on the encoding that we specified in the constructor. For our document, it will look like this:

```
<?xml version="1.0" encoding="utf-8" ?>
```

Next, we call *WriteStartElement()* to create an opening element tag with the name WileyParts.

```
//<WileyParts>
writer.WriteStartElement("WileyParts");
```

WriteStartElement() has a few overloads that allow you to specify things such as a name prefix and a namespace. For our purposes, we just need the simple tag <Wiley-Parts>. We then go into a foreach loop and process every part in arrParts. Each Part element is started by calling WriteStartElement("Part"). Most of the properties of a part are written by calling *WriteElementString()* such as this:

```
//<PartID>xxx</PartID>
writer.WriteElementString("PartID", XmlConvert.ToString(p.PartID));
```

As you can see from the preceding comment, WriteElementString() will write an opening and closing tag for the name specified as the first parameter, in this case "Part-ID". It will insert the value that you specify as the second parameter, inside the tags. Notice also the use of the *XmlConvert* class. PartID is an integer and needs to be converted to a string. XmlConvert provides methods for converting between Common Language Runtime types and XSD types. It also encodes and decodes XML names and takes care of any characters that are invalid in XML names. For our purposes here, we probably could have gotten away with calling the ToString() method on PartID, but when you're dealing with XML it is good practice to use the methods provided by Xml-Convert.

Every Part belongs to a Category. To represent this in XML, we create a Category element with the following code that has two properties, CategoryID and Description:

```
//<Category>
writer.WriteStartElement("Category");
//<CategoryID>xxx</CategoryID>
writer.WriteElementString("CategoryID", strCategoryID);
//<Description>xxx</Description>
writer.WriteElementString("Description", strCategoryDesc);
//</Category>
writer.WriteEndElement();
```

Once again, we call WriteStartElement() and use WriteElementString() to write out the two properties. Last, we need to close the Category element by calling *WriteEnd-Element()*. The XmlTextWriter is smart enough to remember how many times you have called WriteStartElement() and what element names you used. When you call WriteEndElement() you don't have to pass in any parameters. A closing tag will be created for the element for which you most recently called WriteStartElement(). In this case, the tag will be </Category>. In the very next line of code, we call Write- EndElement() again, but this time the tag that is written will be </Part>, which finishes the entry for the current Part.

After all of the parts have been processed, we make a call to *WriteEndDocument()*. But wait a minute, we never called WriteEndElement() for our opening <WileyParts>

tag. While it may be good practice to do so, it is not necessary if you call WriteEnd-Document() because it will close any open elements or attributes for you. The last thing that we need to do is call the *Close()* method on the XmlTextWriter. If we don't, the buffer won't be flushed and our file will end up empty.

We provided a hyperlink on the XmlTools.aspx page that will open up the generated XML file in the browser. A screen shot of what the XML looks like in Internet Explorer, or a snippet of it at least, can be seen in Figure 9.1.

XmlTextReader

The System.Xml.XmlTextReader should be used when you need to read some XML as fast as possible in a forward-only manner. The overloaded constructor allows you to attach the XmlTextReader to several different types of data input including any stream or file. The XML can be read one node at a time by calling the *Read()* method, which will read the next node and return true, or it will return false if there are no more nodes to read.

The XmlTextReader has many properties and methods for retrieving information about the current node and advancing through the XML. Some of the more useful properties are *Name*, which returns the qualified name of the current node. *Value* returns the text value of the current node. The text that is returned depends on the type of the node, which incidentally can be determined with the *NodeType* property. Node-Type will return a value equal to one of the members of the System.Xml.XmlNodeType enumeration. We won't reproduce the fairly long list of node types here; these are readily available in the Microsoft documentation.

In general, you will read through XML by calling the Read() method. Every call to the Read() method will return a new node until there are no new nodes to read. For every node, you can determine what to do based on the type, attributes, and content of the node, which is readily available through the XmlTextReader properties and methods.

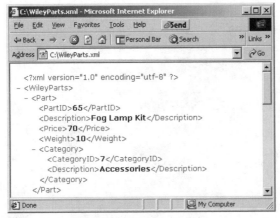

Figure 9.1 Wiley Parts XML sample.

To illustrate a simple example of using the XmlTextReader, we modified the Xml-Tools.aspx page from the XmlTextWriter section. The page now has a single button that will read the newly created file using the XmlTextReader. The handler for the button click event will read the XML and display each part in the file on the page by setting the Text property of a Label control. Here is the code for the handler:

```
try
{
  //Open the WileyParts.xml file with an XmlTextReader
  XmlTextReader reader = new XmlTextReader("C:\\WileyParts.xml");

  //Clear the previous content
  lblParts.Text = string.Empty;

  while (reader.Read())
  {
    switch (reader.NodeType)
    {
      case XmlNodeType.Element:
        switch (reader.Name)
        {
          case "WileyParts":
            break;
          case "Part":
            lblParts.Text += "<br>";
            break;
          case "Category":
            break;
          default:
            lblParts.Text += reader.Name + ": ";
            break;
        }

        break;
      case XmlNodeType.Text:
        lblParts.Text += reader.Value + "<br>";
        break;
    }
  }

  reader.Close();
}
catch (XmlException ex)
{
  Response.Write("An XmlException occurred: " + ex.ToString());
}
catch (Exception ex)
{
  Response.Write("An Exception occurred: " + ex.ToString());
}
```

An XmlTextReader is created and passed in the name of a file that it should attempt to open. If the file can't be opened or does not exist, an XmlException will be thrown. The Text of the Label control is then cleared so that we can begin to write out the content as we read through the XML. The rest of the method is contained inside of a while loop that calls the Read() method. Remember, as long as there are nodes to read, the Read() method will return true and the body of the while statement will be executed. When Read() returns false, there is nothing left to do, so the method will exit after making a call to the *Close()* method of the XmlTextReader, which will close the file.

Now, let's take a look at the body of the while loop. All of the functionality is contained inside of a switch statement on the NodeType property.

```
switch (reader.NodeType)
```

In this case, we are interested only in nodes of type XmlNodeType.Element and XmlNodeType.Text. Here is a look at the format of the XML that we will be reading in.

```
<?xml version="1.0" encoding="utf-8" ?>
<WileyParts>
  <Part>
    <PartID>1</PartID>
    <Description>Engine Long Block</Description>
    <Price>2000</Price>
    <Weight>600</Weight>
    <Category>
      <CategoryID>1</CategoryID>
      <Description>Engine</Description>
    </Category>
  </Part>
</WileyParts>
```

The XML declaration in the first line is of type XmlNodeType.XmlDeclaration. Because we didn't provide a case statement for this type of node, it will be read with the first call to the Read() method, but no processing will be performed for it. The next node is <WileyParts>, which is of type XmlNodeType.Element. Therefore, it will be processed by this case statement.

```
case XmlNodeType.Element:
  switch (reader.Name)
  {
    case "WileyParts":
      break;
    case "Part":
      lblParts.Text += "<br>";
      break;
    case "Category":
      break;
    default:
      lblParts.Text += reader.Name + ": ";
      break;
  }
```

This case statement has another nested switch statement, but this time we're switching on the Name property, which gives us the name of the element. We don't really want to do anything for the <WileyParts> element because it is just a container element for all of the parts. A case statement has been provided for it that doesn't do anything. The same thing goes for the <Category> element; it is just a container element inside each part, and nothing needs to be done for it. If the element is <Part>, we know that we have reached the beginning of a new Part element. In this case, we just want to make sure that we have an empty line between each part for the sake of readability, so a <br> is added to the text of the label.

The default case handles every other element of type XmlNodeType.Element and simply adds the Name of the element to the text stream. It is important to know that for all of the elements such as PartID, Description, and Price, the Value property will be an empty string and not the contained value of the element. For instance, if the reader were positioned on the <PartID> node from the earlier XML snippet, the Value property would be an empty string. With one more call to the Read() method, the reader would be positioned on a node of type XmlNodeType.Text whose Name property would be an empty string, but whose Value property would be 1. This is why two case statements have been provided, one for the Element and one for the Text. The Element case statement is used to print the name of the node, and the Text case statement is used to print the contents.

If we wanted to get the contained value of an Element while the reader is positioned on that element, we could use the *ReadElementString()* method. In the case of the earlier XML snippet, if the reader were positioned on the node <PartID>, a call to Read-ElementString() would return 1. It would also reposition the reader to the <Description> node. The next iteration through the while loop would once again call the Read() method, and now the reader would be positioned on the content of the <Description> node, eliminating the opportunity to retrieve the name of the node, "Description." In addition, we can't just use ReadElementString() exclusively, such as replacing the call to Read() in the while statement with a call to ReadElementString(). ReadElementString() will throw an XmlException if the next node is not a start element or does not contain a textual value. A call to ReadElementString() would throw an exception for the XML declaration, <WileyParts>, </WileyParts>, <Part>, </Part>, <Category>, and </Category> nodes.

The type XmlNodeType.Element does not include closing tags such as </PartID>. These nodes are handled by the type XmlNodeType.EndElement. In this example, we don't need to do anything with the closing tags so a case statement was not provided for that type of node. A screen shot of the XmlTools.aspx page after clicking the Read Parts XML Using XmlTextReader button is shown in Figure 9.2.

XmlDocument

The XmlDocument class provides a complete package for reading and writing XML documents. It has the ability to read an XML document in its entirety with one method call and then provides properties and methods for navigating the XML document in any desired direction. Methods and properties are provided for constructing an XML document from scratch or editing an existing document. At any time, the entire document or pieces of the document contained by an XmlDocument can be extracted with ease.

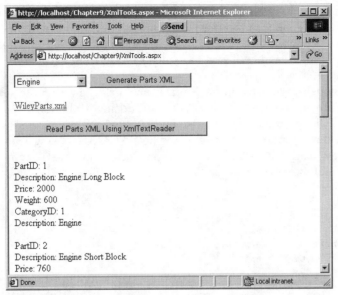

Figure 9.2   Reading parts with an XmlTextReader.

The XmlDocument class inherits from *XmlNode*, which is a class used to represent a single node in an XML document. XmlNode provides properties and methods for reading and writing everything imaginable in an XML node. The *Name* property gets or sets the qualified name of the node. The *Value* property gets or sets the textual contents of the node. The attributes of a node are made available through the *Attributes* property. You can also retrieve a collection of child nodes through the *ChildNodes* property, which will retrieve a collection of XmlNode objects representing any nodes that are contained by the current node. Perhaps two of the most important properties are *InnerXml* and *OuterXml*. InnerXml can be used to get or set the children of a particular node, including the markup. Consider the following XML.

```
<Part>
  <PartID>1</PartID>
</Part>
```

If we have an XmlNode object representing the <Part> node, the InnerXml property would return

```
<PartID>1</PartID>
```

The OuterXml property is read-only and will return the markup for the children of the current node as well as its own markup. For the previous example, the OuterXml property would return

```
<Part>
  <PartID>1</PartID>
</Part>
```

To load an XML document into an XmlDocument object, you can call the *Load()* or *LoadXml()* methods. The Load() method takes one parameter that can be a string representing the path or URL to an XML file, a stream, a TextReader, or an XmlReader. The LoadXml() method, on the other hand, will load the XmlDocument from a string that is preloaded with XML data.

There is a lot of functionality available in the XmlDocument class, much more so than we are going to cover here. As a small example, we will add another button to the XmlTools.aspx page that will read the WileyParts.xml file using an XmlDocument. The output will look just like the output from clicking on the Read Parts XML Using Xml-TextReader button, but the work will be done with an XmlDocument rather than an XmlTextReader. Let's look at the code in the handler for the new button.

```
try
{
  XmlDocument doc = new XmlDocument();
  //Open the WileyParts.xml file with an XmlDocument
  doc.Load("C:\\WileyParts.xml");

  //Clear the previous content
  lblParts.Text = string.Empty;

  //Get all of the parts
  foreach (XmlNode part in doc.GetElementsByTagName("Part"))
  {
    foreach (XmlNode childNode in part.ChildNodes)
    {
      if (childNode.Name == "Category")
      {
        foreach (XmlNode catNode in childNode.ChildNodes)
        {
          lblParts.Text += catNode.Name + ": " + catNode.InnerXml +
            "<br>";
        }
      }
      else
      {
        lblParts.Text += childNode.Name + ": " + childNode.InnerXml +
          "<br>";
      }
    }

    lblParts.Text += "<br>";
  }
}
catch (XmlException ex)
{
  Response.Write("An XmlException occurred: " + ex.ToString());
}
catch (Exception ex)
{
  Response.Write("An Exception occurred: " + ex.ToString());
}
```

This code is perhaps a little easier to understand than the code that was necessary for the XmlTextReader implementation. First, we create an XmlDocument, and then we call the Load() method, giving it the path to the WileyParts.xml file. After we've cleared out any text that might already exist in the Label control, we have a foreach loop.

```
foreach (XmlNode part in doc.GetElementsByTagName("Part"))
```

We're using the *GetElementsByTagName()* method, which will return an XmlNode-List that is populated with XmlNodes whose name matches the passed-in string. In this case, we are looking for all nodes whose name is "Part." Now all we need to do is process each part node, which is done easily by using the ChildNodes property. For each <Part> node we execute another foreach loop on each of its child nodes.

```
foreach (XmlNode childNode in part.ChildNodes)
```

The only child node of the <Part> node that also has child nodes of its own is the <Category> node. For that node, we want to process its child nodes. This is done with the following code:

```
if (childNode.Name == "Category")
{
   foreach (XmlNode catNode in childNode.ChildNodes)
   {
     lblParts.Text += catNode.Name + ": " + catNode.InnerXml +
       "<br>";
   }
}
```

If the Name property of the child node is equal to "Category" then we enter another foreach loop on its child nodes. Inside the foreach loop we are retrieving the name of the node using the Name property and its contents using the InnerXml property.

For all the rest of the child nodes of the <Part> node, there are no child nodes to process so we retrieve the name and contents of the node just as we did for the child nodes of the <Category> node. At the end of the outer foreach loop (the one for all of the <Part> nodes) we make sure that a blank line exists between each part by printing out a <br>. There isn't much use in providing you a screenshot of this in action as it looks exactly like Figure 9.2, aside from there being an extra button for processing the XML using the XmlDocument class.

NOTE The XmlDocument is a bit easier and more intuitive to use than the XmlTextReader. It probably gives up a little in the way of speed, though. If you are doing some simple processing and you need it to be as fast as possible, then use the XmlTextReader; otherwise, we suggest that you go with the XmlDocument. We'll see a practical example of using the XmlDocument class a little later in this chapter.

DataSet

In Chapter 4, "Database Access," we mentioned that the DataSet could be used to read and write XML. The neat thing about this is if you learn how to use the DataSet fairly well for accessing data from a relation data store such as SQL Server, you can apply what you already know to use it for working with XML. As we mentioned in Chapter 4, the DataSet is unaware of its data source. It doesn't know if its data came from SQL Server, Access, or an XML document. Once the data is loaded into the DataSet, we can work with it using the same common interface. We can also load the data from SQL Server and then write the data out to an XML file or any other data source for that matter. For instance, in the XmlTools example, suppose we had retrieved the Parts from the database and loaded them into a DataSet. We could have easily created the Wiley-Parts.xml file by calling the *WriteXml()* method of the DataSet, passing in the path of the file to be created. That's quite a bit of functionality for free, if you ask us.

Because working with XML in a DataSet is nearly identical to working with data from a SQL Server database, we're not going to rehash old ground on the DataSet here. What we would like to do is show you how to load the DataSet with some XML and how the DataSet handles that XML for us. To do this, we'll add another button to the XmlTools.aspx page that will once again read the WileyParts.xml file, but this time we'll use a DataSet to do the work for us. Before we actually process the data in the Wiley-Parts.xml file, let's take a look at the tables and their associated columns that the DataSet creates when the XML is loaded. To do this, we've written some code in the new button's click handler that will load the WileyParts.xml file into a DataSet, and then it will enumerate the Tables collection of the DataSet and the Columns collection of each Table. Here is the code.

```
DataSet ds = new DataSet();
//Open the WileyParts.xml file with the DataSet
ds.ReadXml("C:\\WileyParts.xml");

//Clear the previous content
lblParts.Text = string.Empty;

//Get the created table names and their columns
foreach (DataTable tbl in ds.Tables)
{
  lblParts.Text += "Table Name: " + tbl.TableName + "<br>";

  foreach (DataColumn clm in tbl.Columns)
  {
    lblParts.Text += "  " + clm.ColumnName + " - " +
      clm.DataType.ToString() + "<br>";
  }
}
```

Loading the XML into the DataSet couldn't be much easier. We make one call to the *ReadXml()* method, passing in the path to the WileyParts.xml file as a parameter. We then have a foreach loop that iterates through the Tables collection of the DataSet, and for each table it will iterate through the Columns collection. A screen shot of the output can be seen in Figure 9.3.

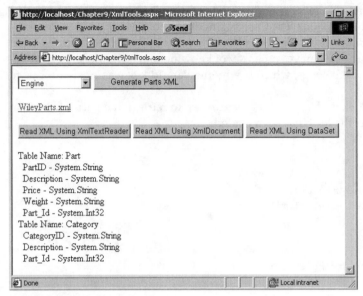

Figure 9.3 DataSet tables and columns.

Because the DataSet is a class for working with relational data, any XML that is loaded into the DataSet must be regularly structured so that the DataSet can determine what to do with it. Loading an XML document into a DataSet provides us with a nice way to access the data in a relational manner.

The DataSet created two tables for us: Part and Category. A parent/child relationship was established between the two tables using a key field that the DataSet created called Part_Id. The Part table is the parent, and the Category table is the child, so there is a foreign key constraint on the Part_Id column of the Category table to the Part_Id column of the Part table. You don't actually see this constraint on the screen shot, but take our word for it, it's there. This makes perfect sense if you take a look at a snippet of the XML again.

```xml
<?xml version="1.0" encoding="utf-8" ?>
<WileyParts>
  <Part>
    <PartID>1</PartID>
    <Description>Engine Long Block</Description>
    <Price>2000</Price>
    <Weight>600</Weight>
    <Category>
      <CategoryID>1</CategoryID>
      <Description>Engine</Description>
    </Category>
  </Part>
</WileyParts>
```

The DataSet created columns for each of the child nodes of the <Part> node that were not merely container nodes. The Category node is a container node for Category-ID and Description, so a new Category table was created to house the Category child nodes. Obviously, we have to have some way of knowing to which category a particular part in the Part table belongs, which is why the Part_Id key was created for us to relate the two tables.

Now let's take a look at the code that we can use to retrieve the part information from the DataSet after the XML has been loaded.

```
try
{
  DataSet ds = new DataSet();
  //Open the WileyParts.xml file with the DataSet
  ds.ReadXml("C:\\WileyParts.xml");

  //Clear the previous content
  lblParts.Text = string.Empty;

  //Get all of the parts
  //Get the Part table
  DataTable tblPart = ds.Tables["Part"];

  foreach (DataRow partRow in tblPart.Rows)
  {
    foreach (DataColumn clm in tblPart.Columns)
    {
      //If this is the Part_Id column, don't do anything
      if (clm.ColumnName == "Part_Id")
        continue;
      else
        lblParts.Text += clm.ColumnName + ": " + partRow[clm.ColumnName] +
          "<br>";
    }

    foreach (DataRelation relation in tblPart.ChildRelations)
    {
      //Get the child rows for this relation
      DataRow[] childRows = partRow.GetChildRows(relation);

      foreach (DataRow row in childRows)
      {
        foreach (DataColumn catColumn in row.Table.Columns)
        {
          //If this is the Part_Id column, don't do anything
          if (catColumn.ColumnName == "Part_Id")
            continue;
          else
            lblParts.Text += catColumn.ColumnName + ": " +
              childRows[0][catColumn.ColumnName] + "<br>";
```

```
        }
      }
    }

    lblParts.Text += "<br>";
  }
}
catch (XmlException ex)
{
  Response.Write("An XmlException occurred: " + ex.ToString());
}
catch (Exception ex)
{
  Response.Write("An Exception occurred: " + ex.ToString());
}
```

We load the DataSet with data just as we did before by calling ReadXml(). Then we get a reference to the Part table of the DataSet and enter a foreach loop on the Rows collection of the Part table. We can go ahead and get the data out of the columns of the Part table and print them out, which is done in the foreach loop on the Columns collection of the Part table. We check for the column name for Part_Id and make sure that we don't print anything out for this column because it would be meaningless data as far as part information is concerned. Last, for every row in the Part table, we need to get the corresponding child row in the Category table. When we loaded the XML into the DataSet, it created a DataRelation for the relationship between the Part table and the Category table. A DataRelation is a class used to represent a parent/child relationship between two tables. It can also be used to retrieve the child rows by passing it in as a parameter to the *GetChildRows()* method of the DataRow class. So, we've created a foreach loop on the ChildRelations collection of the Part table; in this case there will be only one DataRelation, but we're using a foreach loop nonetheless. We then make a call to the GetChildRows() method of the partRow object, which will retrieve the rows from the Category table that are associated with this row in the Part table.

```
DataRow[] childRows = partRow.GetChildRows(relation);
```

Now we can iterate through the returned rows (in this case there will always be one) and then iterate through the columns of each child row, printing out their values.

```
foreach (DataRow row in childRows)
{
  foreach (DataColumn catColumn in row.Table.Columns)
  {
    //If this is the Part_Id column, don't do anything
    if (catColumn.ColumnName == "Part_Id")
      continue;
    else
      lblParts.Text += catColumn.ColumnName + ": " +
        childRows[0][catColumn.ColumnName] + "<br>";
  }
}
```

Notice that we had to retrieve the columns of the Category table by using the Table property of each row and then using the Columns collection on that.

```
foreach (DataColumn catColumn in row.Table.Columns)
```

We could have just as easily gotten the columns by using

```
ds.Tables["Category"].Columns
```

We wanted to show you the former method because you might not always know from which table your child rows are coming ahead of time, as we do with this example. Once again, this code performs exactly the same as the previous examples of reading the WileyParts.xml file. The DataSet is probably one of the better options for reading and writing XML, especially if the XML structure is not overly complicated. We'll see a practical example of using the DataSet for reading XML in the next section.

Freight Calculations

Now that we know how to read and write XML, it's time to put it to practical use and create a real-world component that you can use in your own applications. One of the most common tasks that a business selling physical products needs to do is calculate the proper shipping costs to charge a customer for shipping merchandise. UPS has provided an Internet-accessible service that we can use to calculate dynamic shipping prices. In its simplest form, all we have to do is tell the service from which postal code we want to ship, to which postal code we want to ship, and the weight of the package. The service will then provide information on the shipping methods available for that package between those two locations, including the price and the delivery time. UPS also supplies several other shipping-related services, including services that allow you to track packages. In this section we will create components for using two of the UPS services, Shipping Rates and Address Validation.

All of the UPS tools can be called across the net by posting a request in XML format to the UPS servers. The servers will then send a reply, also in XML format, that we can then parse and from it extract the needed information. How are we going to go about doing this? First, we need to use the XmlTextWriter to create the request to send to the UPS server. We'll have the XmlTextWriter write its content into a MemoryStream (as opposed to a file stream). Then we need a way to send this request to the UPS servers. Requests must be sent to the server via HTTP Secure Socket Layer (SSL). The .NET common language runtime supplies two classes, HttpWebRequest and HttpWebResponse, that we will use for the communication. We'll use the HttpWebRequest class to send our request message to the UPS servers, and then we'll use the HttpWebResponse class to receive the response from the UPS servers. After we have the XML response, we need to be able to parse it and access the needed data. We'll be using the XmlDocument class to do this for the Shipping Rates service and the DataSet for the Address Validation service.

NOTE We're using both the XmlDocument and DataSet only so that we can see both in action. If you have a preference for one over the other, you can certainly reimplement one or both of the components to use what you like.

General UPS Information

To use the UPS tools, you must first visit the UPS Web site (www.ec.ups.com) and sign up for a Developer's Key. Once you have the Developer's Key you can download the fairly extensive documentation on how to access the various tools. To actually use the tools you will need to agree to UPS access terms and receive an Access Key. The Access Key that you receive, as well as your user ID and password, will be sent as part of your XML request each time you send a message to the UPS servers. There is no software that you need to download and install to use the UPS Online services. You have to write your own software to use the services. UPS merely supplies the information that you need to be able to do that.

All of the XML tools that UPS provides have their own specific XML request and response formats. The request messages all have some similarities, however. The requests that we need to send are actually two XML documents concatenated together. In well-formed XML, this isn't really proper, but when the UPS servers receive the message they actually break the message back into two separate documents. The first XML document in the message is the AccessRequest document, and it consists of your AccessKey, user ID, and password. Its format is as follows.

```
<?xml version="1.0"?>
<AccessRequest>
  <AccessLicenseNumber>xxxxxxxxxxxxxxxx</AccessLicenseNumber>
  <UserId>Your User ID</UserId>
  <Password>Your Password</Password>
</AccessRequest>
```

The second document is specific to the service that you are calling and is well documented in the UPS documentation.

WARNING We should take this opportunity to state our disclaimer. The components that we are going to create are not totally complete. We have not implemented the ability to handle any error codes returned by the UPS server. The examples will check whether the request was successful, but if it wasn't, they won't tell you exactly why. When an error occurs, possibly due to an incorrectly formatted request message, the UPS services will respond with an error code and detailed information about the error. We won't be adding the ability to retrieve that detailed information. In addition, the Shipping Rates service is capable of far more than the functionality that we will implement here. That leaves you with quite a bit of room to experiment with the code on your own. Have fun!

Shipping Rates

The first UPS service that we'll be using is the Rates and Service Selection service. The class that we will create will be called UPSRates and will have five properties that we can set: ShipFromPostalCode, ShipToPostalCode, PackageWeight, Residential, and CustomerContext. The first three are self-explanatory. Residential is a Boolean property that will designate whether the package is being shipped to a residence (true) or a business (false). CustomerContext allows us to send some data along with the request that will be echoed back in the response, such as an Order ID or Transaction ID. All five of these properties can be passed in through an overloaded UPSRates constructor, or they can be set individually after the object has been created.

The class will also have three private member variables, m_strUserName, m_strPassword, and m_strAccessKey. For this example, we're going to be hard-coding the username, password, and access key that we acquired from UPS. If you want to try these examples out for yourself, you'll need to get your own credentials from UPS.

There will also be three read-only properties in the class, ResponseStatusCode, ResponseStatusDescription, and RatedShipments. ResponseStatusCode is an integer and will always be 1 if the UPS servers processed the request successfully. This is what we'll be using to determine success or failure. If ResponseStatusCode is 0, you can be sure that the XML response from UPS will contain information about the error, but remember that we won't be providing access to those here. ResponseStatusDescription will either be "Success" or "Failure" and is just a textual redundancy to the ResponseStatusCode. RatedShipments is an ArrayList of RateShipment objects. This is a class that we will define and that will be used as a container for each of the available shipping methods with which UPS responds.

```
public class RatedShipment
{
  private string m_strServiceCode = string.Empty;
  private string m_strServiceDescription = string.Empty;
  private decimal m_decTotalCharge;
  private int m_intGuaranteedDaysToDelivery;

  public string ServiceCode
  {
    get { return m_strServiceCode; }
    set { m_strServiceCode = value; }
  }

  public string ServiceDescription
  {
    get { return m_strServiceDescription; }
    set { m_strServiceDescription = value; }
  }

  public decimal TotalCharge
  {
    get { return m_decTotalCharge; }
    set { m_decTotalCharge = value; }
```

```
   }

   public int GuaranteedDaysToDelivery
   {
     get { return m_intGuaranteedDaysToDelivery; }
     set { m_intGuaranteedDaysToDelivery = value; }
   }
}
```

Listing 9.1 shows an example of a properly formatted request message. As you can see, the first XML document is the AccessRequest. The second document is the actual request for the rates service. The entire document is contained inside of a Rating-ServiceSelectionRequest node. In the Request node, we see a TransactionReference node, which contains a CustomerContext element. The value in this example is "tester". We'll be substituting the value that is passed into the CustomerContext property here. Also there is a RequestAction element, which must be set to "Rate" for this service. This service also uses a RequestOption element, which can be set to "Shop", as it is in this example, or "Rate". The class that we are writing will support only the "Shop" option. This option will return a list of all available shipping methods. The "Rate" option will return the rating for only one method, which must be specified in the request.

The PickupType node is used to specify one of the valid UPS Pickup Types. You can find these in the documentation. We'll be using code 01, which is Daily Pickup. The Shipment node is where we describe the shipment for which we are requesting service. The Shipper node is used to specify the address (PostalCode) of the shipper. The ShipTo node is used to specify the address (PostalCode) of the destination. Also, notice the ResidentialAddress element. If this element is present, it is a signal that the specified destination address is a residential address. If it's not present then the destination address is assumed to be a commercial address. The Package node is used to describe the package itself. We'll always be specifying the PackagingType as code 02, which is a standard Package. Once again, the UPS documentation will give you all of the valid PackagingType codes. Last, we see the PackageWeight, which is where we specify the weight in pounds of the package. As we mentioned previously, there is quite a bit of functionality with this service. We are using only a small portion of it here. For instance, if you wanted to specify the weight of the package in kilograms, there is a way to do that. The default is pounds, which is what we have elected to go with for this example.

```
<?xml version="1.0"?>
<AccessRequest>
  <AccessLicenseNumber>xxxxxxxxxxxxxxxx</AccessLicenseNumber>
  <UserId>Your User Name</UserId>
  <Password>Your Password</Password>
</AccessRequest>
<?xml version="1.0"?>
<RatingServiceSelectionRequest xml:lang="en-US">
  <Request>
```

Listing 9.1 A ratings service request

```
      <TransactionReference>
        <CustomerContext>tester</CustomerContext>
      </TransactionReference>
      <RequestAction>Rate</RequestAction>
      <RequestOption>Shop</RequestOption>
    </Request>
    <PickupType>
      <Code>01</Code>
    </PickupType>
    <Shipment>
      <Shipper>
        <Address>
          <PostalCode>32257</PostalCode>
        </Address>
      </Shipper>
      <ShipTo>
        <Address>
          <PostalCode>32259</PostalCode>
          <ResidentialAddress />
        </Address>
      </ShipTo>
      <Package>
        <PackagingType>
          <Code>02</Code>
          <Description>Package</Description>
        </PackagingType>
        <Description>Rate Shopping</Description>
        <PackageWeight>
          <Weight>10</Weight>
        </PackageWeight>
      </Package>
    </Shipment>
  </RatingServiceSelectionRequest>
```

Listing 9.1   A ratings service request (continued)

The XML response for the request in Listing 9.1 is quite lengthy, so we won't repro-duce the whole thing here, but a snippet of it can be seen in Listing 9.2. The root node of the document is the RatingServiceSelectionResponse node. It will contain one Response node, which is where the CustomerContext will be echoed back. It will also contain the ResponseStatusCode and the ResponseStatusDescription. The rest of the document will consist of <RatedShipment> nodes. There will be one for each available shipping method for the given request. The only elements of this node that we are con-cerned with for this example are the ones seen in Listing 9.2. The Service node gives us the UPS service code of the shipping method. In Listing 9.2, this is 01, which stands for Next Day Air. Once again, a list of all of these service codes can be found in the docu-mentation. The TotalCharges node gives us the total cost of shipping the package via this method, and the GuaranteedDaysToDelivery will specify an integer representing the number of days within which the package is guaranteed to be shipped. If the value is 0, then there is no precise guarantee, such as with the UPS Ground shipping method.

```
<RatingServiceSelectionResponse>
  <Response>
    <TransactionReference>
      <CustomerContext>tester</CustomerContext>
    </TransactionReference>
    <ResponseStatusCode>1</ResponseStatusCode>
    <ResponseStatusDescription>Success</ResponseStatusDescription>
  </Response>
  <RatedShipment>
    <Service>
      <Code>01</Code>
    </Service>
...
    <TotalCharges>
      <CurrencyCode>USD</CurrencyCode>
      <MonetaryValue>22.78</MonetaryValue>
    </TotalCharges>
    <GuaranteedDaysToDelivery>1</GuaranteedDaysToDelivery>
...
  </RatedShipment>
  <RatedShipment>
...
</RatingServiceSelectionResponse>
```

Listing 9.2 A ratings service response

The UPSRates class will have one public method called GetRates(), which will create a request to send to the rates service, based on its property values. It will receive the response, verify that the request was successful, and then populate the RatedShipments ArrayList with RatedShipment objects, which will be filled in from the RatedShipment nodes of the response document. An incomplete listing of the GetRates() method is shown later. The method is quite lengthy, so we've left out most of the code that involves actually writing the request. The entire source can be downloaded from the companion Web site.

```
public bool GetRates()
{
  //Create a MemoryStream and use an XmlTextWriter to fill
  //that stream with our request
  MemoryStream memStream = new MemoryStream();
  XmlTextWriter writer = new XmlTextWriter(memStream, null);
  writer.Formatting = Formatting.Indented;

  //Write a StartDocument element, which will be <?xml version="1.0"?>
```

```
writer.WriteStartDocument();
//<AccessRequest>
writer.WriteStartElement("AccessRequest");
//<AccessLicenseNumber>xxxxxxxxxxxxxxxx</AccessLicenseNumber>
writer.WriteElementString("AccessLicenseNumber", m_strAccessKey);
//<UserId>xxxxxxx</UserId>
writer.WriteElementString("UserId", m_strUserName);
//<Password>xxxxxxx</Password>
writer.WriteElementString("Password", m_strPassword);
//</AccessRequest>
writer.WriteEndElement();
writer.WriteEndDocument();

//Write a StartDocument element, which will be <?xml version="1.0"?>
writer.WriteStartDocument();

//Code for creating the rating service request goes here

writer.WriteEndDocument();

//Flush the writer into the MemoryStream
writer.Flush();

//****************************************************
//Remove this when in production
//Write the request to a file, just so we can examine it
FileStream reqFile = new FileStream("C:\\request.xml",
FileMode.Create);
memStream.WriteTo(reqFile);
reqFile.Close();
//****************************************************

//Create an HttpWebRequest to communicate with the UPS Server
HttpWebRequest request =  (HttpWebRequest)
  HttpWebRequest.Create("https://www.ups.com/ups.app/xml/Rate");
//Set the method to POST, which is required by UPS
request.Method = "POST";
request.ContentType = "application/x-www-form-urlencoded";
//Set the ContentLength in the request header
request.ContentLength = memStream.Length;

//Get the request stream from the HttpWebRequest
Stream reqStream = request.GetRequestStream();
//Write the contents of the memory stream to it
memStream.WriteTo(reqStream);
//Close the request stream
reqStream.Close();
//Close the XmlTextWriter
writer.Close();

//Make the call to UPS and get the response
```

```
HttpWebResponse response = (HttpWebResponse)request.GetResponse();
//Get the response message
Stream responseStream = response.GetResponseStream();

//Create an XmlDocument for reading the response easily
XmlDocument doc = new XmlDocument();
doc.Load(responseStream);

//Close the response stream
responseStream.Close();

//Extract the results
if (!ExtractResults(doc))
  return false;

return true;
}
```

Let's walk through the important parts of this code. First, we create a MemoryStream and hook it up to an XMLTextWriter.

```
MemoryStream memStream = new MemoryStream();
XmlTextWriter writer = new XmlTextWriter(memStream, null);
```

We set the formatting method of the XmlTextWriter to Formatting.Indented. This isn't necessary at all for the code to work. For example purposes only, we will be writing the completed request and the response from UPS to a file so that you can examine them if you like. Setting the Formatting property to Indented will allow you to look at the request file in Notepad easily. Because the request actually has two concatenated XML documents, it is not valid XML, and Internet Explorer will not display it properly for you.

We then write the actual request content with a series of calls to the Write methods of the XmlTextWriter. When we are done, we call the *Flush()* method to make sure that all of the content has been written to the MemoryStream. We then create a FileStream object for the file request.xml in the root of the C drive, write the contents of the MemoryStream to the FileStream, and close the file. We have added extra comments here to remind you that creating this file is for testing and experimentation purposes only. If you were to use this code in a production situation, you definitely would not want to be writing each request to a file.

```
writer.Flush();

//****************************************************
//Remove this when in production
//Write the request to a file, just so we can examine it
FileStream reqFile = new FileStream("C:\\request.xml", FileMode.Create);
memStream.WriteTo(reqFile);
reqFile.Close();
//****************************************************
```

Now that we have the entire contents of the request in the MemorySteam object we are ready to send the request to UPS. This is done through the use of the HttpWebRequest class, which is provided in the System.Net namespace. The HttpWebRequest class is derived from the WebRequest class, which is the .NET Framework base class for requesting data from the Internet. HttpWebRequest allows us to make requests using the HTTP protocol.

We create an HttpWebRequest object by calling the static *Create()* method of the HttpWebRequest class and passing in the URL for the UPS Rate service as a parameter. The Create() method is inherited from the WebRequest class, and as such it returns a WebRequest object, rather than an HttpWebRequest object. This requires us to cast the WebRequest object to an HttpWebRequest object. Once we have the object, we need to specify the request Method, which is POST in this case. We also need to specify the ContentType and ContentLength. We can get the ContentLength from the Length property of the MemoryStream object.

```
HttpWebRequest request =  (HttpWebRequest)
   HttpWebRequest.Create("https://www.ups.com/ups.app/xml/Rate");
request.Method = "POST";
request.ContentType = "application/x-www-form-urlencoded";
request.ContentLength = memStream.Length;
```

Now we're ready to actually write the XML request to the request stream of the HttpWebRequest. We do this by calling the *GetRequestStream()* method of the HttpWebRequest object, which returns a Stream object to us. We can then easily write the contents of the MemoryStream object to the request stream and close the request stream and the XmlTextWriter by calling their respective Close() methods. When we close the XmlTextWriter, it will also close the MemoryStream.

```
Stream reqStream = request.GetRequestStream();
memStream.WriteTo(reqStream);
reqStream.Close();
writer.Close();
```

We now need to actually send the request and retrieve the response from the UPS servers. This is done by calling the *GetResponse()* method of the HttpWebRequest object. The GetResponse() method will return a WebResponse object. HttpWebResponse is derived from WebReponse so we can cast the WebResponse to an HttpWebResponse. We then get the response stream, which will contain the XML response from the UPS servers, by calling the *GetResponseStream()* method of the HttpWebResponse object.

```
HttpWebResponse response = (HttpWebResponse)request.GetResponse();
Stream responseStream = response.GetResponseStream();
```

For this example, we are going to be using the XmlDocument class to read the response, so we create an XmlDocument object and call the Load() method, passing in the response stream. We can then close the response stream. We have separated out the code for parsing through the response document in a separate private method called

ExtractResults(). If ExtractResults() returns false, it means that the ResponseStatus-Code was not a 1 and some error has occurred. If this happens, we return false from the GetRates() method; otherwise, we return true.

```
XmlDocument doc = new XmlDocument();
doc.Load(responseStream);
responseStream.Close();

if (!ExtractResults(doc))
  return false;

return true;
```

Let's take a look at the ExtractResults() method.

```
private bool ExtractResults(XmlDocument doc)
{
  //*********************************************************
  //Remove this when in production
  //Write the returned XML to a file, just so we can examine it
  FileStream rspFile = new FileStream("C:\\response.xml",
    FileMode.Create);
  StreamWriter stmWriter = new StreamWriter(rspFile);
  XmlElement root = doc.DocumentElement;
  stmWriter.Write(root.OuterXml);
  stmWriter.Close();
  //*********************************************************

  //Read the response
  m_intResponseStatusCode = XmlConvert.ToInt32(
    doc.GetElementsByTagName("ResponseStatusCode")[0].InnerXml);
  m_strResponseStatusDescription = doc.GetElementsByTagName(
    "ResponseStatusDescription")[0].InnerXml;

  //If ResponseStatusCode is not 1 then an error occurred
  if (m_intResponseStatusCode != 1)
    return false;

  //Get all of the results
  foreach (XmlNode ratedShipmentNode in
    doc.GetElementsByTagName("RatedShipment"))
  {
    //Create a new result
    RatedShipment shipment = new RatedShipment();
    //Traverse through all of the child nodes, pulling out the data
    foreach (XmlNode childNode in ratedShipmentNode.ChildNodes)
    {
      switch (childNode.Name)
      {
        case "Service":
          foreach (XmlNode serviceNode in childNode.ChildNodes)
```

```
          {
            if (serviceNode.Name == "Code")
              shipment.ServiceCode = serviceNode.InnerXml;

            //Set the appropriate Service Description
            switch (shipment.ServiceCode)
            {
              case "01":
                shipment.ServiceDescription = "Next Day Air";
                break;


                //Rest of the case statements for the available service
                //codes go here
            }
          }
          break;
        case "TotalCharges":
          foreach (XmlNode chargeNode in childNode.ChildNodes)
          {
            if (chargeNode.Name == "MonetaryValue")
              shipment.TotalCharge =
                XmlConvert.ToDecimal(chargeNode.InnerXml);
          }
          break;
        case "GuaranteedDaysToDelivery":
          if (childNode.InnerXml.Length > 0)
            shipment.GuaranteedDaysToDelivery =
              XmlConvert.ToInt32(childNode.InnerXml);
          break;
      }
    }

    //Add this result to the collection
    m_arrRatedShipments.Add(shipment);
  }

  return true;
}
```

The very first thing we do here is write the response to a file just so we can examine it.

WARNING Just as with the request file, this step isn't necessary and shouldn't be done in a production environment.

We create the file by creating a FileStream and a StreamWriter. We then get the root element of the XmlDocument via the *DocumentElement* property and write the OuterXml property of the returned XmlElement to the StreamWriter.

We need to make sure that the request was processed successfully by UPS, so we extract the ResponseStatusCode and ResponseStatusDescription from the XmlDocument.

```
m_intResponseStatusCode = XmlConvert.ToInt32(
  doc.GetElementsByTagName("ResponseStatusCode")[0].InnerXml);
m_strResponseStatusDescription = doc.GetElementsByTagName(
  "ResponseStatusDescription")[0].InnerXml;
```

There is only one node named ResponseStatusCode and one node named Response-StatusDescription, so we can retrieve those nodes using the GetElementsByTagName() method and then retrieve their contents through the InnerXml property of the first XmlNode in the returned XmlNodeList. We then make sure that the ResponseStatus-Code was a 1, and if not, we return false.

We then retrieve all of the nodes named RatedShipment by using the GetElements-ByTagName() method again and enter a foreach loop on this nodes. A new RatedShip-ment object is created at the top of the loop, and we begin to process all of the child nodes of the RatedShipment node with a foreach loop again.

```
foreach (XmlNode ratedShipmentNode in
  doc.GetElementsByTagName("RatedShipment"))
{
  RatedShipment shipment = new RatedShipment();
  foreach (XmlNode childNode in ratedShipmentNode.ChildNodes)
```

We are interested only in the Service, TotalCharges, and GuaranteedDaysToDelivery child nodes, so we use a switch statement on the node name and implement a case statement for each one of these nodes. For the Service node, we will be returned only the service code. The RateShipment class needs us to specify the description of the service (e.g., Next Day Air). Because the UPS service didn't return that to us, we created another switch statement that will fill in the proper service description based on the service code. All but one of the case statements are included in the code snippet. The complete code can be downloaded from the companion Web site. The case handlers for the TotalCharges and GuaranteedDaysToDelivery are pretty straight orward. Notice the use of the XmlConvert class for converting the XML to the needed decimal and Int32 types.

```
shipment.TotalCharge = XmlConvert.ToDecimal(chargeNode.InnerXml);
shipment.GuaranteedDaysToDelivery =
  XmlConvert.ToInt32(childNode.InnerXml);
```

After we have processed a particular RatedShipment node and populated its associated RatedShipment class object, we add the RatedShipment object to the RatedShipments ArrayList.

```
m_arrRatedShipments.Add(shipment);
```

From a client code perspective, all the client has to do is create a UPSRates object, passing in the five properties to the constructor, call the GetRates() method, and then do whatever is necessary with ArrayList of RatedShipment objects. We have created a rudimentary test page called UPSShipRates.aspx that does just that, which you can download from the companion Web site. It looks like Figure 9.4.

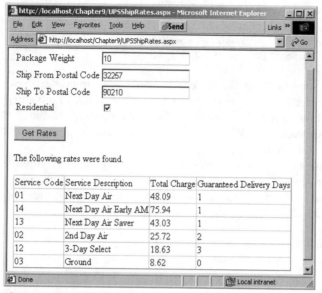

Figure 9.4   UPSShipRates.aspx.

Address Validation

The Address Validation service is quite a bit simpler than the Rates service. We will create a class called UPSAddressValidator that is implemented very similarly to the UPSRates class. Obviously, the Address Validation service requires a different request document and returns a different response document, but the means we use to create the request, send it, and receive the response will be the same with one exception. Instead of parsing the response using the XmlDocument class, we will use the DataSet class. We'll concentrate mainly on this section of the class to prevent covering ground that we just walked on in the previous section.

The Address Validation service requires us to send a combination of city, state/province code, and postal code in our request. As you might imagine, these are write-accessible properties of the UPSAddressValidator class, along with CustomerContext once again. Listing 9.3 shows an example request document.

```
<?xml version="1.0"?>
<AccessRequest>
   <AccessLicenseNumber>xxxxxxxxxxxxxxxx</AccessLicenseNumber>
   <UserId>Your User Name</UserId>
   <Password>Your Password</Password>
</AccessRequest>
<?xml version="1.0"?>
```

Listing 9.3   An address validation request

```
<AddressValidationRequest xml:lang="en-US">
  <Request>
    <TransactionReference>
      <CustomerContext>Tester</CustomerContext>
    </TransactionReference>
    <RequestAction>AV</RequestAction>
  </Request>
  <Address>
    <City>Jacksonville</City>
    <StateProvinceCode>FL</StateProvinceCode>
    <PostalCode>32257</PostalCode>
  </Address>
</AddressValidationRequest>
```

Listing 9.3 An address validation request (continued)

The service will then respond with a list of matching results. A result consists of several properties. Rank is an integer that rates the returned result matches in order, with 1 being the result of the highest Quality. Quality is used to rate how closely the address matches the one specified in the request. It is a decimal number of 1 or less. If the Quality is 1, then the address is an exact match. Each result will also have an Address element that will specify the city and state/province code for the address. Because many cities have several postal codes, there are PostalCodeLowEnd and PostalCodeHighEnd elements that specify the minimum and maximum values for the range of valid postal codes in that city. Listing 9.4 shows a sample response.

```
<?xml version="1.0" standalone="yes" ?>
<AddressValidationResponse>
  <Response>
    <ResponseStatusCode>1</ResponseStatusCode>
    <ResponseStatusDescription>Success</ResponseStatusDescription>
    <TransactionReference>
      <CustomerContext>Tester</CustomerContext>
    </TransactionReference>
  </Response>
  <AddressValidationResult>
    <Rank>1</Rank>
    <Quality>1.0</Quality>
    <PostalCodeLowEnd>32254</PostalCodeLowEnd>
    <PostalCodeHighEnd>32260</PostalCodeHighEnd>
    <Address>
      <City>JACKSONVILLE</City>
      <StateProvinceCode>FL</StateProvinceCode>
    </Address>
  </AddressValidationResult>
</AddressValidationResponse>
```

Listing 9.4 An address validation response

We've created a class called AddressValidationResult that we will fill in from each AddressValidationResult node in the response document. The UPSAddressValidator class will have a read-only ArrayList property called AddressValidationResults, which we will fill in with AddressValidationResult objects when we make an Address Validation request to the UPS servers.

The UPSAddressValidator class will have one public method called Validate(), which will create the request, send it, and receive the response. As we've mentioned previously, the methodology used to create the request, send it, and receive the response is the same as the UPSRates class, so we won't go over that again here. The only difference is how the response is handled. The following is a snippet of the Validate() method, excluding all of the code for sending the request and receiving the response.

```
public bool Validate()
{
  //Create Request
  ...
  //Send Request
  ...
  //Reciever Response
  ...
  //Create a DataSet for reading the response easily
  DataSet ds = new DataSet();
  ds.ReadXml(responseStream);
  //Close the response stream
  responseStream.Close();

  //Extract the results
  if (!ExtractResults(ds))
    return false;

  //Check to see if we have an exact match
  foreach(AddressValidationResult result in
m_arrAddressValidationResults)
  {
    if (result.Quality == 1)
      return true;
  }

  return false;
}
```

A DataSet is created to read the response. The response XML document is loaded into the DataSet by calling the ReadXml() method, passing the response stream as a parameter. Once again, we implemented a private ExtractResults() method, but this time it will be working with a DataSet as opposed to an XmlDocument. Just as before, ExtractResults() will check the ReponseStatusCode first, and if it is not 1, it will return false. If ExtractResults executes successfully, the ArrayList of AddressValidationResult objects should be populated with at least one result. We use a foreach loop to iterate through those results and check for an exact match. If an exact match is found, we return true from the Validate() method; otherwise, we return false.

Now let's take a look at the ExtractResults() method.

```
private bool ExtractResults(DataSet ds)
{
  //*****************************************************
  //Remove this when in production
  //Write the returned XML to a file, just so we can examine it
  ds.WriteXml("C:\\response.xml");
  //*****************************************************

  //Read the response
  //Get the Response table
  DataTable tblResponse = ds.Tables["Response"];
  m_intResponseStatusCode = XmlConvert.ToInt32(
    tblResponse.Rows[0]["ResponseStatusCode"].ToString());
  m_strResponseStatusDescription =
    tblResponse.Rows[0]["ResponseStatusDescription"].ToString();

  //If ResponseStatusCode is not 1 then an error occurred
  if (m_intResponseStatusCode != 1)
    return false;

  //Get AddressValidationResult table
  DataTable tblResult = ds.Tables["AddressValidationResult"];

  //Get the results
  foreach (DataRow rowResult in tblResult.Rows)
  {
    //Create a new result
    AddressValidationResult result = new AddressValidationResult();

    result.Rank = XmlConvert.ToInt32(rowResult["Rank"].ToString());
    result.Quality =
XmlConvert.ToSingle(rowResult["Quality"].ToString());
    result.PostalCodeLowEnd = rowResult["PostalCodeLowEnd"].ToString();
    result.PostalCodeHighEnd =
rowResult["PostalCodeHighEnd"].ToString();

    //Get the address for this result
    foreach (DataRelation relation in tblResult.ChildRelations)
    {
      //Get the child rows for this relation
      DataRow[] childRows = rowResult.GetChildRows(relation);

      result.City = childRows[0]["City"].ToString();
      result.StateProvinceCode =
        childRows[0]["StateProvinceCode"].ToString();
    }
```

```
        //Add the new result to the collection
        m_arrAddressValidationResults.Add(result);
    }

    return true;
}
```

We write the response to a file, for testing purposes only, by calling the WriteXml() method of the DataSet. It doesn't get much easier than that. The DataSet will create four tables for the response: Response, TransactionReference, AddressValidation-Result, and Address. The Response table will have one row containing the Response-StatusCode and ResponseStatusDescription. The TransactionReference table will also have one row that contains the CustomerContext. In this case, a parent/child relationship is established between the Response and TransactionReference table, but having two tables for this is a waste because there will always be only one row. It would be nice if the CustomerContext field were in the Response table, but it's a small inconvenience, particularly because we're not doing anything with the CustomerContext field in this example.

The AddressValidationResult table will have fields for Rank, Quality, PostalCode-LowEnd, and PostalCodeHighEnd. A parent/child relationship will be established between the AddressValidationResult table and the Address table. The Address table will contain the City and StateProvinceCode fields. We can go about extracting all of this information and populating an AddressValidationResult object just as we did in the Xml-Tools.aspx example. Working with a DataSet should be old hat to you by now, so we won't bore you with walking through the rest of the code in the ExtractResults() method.

Our rudimentary test page called UPSAddressValidation.aspx allows the user to enter a city, state/province code, and postal code and call the Validate() method of the UPSAddressValidator class. Again, this code is available on the companion Web site. The page is as shown in Figure 9.5.

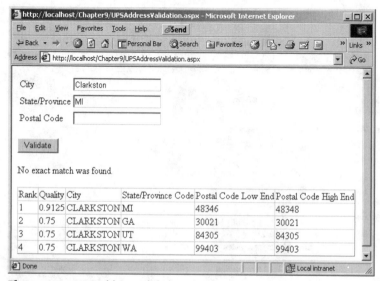

Figure 9.5   UPSAddressValidation.aspx.

Email

One of the more common things that we need to be able to do with applications these days is generate and send email. We might need to send an auto-generated invoice to a customer who has just purchased a product from our Web site or send a reminder to an employee to complete some task. In any case, sending email needs to be a trivial task, and with the System.Web.Mail namespace, it is.

There are three classes in the System.Web.Mail namespace, *MailMessage*, *Mail-Attachment*, and *SmtpMail*. The MailMessage class has properties such as *From*, *To*, *Cc*, *Bcc*, *Subject*, and *Body* that make up the contents of a particular mail message. In addition, we can set the encoding type of the message through the *BodyEncoding* property. This property can be set to any of the members of the System.Text.Encoding enumeration, which are ASCII, UTF7, UTF8, Unicode, BigEndianUnicode, and Default. The format of the body of the message can be specified through the *BodyFormat* property and can be set to one of the members of the System.Web.Mail.MailFormat enumeration, which are Html and Text. The priority of the message can be specified through the *Priority* property and can be set to one of the members of the System.Web.Mail.MailPriority enumeration, which are High, Low, and Normal.

If we have a need to add an attachment to the mail message, we create an instance of the MailAttachment class and specify the path to the file that we want to attach. Once we've created this object we can add it to the mail message by calling the Add() method of the *Attachments* property on the MailMessage object.

The SmtpMail class comes in when we have a complete MailMessage object that we are ready to send. The SmtpMail class has one static property and one static method in which we are interested. The *SmtpServer* property is used to specify the name of the SMTP mail server to use when sending messages. If it is not specified, the name of the local SMTP server for the machine will be used. The *Send()* method is overloaded. One overload allows us to pass a complete MailMessage object in.

```
public static void Send(MailMessage);
```

The other allows us to send a simple email without having to create a MailMessage object. We simply pass in four strings: the From address, To address, Subject, and Body of the message.

```
public static void Send(string from, string to,
   string subject, string messageText);
```

The example is a Web Form called SendMail.aspx. There are text boxes for supplying the From address, To address, subject, and body of the message. There is also a Send button that has the following click event handler.

```
private void btnSend_Click(object sender, System.EventArgs e)
{
  MailMessage msg = new MailMessage();
  //Set the mail message fields
  msg.To = txtToAddress.Text;
  msg.From = txtFromAddress.Text;
```

```
    msg.Subject = txtSubject.Text;
    msg.Body = txtBody.Text;
    //Create an attachment
    MailAttachment attachment = new MailAttachment(@"C:\WileyParts.xml");
    //Add the attachment to the mail
    msg.Attachments.Add(attachment);
    //Send the mail
    SmtpMail.Send(msg);
}
```

This is all that is needed to send a complete email message with an attachment. We have added an attachment to the message, which always attaches the WileyParts.xml file from earlier examples in this chapter. If only everything was this simple. We suppose that if it were, there wouldn't be much need for programmers like us.

Enhancing the WileyParts Project

Now that we have objects to verify addresses and retrieve live shipping costs from UPS, let's add these features to our WileyParts project. To do this, we will need to add the UPSRates and UPSAddressValidator objects that we developed in this chapter to the WileyPartsObjects project. After including these two objects in the project, make sure that they are part of the WileyParts.Objects namespace.

We need to add the address validation to the profile.aspx page of the WileyParts project. This page has a Continue button on it, which saves the information that the shopper has entered and then redirects the shopper to the cart.aspx page. We need to add the following code to the beginning of the click handler for the Continue button:

```
//Verify the address that the shopper entered
UPSAddressValidator validator = new UPSAddressValidator(
   txtCity.Text.Trim(), cboState.SelectedItem.Value, txtZip.Text.Trim(),
   "WileyParts");

if (!validator.Validate())
{
  //Display an error message
  lblValidAddress.Text =
    "The address entered is not a valid address.<br><br>";
  return;
}
```

This code is very simple. All we had to do was create a UPSAddressValidator object passing in the City, State, and Zip to the constructor. We then call the Validate() method, and if it returns false, we display an error message to the user and return out of the click handler, preventing the information from being saved. We added a Label control to the page called lblValidAddress that is used to display the error message if necessary.

To incorporate the UPS shipping calculation into the application, we need to update the GetCartShippingCost() method of the Shopper object in the WileyPartsObjects project. The original version of this method used a static shipping cost of $.50 per pound. We'll change this method to get the shipping rates from UPS for the total weight of all of the items in the cart. We'll use only the UPS Ground shipping rate, just to keep it simple. Here is the new code for the GetCartShippingCost() method:

```
public decimal GetCartShippingCost()
{
   float fltTotalWeight = 0;
   decimal decShipingCost = 0;

   //Calculate the shipping cost on the cart items
   foreach (ShoppingCartItem item in m_arrShoppingCart)
   {
      fltTotalWeight += item.Weight * item.Quantity;
   }

   //Get the UPS Shipping Cost
   UPSRates rates = new UPSRates("10158", m_strPostalCode, true,
fltTotalWeight, "WileyParts");

   if (rates.GetRates())
   {
      //If we were able to successfully get the rates, then use the Ground
      //Shipping Price
      foreach(RatedShipment ship in rates.RatedShipments)
      {
         if (ship.ServiceDescription == "Ground")
            decShipingCost = ship.TotalCharge;
      }
   }
   else
   {
      //If we couldn't contact UPS, just use our default rate
      decShipingCost = (decimal)fltTotalWeight * .50m;
   }

   return decShipingCost;
}
```

This code is fairly straightforward. We calculate the total weight of all of the items in the cart first. Then we create a UPSRates object passing in the FromZip (which is the zip code of Wiley's corporate headquarters), ToZip (which is the shopper's zip code), and true for the third parameter (which specifies a residential address). We then call the GetRates() method, and if it returns true, we look through the collection of Rated-Shipment objects until we find the Ground rate. If for some reason the GetRates() method returns false and we weren't able to get the shipping costs from UPS, we fall back on our static cost of $.50 per pound. This might happen if the total weight of all of our items exceeds 150 pounds.

The last thing we would like to add to the WileyParts application is the ability to email the shopper's invoice after the purchase is made. We will do this at the end of the

Page_Load method in the ordercomplete page. We could send an HTML message to the shopper, but not every email client supports that, and some people just don't like it. To keep everybody happy, we'll send just a plain text message. Add the following code to the end of the Page_Load method of the ordercomplete page:

```
//Email this invoice to the shopper
MailMessage msg = new MailMessage();
//Set the mail message fields
msg.To = m_shopper.Email;
msg.From = "sales@WileyParts.com";
msg.Subject = "Order Confirmation - " + order.OrderID.ToString();
msg.Body = "Thank You for ordering from WileyParts. Your order
information is listed below.\n\n";
msg.Body += "Order ID: " + order.OrderID.ToString() + "\n";
msg.Body += "Sold To:\n";
msg.Body += m_shopper.FirstName + " " + m_shopper.LastName + "\n";
msg.Body += m_shopper.Address + "\n";
msg.Body += m_shopper.City + ", " + m_shopper.StateCode + " " +
m_shopper.PostalCode + "\n\n";

//Add all of the order items
for (int x = 0 ; x < order.OrderItems.Count ; ++x)
{
   OrderItem item = (OrderItem)order.OrderItems[x];

   msg.Body += "Item " + (x+1).ToString() + ":\n";
   msg.Body += "Description: " + item.Description + "\n";
   msg.Body += "Weight: " + item.Weight.ToString() + "\n";
   msg.Body += "Quantity: " + item.Quantity.ToString() + "\n";
   msg.Body += "Price Per Unit: " + string.Format("{0:c}",
      item.PricePerUnit) + "\n\n";
}

//Add the subtotals
msg.Body += "\nShipping Cost: " + string.Format("{0:c}",
   order.ShippingCost) + "\n";
msg.Body += "Tax: " + string.Format("{0:c}", order.SalesTax) + "\n";
msg.Body += "Total: " + string.Format("{0:c}", order.TotalCost) +
"\n\n";

//Add the credit card information
msg.Body += "Payment Information:\n";
msg.Body += strCCInfo;

//Send the mail message
SmtpMail.Send(msg);
```

In a nutshell, what we've done here is create a MailMessage object and dynamically create the Body of the mail message based on the customer's order information.

Adding email to this application was the last thing we needed to do to make the WileyParts Web site feature complete (at least for the purposes of this book). We hope that building this application has been useful for you and that you can build on the techniques we've used throughout the application and apply them to your projects.

Wrapping Up the Chapter

In this chapter, we covered how to add two very important elements to any Web site, freight pricing and email. In doing so, we learned about the XML support classes that are provided by the .NET Framework and how easy it is to work with XML data using those classes.

Debugging and Optimization

Debugging is an integral part of any development cycle. With ASP.NET applications, we can apply some of the same types of debugging techniques that work in all software development projects, as well as apply some more sophisticated methods provided by Windows and the .NET Framework. Optimization is important to any development effort as well, and there are many ways to optimize your Web application to ensure that it runs in the most efficient manner possible. In this chapter, we'll cover some aspects of debugging, optimizing, tracing, and profiling as they are done in an ASP.NET application.

Debugging in an ASP.NET Application

For debugging any Web application, we can resort to writing code to send messages to the browser with useful information such as values, counters, calls, and more. But as with most other programming environments some features provided by the .NET Framework assist us. Tracing is one feature available as part of the framework, and we will experiment with it in this section. When we want to truly debug an ASP.NET application, meaning have the operating system run the executable code into debug mode and allow us to control its execution, we can use the Visual Studio .NET IDE.

Let's use these features to debug the Wiley Parts application.

Tracing

Tracing is a way to write your own output from any part of the application at runtime. But, instead of merely displaying the output in the user interface of the application, when we using tracing, the output is displayed to us in a special user interface generated by the .NET Framework to be used as a programming tool. Even if you don't make the special calls to send your own output to the tracing tool, you can still trace the application and see the default tracing that is already in the Framework code. In ASP.NET, tracing can be enabled on the page level or the application level. When tracing is enabled, ASP.NET sends a slew of information to the browser with each request, appended to the end of the normal page content. This information has sections for the following information:

Request Details. This section displays information about the HTTP request made to the server for the page. This will allow you what was actually sent from the browser to the server.

Trace Information. This section displays the trace message that you included in your code to track variables, state, and more. In addition to your trace messages, those that are in the Framework codeare intended to help you see the flow of the application as it runs, as well as execution times.

Control Tree. This section lists all of the controls in the application, in a tree format according to their containers. With this information, you might be able to spot extra controls, controls of the wrong type, or missing controls that you expected to exist in the page at the time.

Cookies Collection. This section lists the cookies on the browser for this domain. This is helpful when trying to track down values you are expecting to find in a cookie.

Headers Collection. This section lists the HTTP headers that were sent in the request. With this, you can see exactly what is being submitted in a form post from the browser.

Server Variables. This section shows us the server environment variables. This information helps us determine the context and state of the environment on the server on which the page or application is trying to execute.

To cause ASP.NET to serve the trace information with the page, tracing must be enabled via a page directive in the aspx file in question. Code like the following placed at the top of an aspx file will enable tracing for the page:

```
<%@ Page language="c#" Trace="true" Codebehind="trace.aspx.cs"
AutoEventWireup="false" Inherits="Chapter10.trace" %>
```

To try this example, create a new ASP.NET Web Application called Chapter10. Then, create a WebForm called trace, and add a TextBox to it. Make the page directive line at the top of the aspx file look like the preceding line of code. The important part of this line is: Trace="true", which tells ASP.NET to write the trace log. In addition to the tracing output written automatically by the framework, you can add your own output by using the TraceContext object of the Page class, which is exposed as the Trace property. The methods of most interest to us are Write and Warn. Write allows you to send output strings directly to the browser, to appear in the Trace Information section. There are overloads on the method that allow us to optionally send a category name and an exception object in addition to the debug test itself. Warn has the same action, but it renders the text in red in the browser, for notification. Remember that if you have not enabled tracing on the Page, your calls to Write and Warn have no effect. Here is some sample code that shows activity before and after setting text in a server-side TextBox, followed by the output scraped from the browser. You can place this Page_Load into the code-behind file of the your form. You can see the page in action in Figure 10.1.

```
private void Page_Load(object sender, System.EventArgs e)
{
  Trace.Write("Page_Load", "Before set text");
  TextBox1.Text = "Hello World";
  Trace.Write("Page_Load", "After set text");
}
```

When we use Warn instead of Write, we get the output of our calls in red. In this next example, we send an exception to a call to Warn, which will show up in red. ASP.NET will extract the correct values from the exception for display. It knows which properties to call because the exception sent must at least be derived from System.Exception. To cause the exception, we try to divide by zero. This time, create a new WebForm called TraceException, and use the following Page_Load handler. Don't forget to turn on tracing in the page directive of the aspx file. Figure 10.2 shows this code in action.

```
private void Page_Load(object sender, System.EventArgs e)
{
  try
  {
    int i = 0;
    TextBox1.Text = ((int)(10 / i)).ToString();
  }
  catch(Exception ex)
  {
    Trace.Warn("Page_Load", "Caught Exception", ex);
  }
}
```

Hello World

Request Details

Session Id:	obiy5455r0pvey55lm53zu2m	Request Type:	GET
Time of Request:	7/24/2001 10:33:20 PM	Status Code:	200
Request Encoding:	Unicode (UTF-8)	Response Encoding:	Unicode (UTF-8)

Trace Information

Category	Message	From First(s)	From Last(s)
aspx.page	Begin Init		
aspx.page	End Init	0.000147	0.000147
Page_Load	Before set text	0.000256	0.000109
Page_Load	After set text	0.000350	0.000095
aspx.page	Begin PreRender	0.000443	0.000093
aspx.page	End PreRender	0.000542	0.000099
aspx.page	Begin SaveViewState	0.001477	0.000935
aspx.page	End SaveViewState	0.001729	0.000252
aspx.page	Begin Render	0.001827	0.000098
aspx.page	End Render	0.002777	0.000950

Control Tree

Control Id	Type	Render Size Bytes (including children)	Viewstate Size Bytes (excluding children)
__PAGE	ASP.trace_aspx	624	20
ctrl0	System.Web.UI.ResourceBasedLiteralControl	377	0
trace	System.Web.UI.HtmlControls.HtmlForm	226	0
ctrl1	System.Web.UI.LiteralControl	5	0
TextBox1	System.Web.UI.WebControls.TextBox	71	0
ctrl2	System.Web.UI.LiteralControl	4	0
ctrl3	System.Web.UI.LiteralControl	21	0

Cookies Collection

Name	Value	Size
ASP.NET_SessionId	obiy5455r0pvey55lm53zu2m	42

Headers Collection

Name	Value
Connection	Keep-Alive
Accept	*/*
Accept-Encoding	gzip, deflate
Accept-Language	en-us
Cookie	ASP.NET_SessionId=obiy5455r0pvey55lm53zu2m
Host	localhost
Referer	http://localhost/Wiley/DebugAndOptimize/
User-Agent	Mozilla/4.0 (compatible; MSIE 6.0b; Windows NT 5.0; .NET CLR 1.0.2914)

Server Variables

Name	Value
ALL_HTTP	HTTP_CONNECTION:Keep-Alive HTTP_ACCEPT:*/* HTTP_ACCEPT_ENCODING:gzip, deflate HTTP_ACCEPT_LANGUAGE:en-us HTTP_COOKIE:ASP.NET_SessionId=obiy5455r0pvey55lm53zu2m HTTP_HOST:localhost HTTP_REFERER:http://localhost/Wiley/DebugAndOptimize/ HTTP_USER_AGENT:Mozilla/4.0 (compatible; MSIE 6.0b; Windows NT 5.0; .NET CLR 1.0.2914)
ALL_RAW	Connection: Keep-Alive Accept: */* Accept-Encoding: gzip, deflate Accept-Language: en-us Cookie: ASP.NET_SessionId=obiy5455r0pvey55lm53zu2m Host: localhost Referer: http://localhost/Wiley/DebugAndOptimize/ User-Agent: Mozilla/4.0 (compatible; MSIE 6.0b; Windows NT 5.0; .NET CLR 1.0.2914)
APPL_MD_PATH	/LM/w3svc/3/root/Wiley/DebugAndOptimize
APPL_PHYSICAL_PATH	F:\meyneh\Fileshare\Wiley\DebugAndOptimize\
AUTH_TYPE	
AUTH_USER	
AUTH_PASSWORD	
LOGON_USER	
REMOTE_USER	
CERT_COOKIE	
CERT_FLAGS	
CERT_ISSUER	
CERT_KEYSIZE	
CERT_SECRETKEYSIZE	
CERT_SERIALNUMBER	
CERT_SERVER_ISSUER	
CERT_SERVER_SUBJECT	
CERT_SUBJECT	
CONTENT_LENGTH	0
CONTENT_TYPE	
GATEWAY_INTERFACE	CGI/1.1
HTTPS	off
HTTPS_KEYSIZE	
HTTPS_SECRETKEYSIZE	
HTTPS_SERVER_ISSUER	
HTTPS_SERVER_SUBJECT	
INSTANCE_ID	3
INSTANCE_META_PATH	/LM/W3SVC/3
LOCAL_ADDR	127.0.0.1
PATH_INFO	/Wiley/DebugAndOptimize/trace.aspx
PATH_TRANSLATED	F:\meyneh\Fileshare\Wiley\DebugAndOptimize\trace.aspx
QUERY_STRING	
REMOTE_ADDR	127.0.0.1
REMOTE_HOST	127.0.0.1
REQUEST_METHOD	GET
SCRIPT_NAME	/Wiley/DebugAndOptimize/trace.aspx
SERVER_NAME	localhost
SERVER_PORT	80
SERVER_PORT_SECURE	0
SERVER_PROTOCOL	HTTP/1.1
SERVER_SOFTWARE	Microsoft-IIS/5.0
URL	/Wiley/DebugAndOptimize/trace.aspx
HTTP_CONNECTION	Keep-Alive
HTTP_ACCEPT	*/*
HTTP_ACCEPT_ENCODING	gzip, deflate
HTTP_ACCEPT_LANGUAGE	en-us
HTTP_COOKIE	ASP.NET_SessionId=obiy5455r0pvey55lm53zu2m
HTTP_HOST	localhost
HTTP_REFERER	http://localhost/Wiley/DebugAndOptimize/
HTTP_USER_AGENT	Mozilla/4.0 (compatible; MSIE 6.0b; Windows NT 5.0; .NET CLR 1.0.2914)

Figure 10.1   ASP.NET tracing with Write.

Trace Information			
Category	Message	From First (s)	From Last (s)
aspx.page	Begin Init		
aspx.page	End Init	0.001775	0.001775
Page_Load	Caught Exception Attempted to divide by zero. at DebugAndOptimize.traceexception.Page_Load(Object sender, EventArgs e) in f:\meyneh\fileshare\wiley\debugandoptimize\traceexception.aspx.cs:line 31	0.004112	0.002337
aspx.page	Begin PreRender	0.005769	0.001657
aspx.page	End PreRender	0.005934	0.000164
aspx.page	Begin SaveViewState	0.006703	0.000769
aspx.page	End SaveViewState	0.007700	0.000998
aspx.page	Begin Render	0.007806	0.000106
aspx.page	End Render	0.081066	0.073260

Figure 10.2 ASP.NET tracing with Warn and an exception.

Other than calling Write and Warn, and setting the sort order of the trace output with the TraceMode property, there is not much more to adding rich tracing to your Web applications. Remember that if your app is full of trace object calls, they can remain in the production builds because as long as tracing is disabled, which is the default, they will do nothing. Even if tracing is turned on, your application will still run properly; it will just be slower and display a large, user-unfriendly chunk of data at the bottom of the page.

Tracing is also configurable on the application level, meaning that all pages served will be traced. To turn on application-level tracing, add the following lines to the Web.Config file:

```
<trace
enabled="true"
requestLimit="10"
pageOutput="false"
traceMode="SortByTime"
localOnly="true"
/>
```

These lines tell ASP.NET to collect trace information from the entire application, up to the amount to which the requestLimit is set. The pageOutput attribute determines whether the trace log will be displayed on the served pages, as in Figures 10.1 and 10.2. If this is set to false, the output will not be displayed. You can override this by using the TraceMode attribute in the Page directive on a particular page.

If you have enabled application-level tracing but disabled page output, the contents of the collected trace log will be viewable by browsing to a file called trace.axd in the application root directory. In this case, we browse to http://localhost/Wiley/Chapter10/trace.axd, which opens the application trace page. Note that you are not really browsing to this file, and you will not see it in the virtual directory anywhere. The output from Trace.axd is created by ASP.NET when you request it via your browser. If you look in the Application->Configuration->App Mapping section in Web Services Administrator, you will see that .axd files are mapped to aspnet_isapi.dll. Once the aspnet engine is handling the request, it calls on the System.Web.Handlers.

TraceHandler class, which will serve the trace page to you. This is set up by the entry in the machine config file for trace.axd, and it is configured this way by default. Logging the trace information to the trace.axd application is automatically done when you enable tracing in the Web.Config file. Figure 10.3 shows this in action.

Optimization

Session and View state are two powerful parts of Web programming with ASP.NET. They do add overhead and can detract from the overall performance of your application if used inappropriately. We have already learned when and why we would need to use these features, so now let's talk about optimizing their use.

Optimizing Session State Use in Web.Config

When optimizing an ASP.NET application's Session state usage, the first place to start is in the Web.Config file. If you are developing an application that has no need for Session state, you can disable it in the Web.Config file. Turning off Session state helps the overall performance of your application by reducing the memory required and speeding processing of the page. Less memory is used because no session variables are being stored, and pages are processed more quickly because when Sessions are enabled, the session ID cookie must be read and written by the server each time a page is processed, even if no session variables are stored or used. To turn off Session state, set the mode attribute to "Off" in the sessionState section or Web.Config. Here is an example:

```
<sessionState mode="Off" . . .
```

Even when you do need to use Session state, make sure you do so in the most appropriate mode. There are three modes supported by ASP.NET: the in process mode, which is the default, the out of process mode, which relies on a Windows Service to manage the Session state, and SQL Server mode, which uses SQL Server to do the work. Obviously, using the in process mode is the best way in regard to speed performance. This is due to the fact that the objects stored in Session state variables exist in the memory of your Web server, and no cross-process access has to occur when reading or writing them. Storing variables in this kind of state manager means that they are volatile, and they will not be persisted across instances of the application. If the machine or even the Web server is rebooted, session state will be lost. This also goes for compiles of the Web application. When you compile you application, the running application ends, and the first request to your new version starts off a new application. When this happens, all memory is lost from the first application, including the session variables. If you need to keep sessions alive and well during a reboot or restart of the Web server, or even run a compile of your Web application, you may want to use one of the other methods listed. Refer to the MSDN Library for .NET to learn more about these other means, as they are not in the scope of this book Notice that when we simply try to set a Session variable in a page when we have set enableSessionState to "Off," we get the exception in Figure 10.4.

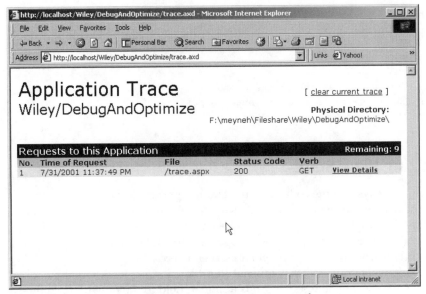

Figure 10.3   Viewing application-level tracing in Trace.axd.

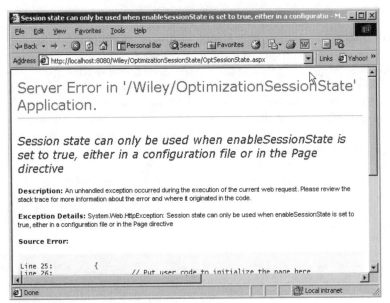

Figure 10.4   Session state turned off in Web.Config.

If we leave Session state enabled in the Web.Config file, we can still disable it on the page level by setting the enableSessionState to false in the Page directive in the aspx file. Doing so will allow you to use sessions only in the pages that need it. This would be done with this line of code:

```
<%@ Page language="c#" enableSessionState="false"
Codebehind="trace.aspx.cs" AutoEventWireup="false"
Inherits="DebugAndOptimize.trace" %>
```

Optimizing View State

There are many ways to write code to ensure that it is performing in the most efficient way and not using more memory than necessary. As with writing any Web application, there are specific ways to make your ASP.NET pages more responsive and engaging. One such way to speed your application's response is to limit the amount of data being sent back and forth between the browser and server. This can be optimized by enabling ViewState only where needed. We discussed ViewState in Chapter 2, "Anatomy of an ASP.NET Page," and how the server sends a hidden field to the browser each time a page is requested. Remember that the hidden field holds information about the controls that are rendered into HTML, particularly the complex controls. This is how the server re-creates the state of your user interface automatically on a postback when a user performs an action in the page that requires a trip back to the server, like clicking a Button control. As an example, if a DataGrid is sent the browser on the first request, it will be rendered as a table. But, if the user then clicks a button that causes code to be run on the server again, that code might need to program against the values in the Data-Grid. Because a DataGrid was turned into a table when it was sent to the browser, and because table elements and their contents are not form controls and would not be sent back to the server as variables, ASP.NET uses the hidden ViewState variable to pass these DataGrid objects' contents back and forth. This also allows the server to rerender the contents into a table on subsequent calls, without having to perform the same code that loaded the initial DataGrid. But, if our code doesn't interact with some user interface elements, then ViewState may not need to be maintained for those controls.

ViewState can be managed for an entire page or any server-side control such as a TextBox, Label, or DropDownList. For any controls on your page that you will never have to access programmatically in server-side code, you can explicitly disable its ViewState where it is declared by setting its EnableViewState property to false. An example for a TextBox may look like the following:

```
<asp:TextBox id="TextBox1" runat="server" EnableViewState="False">
</asp:TextBox>
```

Alternately, you could use the property in code-behind code like this:

```
TextBox1.EnableViewState = false;
```

which would achieve the same results. Any control that has its values set at runtime in the declaration of the control in the aspx file, or by writing to it in the code-behind class, doesn't necessarily need to have ViewState enabled. If, for example, we always set the text of the TextBox above in the Page_Load event, and outside of the IsPostBack, but never read it, we could disable ViewState. One important thing to note is that disabling ViewState in certain types of controls does not render the control unusable by code. In the TextBox example, the text can still be set and retrieved in code for the control, even when ViewState is turned off. A control such as a TextBox is a real HTML Input control once rendered, and it will always have its value passed back to the code-behind class at postback time because the names and values of HTML Input controls are always sent to the server in HTTP Post requests, which is how ASP.NET pages are sent by default. But, more complex controls, which are not represented by Input HTML items, need to have ViewState so that their state is available when the page is loaded in a postback situation. In the case of a ListBox, for example, state is maintained in the ViewState variable, unless you disable it. If, you were displaying items in a ListBox that was for viewing only, and no server-side code would interrogate it for any of its state such as the selected item, you could disable ViewState. Doing so would make the ViewState hidden Input field that gets sent to the browser smaller. For example, a view-only ListBox with these items in it, Hank, Moe, Larry, and Joe, would send the following ViewState variable to the browser and back on each request:

```
<input type="hidden" name="__VIEWSTATE" value="dDwxODU5MTk0OTQ1Ozs+" />
```

If, on the other hand, your code needed to access some state of the ListBox, such as the selected item's text or value, ViewState would need to be enabled just as in the preceding TextBox example and would send this to the browser:

```
<input type="hidden" name="__VIEWSTATE"
value="dDwxODU5MTk0OTQ1O3Q8O2w8aTwxPjs+O2w8dDw7bDxpPDE+Oz47bDx0PHQ8O3A8A8b
DxpPDA+O2k8MT47aTwyPjtpPDM+Oz47bDxwPEhhbms7SGFuaz47cDxNb2U7TW91PjtwPExhc
nJ5O0xhcnJ5PjtwPEpvZTtKb2U+Oz4+Oz47O3Pj47Pj47Pg==" />
```

Obviously, when ViewState is used, the content transferred over the wire is larger. Keep in mind that in a control such as a DataGrid, or another complex control that uses ViewState to hold information about its current state, it will not behave the same when ViewState is disabled. Nor will it repopulate automatically on a postback to the server because it is not a standard HTML control that would normally appear in the request header. When using complex controls such as a DataGrid, the ViewState can become very large. Here is another example, using a DataGrid to display a simple table from the Microsoft NorthWind database. We have seen code like this earlier in the book, so please refer to the sample source code if you need to see it in detail. We won't show you the code or the output here; it is just a plain grid representing the rows and columns in the Products table. Figures 10.5 and 10.6 show you what the browser source looks like when viewed with Internet Explorer 6, both with and without ViewState enabled. And, here is the code snippet required to load the grid:

```
SplConnection conn = new SqlConnection(@"DataSource=(local)\NetSDK;
InitialCatalog=Northwind;
userID=sa;pwd=;");
conn.Open();
SqlCommand cmd = new SqlCommand("select * from products", conn);
SqlDataReader reader = cmd.ExecuteReader();
DataGrid1.DataSource = reader;
DataGrid1.DataBind();
```

Figure 10.5 Browser source from a DataGrid with ViewState enabled.

Figure 10.6 Browser source from a DataGrid with ViewState disabled.

As you can see, the ViewState is huge for this simple table of just 77 rows, and the screenshot shows only a small portion of the source. In fact, by viewing the Properties of the page in the browser, the version in Figure 10.5 with ViewState weighs in at 60,125 bytes, whereas the version in Figure 10.6 without ViewState is only 19,845 bytes—less than a third the size. Of course, as stated several times, you will lose the functionality of re-creating the output automatically after a postback has occurred. In this case, when ViewState is disabled, we would have to requery and rebind the data each time the page loads without regard to whether the IsPostBack property returns true. For this optimization, you have to weigh the benefits of limiting bandwidth usage versus limiting server-side processing and database calls. Also remember that in cases where you are always setting values in controls as runtime in the Page_Load server-side code, you may as well disable the ViewState on that control. It will never be used to repopulate the control, which is one of ViewState's most valuable uses, because you are always doing so yourself with code. In that case, there is just no reason to send the extra content back and forth.

Another way to speed the processing of your pages is to make sure you are using the IsPostBack property appropriately. As explained earlier in the book, this property can be checked when loading the page to determine if the page is being requested due to a postback situation. In the postback situation, you can often rely on the ViewState to load controls on your page; therefore, this optimization needs to be considered along with the previous one regarding ViewState enabling.

Another way to enhance performance is to make use of the robust client-side controls that ASP.NET provides. For example, although it is easy and powerful to handle data validation on the server with ASP.NET, try to avoid doing so whenever possible. By using Validator controls, which will produce client ECMAScript or JavaScript to do much of their intended work, you minimize the number of requests your Web server must process. In a purely World Wide Web-based application, many of your users will have up-level browsers and can benefit from client-side activity. In most intranet applications, the browser version can easily be controlled and will usually be modern browsers, which support client script. Also, don't forget that you are still free to write your own client-side script in your aspx files. Many people get caught up in the power that is afforded with the server-side nature of ASP.NET, but you can still use your existing JavaScript, Jscript, and ECMAScript in the browser to do things where appropriate. Just remember that when doing this kind of client-side programming, you will be responsible for making sure your code works properly in all browsers.

There are other optimizations, like using Stored Procedures whenever possible, refraining from using "select *" in your database queries whenever possible, and compiling your code for release instead of debug. Those techniques are well known, discussed at length in the MSDN Library, and are not inherent only to ASP.NET applications, so we are considering them as outside the scope of this book.

Optimizing Using Caching

Caching is a common technique used in all types of applications, and it plays a major role in speeding up the response time and overall performance of your program. Caching simply means storing data or objects in memory so that a program can access them quickly at any time. If data is left on a permanent storage device such as a disk drive or database server, it takes longer to retrieve it for use when needed. If it can be determined that a piece of data or an object does not need to be dynamically loaded before every use, caching is a good optimization for any application, including those written for ASP.NET.

Output Caching in an ASP.NET Page

Many applications can benefit from caching in some way or another. *Output caching* is a means by which a page request may be filled from a cached version of the page in memory rather than from a stream of HTML that is returned by the Web server, if the page has been cached recently. For example, if you have a page that displays a list of all of your products on a shopping cart type page, you could cache this and probably reap some speed increases or load decreases in your application. Caching can be done on several levels, but in all cases it is handled for you, without your having to write code to store the cached content. In the example of the full product list for a shopping page, that data may not change very often, so the server code doesn't need to query the data source every time the page is requested.

To show the improvements in response time that can be gained, we performed a simple test. Returning the same data as in the last example, the Products table from the Northwind database, we can see varying results when enabling and disabling caching. For the experiment, we request the page 10 times and look at the IIS Log to see the times posted for processing each request. Here are the times with caching enabled: 460, 421, 481, 531, 500, 481, 400, 451, 480, 501.

These times yield an average of about 470 ms. Next, we ran the same test with caching enabled and a duration of 120 seconds, so we would have plenty of time to request the page 10 times. Here are the results: 0, 10, 0, 0, 0, 0, 10, 0, 0, 10, 0. This time, the response times were drastically reduced. This makes sense considering that the server doesn't have to serve the content, just negotiate with the client that the data is retrievable from cache. Also, in the server log, we can see that when the page is served the first time, over 60K of data is sent; the cache hits saw only about 200 bytes being sent—an obvious boon if you have a slower network or are paying by data traffic for your ISP service. In the browser, where the previous example seemed to pause for a second and the IE globe icon made about a quarter turn, these requests were filled so quickly, it was hard to see the browser reloading. In addition to the times used to process the request, IIS logs the return code for the requests as well. When we were returning the page in the first test, it was being created normally and returning HTTP 200, which means normal execution occurred. In the latter test, the return code logged is HTTP 304, which means that the browser was told not to reload the page because it has not been modified in a certain amount of time: the cache duration. One thing that this tells us is that ASP.NET caching employs the caching mechanisms built into HTTP/1.1, which is supported, at least, by the browser we used for the tests. The return value of 304 sent out by the server tells the client not to expect content to fulfill the request, but to retrieve it from cache. If there is any server downstream from the server that caches HTTP data, like a proxy server, it may provide the caching storage there. If the browser is the first HTTP client that the data goes to, it will cache the page in its own temporary area to fill any unexpired subsequent requests for the same resource.

To illustrate this clearly, we wrote a simple HttpClient as a WinForms C# application, which requests the URI and displays the response. When requesting a page with caching enabled, the server sent the following response headers:

```
Server: Microsoft-IIS/5.0
Date: Mon, 13 Aug 2001 05:32:55 GMT
Cache-Control: public
Expires: Mon, 13 Aug 2001 05:33:00 GMT
Last-Modified: Mon, 13 Aug 2001 05:32:40 GMT
Content-Type: text/html; charset=utf-8
Content-Length: 60115
```

Notice that there is a Cache-Control header present and set to public, as well as the Expires and Last-Modified headers. An important issue with caching is that if you are relying on the browser caching client for performance, there will be much less benefit achieved than if you use a middle caching piece, such as a proxy cache server, for example. Even though you have served the requested page at least once to a client and it is cached in his or her browser, the server will have to process and serve the same page again when another browser requests it, even if it is on the same machine as a previous one. The new user or browser can't load the page from cache if it doesn't have it in cache. Of course, there is still a benefit when the same user requests the same resource multiple times; it will be retrieved from the server only the first time. The real benefit of caching comes in when there is a server in between all of the users and the server. This caching server can cache the page from the server the first time any user requests it and then serve it out from fast memory to any other user or browser until it expires.

The actual location of the caching can be set by the Location attribute of the Output-Cache directive, if so desired. There are several different options for the location of the cached data, and the following are the ones most commonly used. When set to Any, the data is cached by whichever caching application gets the data. It could end up cached in a downstream caching server or in the client's browser if no other server is in the stream. When set to Client, the cached data is stored in the client's browser. This is the most common location, and it works whether there is a dedicated caching application between the browser and Web server. When set to Downstream, any caching application that is between the client browser and the server will cache the data. This location is useful when running a caching server of your own in front of your Web server.

As far as the overall application performance goes, a tremendous load is taken off the server when caching is used properly. In addition to the Web server not having to restream the same data over and over to the clients, the database is also spared excessive connections and queries. Of course, performing this kind of caching is not appropriate when the user always needs to see the current version of the content. An example of putting caching to good use would be a page that returns daily company headline from a database. This data is unlikely to change every time a client requests the page. If it is cached, then that is one less page for your server to have to process while it is trying to process more important pages that must be fresh for every request. One important thing to note is that as of the writing of this book, the caching features of ASP.NET are available only in the ASP.NET Premium version, which is an up-rated version of the server available for free from Microsoft. If you attempt to use caching on a server that has only the standard .NET Framework installed, it will have no effect. You will receive no error or warning that caching is not working; you must know the version of the server you are using.

Caching in a User Control

In some cases, you may need to cache only a portion of a page. For example, maybe you have a shopping site that has daily specials to be displayed at the top of every page. These daily specials come from the data source, so they must be refreshed at least once a day. But because they change only once, they don't need to be reprocessed every time a page is requested. If this daily specials area needs to appear on a page that does have to be refreshed on every request, such as a shopping cart, how can we keep it from being processed as well? An ASP.NET user control may be the solution. These controls were discussed earlier in the book, so we won't explain them again here. Just know that user controls, like pages, can be cached, and separately from the pages in which they live. This makes for some nice performance capabilities in that you can control caching not just on a page level, but in certain areas in the page as well. This technique is often referred to as fragment caching. In this example, we will simulate a page that needs only part of it to be dynamic all of the time. To do this, we simply add a new Web Form to our Chapter10 project called UserControlCaching. Also, add a user control called SampleUserControl that has caching set with the OutputCache directive in the aspx file. Add this user control to the to the UserControlCaching page and disable its caching. The code for the UserControl- Caching is in Listing 10.1.

```
<%@ Page language="c#" Codebehind="UserControlCaching.aspx.cs"
AutoEventWireup="false" Inherits="Chapter10.UserControlCaching" %>
<%@ Register TagPrefix="SampleControl" TagName="ProductsControl"
src="SampleUserControl.ascx" %>
<!DOCTYPE HTML PUBLIC "-//W3C//DTD HTML 4.0 Transitional//EN" >
<HTML>
  <HEAD>
    <meta name="GENERATOR" Content="Microsoft Visual Studio 7.0">
    <meta name="CODE_LANGUAGE" Content="C#">
    <meta name="vs_defaultClientScript" content="JavaScript
      (ECMAScript)">
    <meta name="vs_targetSchema"
      content="http://schemas.microsoft.com/intellisense/ie5">
  </HEAD>
  <body>
    <SampleControl:ProductsControl runat="server" ID="ctl1" />
    <form id="UserControlCaching" method="post" runat="server">
      <P>
        <FONT face="Verdana" size="2"><STRONG>This is a non-cached page
          <BR>
          <BR>
```

Listing 10.1   UserControlCaching.aspx

```
        </STRONG>Last updated time:
          <asp:Label id="lblDateTime" runat="server">Label</asp:Label>
      </FONT>
    </P>
  </form>
 </body>
</HTML>
```

Listing 10.1   UserControlCaching.aspx (continued)

And here is the Page_Load handler for the page:

```
private void Page_Load(object sender, System.EventArgs e)
{
  if (!IsPostBack)
  {
    //Set datetime stamp control
    lblDateTime.Text = DateTime.Now.ToString();
  }
}
```

Next, in Listing 10.2, we see the aspx code for the user control itself. Notice that the page directive has caching set to 60 seconds and is not varied by parameter.

```
<%@ OutputCache Duration="60" VaryByParam="None" %>
<%@ Control Language="c#" AutoEventWireup="false"
  Codebehind="SampleUserControl.ascx.cs"
  Inherits="Chapter10.SampleUserControl"%>
<P>
  <asp:Panel id="Panel1" runat="server" Width="420px" Height="69px"
    BorderStyle="Solid" BorderColor="#0000C0" BorderWidth="1px"
    BackColor="#C0C0FF">

  <FONT face="verdana" size="2"><B>This is a cached user control</B>
    <BR>
    <BR>
    Last updated time:
    <asp:Label id="lblDateTime" runat="server">Label</asp:Label>
    </asp:Panel>
  </FONT>
</P>
```

Listing 10.2   The user control code

In Figure 10.7, notice that the times match because both pages are processed on the server. Then, notice that in Figure 10.8, the user control shows the same time, but the page shows a time different by more than 30 seconds. The page was refreshed, but the control was cached; therefore, it remained unchanged.

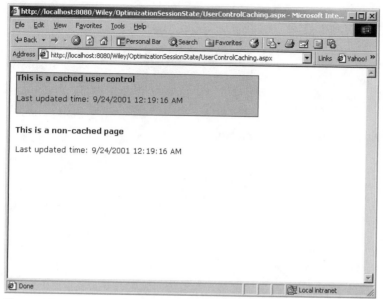

Figure 10.7   A noncached page with a cached user control on the first visit.

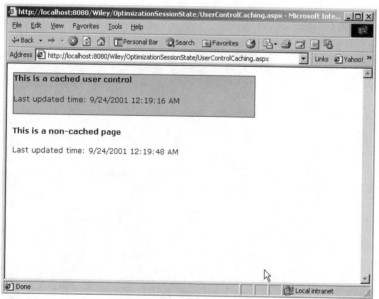

Figure 10.8   A noncached page with a cached user control on the second visit.

The Cache Class

Another way to cache data so that your server application doesn't have to perform lengthy processing is to use the Cache class, which is part of the .NET Framework. This class resides in the System.Web.Caching namespace, and it is exposed in all ASP.NET pages via the Cache property. This type of caching is called *ASP.NET Application Caching*.

The Cache is an object that holds other objects in memory and allows programs to store any type of object and retrieve it again at will. This is perfect for storing an object that doesn't change often and that taxes the system in a lengthy or processor-intensive manner when it is first created. An object with these characteristics could be stored in the Cache so that the heavy processing needed to load it happens only periodically. This kind of caching is completely different from Output Caching. Where Output Caching uses HTTP/1.1 features to support the storage of Web pages (and portions of Web pages when using User Controls, which are really just small Web pages themselves) on a piece of software that has a storage facility, using the Cache is similar to storing data or an object globally at application startup. We say globally because the Cache is accessible from any page in the Web application.

Let's revisit the daily specials data example. If we were writing an application and we somehow knew that all browser caches were disabled, and if we had no downstream caching application like a proxy server, then we would want to come up with another way to keep from having to requery for the daily specials on every page request. After all, if this were a rich client application that stayed running all day, we could always load the specials into memory and pull them from there instead of the real data source. In ASP.NET, we could query the specials and put them into the cache, and on each new page request, we could simply read them from there. We would reload them into the cache only when their cache time expires, about which we would be notified by a callback function into our code.

For this example, we queried the same table as before, the Products table in the Northwind database. This time, however, most requests for this data can be fulfilled from the Cache object. To achieve this, the first thing we do is check for the existence of the object in the cache. We can do this by its name, which in this case is ProductArray:

```
Object objCacheItem = Cache["ProductArray"];
```

If the object does not exist in the cache, we will be left with a null reference, at which point, we will create our cached data object and store it for later use. The data is read from the database via the ODBC providers OdbcDataReader. Notice, however, that we can't just store the reader object because it is forward-only, and only the first request to read it would have success. So, instead, we create ProductDataItem objects from the rows of data in the reader, and we add them to an ArrayList collection object. For brevity of the example, we didn't create a property for every column in the table. We then store the collection in the cache. The next request that comes in will see that the data has been cached, so it will simply bind to the cached version and display it to the user. This example uses a simple page with a DataGrid on it, and all processing takes place in the Page_Load event handler. Create a new Web Form in the chapter example called ApplicationCaching. Figure 10.9 shows us the page in action. Here is the code for the the Page_Load handler:

```
private void Page_Load(object sender, System.EventArgs e)
{
  if (!IsPostBack)
  {
    object objCacheItem = Cache["ProductsArray"];
    if (objCacheItem == null)
    {
      SqlConnection conn = new SqlConnection(@"DataSource=(local)\NetSDK;
      InitialCatalog=Northwind;userID=sa;pwd=;");
      conn.Open();
      SqlCommand cmd = new SqlCommand("select * from products", conn);
      SqlDataReader reader = cmd.ExecuteReader();

      //Create a collection or product items.
      ArrayList arr = new ArrayList();
      ProductsDataItem item = null;
      while (reader.Read())
      {
        item = new ProductsDataItem();
        item.ProductID = Convert.ToInt32(reader["ProductID"]);
        item.ProductName = reader["ProductName"].ToString().Trim();
        item.SupplierID = Convert.ToInt32(reader["SupplierID"]);
        item.CategoryID = Convert.ToInt32(reader["CategoryID"]);
        item.QuantityPerUnit = reader["QuantityPerUnit"].ToString().Trim();
        arr.Add(item);
      }
      reader.Close();

      //Store the collection in cache.
      Cache.Add("ProductsArray",
        arr,
        null,
        DateTime.Now.AddSeconds(20),
        new TimeSpan(0),
        CacheItemPriority.Normal,
        null);

      Response.Write(
        string.Format("Loaded products into cache at {0}<br>",
        DateTime.Now.ToString()));
    }

    //Data bind from cached products array.
    DataGrid1.DataSource = (ArrayList)Cache["ProductsArray"];
    DataGrid1.DataBind();
  }
}
```

The code for the aspx code is simply a DataGrid that looks like this:

```
<asp:DataGrid id="DataGrid1" runat="server" Font-Size="X-Small"
  Font-Names="arial" CellPadding="0" BackColor="White"
  BorderColor="Silver" BorderWidth="1px"
  BorderStyle="None">
</asp:DataGrid>
```

This technique would have the most impact on performance if the query for the products were a lengthy one; here it is a very fast query so the performance gain is negligible. Also, this technique doesn't save any on the front-side bandwidth consumption as the same data is still sent to the client on each request. This would consume less internal bandwidth by requiring less traffic from the Web server to the data server.

There are a few more things that can be done with the cache object. We can set up a sliding expiration time. This would make the expiration time extend itself each time the object was accessed in the cache. Here is a situation in which this could be helpful. If you have a Web application that stays very busy during the normal working hours, such as a heavily used intranet application in a corporation, you may not want the cache expiring while there is heavy traffic on the server. Making the expiration slide by a small amount each time the cached object is used, it will only expire when the traffic slows down enough so that there are no requests before the timeout slide time. So, if the slide time is set to a time span of five minutes, as long as the requests for the cached item at intervals less than five minutes, it won't expire. Once the requests slow down and are ever more than five minutes apart, the time will expire and the object cached object can be refreshed. This somewhat achieves load management in that the lengthy code is run only during idle times.

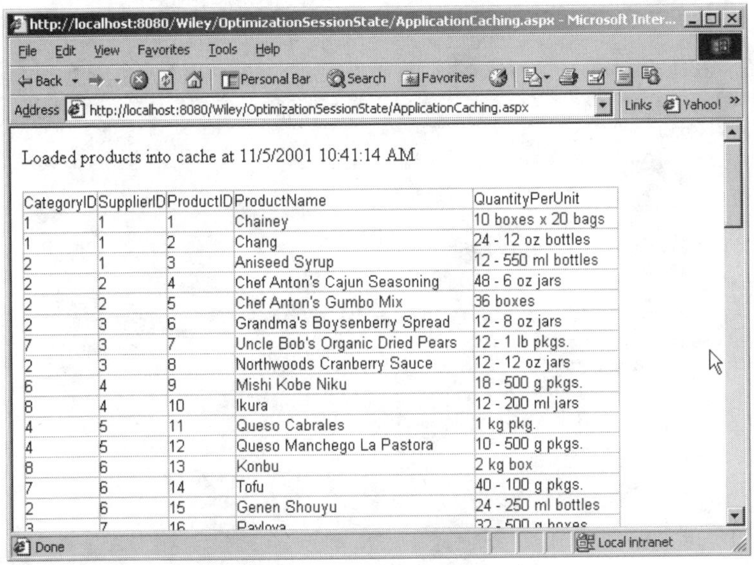

Figure 10.9 The cached page in action.

Another feature of the cache is its ability to alert us when an object has expired. This allows us to refresh it even periodically as opposed to doing so when we encounter a cache miss due to a request for the page. This may help the user experience by having the cached object kept up-to-date without having to be refreshed when one unlucky user requests the page.

To accomplish this, we need to set up a delegate—an event handler method—for the caching system to call when it removes an item. Once the event handler is in place, we can send its delegate into the Cache.Add method, as the last parameter. In this example, we check for a cache miss when the page loads, and we load the cache item at that time if needed. This is just like the last example, but we are now using a simple string for the cached item, to make the example easier to read. When the cached item expires, the event handler is called, and the expiration is logged so we can have proof that the code works. Then, the cache is reloaded with a fresh version of the string data. Create a new WebForm called AdvApplicationCaching. The aspx file requires no code modifications, and here is the required code for the code-behind file:

```
//The one static cache removal callback delegate.
private static CacheItemRemovedCallback onRemove = null;

private void Page_Load(object sender, System.EventArgs e)
{
  //Instance the callback delegate.
  onRemove = new CacheItemRemovedCallback(RemovedCallback);

  if (!IsPostBack)
  {
    //Check for a cache hit.
    object objCacheItem = Cache["Note"];
    if (objCacheItem == null)
    {
      //Cache miss - so load item into cache.
      DateTime t = AddCacheItem("Hello from Page_Load");
      Response.Write(string.Format(
        "Loaded item into cache from Page_Load at {0}<br>",
        t.ToString()));
    }

    //Display item.
    Response.Write(Cache["Note"].ToString());
  }
}

private DateTime AddCacheItem(string s)
{
  //Store the data in the cache.
  Cache.Add("Note",
    s,
    null,
    DateTime.Now.AddMinutes(1),
```

```
        new TimeSpan(0),
        CacheItemPriority.Normal,
        onRemove);

    return DateTime.Now;
}

public void RemovedCallback(string k, object v, CacheItemRemovedReason r)
{
    //Only handle cache removals if config says to.
    bool b = Convert.ToBoolean(
      ConfigurationSettings.AppSettings["HandleCacheRemovals"]);

    if (b)
    {
        //Cached item was removed, so log it.
        StreamWriter sw = new StreamWriter("c:\\cacheremove.htm", true);
        sw.WriteLine(string.Format("Removed: {0} at: {1} reason: {2}<br>", k,
          DateTime.Now, r.ToString()));

        sw.Close();

        //Add fresh item to cache.
        DateTime t = AddCacheItem("Hello from RemovedCallback");
    }
}
```

The first things of note in the code are the lines:

```
private static CacheItemRemovedCallback onRemove = null;
. . .
onRemove = new CacheItemRemovedCallback(RemovedCallback);
```

These lines set up the delegate to the event handler method for the callback to use. Notice that it needs to be static so that the system can call the method even when there is not a request, and therefore not necessarily an instance of the page class running. If this weren't static, then the method that it points to, RemoveCallback, would have to be static, but that would require other code to be able to access the cache because a static method would not have access to the "this" pointer, which would be the page where the cache property exists. We make the delegate static, which allows the call to occur at any time; the system can call the function on your page class from its class name instead of a running instance. If the delegate and the event handler were both nonstatic, then the system would have to wait until a request comes in and a page object is instantiated, to call the callback method. The Page_Load code is self-explanatory; it just checks for a cache hit and loads the cache on a miss, then prints the cached data value. In the call to Cache.Add, we can see the last parameter tells the cache to call RemoveCallback whenever an item is removed from cache. At that point, we simply load a new, fresh item in the cache. The next time a request comes in for the page, there will probably be a cache hit, resulting in a quick serve of the page. We shouldn't write to the content stream from this function because it will likely be called when there is not a valid context to which to return HTML.

Another tidbit we used is this line:

```
bool b = Convert.ToBoolean(
    ConfigurationSettings.AppSettings["HandleCacheRemovals"]);
```

which looks at the application configuration settings to determine whether the code should refresh the cache and log the event. The value is entered into the Web.Config file, as text, and can be changed at any time. This is a simple way of controlling settings in the application at runtime, similar to using a registry entry that the code reads. The difference is that we don't have to write code to read the registry, and these types of settings can be changed on the fly. The application will keep in sync with them automatically without our having to restart the Web server or the application. To use this application configuration setting, we must create an appSettings section in the Web.Config XML like this:

```
<appSettings>
  <add key="HandleCacheRemovals" value="false" />
</appSettings>
```

Keep in mind that the event will still fire, and the handler method will still be called; we have just prevented it from filling our hard drive full of removed cache item log entries. In fact, if you run this kind of example, you should restart the Web service after you are finished; don't request the page again, or else it will keep on refreshing in the background.

Optimizing via Performance Profiling

Performance profiling is a way to keep track of the efficiency of an application by tracking various parameters at runtime. This is done throughout the Windows operating system components as well as many applications written for Windows already likely running on your machine. The main tool for viewing these parameters in Windows is the Performance Monitor. Like any other type of application, ASP.NET Web applications can write information into the performance logs in Windows, so that it can be gathered and viewed with Performance Monitor.

perfmon and Performance Counters

ASP.NET creates a robust set of performance counters that can be read with perfmon, or any other performance counter reading application. These can be useful in tracking the performance of your Web applications, as well as other measures, such as how many sessions are active. To view performance statistics for ASP.NET in general, open perfmon by typing perfmon at a command prompt. To view current activity in ASP.NET, click the + button on the toolbar, which opens the Add Counters dialog. The most important counters to a Web application programmer are in the ASP.NET applications performance object. Selecting this in the Performance Object list shows you all of the available counters that are related to ASP.NET applications themselves. Select a counter from the list, and you will notice that there is an entry for each ASP.NET application currently running on the server. In Figure 10.10, you can see that two applications are running: gm and BugMan. Notice that their application names are preceded by W3SVC_1 because they are running on the default Web site. If we browse to an application on our server running on another Web site, it would be shown in the list as well, with a different prefix to the application name.

One of the counters that may be of interest to you is the session active, which may determine when you do a reboot or restart of the server. If you have hundreds of active sessions, you may want to postpone a software update until later; you don't want to unnecessarily cause a "session not found" error for a bunch of users if it can be avoided. Also, the cache miss counter may help you tune your application caching design. Maybe your cached content needs to last longer before expiring. Maybe you see that you have so many cache misses because the queries to the server vary more that you had anticipated. In that case, maybe you would want to take out the caching code altogether if it is using a lot of memory but not being hit often enough to justify its use.

Programming Your Own Performance Counters

In many cases, the standard ASP.NET counters are helpful in diagnosing performance bottlenecks or uncovering potential optimizations.There may be times when you can benefit from having your own custom counters in place. Fortunately, the .NET Framework makes this relatively simple to do.

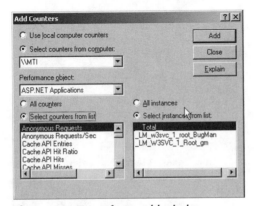

Figure 10.10   perfmon add window.

When creating performance counters, we first need to check to see if the category exists, and if not, create it and then update its value. The category is actually the item shown in the object list on the Add dialog box of the perfmon application. In this case, the easiest way to check for its existence is to try to access it and catch the exception if it doesn't exist. If the object needs to be created, we can do so and then access it for modification or reading. In this example, we will create a simple counter to keep a tally of how many times a user accesses the page. This is done by placing the code in the Form_Load, but it might be a good candidate for a base class method in a base page. While it is true that we could accomplish the same thing (counting page hits) with a database, file, or many other means, writing to a performance counter is handy in that it can be accessed from another machine (one machine can read performance information from another machine on the network) and it doesn't require the user to access the database just to see these statistics. In addition, the performance counter system in Windows supports more advance features such as averages, different refresh intervals, and graphing. Create a new WebForm called PerfCounters in the chapter project. Add the code listed here for the writing of a counter when the page loads. In this case, no code in the aspx file is needed other than the default generated form.

```csharp
string strCategoryName = "WileyParts";
string strCounterName = "Vehicle Selections";
private void Page_Load(object sender, System.EventArgs e)
{
  if (!IsPostBack)
  {
    try
    {
      PerformanceCounter objCounter = new
        PerformanceCounter(strCategoryName, strCounterName, "Inst01",
        false);

      objCounter.IncrementBy(1);
      Response.Write("Incremented to: " +
objCounter.RawValue.ToString());
    }
    catch
    {
      CreateCounter();
    }
  }
}

private void CreateCounter()
{
    CounterCreationDataCollection objCounterDataCollection = new
      CounterCreationDataCollection();

    CounterCreationData objCounterData = new CounterCreationData();
    objCounterData.CounterName = strCounterName;
```

```
        objCounterData.CounterHelp = "Number of vehicle selections";
        objCounterData.CounterType = PerformanceCounterType.NumberOfItems64;

        objCounterDataCollection.Add(objCounterData);

        PerformanceCounterCategory.Create(strCategoryName, strCounterName,
            objCounterDataCollection);
}
```

Notice that in the code we use the CounterCreationDataCollection object to which we add new CounterCreationData objects. We are adding only one object to the collection, but if we needed to create multiple counters quickly, we could do so by adding more data objects to the collection before passing it to create. Also, we put the calls inside the try block without any other code. The exception thrown when the counter doesn't exist is of type InvalidOperationException, which could be thrown by other code if it were present.

Another example of good use of counters is code that looks at the recent page hits or the request count for the last few minutes. This could be displayed to users to tell them how busy the server may be at the time. This could be useful for intranet applications, especially when a user has the option of postponing use of the system until a later time when it is not so busy.

Wrapping Up the Chapter

There are a host of options available to you for debugging, tracing, optimizing and profiling, and collecting performance data about your ASP.NET applications. This can go a long way toward making our Web-based applications as robust and scalable as our rich client applications.

Index